LLOYD'S
IN CRISIS

LLOYD'S IN CRISIS

The Insurance Scandal of the Twentieth Century

or,

The Farce Surrounding Syndicate 334

(1985) Names Association

EDMUND LESTER

First published in Great Britain in 2025 by
6 Figures Ltd, in partnership with Whitefox Publishing Ltd

www.wearewhitefox.com

Copyright © 6 Figures Ltd, 2025

ISBN 978-1-916797-50-5

Also available as an eBook
ISBN 978-1-916797-51-2

6 Figures Ltd asserts the moral right to be
identified as the author of this work.

Designed and typeset by seagulls.net
Cover design by Tomás Almeida
Project management by Whitefox Publishing Ltd

Dedicated to the late Clive P. Francis, the indefatigable Chairman of the Association; to Carol, with love, and all those entangled in the crisis.

Clive Francis (1928–2018), a gentleman warrior
and formidable foe.

TRIGGER WARNING

This true story is about insurance underwriting risk, legal issues, insurance broking, management, politics, auditing, accounting, taxation, severe mental stress and suicide.

CONTENTS

Appendices

The bell of HMS *Lutine* was recovered from the ship in 1858, after it foundered in 1799. The loss of the ship was a massive financial hit to Lloyd's. The bell is rung occasionally for important news: once for bad news and twice for good news.

LLOYD'S STRUCTURE

Lloyd's Act 1982, effective 23 July 1982

(incorporating sections of Lloyd's Acts currently in force, 1871, 1911 and 1951)

Corporation of Lloyd's

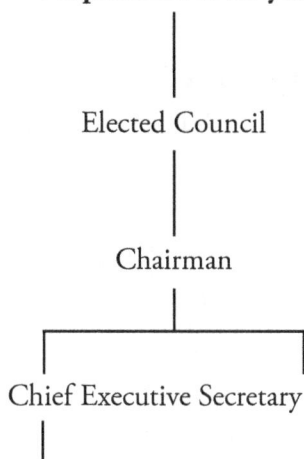

|

Elected Council

|

Chairman

|

Chief Executive Secretary

|

Departments

Legal Services

Lloyd's Claims Scheme

Lloyd's Financial Recovery Department

Lloyd's Regulatory Services

Membership

Names' Interest

Public Relations

Specialist Claims Unit

Lloyd's Administration:
1 Lime Street, London, EC3M 7HA

INDEPENDENT BUSINESSES STRUCTURE POST-LLOYD'S ACT 1982 IN THREE PARTS

There are three sorts of independent businesses:

1. Lloyd's Broking Companies, comprising insurance brokers.
2. Underwriting Agents that operate and run the syndicates.
3. Names' Managing Agents that support Names.

1. Matthews Wrightson Group PLC

(taken over by Sedgwick Group PLC, subsequently Willis Faber Group then Willis Corroon; eventually Marsh & McLennan Companies Inc.)

Subsidiaries

Matthews Wrightson Pulbrook and Stewart Wrightson Ltd
Syndicate stable of Matthews Wrightson Pulbrook
Syndicate 334 (including 85) Marine
Syndicate 90 (including 82) Non-Marine

Insurance Broker History

Stewart Wrightson Ltd (taken over by Sedgwick Group PLC)
Sedgwick (taken over becoming Willis Faber Group)
Willis Faber (merged with Willis Corroon, taken over by Marsh & McLennan Companies Inc.)
Winchester Bowring – a subsidiary of Marsh & McLennan

2. Underwriting Agents

Merrett Underwriting Agencies
Matthews Wrightson Pulbrook Ltd (became a Names Agent only)
Pulbrook Underwriting Management Ltd
Cox & Bell
Fielding & Partners
Gooda Walker Names

Underwriting Agents (cont.)

Gooda Walker Partners

John Poland Agency

Meacock Underwriting Management

Oakley Vaughan Agency

Outhwaite

Rose Thomson Young

Warrilow Agency

Whittington Syndicate Management Ltd

3. Names Agencies

Willis Faber & Dumas (Agencies) Ltd

Cox & Bell

Cuthbert Heath Agency

Feltrim Agency

Fielding & Partners

Hayter Brockbank Agency

Matthews Wrightson Pulbrook Ltd

London Wall Members Agency

SYNDICATE 334 (1985) NAMES ASSOCIATION STEERING COMMITTEE

Syndicate 334 Names

Clive Francis – *Chairman*	Former RAF Squadron Leader
Keith Lester – *Treasurer*	Chartered Accountant
Charles Baron	Chartered Management Accountant
Raymond Cook (Ray)	Businessman
Alasdair Ferguson MBE	Engineer businessman
Harry Purchase	Chartered Accountant and former Lloyd's Broker
Adam Raphael	Journalist
Jasper Salisbury-Jones	Barrister

Syndicate Committee Members Not Names on Syndicate 334

Guy Wilson – *Secretary*	Chartered Certified Accountant
Dr **David** Tiplady – *Solicitor*	Partner, D J Freeman & Co

Supporters

James Sinclair	Managing Director, Willis Faber & Dumas (Agencies) Ltd
Nicholas Strauss QC	Counsel
Ian Taylor MBE MP	Member of Parliament for Esher

The Opposition

Stephen Merrett	Managing Director, Merrett Group, sometime Deputy Chairman of Lloyd's

The Establishment

Sir Peter Miller	Chairman of Lloyd's 1984–87
Murray Lawrence	Chairman of Lloyd's 1988–90
David Coleridge	Chairman of Lloyd's 1991–92
Peter Middleton	Chief Executive Officer of Lloyd's 1992–95
Sir David Rowland	Chairman of Lloyd's 1993–97

INTRODUCTION

Who prologue-like your humble patience pray,
Gently to hear, kindly to judge, our play.

Shakespeare, *Henry V*, Prologue

This is a story of people brought together by financial catastrophe. During the 1980s a crisis arose in the international insurance industry regarding three long-term risks. These were asbestosis, diethylstilboestrol (DES) and environmental pollution. This story is about huge losses in the Lloyd's Market incurred by Names, who provided trading capital for Lloyd's, the development of what many considered to be unjustified losses and the way Lloyd's was persuaded to resolve the crisis. The insurance industry was based on the premise that people would buy insurance cover so that in the event of a loss, a claim on the policy would fund the loss, or part of it, according to the terms of the policy. Insurance businesses were highly regulated and generally made a profit each year that enabled them to continue in business.

Asbestosis or mesothelioma is a fatal cancerous disease resulting from asbestos dust arriving in the lungs, causing breathing difficulties, or in other internal organs of a human being. Asbestos is a mineral that is composed of very fine fibres which are extremely durable, fireproof and add strength when bonding with other materials. It has been mined and used for hundreds of years. Disturbed fibre particles may float in the air as dust. Fatalities were reported in the early part of the twentieth century. There was increasing concern as insurance claims from policies written by Lloyd's underwriters in the 1940s and 1950s began to be received in London, escalating exponentially in the 1980s. Asbestosis claims increased right across the Lloyd's Market. Paul Brodeur's book *Outrageous Misconduct* tells how the American asbestos industry kept the knowledge of the dangers of working with asbestos to itself as a deliberate policy from the 1920s to the 1970s. The Johns Manville Corporation knowingly concealed the information from their employees for five decades. Primary insurers of various asbestos companies were aware of what was going on and acquiesced in a conspiracy of concealment. Two American lawyers in the 1970s exposed the conspiracy. By 1981 individual claims that had been settled for many years in the region of $3,000 suddenly leapt to $750,000 each, including punitive damages for concealment. Several American asbestos companies went into Chapter 11 of the United States Bankruptcy Code and the primary insurers were inundated by claims. These primary insurers turned to Lloyd's as their reinsurers. One Lloyd's Managing Agent's Board Meeting minutes recorded, 'We dare not tell the Names otherwise they will desert in droves.' The book mentioned estimates of total compensation payments for asbestosis-related disease over the next twenty to thirty years at probably around $40 billion.

The second risk was diethylstilbestrol or diethylstilboestrol (DES), a synthetic form of oestrogen hormone developed in 1938 in England. It was prescribed to pregnant women and gave rise to an increased cancer risk for their daughters as well as other long-term issues as some babies were deformed. DES was known as the 'silent Thalidomide'. The drug could prevent miscarriage and premature labour and stop lactation. It was prescribed between the 1940s and 1971, when an influx of claims arose against Lloyd's policies.

The third risk was environmental pollution. There were thousands of contaminated sites of hazardous waste being dumped, left out in the open or badly managed in the United States of America in the 1970s. Congress established the Comprehensive Environmental Response Compensation and Liability Act in 1980. The Act allowed the Environmental Protection Agency to clean up contaminated sites and charge the costs of the clean-up to the polluter or owner. Some polluters were insured at Lloyd's against such costs, and consequently implementation of the Act resulted in a rapid increase in contaminated land and pollution claims against Lloyd's underwriters.

The 300-year-old Lloyd's Insurance Market evolved as wealthy traders were intent on carrying out business overseas. Several merchants gathered together to provide funds for costly voyages that might last two or three years. If their ships returned safely, profits were divided, but if a ship was lost, so too was the traders' investment. This gave rise to the concept of syndication where a number of people were able to take a small share of large risks.

Over time multiple syndicates gathered together to form a market, collectively called the Society of Lloyd's. This was established in 1871 by the Parliamentary Act of Incorporation and the Society was allowed to regulate itself. Syndicate Members who backed the syndicates financially were known as Names – 'Internal Names' for those working within the Market and 'External Names' for those who were outside the Market. Syndicates accounted for underwriting on a calendar-year basis. Some claims took time to materialise and syndicates closed off each calendar-year account after three years. Lloyd's was governed by a Council that was restructured under the Lloyd's Act 1982 and comprised sixteen Working Members, eight External Members and three nominated by Council and confirmed by the Governor of the Bank of England. While Council could increase or decrease the numbers, there was a restriction such that Working Names did not exceed two-thirds of the Council.

A client wishing to insure with a Lloyd's policy firstly had to find an insurance broker approved by Lloyd's. The risk and the cover required would be discussed. The broker then visited the Lloyd's building and asked one or more syndicate underwriters if they would take a part of the risk. The broker had a piece of paper known as a 'slip'. Each underwriter would indicate the proportion of the risk the syndicate would take and 'initial' the slip. The client would pay the broker, who would pay the syndicate after deducting a commission for the broking service. In essence, a customer making a claim resulted in the process being reversed. The relationship between the client, broker and syndicate was one of trust. Lloyd's basis of trading promulgated *uberrima fides* (utmost good faith) and touted that it always paid valid claims.

Monies received as premiums for a risk were put on deposit and the syndicate received interest. This was a particularly important contribution to syndicate income when interest rates were typically around 10% per annum. Based on actual and historical statistics the underwriter estimated that the premium and interest receivable would cover estimated claims enabling a profit to be made for the syndicate. At the end of three years the underwriters made a calculated estimate at the value of unknown claims, known as incurred but not reported (IBNR). The underwriters created a suitable provision in the accounts before striking the profit or loss for the year. This provision was known as the reinsurance to close (RITC).

Most likely a syndicate would have different participants in the following calendar year. Consequently, arrangements had to be made for the syndicate to continue the business. The following year's syndicate was called the successor syndicate. The RITC provision was carried forward to the successor syndicate and included in the syndicate's next year of account. It was deemed sufficient to allow late claims to be paid without affecting the profit or loss account of the new accounting year. The syndicate's profit or loss for the year would then be determined. Names would be paid profits but would be liable for losses as notified by a 'cash call'. Losses may be mitigated by recoveries of tax.

Tax legislation allowed Names' losses to be set against trading profits of the same year elsewhere, or trading profits of a previous year. The loss could also be set off against other taxable income for the year. In 1987–88 the tax rate for high earners was 60%. Names often paid a tax-allowable premium for a 'stop-loss insurance policy' where a claim reduced the effect of a loss.

An underwriter might lay off some of a syndicate's risk by reinsuring it in part or in total, with other syndicates or with regulated commercial insurers outside the Lloyd's Market. Some large risks were divided into layers and underwriters were able to write all or part of one layer or more. Layers might be in bands such as £0 to £10,000, £10,001 to £25,000, £25,001 to £50,000, £50,001 to unlimited.

Lloyd's syndicates could underwrite risks where claims could arise many years after the year in which the cover was written. These were known as 'long-tail' risks. Statistical information, market knowledge and the underwriter's judgement were critical to estimate the risk and premium charged for the policy. Sometimes an underwriter reinsured such risks, for example, with a specialist 'time and distance policy'. The maturity of these policies was designed to provide cash flows likely to match anticipated claims by the insured client, decades into the future. The premium for the risk related to prevailing and forecast interest rates as well as the length of time involved.

The story in this book has two themes. Firstly, it focuses on severe losses attributed to Syndicate 334 Names and how matters were successfully resolved. Secondly, it records the personal story from start to finish of how one Syndicate 334 Name became involved with Lloyd's, suffered substantial losses and how he eventually left the Society. There is many a slip 'twixt the cup and the lip, but in this instance the slip was between 'broker and underwriter', giving rise to an ominous cloud threatening the financial integrity of Names and the possible demise of Lloyd's itself.

Winchester Bowring Ltd	WIN 961	81134002

POLICY NO. 81134002   REF. NO.

REGISTRATION   V.A.T.   T.O.C. TRIBUNAL

D.O.T. CODE   REGISTRATION CATEGORY   YEAR 81   MONTH 9

ASSURED/ACCOUNT: R.G.T. Verrall & others   ADJUST. SCHEME YES / NO

COUNTRY OF ORIGIN: UK   MARINE / NON MARINE / AVIATION

CURRENCY US$ SIGNED LINE   GROSS PREMIUM

TOTAL 100% $425,000.00

LLOYDS 100% $425,000.00

HLU

PRAC

OTHER COMPANIES

CLASS	AGENT	GEOG LOCH
RR	XX	HH
New		

5 REASSURED: SYNDICATE NO.'S 333, 334, 335, 426 AND 427 AND/OR THEIR QUOTA SHARE REINSURERS, IF APPLICABLE, CURRENTLY UNDERWRITTEN FOR BY R.G.T. VERRALL ESQ. & OTHERS AND OR HIS PREDECESSORS, AND/OR HIS SUCCESSORS, AS APPLICABLE AND INCLUDING ANY PREVIOUS SYNDICATE CARRIED FORWARD OR TRANSFERRED INTO THE CURRENT SYNDICATES.

6 PERIOD: ALWAYS OPEN WITH EFFECT FROM 1ST JANUARY, 1981. NON CANCELLABLE.

7 TYPE: AGGREGATE EXCESS LOSS REINSURANCE.

8 CLASS: IN RESPECT OF ALL LIABILITY WHICH THE REASSURED MAY INCUR ON ITS 1976 AND ALL PRIOR UNDERWRITING YEARS OF ACCOUNT.

NO EXCLUSIONS.

TERR. SCOPE: LOSSES WHERESOEVER OCCURRING.

9 LIMIT: TO PAY ALL LOSSES HOWSOEVER OCCURRING IN EXCESS OF AN ULTIMATE NETT LOSS OF US$12,000,000 IN THE AGGREGATE.

SUM REINSURED: UNLIMITED.

CO. R/I: Not Applicable.

F/I/B: Not Applicable.

REINST: Not Applicable.

10 PREMIUM: US$425,000 in full-payable by 1/10/81. by Special Settlement.

DEDUCTIONS: 5% Brokerage.

PRM./LOSS RESERVE: Not Applicable.

BJB/MG/MEH/16.9.1981.

CLASS / AGENT / GEOG LOCH

RENEWAL/NEW   MAG CARD NO   Track's 20/21   ILL TREATY NO

HERON 100%

WRITTEN LINES PERCENTAGES OF WHOLE

SIGNED LINES PERCENTAGE OF WHOLE

LPG TREATY NO.

3

14

TREATY

15 Winchester Bowring Ltd

R.G.I. Verrall Esq. & other
Aggregate Excess Loss R/I

J/L xs $12,00,000 in ويل
Always app_ ويل 1.1.1981 iro
1975 & Prior U/w Years   61

16

---

11 SIGNED LINE

GEN. CONDS: Reassured to supply annual advices of settled and outstanding losses.

Reinsurers to benefit from all Salvages, Recoveries, Additional Premium and the like and from any applicable Reinsurance recoveries actually received by the Reassured. Likewise Reinsurers to be liable for all return premium, and the like.

Amounts recoverable hereunder shall be payable solely in United States Dollars and for the purposes of establishing the aggregate deductible under this contract the total annual settlements made by the Reassured in Sterling and Canadian Dollars shall be converted into United States Dollars at the applicable Lloyd's Audit Rates for that calendar years settlement.

It shall be understood however that the settlements of the Reassured in Sterling will include loss or losses if any, paid by the Reassured in currencies other than Sterling, United States Dollars and Canadian Dollars which are converted into Sterling at the rates of exchange as used by the Reassured in their books.

All Periods, Terms, Clauses, Conditions and Warranties as original and to follow original fortunes and settlements including ex-gratia payments in every respect.

UNL Clause amended to read 'Losses Actually Recovered'.

Claims payable annually by Special Settlement on or after 1st April following the 31st December each year.

However, if settled losses amount to US$100,000 or more in any one calendar year, Reassured may recover within 30 days of notice to Reinsurer the aggregate of losses settled to date of notice. Thereafter claims settled in same calendar year to be recovered following 1st April.

12 Reassured to have sole benefit of any underlying 'Run-Off' reinsurances.

WORDING: Full wording to be agreed Leading Reinsurer only (Arbitration at Lloyd's).

13 100%

100%   RJM 418

Winchester Bowring Broker's Slip (Key)

1. Winchester Bowring Ltd
2. Assured's AccountR G I Verrall & Others
3. Marine Syndicate
4. Premium: US$425,000
5. Reassured: Syndicate 334 (and others)
6. Period: from 1 January 1981, always open, non-cancellable
7. Type: aggregate excess of loss
8. Class: all liability that the reassured may incur on its 1975 and all prior underwriting years of account, no exclusions, losses wheresoever occurring
9. Limit: in excess of an ultimate net loss of US$12,000,000 in the aggregate
10. Premium: $425,000 payable by 1 October 1981
11. General conditions
12. Arbitration clause
13. Syndicate 418 underwriter accepting 100% of the risk. XLXXI.3.7 (3 July 1981)
14. Policy Number: 81134002
15. Policy details
16. Contract formalised at Lloyd's Policy Signing Office (LPSO), 30 September 1981

CHAPTER 1

Many a Slip 'Twixt…
Broker and Underwriter

It must be thought on. If it pass against us,
We lose the better half of our possession…

Henry V, Act 1 Scene 1

In 1981 the underwriter of Marine Syndicate 334 had reinsured the syndicate against potential losses arising prior to 1975, but had recently learnt that the reinsuring syndicate refused to accept liability. On a cloudy summer's afternoon, 6 June 1990, seven men, six of them Members of Lloyd's Marine Syndicate 334 and one of them a solicitor, gathered in the London office of the Association of Lloyd's Members (ALM) to discuss ballooning losses arising from their underwriting activities. This decision had far-reaching consequences and would destroy the wealth and lives of numerous Syndicate 334 Members.

The meeting's deliberations concerned the 1985 year of account which remained open and not closed by a reinsurance to close (RITC). Ron Verall, the Syndicate 334 underwriter, was unable to quantify the likely claims to come on Syndicate 334's 1985 account. During the 1960s and 1970s various syndicates had been writing environmental policies giving cover for such risks as pollution, asbestosis and diethylstilbesterol (DES). Syndicate 334 specialised in marine risks but had been permitted to underwrite a few 'incidental' non-marine policies.

Many claims were against policies that were written for USA policy-holders thirty or more years ago. By 1980 asbestosis could no longer be ignored by Lloyd's. However, it was doubtful if all underwriters understood and appreciated the scale and extent of losses to come. Information about the risks associated with these liabilities was not given to External Names, that is, Names not employed by Lloyd's. Managers and underwriters who did realise the extent of potential claims aimed to add enough capital to ride out the losses by rapidly increasing the number of Names or encouraging existing Names to increase their assets held by Lloyd's.

It was the incidental non-marine risks that caused concern for Syndicate 334. Verall was aware of the risk of potential claims. A Lloyd's broker, Winchester Bowring, had placed an aggregate excess of loss reinsurance for Syndicate 334 – reinsuring risks on the 1975 and all prior underwriting years of account – with Merrett Syndicate 418. The terms of the insurance policy stated that losses were reinsured wheresoever occurring and unlimited in excess of an ultimate net loss of $12 million in the aggregate and it was not cancellable. In other words, the maximum liability for the syndicate was $12 million. The premium for this reinsurance cover was $425,000. The contract for the reinsurance followed customary Lloyd's procedure of initialling a 'slip'. Thus on 18 September 1981 the underwriter laid off the total risk for old years' liabilities prior to 1975, subject to the excess of $12 million. Syndicate 418 was a well-established syndicate dealing with long-tail risks. Ron Verall felt assured that the Syndicate 334 Names had no liability for claims arising earlier than 1976. He was very comfortable with the 'sleep easy' insurance cover.

On 4 May 1989 the Syndicate 418 underwriter gave notice to void the reinsurance policy. The decision to void the policy went to arbitration. Arbitrators were appointed by each party and a third one, Sir William Stabb QC, had a casting vote. The hearing lasted nine days. Each party to the contract owed to the other a duty of *uberrima fides*, utmost good faith. Syndicate 334 had provided a summary of the risks and there was sufficient information for the underwriter to make intelligent enquiries. Syndicate 334 did not explain or reveal the figures for outstanding claims reported as 'short-tail'; these were claims which typically arose close to the date the insurance policy was written. The arbitrators considered this was misleading because these claims related to 'long-tail' risks where claims might arise many years later. Such liabilities should have been properly reserved and explained by Syndicate 334. It was also acknowledged that there was poor underwriting by the reinsurer, Syndicate 418.

On 2 February 1990 an arbitrators' interim award was made favouring the claimant, Syndicate 418. Two arbitrators found in favour of Syndicate 418 that the contract was lawfully avoided. The third arbitrator found in favour of the respondent, Syndicate 334, as he considered that there was no 'nondisclosure', as in his view sufficient information had been provided. Leave to appeal the arbitration award to the High Court was unsuccessful.

The voided policy meant that Syndicate 334 had lost the reinsurance cover for the years prior to 1976. Syndicate 334 Names who thought they had been insured suddenly found that they had dire actual and potential liabilities. For some Names, Syndicate 334 losses, together with losses elsewhere in the Market, were potentially catastrophic. A severe storm was beginning to overshadow not only Syndicate 334 Names but involving the finances of the whole of Lloyd's Society and its Market. Angry Names were up in arms. They demanded explanations. Some refused to pay cash calls, others threatened legal action, cries for the resignation of responsible officials were heard, many contacted their Members of Parliament, made complaints to appropriate authorities and wrote to the press. A great furore of unbelievable anger was created.

It was in this highly charged atmosphere that, on the cloudy June afternoon, seven serious-minded men gathered together. The solicitor present was Dr David Tiplady, from D J Freeman, a City firm of solicitors, who summarised the implications of legal action necessary to overturn the arbitration. Dr Tiplady emphasised, 'No one should be in any doubt about the severe difficulty of overturning the arbitration.'

The vision for a proposed Association was to recover losses, if necessary, by winning a legal action. It was agreed to form a provisional Steering Committee of Syndicate 334 Names with a view to starting an Association to take legal action to recover the losses. Those present were

Alasdair F. Ferguson MBE and Ray Cook, who were businessmen; Jasper Salisbury-Jones, a barrister; Keith Lester and Harry Purchase, Chartered Accountants; and Clive Francis, a retired Royal Air Force squadron leader, whom Keith had met at a recent ALM lunch and persuaded to attend the meeting. Clive was proposed as Chairman.

Initially, Committee Members were faced with immense uncertainties over funding and expertise in their attempt to achieve a successful outcome. To address the enormity of the task it was vital to recruit enough Syndicate 334 Names to finance the proposed Association's activities.

It was agreed to arrange a meeting on 3 July for Syndicate 334 Names, and Alasdair Ferguson agreed to prepare a background paper.

Syndicate 334 Names were subject to cash calls to fund the losses on the 1985 account. A Name's capacity to underwrite was expressed in units of £10,000, known as 'lines' and supported by assets pledged to Lloyd's. Losses were given as a percentage of the line. Thus, as an example, a 100% loss would be £10,000. In other words, the Name would have to find cash to replace the £10,000 lost. Following the arbitration, the cash call was 180%, needing £18,000 to fund the £10,000 underwriting capacity.

For someone underwriting £1 million capacity on a number of syndicates in the Market at 180% loss, the amount to be paid to Lloyds would be £1,800,000. In dire circumstances it was possible to become bankrupt. The next chapter describes how someone became a Name at Lloyd's and landed up in quite a pickle.

Summary of Key Issues

1. A reinsurance policy for Syndicate 334 was voided and went to arbitration. Syndicate 334 lost the arbitration. There was unbelievable anger.
2. Six Syndicate 334 Names gathered to receive advice about taking legal action to overturn the arbitration.
3. The immense difficulty in overturning the arbitration should not be underestimated.

CHAPTER 2

Background to a Name's Recruitment, Underwriting and Contemporary Events

To find his title with some shows of truth,
Though in pure truth, it was corrupt and naught

Henry V, Act 1 Scene 2

In the 1970s Harry Purchase and Keith Lester were employees of Stewart Wrightson Ltd, which had as its Managing Director David Rowland, often referred to as JDR by his staff. Stewart Wrightson was a subsidiary of Matthews Wrightson Group PLC, the international insurance brokers. Another subsidiary of the Matthews Wrightson Group was Matthews Wrightson Pulbrook Ltd, a Members' underwriting agency that managed both Lloyd's Names and underwriting syndicates. There were two syndicates in the Matthews Wrightson Pulbrook stable, Marine Syndicate 334 and the specialist Non-Marine Syndicate 90.

Harry Purchase was the Managing Director of a UK regional insurance broker, a subsidiary of Stewart Wrightson Ltd. He was a Working Name at Lloyd's. Stewart Wrightson liked its senior staff to have an interest in underwriting at Lloyd's. Consequently, the company provided guarantees for Harry as the asset supporting the 'means' given to Lloyd's, enabling him to become a Name and engage in underwriting in the Lloyd's Market. Using the company guarantee route, the individual was called an 'Assisted Name'. Such individuals were likely to have a weaker personal asset base.

Keith Lester met David Carrington, the Managing Director of Matthews Wrightson Pulbrook, in 1978 at a Stewart Wrightson Executive Management course in Oxford, and expressed an interest in underwriting. He was prepared to show personal assets as 'means', enabling him to become a Name. He was nominated by his Managing Director, David Rowland, as an 'External Name', someone who was not working in the Market. Prospective Names were interviewed at a rota meeting with the Lloyd's Membership Committee sometimes in the Adam Room, Lloyd's Council Chamber, originally part of Bowood House. Attendees at the rota meeting included, for example, the Secretary of the Society of Lloyd's, a Member of the New Names Department and an active underwriter. They explained the possible consequences of unlimited liability concentrating primarily on the severity of the downside risk. Names' assets had to be held in the sole name of the individual. They said assets held by a spouse could not be acquired to satisfy any liability that exceeded the assets of the Name. Keith was accepted and started underwriting from 1 January 1981.

He started underwriting as an External Name through Matthews Wrightson Pulbrook, joining Marine Syndicate 334, Non-Marine Syndicate 90 and Motor Syndicate 533. Keith's premium limit (or line) for Syndicates 334 and 90 was £25,000 each, with an additional £10,000 on Motor Syndicate 533. The limits were the value to which an underwriter could allocate premium for policies written by his syndicate and related to the value of assets accepted by Lloyd's as security, or 'means'. Syndicate 334 capital gains for 1982 exceeded the trading loss leaving a small net profit overall. This was enhanced by income tax recoveries on trading losses which could be set against other personal income. Marine Syndicate 334 was permitted by Lloyd's regulations and bylaws to underwrite a small 'incidental' proportion of non-marine insurance business and this took the form of long-term businesses such as environmental pollution and exposure to latent diseases including asbestosis and DES. As described in Chapter 1, Syndicate 334 sought reinsurance cover for 1975 and earlier years to give comfort to Names that the liability of all the incidental non-marine long-term risks had been reinsured. In July 1981 Carrington contacted Keith, explaining that, 'I am able to tell you the Special Reinsurance referred to in the Marine Underwriters report has now been placed and I am reasonably confident that the 1979 and 1980 accounts of these syndicates will not be negative.' However, the cover had been placed but was not recorded at the Lloyd's Policy Signing Office until 18 September. Carrington's optimism subsequently proved to be quite misplaced.

Parliament passed the Lloyd's Act 1982 which came into force that year on 23 July, and various changes occurred at Lloyd's. Underwriting and Names' agency activities, previously operated by one company, were divided into component parts. Matthews Wrightson Pulbrook retained the underwriting agency. A new company was formed to look after the Names' affairs called Stewart Wrighton Members' Agency. This company subsequently merged into Willis Faber & Dumas (Agencies) Ltd. In January 1985 Matthews Wrightson Pulbrook Underwriting Management was taken over by Merrett Underwriting Agencies, becoming part of the Merrett Group. Thus, the reinsuring Syndicate 418 and the reinsured Syndicate 334 became part of the same financial entity, the Merrett Group. This resulted in a severe conflict of interest as the owner was both the insurer and the insured. Stephen Merrett was the Chairman and largest shareholder in the Merrett Group and was responsible for voiding the Syndicate 334 insurance cover for years prior to 1975. Merrett had been a prominent Member of Lloyd's for many years. He was a Member of Lloyd's Council from 1981 to 1984 and from 1987 to 1990. He was Deputy Chairman of Lloyd's in 1993. Since 1980 he had been a member of twelve key Committees including: Accounting and Auditing Standards; Audit; Inception Date and the Accounting Work Group which dealt with solvency and security; and Finance and General Purposes, concerned with terms of credit. He was entrepreneurial and a very experienced underwriter.

Carrington reported that there was an immense amount of work to be done on the RITC for closing Syndicate 90 in 1983 and into 1984. Accounts for 1983 would require audit certificates, a new requirement following the implementation of the Lloyd's Act 1982. However, after tax, he thought there would be a net profit on the 1983 account. Bad news came from James Bazell, Chairman of Stewart Wrightson Members' Agency Ltd, in April 1986. He reiterated his letter of March 1985 that Syndicate 90 had a serious loss and the 1982 account would continue to remain open as the RITC had not been quantified. He forecast a 20% trading loss for Syndicate 90 in 1983. However, there was a profit forecast of 7% on Syndicate 334 for that year. He confirmed these results on 18 June 1986.

In 1983 Ian Hay Davison CBE FCA, a high-flying Chartered Accountant, had returned from the USA and become the managing partner of the infant Arthur Andersen practice. *The Sunday Times* reported on 2 September 1984 that Davison had expressed his concern about the failure to bring criminal actions against insurers who made secret profits in offshore reinsurance companies. He pointed out that it was over two years since this reinsurance scandal had surfaced publicly. Reportedly he had written to the Prime Minister accordingly. Many within Lloyd's believed that the Government lacked the will to carry out the necessary proceedings to prosecute. Furthermore, the Department of Public Prosecutions considered that any case brought would be so complicated that it would be impossible to explain the facts adequately to a jury. There were strong hints from the authorities that a public washing of Lloyd's dirty linen would damage both Lloyd's and the City in the important American market. At the prompting of the Governor of the Bank of England, Lord Richardson, Davison was appointed as CEO to clean up Lloyd's.

By 1985, Keith Lester's underwriting capacity had increased to £250,000 spread over twelve syndicates. The 1985 years for Syndicates 334 and 90 did not close at the end of 1987 and remained as open years, clocking up losses each year.

Keith's loss for syndicates at the end of 1987 that should have closed at the end of 1989 amounted to £33,200 for Syndicate 334 plus £30,000 for the Non-Marine Syndicate 90, totalling £63,200. However, there were profits from other syndicates of £5,500, resulting in a net loss of £57,500, payable in June 1990. Some stop-loss insurance was available to reduce the loss.

Stop-loss protection insurance is provided after an excess of a certain amount – say, £12,000. A premium is paid to cover losses in a band – say, from £12,000 to £30,000. Beyond £30,000 the loss falls upon the Name again. Using the above example of £57,500 loss, Keith bore the first £12,000, the stop-loss underwriter the next £18,000, leaving an excess of £27,500, again borne by Keith. Thus, the net loss to be settled in cash for the losses was £39,500.

The stop-loss excess and banding were judgements at the beginning of the relevant calendar year of account (e.g., 1981), depending on current and expected circumstances. Cover lasted for the three years of the account at the same annual cost. In this case, the annual tax-allowable premium for stop-loss cover for £18,000 excess £12,000 spread over three syndicates was typically £415 per annum. The premium reduced any profit or increased the loss for the year of account. At the beginning of 1980, seemingly, there was no Market information available to stop-loss underwriters that such an excessive loss was likely. With hindsight, a total of £1,245 paid for the three years to settle a claim of £18,000 was a good bargain.

Syndicate performance information was provided each year by the Names' agency. An employee of Willis Faber & Dumas (Agencies) suggested that Keith could increase underwriting on Syndicates 90 and 334. Keith told him, 'I do not intend to increase underwriting on these syndicates as both syndicates have a poor record, whilst the former appeared to be trading badly, the latter was steady. I am considering withdrawing from them altogether!' Often a syndicate made an underwriting loss, but the capital gains on investments held as reserves to pay claims exceeded the loss. After taking account of tax recoveries on trading income, a Name might receive overall a net 'profit' as a cash receipt.

By 1985 Keith's premium limit had risen to £250,000 on twelve syndicates across the Market. However, in view of the disappointing results and forecasts for the 1985 year, premium limits for underwriting on Syndicates 90 and 334 were reduced from £25,000 to £15,000 and £20,000 respectively. Keith wrote to Carrington expressing concern about the poor results, observing that the syndicates to which he belonged were almost wholly in the lower quartile of Lloyd's published syndicates' results. Syndicate 334 looked like a high-risk long-tail syndicate. Keith wished to come off poor-performing syndicates, particularly mentioning Syndicates 334 and 90. The losses on the 1992 account for Syndicate 90 were five times higher than the premium underwritten. The stop-loss was set to cover reasonable underwriting losses but not those of professional negligence and fraud. He observed that these points were relevant to Carrington personally as he was a Name on both syndicates. Carrington commented that he was writing closer to his premium limit and thought Syndicate 334 should improve its overall performance. He did not consider that Syndicate 334 was a long-tail syndicate. He mentioned that Michael Turner, the syndicate's Deputy Underwriter, had brought in an excess of loss underwriting team in the autumn of 1983 to address performance issues. Excess of loss related to liabilities that were largely non-marine long-tail policies in this instance, and it was difficult to obtain reliable information as to the extent of the loss. Hence a specialist team was set to work on these claims and potential liabilities.

Her Majesty Queen Elizabeth II opened the iconic new Lloyd's building designed by Richard Rogers on 18 November 1986. There was a ballot of Names for an invitation to attend the opening. During her gracious speech Her Majesty commented, 'Alongside its successes of recent years, the community of Lloyd's has been faced with some major problems. Much time and effort has been spent in developing self-regulatory requirements. Steady progress has been made and I am sure will continue to be made, towards a better supervised Market.' The *Financial Times* reported that this referred obliquely to scandals that had surfaced in 1982.

The Annual General Meeting of Willis Faber PLC was held on 24 May 1990 and shareholder Keith asked Chairman David Rowland questions about Syndicate 334. He complained about the incompetent management and enquired whether there was any provision for liabilities arising from such incompetent management, and about training of young people in the business. The Syndicate 334 Annual Report made no mention of the directors' entrepreneurial skills, or their professional or academic training. The Chairman said there was no provision in the company's financial statements for losses by Lloyd's syndicates. There was no follow-up question or comment.

In June 1987 James Bazell, Chairman of Willis Faber & Dumas (Agencies), provided the underwriting results for the 1984 account for Syndicate 334 and showed a small trading profit overall and a capital gain. Once again there was a significant loss for Syndicate 90 and the 1982 account remained open.

A circulated 'Statement of Disclosures of Interests' from Bazell received on 28 March 1988 showed syndicates' capacity, on which directors were underwriting. Bazell's lines on Syndicates 334 and 90 showed capacity of £65,000 each, and Carrington £20,000 each. It is not known whether they realised the extent of potential losses from long-term liabilities facing the Market. If they did know they obviously thought they could trade through any unprofitable situation. A £65,000 capacity at 180% prospective loss, mentioned in an earlier example, would incur a liability of a £117,000 cash call for Syndicate 334 alone.

Elizabeth Le Sueur of Salisbury wrote to Carrington and Murray Lawrence, Lloyd's Chairman, on 27 June 1989. She said that she had never been informed that she could be liable for claims arising out of events which occurred prior to her joining Lloyd's. Now she understood there was a 'very large' bomb about to explode in the form of escalating claims from asbestosis. Between 1980 and 1982 her concern had been allayed by the clear impression conveyed in underwriters' reports that 'appropriate provisions' had been made and a 'substantial measure of reinsurance protection' had been placed. Le Sueur's primary concern related to Syndicate 90, however, she had been informed that a similar asbestosis-related problem had arisen on Syndicate 334. She would have attended a rota meeting before she joined Lloyd's, where the downside risk of unlimited liability would have been explained.

Bridget Milling-Smith of High Wycombe wrote to Lawrence on 20 June 1990 about her call for £44,232 on the 1982 account which had subsequently increased to £76,524. In 1977 at the age of twenty-six she had lost her Royal Marine husband in a helicopter accident in Oman and was left with two small boys. She was not wealthy. She explained she had handed her financial affairs to David Bentata of broker Charterhouse Japhet, who suggested she become a Name at Lloyd's. He introduced her to Brian Bell of the underwriting Agent Cox & Bell, whom he said she could trust and would look after her underwriting. She had asked Brian Bell not to put her on any high-risk syndicates. Lawrence replied that Names were given the opportunity to confirm their understanding of Lloyd's, and to ask questions. He commented that she had £24,500 profit from another agency, R. F. Kershaw. She also had some stop-loss insurance. It would be improper for him to advise her regarding her Lloyd's Membership. This was the 'Establishment' batting with a straight bat and taking no responsibility for individual Names' predicaments. Guy Wilson, who was acting as the 'Association's' Committee Secretary, contacted Milling-Smith, suggesting she should consider applying to the Hardship Committee for relief. Milling-Smith featured in the *Daily Telegraph* on 21 June 1991. The headline was 'What It Means To Be A Lloyd's Loser'. Lloyd's professionals say she should never have been a Name.

As the two cases above indicate, preparations for an association became imperative as an increasing deluge of stories of distress were received by mail, email and telephone.

Summary of Key Issues
1. Steps needed to be taken to become a Name at Lloyd's, including sample details of risks.
2. Information provided about syndicate performance and relations with Names' agencies.
3. Details of complaints received by Names.
4. Even HM The Queen was moved to point out the need for reform. That's how (arguably) corrupt or poorly managed the Society of Lloyd's had become.

CHAPTER 3

Preparations to Form an Association: To Get 'Our' Money Back with Costs

He [King Henry] wills you [the King of France] in the
name of God Almighty,
That you divest yourself and lay apart...
'Tis no sinister nor no awkward claim.

Henry V, Act 2 Scene 4

On 3 July 1990 the Chairman of the Steering Committee, Clive Francis, welcomed some 160 Members (out of a total Membership of 562) of Syndicate 334 to the Old Library at Lloyd's. Other attendees included solicitor Dr David Tiplady, representatives of the Association of Lloyd's Names, and Stephen Merrett of Merrett Underwriting Management, Chairman of the Merrett Group.

Clive informed attendees:

When Names joined Lloyd's they were aware of the external risks they ran but were never warned of Lloyd's internal risks. Names should not have to pay the penalty of funding the negligence or breaches of good faith by Managing Agents. Lloyd's *prime* responsibility must be to the security of its policies to meet valid claims and to preserve the good name of Lloyd's for the future prosperity of the Market generally. It was Syndicate 334's reinsurance policy that had been voided and the Syndicate had been left unprotected. The

Council of Lloyd's appeared wholly unconcerned by aspects of gross negligence and bad faith shown by a Managing Agent.

Clive continued, 'I have received many letters from Names including one from Karl Ziebarth of Dallas.' Ziebarth's letter was read out and it mentioned the recent insurance case about the sinking of the MTS *Oceanos* in 1991 that had changed the legal framework under which the Lloyd's community must be judged. The law now made the underwriting Managing Agent and the reinsurance broker responsible for their errors. The Agent had the discretionary authority to purchase a contract of reinsurance. Failure to disclose fully all the facts that allowed the contract to be voided subsequently was a gross breach of contract. It appeared that the Managing Agent, its officers, directors and successors were completely liable and the policy should not have been voided.

Merrett addressed the meeting. 'I am very sympathetic and deeply regret the losses which have caused many Names great worry. The premium plus interest for the voided contract has been repaid and the parties concerned should abide by the decision of the Arbitrators.' Clive observed, 'There is absolutely no sign of any compromise from Mr Merrett. This is cold comfort for me and other Names. I am very disappointed in what Mr Merrett has had to say. His stance appears to be "catch me if you can".'

Martin Bakes of Herbert Smith, solicitors for Syndicate 334, outlined the legal position identified at the arbitration. He identified three counts of nondisclosure including: failure to disclose long-term liabilities including asbestosis, failure to disclose IBNR reserves of $1.5 million and failure to disclose Johns Manville asbestosis claims. Johns Manville was a US corporation that produced asbestos products. There was awareness of asbestos causing ill health in the 1940s and it was company policy not to inform the workers about the disease. Serious illnesses caused by exposure to the company's asbestos products started appearing in the late 1970s and into the 1980s. Legal actions were started against Johns Manville. The liability from asbestos-related claims became enormous. The company filed for bankruptcy in 1982.

Bakes maintained that Syndicate 418 was provided with substantial information and had waived its requirement to further disclosure. However, for the risks mentioned above there were no IBNR reserves. Syndicate 334 was substantially under-reserved. Nevertheless, he thought the arbitrators' decision was wrong as they did not take due notice of dissenting comments.

Dr David Tiplady, the proposed association's solicitor, had circulated a detailed legal position statement and mentioned three ingredients for a valid claim. These were, firstly, the underwriting Agents owed a duty of care; secondly, that duty must have been broken; and thirdly, a loss must have occurred. He said that Members' Agents had a *prime* responsibility to Names but the extent of their duty was unclear. He observed that while the arbitrators said Pulbrook Underwriting Management had failed in making disclosures, they did not say Pulbrook Underwriting Management was negligent. He thought there may be a claim in both tort and contract against the Lloyd's brokers, Winchester Bowring. There may have been some form of misrepresentation or negligence regarding those Names who joined in 1982. Full disclosure of events prior to that time would not have been given to potential Names. It was pointed out that having agreed to a policy with Syndicate 418, Syndicate 334 had lost the opportunity of placing the business elsewhere.

Some Names were stating categorically that they would not pay calls. David Tiplady confirmed that Names had contractual liabilities and should pay calls.

There was an overwhelming vote in favour of forming a Steering Committee with an initial contribution of £250 per Name. The purpose would be to explore the possibilities of conciliation and settlement and advising Names on all aspects of full legal action.

Merrett commented that he could not give a formal response and it was unclear who would indemnify the Names. He added that there would be a thorough investigation of the books and he would let Names know in due course if there would be further cash calls. Jasper Salisbury-Jones, as a barrister, doubted whether conciliation would get anywhere.

Harry Purchase spoke vehemently, saying, 'I'm not going to pay my cash calls. There was gross negligence and serious mismanagement. No way am I going to pay, furthermore, where would I find the cash?' On a show of hands, seventeen Names indicated that they would refuse to pay their cash call.

Guy Wilson, as a Lloyd's Name and Chartered Certified Accountant but not a Member of Syndicate 334, represented two Syndicate 334 Names with cash calls amounting to £320,000. He asked about the effect of unpaid calls. The famous 'pay now, sue later' clause was in the underwriting contract. If Names refused to pay calls the liability would be met from the Central Guarantee Fund (CGF) and Names would have their Membership suspended until the calls were settled. Ultimately, defaulting Names would be sued by Lloyd's.

Membership of the provisional Steering Committee was confirmed by the meeting and comprised Clive Francis, Chairman; Keith Lester, Treasurer; Alasdair Ferguson MBE; Harry Purchase; Charles Baron; Raymond Cook; and Jasper Salisbury-Jones. David Tiplady was appointed to act for the Association. Clive instructed those at the meeting in a strongly assertive tone, 'You must write to key Lloyd's personnel, their Members of Parliament, the press, and cause as much trouble as you possibly can.' There was appreciative applause for the event's organisers.

A month later David Tiplady said he had received contributions from over 180 Names and would be disappointed if fewer than 300 would eventually subscribe. Subscriptions were received from overseas including Australia, New Zealand, USA, Canada, France and Portugal, as well as from England and Scotland. David Tiplady explained that finding an expert opinion was a real problem as no Lloyd's Working Name would challenge the acting Working Name who held the underwriter's pen. He had instructed an expert, Brian Wood, the chief marine underwriter for Norwich Winterthur Reinsurance Corporation Ltd, to prepare a report.

Some Names had died and their liabilities were in the hands of the trustees of their Estates. Other Names were Working Names like Gervase Tinley and Harry Purchase. Both were 'Assisted Names' with

Stewart Wrightson, and relied on the Agent's advice to be satisfied they would not be making substantial losses. Harry's loss was £47,882 and he alleged negligence.

On 9 July a list of questions was sent by Keith Lester to James Sinclair, Managing Director of Willis Faber & Dumas (Agencies) Ltd, the Members' Managing Agent, including:

1. On what grounds were losses of Syndicate 334 a liability of Names and what action has been taken to mitigate the losses?
2. If Mr Merrett and his company were not working on behalf of Names on syndicates then who was he working for and what service was he providing?
3. Would Mr Sinclair agree that he had entrusted Names' affairs to an incompetent underwriting management company?
4. Can a Name be satisfied those costs had been properly attributed to a syndicate and does the syndicate make a charge to the Agent for using time of syndicate employees in researching aspects of litigation that may be taken against them?
5. Was there a charge in respect of lost business opportunities?
6. Was there a claim being made on Names' behalf against the Managing Agency for gross professional negligence?

The arbitrators concluded there were three areas of gross managerial incompetence and the underwriter's conduct had 'bordered on gross negligence'. Merrett's company took over the management of Syndicate 334 and must have been aware of the reinsurance policy between Syndicates 418 and 334 immediately inferring conflicts of interest. The reinsurance policy was judged voidable five years after it was signed. Consequently Syndicate 334 had lost an important contingent asset, contingent on claims being presented for settlement. Names were misled for five years into believing the asset was theirs and claims against the syndicate would be settled.

First Steering Committee Meeting, 16 July 1990

The first meeting was held in Michael Jump's Chambers at Lincoln's Inn. In addition to the elected Committee, Jump, a Syndicate 334 Name and a tax barrister, joined the meeting. Oliver Carruthers, the Editor of the *Digest of Lloyd's News*, also attended for about half an hour. Guy Wilson was co-opted to the Committee and appointed as Secretary. As he was not a Member of Syndicate 334 it was agreed to pay for his services at £12 per hour. Other Committee members were voluntary and unpaid.

Karl Ziebarth's draft letter to Alan Lord, Lloyd's Chief Executive, concerned the re-registration of Merrett Underwriting Agencies Ltd, and questioned its fitness – or lack thereof – to act as a Names' underwriting Agent. It was suggested that Ziebarth should be encouraged to send the letter personally from Dallas. Clive opined, 'It is preferable to manufacture "bullets" for others to fire. Furthermore, the Committee should take an extremely considered approach to correspondence with Lloyd's in view of the vast sums at stake. To control correspondence, I propose that barristers on the Committee should vet direct approaches to Lloyd's'. The Committee approved the proposal unanimously.

Clive wondered where the impetus came from for Willis Faber & Dumas Names' Agent to upset their very comfortable applecart by taking up cudgels on the Names' behalf against a fellow Agent. 'There isn't any', he said, 'unless the Name points out in strongest terms where legal duty lay'. He exhorted Names to ask their solicitors to write demanding that Agents and Lloyd's Council perform their legal duties.

Committee member Jasper Salisbury-Jones agreed to provide some rules for the Association. The objects were:

1.   to progress the legal case.
2.   to spearhead aggressive attacks on the various 'targets' which David Tiplady outlined later in the meeting.
3.   to obtain appropriate publicity in quality newspapers with the aim of alerting the general public as to the dangers of Lloyd's Membership.

4. to embarrass Lloyd's officials who were already worried about the decline in Membership and its effect on capacity.

Lloyd's had issued Membership suspension notices regarding unpaid cash calls to various Names, including Jasper Salisbury-Jones. Jasper had requested an oral hearing as Lloyd's had said no suspensions would occur whilst oral representations were being made. Oral representation would keep the pot boiling.

It was suggested that Matthews Wrightson Pulbrook should make a claim under its own errors and omissions (E&O) policy and shown in Syndicate 334 as a debtor. This may not have been considered, as it was easier for Matthews Wrightson Pulbrook to extract money from Names.

David outlined the legal targets for action:

1. Herbert Smith the solicitors acting in the arbitration case may have been in breach of duty and may be sued in tort.
2. Pulbrook underwriting management.
3. Various Members' Agents and possibly some Directors.
4. Other legal targets were suggested by several Committee Members. There would have to be a 'reasonable cause of action' before counsel would agree to their inclusion as likely defendants.

David said the arbitration had no binding effect regarding litigation even though leave to appeal to the House of Lords was refused. He had asked the stop-loss underwriters for a contribution to the fighting fund but they declined to become involved at this stage.

Jonathan Gaisman QC was proposed as counsel. Michael Jump and Jasper Salisbury-Jones agreed to discuss preliminary instructions prepared by David, who anticipated issuing a writ within six months and it would then be valid for four months.

Oliver Carruthers gave the Committee some ideas on how to use the press to best advantage. It became clear that one of Lloyd's principle aims for publicity was to make Lloyd's a better institution. The Corporation and Council of Lloyd's were very worried about adverse publicity.

In the Merrett Group the normal procedure for approving policies was explained. John Emney, the active underwriter for Syndicate 418, would take details of the reinsurance policy to be written for Syndicate 334, for example, for 'rubber-stamping' by Merrett. Apparently, they never thought the policy would be invoked. Once the policy was voided Syndicate 334 was a bleeding wound with unquantifiable losses, and the cash call in 1991 may have been at least 25%. Names with 48% of their underwriting on Syndicates 334 and 90 were reckoned to have a very good cause for action.

Nominations for election to Lloyd's Council had to be submitted by 21 September and be supported by sixteen External Members. A likely candidate was Committee Member Keith Lester, who, to be eligible, must not become suspended from underwriting.

David Tiplady gave a report on the finances of the proposed Syndicate 334 (1985) Names Association (the Association) and informed the Committee:

> I have received subscriptions from 180 Names. This shows substan-
> tial support for the proposed actions of the Steering Committee
> even though it is highly doubtful that a legal challenge would be
> successful. I have £50,000 for the fighting fund. Every day Names
> have given me their stories. I would like to receive any informa-
> tion or records that may be of assistance. I have analysed five large
> lever arch files of arbitration documentation and am now able to
> instruct an expert witness. Although there are few people in the
> Market willing or able to act as experts I am awaiting a report
> from Mr Brian Wood, the Chief Marine Underwriter for Norwich
> Winterthur Reinsurance Corporation.

David also reported that his firm's bill amounted to some £25,000 and reckoned he had worked quite hard for the Association. A counsel's opinion was likely to cost £10,000 or more.

Following the Committee meeting Jasper Salisbury-Jones provided a press release. Articles were published in *Lloyd's List*, the *Guardian*, the *Financial Times* and the *Daily Telegraph*.

Assisted Name Harry Purchase wrote to Alan Turner, the Secretary of Willis Faber & Dumas, saying that he was told by both James Bazell and David Carrington that Syndicates 334 and 90 were conservative and unlikely to make much in the way of large profits or suffer large losses. In his discussions with them they confirmed that the syndicates were fully reinsured and did not underwrite long-tail business. He had not been offered any other syndicates. Harry had resigned as a Name and had no reserves at Lloyd's. There was obviously a serious management failure as no proper check was in place to ensure that a marine syndicate underwriting incidental non-marine risks took on such horrendous liabilities as those associated with asbestosis and pollution. He protested, saying he was not going to fund the loss which overall might eventually amount to £250,000.

Kenneth Lavery, a Chartered Accountant in Ontario, wrote on July 25 to Lloyd's Chairman Murray Lawrence about Syndicates 334 and 418. He said the fact that the syndicates were in the same group boggled the mind – it smelled, even across the Atlantic. He requested a written explanation from Ernst & Whinney, the auditors, on how they were able to give a clean audit report for Syndicate 418 for the closed 1982 year. He had sent funds to the Cuthbert Heath Agency with strict instructions to retain the funds until he received satisfactory responses to his questions. In his view, the 1982 year for Syndicates 334 and 418 should have been kept open. He would then have missed the loss, as he only joined the syndicates in 1984. He queried how he was put on high-risk syndicates unbeknownst to him, and why any Name in their right mind would stay in Lloyd's.

He also wrote to C. K. Murray, the Deputy Chairman of Lloyd's, wondering how the auditors could have given a clean audit report for the 1982 year, and how it was Lloyd's Council had been satisfied. He thought it was a bit like sending in the fox to check on the security of the hen house. One Name contacted Alan Turner, the Company Secretary of Willis Faber & Dumas (Agencies), complaining, 'On 2nd August I had a call of £22,111 as an "on account stop-loss claim" and I have already sent a cheque for £7,200 in respect of Syndicate 56.'

Alistair, Lord Strathnaver of Golspie, said:

> I am not prepared to send any more money and would resist any
> suspension attempt. I understand that Syndicate 334 has Errors and
> Omissions (E&O) cover with the same reinsurers, i.e., the Merrett
> Group, and think it would be difficult for a subsidiary to proceed
> against its parent in a matter of this type. My family has been asso-
> ciated with Lloyd's for three generations but now I have resigned
> with effect from 31 December 1990. When I joined Lloyd's, I was
> assured that all the recent scandals had been ironed out and that
> once again the Corporation was a collection of individuals of integ-
> rity. I just do not know who to trust at Lloyd's anymore.

He was just one of 1,400 Names who resigned in 1990. There were
only 325 joining in 1991, with 7,000 continuing Names proposing to
increase underwriting. Those increasing capacity were either making
profits or little loss, or decided to trade through potential losses. However,
Membership had fallen for four years from a peak of 32,433 in 1988 to
some 27,000. About 120 Names had applied for Hardship. This was a
scheme that supported Names who could not pay calls, preventing them
from becoming bankrupt. The Hardship Scheme allowed sufficient assets
and income for such Names just to survive. The downward phase of
the insurance business cycle meant that Lloyd's was only underwriting
60% of its capacity.

The letter to Keith Lester of P. R. Judges, Manager of the Membership
Department, explained the effect of suspension for nonpayment of calls.
It included a copy of the Central Fund and the administrative suspension bylaws. After suspension from underwriting, it could only be
recommended if all the dues to Lloyd's had been paid or assets at Lloyd's
earmarked. Representations regarding the reasons for nonpayment should
be sent to S. D. Marks of the Administrative Suspension Committee.
Keith complained to Judges:

Syndicate 334 has omitted the statutory report of an independent actuary as required by bylaw 17. On a technical point I have a solvency margin of £11,562. Without a certified actuarial report could anyone be certain that the cash call numbers were correct? I suggest that the £33,433 call is far in excess of solvency needs. I am so incensed by the grave injustice meted out to Names that I have not so far met the required legal obligations. I protest most strongly that former colleagues of mine in 1980 encouraged me to join three syndicates, two of which were poor performers and behaving disastrously. I am a conscientious objector when it comes to paying for professional, managerial and insurance incompetence.

He had to make arrangements to borrow funds on overdraft in case he had to settle the liability.

In a letter to Roger Wooderson, Chairman of Willis Faber & Dumas (Agencies), on 15 August Keith Lester complained about the quality of its management. He noted with concern the supplementary information supplied by the Agency did not include any professional qualifications among the directors of the company. No actuaries, accountants or lawyers or Fellows of the Chartered Insurance Institute were board Members and only one person declared a degree. 'Surely it was not true that the most able go to university and the others go to Lloyd's?' This question reflected an apparent lack of rigour in the training of persons in managerial positions of responsibility in the business of managing Names' interests.

David Rowland, as Managing Director of Stewart Wrightson, was keen to strengthen his team. He established training programmes for executives and staff, and employed graduates and professionally qualified individuals. Keith Lester concurred with this policy and had received such support when working at Stewart Wrightson. At the time in question Rowland's influence on training seemingly had not spread to Matthews Wrightson Pulbrook. Rowland had studied medicine at Cambridge but decided he should do something he was naturally good at. His father

introduced him to Matthews Wrightson in the City. He was a politician
and excellent communicator determined to further his ambitions in the
web and turmoil of business, which happened to be in insurance.

Second Steering Committee Meeting, 16 August 1990

Gratefully accepting an offer of accommodation, the Steering Committee was again able to meet at Michael Jump's Lincoln's Inn Chambers. It
was agreed to form the 'Syndicate 334 (1985) Names Association' and
consider adopting objects and rules similar to those of the Syndicate 90
Association. A formal launch of the Association was to be delayed while
legal implications were considered. By now, 200 Names had subscribed
but recruitment had diminished as Willis Faber & Dumas (Agencies) Ltd
had refused to release the Syndicate 334 Names and their addresses to the
Association's Committee.

Administration of detailed records would be held and maintained
by Louth Secretarial Services (LSS). The firm would provide a registered
address, and handle correspondence and newsletters. Organising an
efficiently managed enterprise would be fundamental to achieving the
Association's objectives.

Keith Lester did not pay his cash call and, assisted by Jasper Salisbury-
Jones, prepared lengthy solvency representations to S. D. Marks of the
Administrative Suspension Committee. He added that Syndicate 334's
audit report failed to mention non-compliance. He sent a cheque for
£33,000 and requested that it was not cashed until the representations
had been considered.

Clive sent a form to prospective Members of the Association asking
them to let him know if they did not intend to pay their calls. He said
that suspension could be a lengthy process and circulated a copy of Keith
Lester's representations. The more who stood their ground, the longer and
more difficult the process must become for the authorities.

Brien Symes had written to Clive Francis that Merrett received a
roasting at the 3 July meeting and looked extremely worried, suggesting
he had given a weak, complicated and worthless explanation.

Merrett, on tour in North America, had told Names that he was clapped at the end of the 3 July meeting. In truth the applause was for Clive as Merrett had been most unhelpful. Frank Wright informed Clive that he had attended a reception at the Willard Hotel in Washington, DC attended by the Chairman of Lloyd's and Merrett. Frank mentioned to Merrett that he had had a hard time at the meeting on 3 July. Merrett looked Frank square in the eye and stated, 'Absolutely not, as a matter of fact, I was applauded and complimented by the group.' Frank said he learnt that the Merrett syndicate underwrote the E&O policy for Stewart Wrightson, at the time the ultimate shareholder managing Syndicate 334. He was appalled at the apparent conflict of interest following the takeover by the Merrett Group between insuring Syndicate 418 and the insured Syndicate 334.

Committee Members Harry Purchase and David Tiplady circulated details of the merger documents of Willis Faber and Corroon & Black which stated that *any potential liability of the Matthews Wrightson Pulbrook Agency was fully covered by their E&O insurance.* Disclosures in the merger documentation indicated that Willis Faber expected to be sued by Syndicates 334 and 90 and they could lose the case. However, it was expected that the E&O insurance should cover the situation although the amount of cover or potential loss was not quantified.

Marks replied on 10 September to Keith's solvency representations letter saying that there was no committee within Lloyd's empowered to look behind the results of the annual solvency test but he copied the correspondence to a Mr Nunn at the Solvency and Reporting Department. In the light of misconduct allegations, he had passed the letter to the Secretary of the Investigations Committee and mentioned that the Lloyd's Members' ombudsman was Sir Kenneth Clucas.

Willis Faber & Dumas (Agencies) wrote to all Syndicate 334 Names on 12 September 1990 saying that D J Freeman, solicitors, had asked for the names and addresses of all Syndicate 334 Names. If Names did not wish their details to be submitted, they should advise Willis Faber & Dumas (Agencies) accordingly.

Guy Wilson went with two clients to see Willis Faber & Dumas (Agencies), where they met the Managing Director, David Carrington, and his Assistant, David Garner. Guy stated the married couple 'were both put on the same syndicates; this was seriously negligent as the Agency owed a duty of care to their Names'. The visitors thought the Agent's representatives looked distinctly nervous about the allegations that they strenuously denied. Though they appeared quite arrogant initially, their attitude ameliorated as the two visitors 'laid into them'. The visitors were left with the impression that the Association had no hope of making any impact on the Agency. Guy's clients intended to serve notice to change their Agent.

Keith Lester decided to obtain sixteen proposers for him to stand for election to Lloyd's Council. Dr John Maxwell of London was delighted to nominate Keith. He said he would be resigning from Lloyd's and explained that apart from the Syndicate 334 losses he had received notification of a 50% loss on two Feltrim Agency syndicates that had been forecasting a breakeven position a few months earlier. Adding fuel to the fire, he complained, 'My boat had been insured with Lloyd's and following a major collision with a floating object I made a claim. I obtained and supplied a surveyor's report and evidence from the boat repairer. To my astonishment my claim was rejected. I am totally unimpressed with the integrity of a Lloyd's policy.'

A Name from Raynes Park reported on 29 August that he was also very unimpressed with Lloyd's, as Syndicate 334 claimed £41,777.46 from him. He considered this a loss from nondisclosure and from negligence by Pulbrook Underwriting Management Ltd.

Karl Ziebarth's discussion with David Tiplady on 12 September included any potential criminal aspects of the 1982, 1983 and 1984 Syndicate 334 reports and certificates. It was wondered whether the Merrett Group had used the knowledge of Market weakness in the reinsurance sector to hammer down the purchase price of Syndicate 334.

James Sinclair, Managing Director of Willis Faber & Dumas (Agencies), wrote to all Syndicate 334 Names that Michael Turner, the underwriter, had resigned with effect from the end of the year. In future a much larger syndicate would be created with the merger of Syndicates 334, 522 and 264. Sinclair said the arbitration judgement of 2 February was a very harsh decision for Syndicate 334 Names, and it was most disappointing that the court would not give leave to appeal. The underwriter had disclosed in 1981 that he had an asbestos and pollution problem when buying the reinsurance. His agency would have liked the case to go to the House of Lords to test the 1984 decision in the *Oceanos Mutual Underwriting Association v Container Transport International Inc (Oceanos v CTI)* case. This 1984 case effectively changed the emphasis on disclosure. The *Oceanos* decision required the proposer of an insurance policy to disclose every fact that the underwriter may wish to be aware of during his decision-making process. Syndicate 334 made a claim for the first time in 1988 only to find that the Merrett Syndicate 418 were able to use the 1984 case to void the contract. Sinclair did not like the Merrett tactics, although they were supported by law, and the Merrett Group had the Syndicate 418 Names to consider. Sinclair said this was all very distasteful and very damaging to Lloyd's. In 1981, at the time the slip was signed, the parties had agreed to arbitration for any disputes that might arise. Lloyd's did not see it as their problem and could not get involved in reversing a decision finalised by arbitration and supported by the court. His agency could not get involved in helping Names with action groups as there would be a conflict of interest.

In May 1981, Ron Verrall, the underwriter for Syndicate 334, thought the IBNR fund to be 'very comfortable'. However, he purchased a limited layer of protection from 1st State Insurance Company, $8 million excess of $4 million at a premium of $2.5 million. This was a time and distance policy. The level of cover then slightly exceeded what the underwriter thought was 'an already generous reserve'.

Verrall was worried throughout 1981 about asbestosis. He had made the first specific provision for asbestosis claims in 1978. He planned to retire and thought that the Merrett Syndicate 418 layer would provide a belt-and-braces cover. This would mean that Michael Turner, the current deputy underwriter, would effectively take over a 'young' syndicate, i.e., having no long-term liabilities. Furthermore, it could enable a release of reserves into the next year, which was looking rather lean.

Brian Wood's report was circulated to the Committee in the matter of *Merrett v Turner Arbitration Award*. An Opinion was required on whether information presented by brokers Winchester Bowring Limited to Merrett Syndicate 418 regarding the reinsurance contract was misleading; furthermore whether Pulbrook Underwriting Management Ltd and/ or Winchester Bowring Limited should have known this. At the 1990 arbitration, the reinsuring underwriter of Syndicate 418 indicated that the Syndicate 334 underwriter was seriously exposed to legal jeopardy regarding asbestosis and was aware of the coming flood of claims, but failed to make proper disclosure of these facts to him.

Prior to placing the Syndicate 334 risk with Syndicate 418 in 1981, Winchester Bowring Limited had attempted to broker a similar Syndicate 90 risk to John Emney, the deputy underwriter of Syndicate 418. The approach was rejected and Ray Barry of broker Winchester Bowring reported John Emney as 'very rude'.

The report stated that during the 1940s, 1950s and 1960s, in common with other marine syndicates, Syndicate 334 had written US non-marine casualty business, relating to accident and health, for small premiums. A conservative legal situation prevailed in the United States. Insurance risks covered included negligence for product liability and bodily injury claims. There were moderate court awards and punitive damages were not a feature. The legal situation changed in the United States particularly in respect of bodily injury. Asbestosis disease manifested itself many years after exposure. Frequency and claims costs changed dramatically with greatly increased court awards.

The contention arose because a marine syndicate wrote long-tail non-marine policies and treated them as short-tail in accordance with accepted practice in the Market. This categorisation gave a false impression of the risk. John Emney should have expected some long-tail business included in the short-tail cargo or voyage accounts and put on notice to make further enquiries as to custom and content.

It appeared that in 1981 Winchester Bowring Limited copied the information about the business from the books of Syndicate 334 without any thought that the presentation was fair. The Syndicate 334 internal auditor had noted relevant figures as asbestos-related business but no such note was provided with the document placing the insurance. *This was thought by Mr Wood to be totally misleading.*

In his report Wood commented on the IBNR, which technically covered claims that had occurred but of which the insurer had not been advised. It may also apply to matters that had not been officially advised but arise through general knowledge. Syndicate 334 IBNR reserves for 1975 and prior years of account for non-marine business included $1,050,000 established specifically to meet anticipated asbestosis and DES claims. The placing information was originally compiled for 1st State Insurance Company, which was offering a type of time and distance cover that did not require a great deal of detailed information. *In Mr Wood's Opinion presenting essentially the same information in order to place an unlimited whole account run-off reinsurance was insufficient to discharge the duty of full disclosure.* Pulbrook Underwriting Management should have been aware of this. John Emney told the arbitration tribunal that he relied on the description and did not think he needed to question it.

The arbitrators had agreed that there was no necessity for the total IBNR figure to be disclosed as it formed a subjective assessment of what sum additional to reserves should be allowed for possible future claims. Nevertheless, the majority decision was that the reserves included in the IBNR should have been disclosed. The dissenting arbitrator found there was no need to disclose the IBNR and Emney had quoted for the business without the IBNR figures. By agreeing to write the reinsurance without these figures Emney had waived his right to that information.

For Syndicate 334 there was additional exposure to Johns Mansville regarding four lines written in the 1950s and 1960s that had not been reserved. Johns Mansville was a total loss and claims were first advised in February 1981. There was further information in June and July 1981 which Verrall said he did not see. Turner thought these four lines should have been reserved.

In conclusion, *In Mr Wood's Opinion the underwriters should have been aware of the full extent of this exposure to Johns Manville amounting to approximately $900,000 before placing the Merrett reinsurance contract.*

The *Merrett* case rested on the decision of *Container Transport International Inc v Oceanos Mutual Underwriting Association (Bermuda): CA 1984.* The plaintiffs operated a scheme relying upon insurance. Their insurers refused to renew. The plaintiffs then approached and obtained insurance from the defendants, but, it was alleged, without disclosing the full history.

David Tiplady's covering letter enclosing Wood's report said that he regarded it on the whole as highly encouraging. Wood had concluded that for two of the three grounds of nondisclosure the arbitration panel found in favour of Merrett, but Pulbrook Underwriting Management and Winchester Bowring should have known better than to act as they did. In lawyers' terminology, this was actionable negligence.

Third Steering Committee Meeting, 26 September 1990:
Standing for Election to Lloyd's Council
The Steering Committee met at Clive Francis's house in Elgin Crescent. Tom Benyon, a former Member of Parliament and former Chairman of the ALM, addressed the Committee. Based on his experience he said Lloyd's would not be helpful in any way. He agreed that the Steering Committee should form an Association of Syndicate 334 affected Names, although some Names with substantial stop-loss, for example, were not affected by the losses. Tom said the Association must be large, mean and rich enough to proceed without exhausting resources. There was a 50% chance of getting money back. Press coverage and retention of Association Members was essential. Legal matters tended to drag on and people might lose interest. He never advised anyone to go to the Suspension Committee and argued Lloyd's would prefer to settle out of court. Once the Association had been formed it should collectively handle all legal activity as it would be too expensive for individuals to handle it alone. D J Freeman solicitors had a wealth of experience with Lloyd's.

Jasper Salisbury-Jones, with Clive Francis in support, had spent two hours in front of the Suspension Committee the day before, setting out his reasons for not being suspended.

A legal Opinion indicating the strength of a possible Syndicate 334 legal case was required. David Tiplady forwarded a detailed copy of 'Instructions to Counsel' addressed to Jonathan Gaisman QC, requesting a final draft of his advice by the end of the month. A second expert was engaged regarding the liability of Winchester Bowring.

David acted for both Syndicates 334 and 90. He thought the Syndicate 334 case was relatively straightforward and Syndicate 90 case was much more complex. His preference would be for this Association to be in court before the Syndicate 90 Association.

Keith Lester had received sixteen nominations for election to Lloyd's Council as an External Name and the documents were submitted to the Secretary of Council. He had produced a publicity leaflet which included a note about voting strategy since two persons would be elected.

To increase the chances of winning the leaflet suggested voters only voted for him and no other. The leaflet would be sent with next newsletter mentioning Keith Lester as a Member of the Steering Committee but without any other comment. An advert would also be placed in *Lloyd's Digest*.

The Committee decided that the Association would not be formed formally until the report of counsel had been received. Legal fees of some £1,250,000 would be required to reach the court door. To achieve this, staged payments over eighteen months would be requested based on the premium income limit of each Name. Approximately 10% of Names' premiums limit might be required. To effect tight financial control over cash it was requested that D J Freeman should render monthly invoices to the Treasurer supported by an analysis of time.

It was proposed that the Committee of the new Association would have a maximum of ten Members of whom eight would be Members of Syndicate 334. The Association's Secretary, Guy Wilson, would be paid fees at a nominal rate of £25 per hour and settled by the Association when

KEITH LESTER BSc FCA FBIM

draws your attention to his candidature for election to

THE COUNCIL OF LLOYD'S

---

and seeks your support

Lloyd's policies have been made void because of non-disclosure and misinformation as has happened with some reinsurance policies.

This has resulted in cash calls to Members rather than recompense from those responsible for omissions and errors. Syndicate management must not evade their responsibility for professional shortcomings by inappropriate application of Member's funds, which are made available to underwrite risk *external* to Lloyd's.

Keith Lester will be pleased to discuss your own circumstances on writing to:

Keith Lester & Co.
St. Andrew's House
26 Brighton Road
Crawley
RH10 6AA

Fax No. 0293 553273

When you vote please consider the mechanics of multiple voting. Because all candidates are in competition for your votes, if you cast more than one vote then second and subsequent votes **diminish** *the likelihood that your preferred candidate will be elected.*

it was formed. Similarly, LSS would provide administration services at £12 per hour. These costs would be a drain on resources when cash flow was so uncertain, even though the agreed rates were quite paltry.

Subsequently, A. P. Barber, the Secretary of Council, wrote to Keith Lester that ten External Members had been nominated for two places on Lloyd's Council, necessitating a postal ballot closing on 14 November. Subsequently, following the advice of Lloyd's solicitor, some of Keith's proposed information about the election was deleted by Barber, who said on 8 October, the information was not to be used for the ventilation of personal grievances involving identifiable entities. He explained that the Council could not publish anything that was potentially damaging or otherwise actionable, or factually incorrect. A document prepared by Keith titled 'Quality and Profits' was published in the candidates' information document. A photograph and brief biographical details were also printed in the October 1990 Lloyd's newsletter. Keith Lester replied to Barber on 3 November and thanked him for amending the 'Other Information' being published in the candidates' information documents and concurred that the Council should not publish defamatory or actionable material. He put his name forward for election precisely because Names had the right to be made aware of issues even if they had not been proven in court. He would have preferred to have seen a final draft of the text before publication.

Newsletter, October 1990
In October 1990, a newsletter was distributed to Syndicate 334 Names as potential Association Members, stating that no one should underestimate the tactics that would be met from the Lloyd's Market. Legal action was lengthy and costly. Clive had been in contact with the Chairmen of other Action Groups, including Syndicates 90, 317 and 533, to establish joint approaches. Tom Benyon was the Chairman of Syndicate 533 and had been campaigning for two years. The newsletter mentioned that a Committee Member was a candidate for election to Council.

The Committee proposed two main thrusts of action: to direct and progress the lengthy legal action, and to consider and devise every possible means for applying pressure to the Lloyd's regulatory authorities, members of the Council, and the Chairmen of Suspension and Hardship Committees. Publicity pressure should be exerted in the form of written and verbal representation and the use of newspaper columns. Names were urged to write to the Names' Interest Department and report the facts as they saw them. A summary of topics and suggestions was detailed as an informed prompt. Names could also write to the Agency Regulation Department and the Lloyd's ombudsman, setting forth objections to the continuance of protagonists as underwriting Agents and as Members of Council.

Clive decided to send the newsletter, together with letters from Names as appendices, to all underwriters. This was a bold and unexpected step to force consideration of the issues throughout the Market. The list of 400 underwriters' addresses did not include the relevant syndicate number, which had to be entered manually. The letter covered issues of self-regulation, bureaucracy and bylaw 11 regarding misconduct. It was thought that Rt Hon John Redwood at the Department of Trade and Industry (DTI) might take an interest, particularly regarding the protection of policyholders' interests. Letters were sent to the Minister through Members of Parliament, and to the Opposition Spokesman for Trade and Industry. Clive's covering letter on 31 October to his MP, Dudley Fishburn, explained that self-regulation at Lloyd's was not working, as conflicts of interest were so interwoven. He also wrote to the Chairman and Deputy Chairman of Lloyd's. The former eventually responded on 20 November, explaining that the Lloyd's Acts do not include any powers for compensation or restitution.

At the 1990 Lloyd's Annual Meeting, Keith Lester asked Chairman Murray Lawrence whether Names should pay losses where policies have been voided. Lawrence replied that policies were voided all the time – there were arbitration clauses, and resort could be made to the law. This was the course to be taken by the Association.

Some Members had difficulties in paying the subscription. For example, one Member, from Vermont, expressed his concern about the second subscription instalment of £1,500. He said his UK funds were held by the Bank of Credit and Commerce International (BCCI) which was under investigation for poor regulation and he was in process of opening new bank accounts with Lloyds Bank. He would send the second instalment of £1,500 as soon as possible.

Seascope Special Risks Limited was a company that arranged stop-loss insurance for Names. For example, for an underwriting capacity of £245,000 the premium was £3,495 per annum. Some 10% of this risk was insured with Municipal and General Insurance Limited which went into compulsory liquidation on 9 March 1994 owing money to Seascope. The claims were settled over a long-drawn-out period, taking many years – one Name had the final balance paid on 11 February 2010, some twenty-five years after the insurance was placed, and well into the next century.

Clive, Guy Wilson and Nicholas Gratwick met Mrs S. Buchanan of the Names' Interest Department on 3 October. The meeting was reported in the October newsletter to which item Buchanan objected. She complained that the newsletter 'TOTALLY MISREPRESENTED' the discussions. Clive responded that it was never the intention to misrepresent her views and they could find nothing in the newsletter which misrepresented the meeting. He informed the Committee that the interview with the Manager of the Names' Interest Department was a wholly sterile exercise confirming the worst fears that the title was a misnomer. It should be called the Names Indifference Department. Buchanan was receiving correspondence from many Names. For example, a Name from Glasgow made a formal complaint saying he had lost almost £50,000 and was anticipating further losses. Kenneth Lavery of Ontario complained under Lloyd's bylaw 11 of misconduct by Stephen Merrett, the auditors Ernst & Young, Winchester Bowring, Pulbrook Underwriting Management and Syndicate 334 underwriters.

The Committee had received quantities of correspondence at a fast pace over the last ten days. Clive said Nicholas Gratwick had applied in person for a writ of mandamus, which is an order to a public officer to carry out his duty, naming a host of people, including the Suspension Committee and the Chairman of Lloyd's. He deposited the relevant papers in person in Lloyd's Chairman's office where the Chairman's assistant went 'slack-jawed' and was somewhat ruffled. Resulting from the newsletter both Lord Nelson of Stafford and the Rt Hon Lord Davies had been in contact with Clive as it had been suggested that they had an unconstrained right to air the issue in the House of Lords.

Clive also wrote to the Chairman of Lloyd's on 31 October, pointing out that his dealings with Merrett must make it difficult for him to have a detached position. He mentioned he had sent correspondence to the DTI as there had been no news of a disciplinary action under bylaw 11. There was an apparent failure of Lloyd's to regulate itself. The Chairman replied on 7 November to say he thought Lloyd's continued to regulate itself and he and his Council Members ensured that their private interests did not influence decisions. Charles Baron thought Clive's initial draft was unnecessarily abrasive and would put off attempts at conciliation.

Clive subsequently wrote thanking Lloyd's Chairman Lawrence for identifying Pulbrook Underwriting Management as the culprit and suggesting arbitration under the auspices of Lloyd's. He pointed out that Names had been writing to him for the past five months on this subject. Pulbrook Underwriting Management said in their May 1984 report there was unlimited reinsurance cover for 1975 and earlier years. Names were assured the reinsurance policy would respond to any strain caused by new advices or increased claims falling on old years. If this was untrue, then under company law criminal charges could arise. However, if true, then a claim could be made under the E&O policy. He also said that the Committee's files were full of vitriolic letters from defenceless impoverished Names. Many had been received from Names who were also brokers, using descriptive words such as chicanery, skulduggery, dishonesty and alley-cat morals, for example. Whilst he welcomed the initiative in setting up arbitration, he would have expected any reputable commercial organisation to have dealt with the situation with more probity, speed and authority than had been the case to date. He finished the letter by reassuring the Chairman that there was no bitterness in the proceedings – just a resolute determination to see those who had entrusted their money to his care in underwriting insurance risks the world over not be deceived and cheated by internal *legerdemain* at Lloyd's.

The 3 November issue of the *Spectator* published an article by Christopher Fildes about the ten prospective candidates for election to Lloyd's Council. It said that the days had gone when Lloyd's Names voted like tame electors in pocket boroughs waiting to be told which way to vote. With fewer cheques being distributed the voters had emerged with the ancient cry, 'Throw the rascals out!' Keith Lester was quoted stating that, 'Names were customers of Agents and satisfied customers do not complain.'

A report by Hugh Malcolm Thompson dated 29 October commented on the possible culpability of Syndicate 334 Managing Agent Pulbrook Underwriting Management and Winchester Bowring, which acted as intermediary in the unlimited stop-loss contract. The conclusion was that there was a weak case against them, especially as John Emney refused to quote for Syndicate 90. There was an observation on whether earlier and later joiners of the Syndicate had a different legal position. In addition, there was a question of a time bar, which started on 4 May 1989, affecting Names joining before 1981.

When the October newsletter was sent out to underwriters, it included copies of correspondence from Kenneth Laverey and John Speirs. Titmuss Sainer & Webb, solicitors, contacted Clive and Keith on 7 November. To Keith they postulated:

> You have made a serious libel and further publication constitutes additional libel. The distribution of this literature is considered unbecoming for a prospective Member of Lloyd's Council and we propose to report you to the Council. An undertaking not to permit or authorise further publication is required by 5pm on 8 November.

In consultation with David Tiplady, Keith replied:

> Firstly, the material in question was published and distributed without my knowledge, authority or consent. I would not have

authorised libellous material to be distributed. Secondly, the election address leaflet which was published with the newsletter was from the Committee and not the other way round. Consequently, the requirement for an undertaking from me is meaningless. Thirdly, your threat to report me to the Council of Lloyd's is itself potentially defamatory. I require an undertaking from your client by 5pm on 9 November that your client will not carry out the proposed action.

The solicitors replied the following day accepting the contents of Keith's letter. The faxed copy was received in Keith Lester's office in Horsham. 'The attached made my day!' was penned by Gervase Tinley, Keith's Co-Director, on forwarding the fax.

Clive replied to Jane Plumptre of Titmuss Sainer & Webb saying he had returned to his desk that morning and hastened to reply. He was happy to give an undertaking in respect of any matter which may be regarded as libellous. He asked for a definition of the areas of disagreement so that matters could be corrected with an apology or withdrawn, and requested her to specify precisely the words to which she objected. Clive explained that much of that in the correspondence enjoyed absolute privilege, was factually supportable or otherwise fair comment. He suggested that the demands made in the solicitor's letter could well be construed as seeking to stifle proper comment and could be regarded as unduly oppressive, but he would give suitable undertakings. Plumptre replied promptly with a series of demands requiring an undertaking that he should not *further* publish the words 'Stephen Merrett has the business ethics and morals of XX.' Furthermore, he was not to publish that Merrett or any director within his Group may be guilty of fraud or guilty of any disciplinary offence under Lloyd's bylaws. Clive lost no time in responding and said he was astonished to find the words set out in her requirement. He could only conclude that somehow in the Committee Chairman's absence abroad, the wrong papers had been sent out. Under the circumstances he had no hesitation in giving the precise undertaking required subject to the word *further* being deleted from their letter, to remove any ambiguity of commission which he called 'a small syntactic infelicity'. He regretted any distress which may have unwittingly been caused to their clients. The undertaking was given with a reiteration of the injustices faced by Syndicate 334 Names.

From Lapworth in the West Midlands, Douglas Hanmer's handwritten letter said:

> Dear Mr Lester, I wish you success in the election. I have been underwriting since 1959 and have given most of my wealth to my wife and young children. I expect to be cleaned out, especially as I had a £50,000 line on Syndicate 334 and a £60,000 line on Syndicate 90. I think the disaster is likely to go on until the next century and the lawyers are on to a 'field day'. At 72 years old I hope I can survive on my wife's charity.

In reply, Hanmer was asked to write to the Names Interests Department emphasising astonishment at the losses resulting from voided policies.

Keith Lester had written to S. D. Marks, the Secretary of the Administrative Suspension Committee, on 5 October, to whom he had sent a cheque for £33,000 that Marks held, pending a review. He asked that his letter be sent to a Mr Nunn at the Solvency and Reporting Department and the letter should also go to the Manager of the Names' Interest Department, the Lloyd's Members' ombudsman and the Secretary of the Investigations Committee. Marks phoned to say he wished to meet Keith at 9.15 am on 11 December in the Special Dining Room at Lloyd's.

On 15 November, James Sinclair wrote to R. A. C. Hewes, the Head of Regulatory Services, discussing the unhappy situation of the Names of Syndicates 334 and 90. He wrote, 'it is quite disgraceful of Agents in a section of Lloyd's community wriggling again, particularly when the 1987 contract reconfirmed Agents, duty of care and again in 1990 when Names were obliged to sign a new contract enhancing Agents, duty of care. How can Agents in 1991 pretend they did not have a duty of care back in 1982 and why buy expensive E&O insurance if Agents had no responsibility?' He concurred with the views generally expressed, that Lloyd's stank and was suffering a breakdown of Market discipline. Names were wondering if Lloyd's contracts with other syndicates would not suddenly fail. He said that Lord Wiedenfeld, a press baron, was putting a major article in the US edition of *Forbes* magazine centring on the failure of Lloyd's contracts. Lloyd's would have a very high price to pay for the clottish underwriting policy of a few greedy underwriters.

Fourth Steering Committee Meeting, 16 November 1990: Inadvertent Libel

David Tiplady led the discussion at a Steering Committee meeting at D J Freeman's offices and aired the technical legal arguments. He introduced the concept of 'material disclosure of a reasonable underwriter'. He said that underwriting in 1981 applied the Marine Insurance Act of 1906, and the *Oceanos* case of 1984 was not relevant. Had full disclosure been made, questions arose as to whether Emney would have underwritten the reinsurance. If so, there might have been a higher premium, estimated at up to $2 million. The next question was whether Ron Verrall would have paid the higher premium. However, it was apparent Verrall did not know the extent of his book of business.

It was unanimously decided to take legal action and to hope that Clive's pursuit of arbitration with Murray Lawrence would bear fruit, thus avoiding litigation.

Clive said to the Committee:

> You may not be aware that Keith and I had a strongly worded letter from a solicitor alleging libel. It seems vitriolic letters that I had received from Kenneth Laverey and John Speirs had inadvertently been included with the newsletter that had been sent to active underwriters. Keith and I have had to smooth things down and give undertakings that this will not happen again. Does anyone know how these seemingly libellous letters came to be sent out?

There was complete silence; and some looks of astonishment. A few eyes wandered around a bit. *No one* had any knowledge of the matter. Clive, looking down at his papers, could not hide the broad grin that creased his face and he uttered a little chuckle.

Counsel Jonathan Gaisman and Christopher Butcher's Joint Opinion was distributed. They commented that litigation would be a lengthy and expensive process but was the only hope of redress. Syndicate 334 was assessing the full exposure of 1985 long-tail risks. Until this was complete, it was not possible to assess the quantum of further calls. D J Freeman restated the claims against Pulbrook Underwriting Management, including negligent misrepresentation and nondisclosure, and failing to keep an earlier year of account open. There would be valid grounds to contend that Names would not have joined the Syndicate if there had been proper disclosure. Assisted Names on Syndicates 334 and 90 were special cases.

It was decided to take steps to form the Names' Association immediately and the LSS's address should be used for all correspondence. It was now urgent to fund the Association. David Tiplady had written to 562 Names on Syndicate 334.

The Rules of the Association (Appendix 5) stated that only those who contributed to litigation would be entitled to join the Association and benefit from any success. Conduct of the litigation would be at the sole discretion of the Steering Committee. Should anyone wish to withdraw once litigation had started, then funds would be applied to litigation costs and they would be only entitled to any remaining balance once the proceedings had been finally settled. If there was an appeal against any judgement, Names may be asked to make a further contribution. The litigation would only take place once enough Names had subscribed.

Keith Lester was congratulated on coming third of ten contestants in the election to Lloyd's Council with 1990 votes. This was not sufficient for him to become an External Member of Lloyd's Council.

On 16 November, Keith wrote to Titmuss Sainer & Webb following their letter of 9 November to set out the reasons for the distribution of the Syndicate 334 newsletter. He said:

A critical Syndicate 334 reinsurance policy was voided by their client, seemingly highlighting a lack of integrity in a Lloyd's policy. In future underwriters will need to pay greater attention to policy detail. Litigation does not engender harmony and is very expensive. Additionally, a message is being sent to the outside world of incompetence and deviousness. Scarce resources are being poured into legal action instead of increasing Market share and profitability. Voiding policies is responsibility without accountability. When errors and omissions were made, it could not be just and equitable for the managers to receive remuneration while charging any ensuing losses to Names. External Names are customers and should always call the tune. Lloyd's policies which did not have integrity, did not truly form part of the business of insurance but were more akin to gambling and lottery.

Keith requested the letter was copied to Lloyd's Chairman Murray Lawrence, Stephen Merrett and his board members. Three days later, Jane Plumptre confirmed she had circulated the letter as requested.

To maintain pressure, Keith wrote to his MP, Ian Taylor, to Norman Lamont, the Kingston MP whom he had met in connection with the Kingston Branch of the British Institute of Management, and to the Rt Hon John Redwood, the Secretary of State at the DTI, asking them to raise in the House of Commons serious failings of self-regulation at Lloyd's. Dudley Fishburn MP informed Clive that he had already written to the DTI.

Clive wrote to the Governor of the Bank of England and received a reply from Mr Pen Kent, an Associate Director, on 3 December. Kent said self-regulation fell to the DTI rather than the Bank of England and complaints should be sent to them. However, the Bank took an interest in the evolution of the Insurance Market and its regulation. He avoided responding to the substance of the letter.

There was increasing interest from the Press. *Business Insurance* on 3 December said Lloyd's Members were urging the Council of Lloyd's to investigate disputes over run-off reinsurance policies. The cash call for Syndicate 334 of £29.4 million was mentioned and it included a detailed account of the arbitrated issues, with comments by Canadian Member Kenneth Lavery, as well as Clive Francis, who was identified as the Chairman of the Syndicate 334 Names Association.

David Tiplady obtained and distributed the contentious placing slip for the voided Syndicate 418 policy and a copy of the treaty wording.

Under the heading 'Willis Chief Hits Out at Lloyd's', James Sinclair accused Lloyd's of trashing the value of its contracts by clottish underwriting and forcing Names out of the Market. This report in the *Evening Standard* on 4 December explained that Syndicate 334's voided reinsurance policy meant its Names were facing asbestosis losses of £28.7 million because of an unfavourable arbitration result. Names would not know the potential extent of their losses until February 1991. Estimates of losses varied.

The following day, *The Times* ran the headline, 'Utmost Bad Taste at Lloyd's of London'. It reported that Lloyd's would have a high price to pay within the next two years for the failure of Lloyd's contracts and tactics of bouncing liability around the Market. Dr Mary Archer, who chaired the Hardship Fund, would be asked to go easy on unfortunate Names. Her husband was Jeffrey Archer, the novelist. On the same day the *Financial Times* exclaimed, 'Leaked Letter Criticises Lloyd's', and repeated details of the issues, as did the *Daily Telegraph*, with 'Members Warn of Exodus from Lloyd's'. The *Independent* headline was 'Letter Denounces Lloyd's'.

LSS wrote to all Members stating the object of the Association was to 'GET OUR MONEY BACK WITH COSTS'. In summary, there was a negligence case against Pulbrook Underwriting Management. Success in legal action may depend on the dates on which Names joined the syndicate. The estimated legal cost for the worst-case scenario was £1,500,000, which would include the other side's costs if the action was lost. Members should be prepared to pay 10% of line in four stages at six monthly intervals, two at 3% and two at 2%, commencing on joining the Association. A draft copy of the Association's Rules was enclosed (Appendix 5).

On 14 November, Clive had written to Tom Sharp, the General Manager of the Names' Interest Department. The Chairman of Lloyd's had suggested that it might be profitable to have a further meeting. Sharp eventually replied fifteen days later stating that if Clive understood the procedures, a further discussion would serve no useful purpose.

Clive responded on 7 December:

> It hardly rebounded with credit to the Lloyd's Regulatory Authorities that it took some 15 days to answer a letter of unambiguous simplicity. It laboured all too successfully to convince me of the misnomer of your Department. This was especially the case when a group of Names are seeking assistance. Your reply is a delectable evasion and there is a suspicion that between the Chairman and Lloyd's Regulatory Authorities the injured Names are being given the old-fashioned run-around.

The Rt Hon John Redwood, Secretary of State at the DTI, wrote to Dudley Fishburn MP on 8 December. He explained that the Government set up a Committee of Inquiry into Regulatory Arrangements at Lloyd's to consider whether the protection of the interests of Members of Lloyd's was comparable to that in the proposed Financial Services bill. The Chairman, Sir Patrick Neill QC, had reported in 1983 and made seventy recommendations. One significant conclusion was that it would not be advantageous for Lloyd's to be closely regulated by an external body. However, it did recommend that the balance of Membership of the Council be shifted away from Working Names, and this was implemented in 1987. Staff of the Corporation of Lloyd's, who exercised regulatory powers, were not allowed to have any financial interest in the business. Clive thought it was difficult to sustain a convincing argument that Lloyd's was wholly self-regulated. Ten of the recommendations related to 'Complaints and Disputes, Indemnity and Compensation Schemes'. The Council had implemented these in line with the recommendations. If External Names were not satisfied, it was open to them to make representations for changes to the Council of Lloyd's. The Secretary of State was pleased to see that Clive Francis and others were putting their concerns to the Chairman of Lloyd's and the Head of Lloyd's Regulatory Services Group.

The Times reported on 10 December that David Coleridge was appointed the new Chairman of Lloyd's, who said that confidence amongst Names had reached a low for as many as 2,000 Names were resigning in 1990. The challenge facing the Market was to prove that its famous boast of being able to meet any legitimate claim was as valid today as at any time in the past 300 years.

Fifth Steering Committee Meeting, 10 December 1990

The Committee feared that the Gaisman Joint Opinion was not strong enough to recommend litigation. Jonathan Gaisman was a Name himself, and came from a very wealthy family. This might have coloured his Opinion. Concern was expressed that if the Opinion was released the defendants would almost certainly obtain a copy. An Opinion from another counsel would cost £6,000 to £7,000. It was resolved to ask Gaisman to amend his Opinion or, failing that, to appoint an alternative counsel with immediate effect. Subsequently, David Tiplady said he had already been trying to get the barristers to amend the conclusion of their Joint Opinion and they had declined. It was now time to seek another QC.

Some 249 Names had contributed £250 each, totalling £62,250. To increase awareness and recruitment, a petition to 12,000 Names in January was proposed along the lines 'Do Names think that Lloyd's policies' valid claims should always be paid?'

The *Lloyd's List International* headline of 11 December was 'Difficult Year Facing Stop-loss Insurers', opining that being a Name at Lloyd's can be dangerous to your financial health if you are unlucky, particularly if you are on one of those syndicates clobbered by catastrophic losses. Arguably the greatest need for stop-loss cover was for the less wealthy Names. About 45% of Names had bought some stop-loss cover in the past but for 1991 it could go as high as 66%. There were different, complex products provided by stop-loss underwriters. In some cases, there could be substantial scaling back of cover depending on demand and the underwriters' perception of the risk. In others, premiums could amount to over 50% of the cover; say, for a premium of £3,265, only £6,000 of loss would be covered. Stop-loss premiums reflected Names and underwriters taking account of prevailing Market conditions.

Clive, and David Garner of Willis Faber & Dumas (Agencies), attended Keith's meeting with the Suspension Committee on 11 December and a copy of the Syndicate 334 voided reinsurance policy was distributed. Keith asked that his cheque be placed next to the policy and explained that both were contingent. The cheque was contingent on it being banked and the policy was contingent upon a valid claim being made. Members of the Committee were unable to answer key questions. The solicitor, Mr J. R. Mallinson, was asked on what conditions a valid claim would not be paid. Mr H. R. Dobinson and Mr M. H. Cockle were asked how a profitable business could be built upon policies which fail to pay claims and how a director of an insurance company could responsibly place reinsurance business with Lloyd's. The qualified accountant, Mr N. C. T. Pawson, was asked how he could justify signing an unqualified audit report when key policies protecting the interests of Names may well fail when tested with a claim. As he was also an actuary, he was asked how he might assess the liabilities and matching of assets when insurance policies are subject to failure. Then Mr S. D. Marks, as Chairman, was asked why Council agreed to waive bylaw 17 which required the provision of an actuarial report to be published with open years of account. He was unable to comment when it was riposted that the only reason Keith Lester was appearing was because a Lloyd's policy had failed. Marks maintained that the Council was the highest appellate body to which a Name could appeal. When asked what might be the object of suspension, Marks replied, 'to protect the sanctity of the Lloyd's policy'. When the laughter of the two Names subsided, one remarked that the only reason they were appearing in front of it was because a Lloyd's policy had failed. Where was the sanctity of that policy now that mere Names needed it? There were now those who were starting to aver that Lloyd's would shortly become insolvent. It was facing huge and mounting claims for asbestosis and pollution. Whilst tales of financial bankruptcy might have been over-stated, sadly those of moral bankruptcy did not appear to be.

Keith asked that the meeting be adjourned *sine die*, i.e., without an agreed date to resume, pending the integrity of Lloyd's policies being reviewed by Lloyd's Council. Following the meeting in a letter the next day enclosing the meeting transcript, he was given until December 31 to clear his solvency shortfall.

Ian Taylor MP wrote to Keith Lester, his constituency Member, to say he had already noted the matter of self-regulation at Lloyd's. However, because of the information sent by Keith he would go into it in more detail.

In a letter to James Sinclair, Managing Director of Willis Faber & Dumas (Agencies), on December 13, Keith suggested that as a policy-holder whose valid claim had not been met, the full Council of Lloyd's be addressed and seek its protection. Sinclair replied promptly recommend-ing an appeal to a higher authority and to write directly to the Chairman of Lloyd's requesting an audience. He further explained that Members' Agents were in court in 1991 to contend that they were not responsible for the appalling losses as there was no direct contract between a Name and the Managing Agent. In conclusion he understood that Keith was in shock, an unhappy and damaged Name. Lloyd's was an £11 billion busi-ness and trading for some 300 years, but neither the Agent nor Lloyd's maintained they owed a duty of care to Names. It was right that Keith took independent legal action.

Sinclair enclosed an internal memorandum from Heather Thomas of the Willis Faber Legal Department setting out their legal position. She said it was a classic case of conflict of interest on the part of the Members' Agent at the point the Managing Agent was accused of negli-gence. The Members' Agent was disabled from determining on behalf of Names whether there was a good case to pursue because they would be on the receiving end of any suit brought as a result. Names were exasperated when Willis Faber & Dumas (Agencies) adopted a neutral stance, precisely because they, the Names, now urgently needed vigorous assistance from within the Market.

By now, 249 Names had contributed to the Association and 155 of these Names were on Syndicate 90 as well as Syndicate 334. There were also sixty-four late joiners. If in 1992 Syndicate 90 Members had been given full information at the relevant time, they had valid grounds for asserting that they would not have joined Syndicate 90. It seemed to follow they would not have joined, or they would have left Syndicate 90, and this would also have applied to Syndicate 334.

Counsel advised that the 155 Association Members and the 64 late joiners, a total of 219, appeared to have compelling claims. The remaining 30, they advised, may also have strong claims.

The *Financial Times* reported that overall Lloyd's capacity would fall from £11.4 billion to under £10 billion in 1991. This reflected the substantial fall in the total number of Names from 32,433 to some 27,000. However, the Hayter Brockbank Agency Group had announced it would increase its underwriting capacity.

Keith Lester's letter of 5 October to Marks eventually resulted in a reply from the Deputy Chairman of Lloyd's, Alan Lord. He said the facts that were reported under the misconduct reporting bylaw 11 would be given careful consideration. The powers under the Lloyd's Acts concerning the investigation and the bringing of disciplinary proceedings for misconduct did not include any power to direct compensation or restitution to anyone who may be shown to have suffered loss as a consequence of misconduct.

Keith Lester wrote to the Chairman of Lloyd's seeking to appeal the decision of the Suspension Committee. Enclosed was a copy of his address to Names for election to Council, James Sinclair's letter of 13 December, and a letter from Clive about legal action. On 20 December, Clive also wrote to the Chairman in support of the appeal. He concluded that the Council might well benefit from Keith Lester's considerable experience and record in the realms of accountancy, insurance and management.

Murray Lawrence, Chairman of Lloyd's, responded on 19 December to Clive's letter of 26 November and an anonymous letter of 2 December which was sent to all Members of the Council of Lloyd's and which had invited contact with Clive. He said he had decided to review the matter fully and wished to clarify three points:

1. Lloyd's was not unsympathetic with the situation in which Syndicate 334 Names had found themselves. However, following the arbitration award that resulted directly from the due legal process of the arbitration, the court declined to grant leave to appeal. It was not within the powers of the Council of Lloyd's to take intervening action to set aside or question such a decision.

2. Various letters asserted and alleged in emotive terms that there had been improper conduct on the part of various parties involved. The assertions had been advanced without the full facts and evidence to support the conclusions drawn. With the possibility of legal action, it would be quite wrong for Lloyd's to prejudice the possible outcome.

3. Lloyd's would be open to an approach from the parties on possible arbitration or conciliation to be conducted under Lloyd's auspices.

The Chairman of Lloyd's sent a copy of the above letter to all Members of Council. The Chairman's reply stated that there was no mechanism for an appeal as 'solvency is a fact'. Keith wrote to James Sinclair giving permission for a cheque of £11,562 to be banked, to ensure his minimum solvency at Lloyd's. He expressed grateful thanks to Sinclair for his advice and assistance. Mr P. B. Lutman of the Membership Department wrote that Keith's premium limit would be reduced from £250,000 to £75,000 as the first reserve at Lloyd's was deficient by £18,750. He wanted an amended syndicate list from Willis Faber & Dumas (Agencies) by 31 December.

Lloyd's Newsletter of January 1991 welcomed David Coleridge as the new Chairman of Lloyd's. It also announced the formation of a reinsurance company which would offer run-off reinsurance to Lloyd's syndicates with open years. It said there was an encouraging reduction in the number of run-off years from 115 to 92. However, there were some syndicates where the Managing Agent could not determine the RITC because of the deterioration of long-tail liabilities. The Council was concerned that Names on such syndicates could resign from Lloyd's but were still responsible for the claims arising from policies underwritten on their behalf. Such liabilities would remain with a Names' Estate even after death.

The Administration Suspension Committee informed Keith on 2 January 1991 that he had failed the Lloyd's Annual Solvency Test. Consequently, he was suspended, and a notice would be posted in the Underwriting Room. Suspension would remain until the Council of Lloyd's was satisfied with compliance. However, James Sinclair said Keith's cheque for £11,562 would be banked and suspension lifted. He also requested a cheque for £18,750 to allow him to write to the full premium income limit. Following the temporary suspension, Keith would not be allowed to underwrite in respect of contracts written between 1 and 3 January 1991. This was confirmed in letters from P. B. Lutman of the Membership Department and S. D. Marks of the Administrative Suspension Committee.

A detailed background note about the Syndicate 90 situation regarding arbitrations and the Syndicate 90 Association was sent to Association Members by LSS on 2 January 1991. A Syndicate 90 (1982) Names Association had been formed when Syndicate 90 had 478 Names with an aggregate premium limit of £17,000,000. Like Syndicate 334, Syndicate 90 was managed by Matthews Wrightson Pulbrook Underwriting Management Ltd (previously a subsidiary of Matthews Wrightson Group but now part of the Merrett Group). Most of the Names were introduced by Names' Agent Matthews Wrightson Pulbrook Ltd, then a subsidiary of Matthews Wrightson Group and now part of the Willis Faber Group.

In the early 1980s Names were informed of the growing significance of American liability claims principally from asbestosis but advised there were adequate reserves and reinsurance. The Syndicate 90 1981 year was reinsured into 1984 (in 1984). The active underwriter Mr D. P. Taylor died and was replaced by Mr E. A. Moore, who took a more rigorous view of old year risks. Subsequently Names were informed that the 1982 year would be kept open as reinsurers were disputing the run-off reinsurance contracts, which were in arbitration. Matthews Wrightson Pulbrook made further calls on Syndicate 90 Names up to 200% of line and the 1982 year remained open with no prospect of closing. This was very bad news for Syndicate 90 Names.

There were other disputes over arbitrated losses. Outhwaite Syndicate 661 originally covered 50% of excess of loss without limit and the dispute went to arbitration. The unfavourable arbitration decision resulted in an agreed compromise to cap the losses. The Syndicate 90 Association Committee was unable to establish the facts and arguments underlying the settlement with Outhwaite. It was not known to what extent Outhwaite had been informed of the deterioration in the asbestosis claims position. It appeared that placing the reinsurance was concluded in a most informal manner. Much of the discussion was alleged to have taken place over dinner at Frederick's Restaurant without any written record. Board minutes of Matthews Wrightson Pulbrook referred to 'internal reinsurance arrangements'. In March 1990 copies of these documents were requested, and incomplete files were received some seven months later. The Committee reminded Names' Agents of their duties under the general law of agency. In particular, 'A Name shall be entitled to inspect the underwriting books and accounts and at all reasonable times to make extracts or copies.' However, counsel advised solicitors for Matthews Wrightson Pulbrook, Cameron Markby Hewitt, that they were not obliged to disclose documents to Names. If a request was made by a Members' Agent, they would reconsider the position. The Syndicate 90 Association's Committee concluded that Names were victims of elaborate measures of procrastination and filibustering attempting to deter them by escalation of legal costs that were ultimately payable by Names. The deadline for serving writs for the Syndicate 90 Association would be April 1991.

During 1990, the Syndicate 90 (1982) Names Association instructed D J Freeman to protect such legal rights as they may have. Because of the acute danger of any legitimate claim being time-barred, a stand-still agreement was not accepted and writs were taken out against all parties likely to be involved in judicial proceedings. Once it was apparent that Names were going to take legal action, Names' Agents withdrew all but minimum cooperation. They declined to provide Syndicate Members' names and addresses until their own E&O insurers had been consulted.

Some 'Insider Names' had joined the Syndicate 90 Association but had not subscribed funds. The Committee would take an exceedingly serious view if the Insider Names were treated differently from the External Names, as no such disclosure had been made to Association's Members.

D J Freeman sought the advice given to Matthews Wrightson Pulbrook by their solicitors as to the reasons why Matthews Wrightson Pulbrook did not proceed against Winchester Bowring for their failure to effect proper reinsurance. D J Freeman received some answers but only after months of delay.

A meeting of the Syndicate 90 Association had been arranged for 12 March 1991 in Central Hall, Westminster, when it was proposed to consider and approve the next stage for action. The Chairman of the Association, Sir Ian Fraser, had met Brian Pomeroy, Chairman of Lloyd's Names' Interest Committee, to press points of complaint. It was suggested that Names write in the strongest terms to Pomeroy and copy the letters to the Chairman of Lloyd's. It was important to project a powerful united front. Names were requested to supply the Association with relevant evidence and documents which would show misrepresentation and nondisclosure.

Investigations were taking place into Jonathan Mance QC's Opinion which referred to internal reinsurance schemes. The more the situation was probed, the more the Syndicate 90 affairs appeared to be a 'can of worms'. The Committee concluded that Syndicate 90 Names had not been treated with 'utmost good faith', the proud slogan under which Lloyd's was meant to trade. They suggested that Names vented their feelings on those responsible.

Another planned arbitration was with the Meacock Syndicate and scheduled for 14 January 1991. The Syndicate had covered 20% of the excess of loss without limit. If the arbitration was lost there could be a further cash call of 70%.

A letter was published in *The Times* on 4 January from Murray Lawrence answering one from Dr John Maxwell, stating that in a dispute subject to arbitration, it was not the task of Council to intervene in commercial aspects of Lloyd's, where these related to the transaction of insurance business. Lloyd's task was to regulate the conduct of all at Lloyd's, within the framework of the 1982 Lloyd's Act and following the recommendations of the 1987 Neill Enquiry into Regulatory Arrangements at Lloyd's.

Four days later a letter in *The Times* from Roger Bradley explained that the Council was distancing itself from Names who had been hurt, especially when any underwriter or Agent needed official approval from Lloyd's Council. He quoted the Lloyd's Act 1982, which stated that 'the Council shall have the Management and Superintendence of the Affairs of the Society and the power to regulate and direct the business of insurance at Lloyd's'. The business of insurance must include commercial aspects. A Name may become bereft of any help because of so many conflicts of interest. The Council could not be sued as the 1982 Lloyd's Act provided immunity and the Name's Agent may well put up the shutters.

Clive wrote to Dudley Fishburn MP on 8 January 1991 following up on Minister John Redwood's letter in December stating that the realities were very far removed from that which his letter portrayed. The Committee of the Syndicate 334 (1985) Names Association included two eminent barristers, four chartered accountants, a JP and a leading solicitor. He said that it was highly unlikely that the Committee would have bothered the Minister if all avenues had not been fully explored prior to such a move. He would not wish to waste the Minister's time if he had not come to the considered opinion that the relevant Neill recommendations had been cleverly emasculated to the point where no redress was possible for an aggrieved Name.

The Minister had mentioned that there was a Lloyd's ombudsman, however, the terms were so adroitly drawn as to render his position impotent. Clive commented with an illustrative example. 'If a head waiter has failed to reserve a favourite table in The Captain's Dining Room (Lloyd's dining suite) and was subsequently rude to you, the ombudsman may hear your complaint. However, if your Agent robbed you of £45,000, he may not!'

The Minister had pointed out that the Neill recommendations had been speedily and fully adopted. Clive suggested that two recommendations were incomplete. Firstly, that Lloyd's must ensure their own arrangement for compensating Names against losses which arose other than because of normal risks of underwriting and, secondly, Lloyd's must facilitate the investigation and resolution of Names' money claims against their Agents by arbitration. Money claims by Names against Agents were limited to a specific amount of £40,000. However, if two Names had the same problem with their Agent for this amount, the mechanism could not be used. He referred to Roger Bradley's letter in *The Times* which would allow the Minister to understand that the 'Names' Interest Department' was regarded as a risible misnomer. The saga of Syndicate 334, he suggested, was one of astonishing mismanagement, lack of scruple, conflict of interest and fat-cat fudge at Lloyd's.

Finally, Clive commented on the unwieldy size of the Council. Council Members informed him that thirty people met once a month, never got to converse with one another and were submerged in paper from the secretariat. All the effective decisions of Council were taken safely by an inner cabal of Market Men.

David Coleridge, the new Chairman of Lloyd's, replied to Keith Lester's letter to the former Chairman, Murray Lawrence, on 31 December and explained that there was no mechanism or any entitlement to appeal to Council. He also said the Administrative Suspension Committee was properly constituted.

Gervase Tinley was married and divorced while serving in the US armed forces. On returning to the UK he qualified as a pensions and life assurance consultant, becoming employed by Stewart Wrightson in the early 1970s. At the time of the damaging 'three-day-week strikes', high inflation and high taxes, there was a cap on salary increases. Tinley was offered Membership of Lloyd's as an Assisted Name. He was told this was a bonus as a way to legally increase his income. Through Matthews Wrightson Pulbrook he joined both Syndicates 334 and 90. Suffering disproportionally huge losses he wrote to Pomeroy of the Names' Interest Committee. He explained:

> I have devoted myself to professionalism in pensions and life assurance. I feel pressurised and penalised by dubious practices in the one organisation, Lloyd's, that I have always held out to be an exemplar of good faith. Furthermore, now I am a pensioner with a gross annual pension less than either of the lines on Syndicates 334 or 90. I have no assets to settle cash calls. In this immensely worrying situation what assistance and advice can you give me?

Sixth Steering Committee Meeting, 16 January 1991: Inflicting Commercial Damage

David Tiplady informed the meeting that Matthews Wrightson Pulbrook had obtained a copy of the counsel's Opinion for Syndicate 90. He thought it unwise to release the Gaisman Opinion regarding Syndicate 334 as it was not very favourable. Late joiners to Syndicate 334 had a stronger case than early joiners.

A discussion arose about costs, especially if the case was lost and funds were needed to pay the other party. All Members would be expected to pay but if there was a shortfall the wealthiest may become a target for the shortfall costs. This emphasised the importance of receiving sufficient subscriptions to cover all potential costs.

The *Financial Times* of 17 January reported on 'Reforms at Lloyd's' in which it said there were 'wide consultations'. Among Council's six priorities were a high-level compulsory stop-loss scheme, ways in which the Corporation's reinsurance company CentreWrite could reinsure open years, and the introduction of limited-liability capital to Lloyd's. Reaction among some of the 2,000 US-based Names to a Lloyd's reform package said the proposals were too late.

It was agreed to form the Association and send its Rules and copies of press cuttings to all Syndicate 334 Names while D J Freeman would set out the current prospective legal case. In summary, an action for negligence was to be brought against Pulbrook Underwriting Management Ltd for failing to make full disclosure to Syndicate 418. On full disclosure reinsurance cover would have been available from Syndicate 418 or elsewhere, although probably for a larger premium. There was negligence in failing to keep open an earlier year than 1985. This also meant negligent misrepresentation and nondisclosure to new or existing Names who might have decided not to join or to leave the Syndicate. Pulbrook Underwriting Management was in breach of its duty to inform Names that the reinsurance was defective. There were individual or subgroup claims, for example, where Members of the same family were placed on the same syndicates or with lines that were arguably too large, being inadequately or improperly advised. There were 232 Names on both Syndicates 334 and 90. Had proper disclosure been made, Names might not have joined Syndicate 90 and it may follow that the Names would not have joined Syndicate 334 also. There may be a parallel cause of action against the Members' Agent for breach of contract or negligence. Negotiations with Members' Agents had already begun and if unsuccessful it would be necessary to litigate the claims.

The *Financial Times* reported on Merrett Holdings' profits on 1 February. There was a sharp decline from £9.87 million in 1989 to £6.96 million in 1990. More than half the revenues came from agency activities. It also reflected a decline in the profits of the 1987 Lloyd's year of account and Merrett Holdings voluntarily waived profit commission of £2.3 million in respect of Names participating in Syndicate 418 for both the 1985 and 1987 underwriting years. Syndicate 418 had sustained heavy losses on its 1985 year. Merrett had been unable to assess accurately future claims and close the 1985 year.

The February 1991 issue of *Association of Lloyd's Members News* detailed the proposals for setting up a Lloyd's Capital Base Task Force Enquiry.

This would be chaired by David Rowland, who was now Chairman of Sedgewick Group PLC, the largest Lloyd's broker. The newsletter identified Stephen Merrett as a Member of the Task Force.

The letter on 25 February from an Association Member, Jack Scheinuk of New Orleans, quoted a 1931 issue of *Syren and Shipping* in which Cuthbert Heath, who was regarded as the father of non-marine business, stated:

> One thing shines as brightly as ever. It is the honourable feeling that, privileged as we are among traders, our contracts are those of *uberrima fides*. Our good faith must also be the supreme law of our existence. I feel certain that underwriters generally are still as determined as ever to do what is fair, rather than to insist on legal rights.

Scheinuk commented on the failure of a Lloyd's policy that had caused a loss to Names on Syndicate 334. He said that coupled with Lloyd's current lack of leadership, both administrative and underwriting, he could no longer feel that Lloyd's would always pay its policy obligations in the fair manner so cogently expressed by Cuthbert Heath. He had now advised all his business associates to select underwriters other than Lloyd's.

David Coleridge, Chairman of Lloyd's, writing to Keith on 5 March 1991, said he had seen a letter from the Chairman of the Syndicate 334 Names Association indicating legal action may commence against various parties. Consequently, it would be inappropriate for him to pass comment.

Clive responded to an earlier letter from the Chairman of Lloyd's on 5 March saying he regretted the Chairman's inability to deal with a simple question without resorting to 'argumentum ad hominem', in a woefully laboured attempt to dodge the question and avoid the logic or premise of the argument itself. He also said that his predecessor had impugned slyness over an anonymous letter and explained that this Committee did not need to resort to any methods sly or underhand. Quite the converse, he argued, when it was the underhand dealing at Lloyd's which formed the nub of their reprehension. He restated that Pulbrook Underwriting

Management in their May 1984 report to Syndicate 334 stated that the reinsurance for 1975 and prior years was on an unlimited basis. This had proved to be untrue. He quoted Sir Peter Miller, a former Chairman of Lloyd's, that the Lloyd's Acts 1871 to 1982 imposed upon the Council the task of managing and superintending the affairs of the Society, regulating and directing the business of insurance at Lloyd's. He enclosed the letter from Jack Scheinuk describing in compelling terms the commercial damage being done to Lloyd's by Merrett-style repudiations. Such obloquy conveyed a shabby tribute to the degeneration of a once great British institution. The size of Lloyd's Council was also criticised as being unable to exercise effective, let alone courageous government.

On 8 March Clive wrote to D.J. Freeman, the senior partner of D J Freeman & Co, as it had been reported that possible defendants had derived some satisfaction because the Committee of the Association was not being guided by someone who was a partner in his firm, concluding that 'our case cannot be taken very seriously'. In addition, the reports suggested that the Committee had received an Opinion so weak that they were afraid to circulate it. Clive explained that the Committee held Dr Tiplady in the highest regard and could not fault the guidance he had given. When the Opinion was received it contained certain weaknesses which David Tiplady perceived and it was returned for revision. However, the revision proved to be of little help and another counsel was sought. The Committee was astonished to find that Dr Tiplady had been dissuaded by others in his firm from putting this proposal into effect. Furthermore, the Association had been unable to send out a bullish Opinion in response to its call to arms and the viability of the project must be very much in question. Clive said he was seeking assistance from Freeman to rescue the situation.

The Economist had published on 26 January a lengthy article titled 'Leaking at the Seams'. It said that the Market was 300 years old and queried whether it would last another ten. A further article on 9 March was titled 'A Lutine Peel at Lloyd's'. It said there was a steady stream of Names leaving the Market. It pointed out that within fifteen years death would have claimed half the current Names, thinning the ranks even further. It suggested that one way or another the coming losses at Lloyd's were slowly and surreptitiously being 'mutualised'. There was a need to wake up to reality and call swiftly for the end to unlimited liability. Otherwise, it suggested, 'Do not ask for whom the bell tolls. It tolls for Lloyd's.'

The Times reported that 150 Names attended the first Annual General Meeting of the Syndicate 90 (1982) Names Association. Names voted unanimously to serve a writ on the Merrett Managing Agency as Matthews Wrightson Pulbrook's owner, alleging negligence. This Syndicate 90 decision rather endorsed the actions of Syndicate 334.

Events were moving quite quickly in identifying the legal case or cases and the amount of support from Syndicate 334 Names for legal action. Caution had been urged before formally launching an Association, to ensure a proper control and structure to the organisation. Also, an estimate of funding likely to be required for success in court, including sufficient funds to settle the costs if the case was lost. There were many uncertainties. Success was not a foregone conclusion. The next chapter formally established the Association.

Summary of Key Issues

1. There were escalating asbestosis claims and a strengthening legal case.
2. The Association's Rules were issued following a strong growth in Membership.
3. Communications were received from Names with heart-rending stories.
4. Mr Wood's Opinion was in favour of the Association.
5. Publicity included letters to MPs, the press and a candidacy for Lloyd's Council.
6. Alleged libellous material was circulated.
7. Suspension Committee decisions were received and Names' solvency matters discussed.
8. Contraction in Lloyd's business and number of Names was very concerning.
9. The background was given to Syndicate 90.

CHAPTER 4

Formation of the Syndicate 334 (1985) Names Association

The well-appointed king at Hampton pier
Embark his royalty; and his brave fleet

Henry V, Act 3 Prologue

Seventh Steering Committee Meeting, 13 March 1991

Adam Raphael, a journalist, was invited to join the Committee at D J Freeman's offices. He was a Member of the Committee of the Syndicate 90 Names Association.

A list was provided of 148 subscribers to the Association. Clive indicated that the Association had been properly formed and he proposed that D J Freeman & Co be formally appointed as the firm of solicitors to act for the Association and working with Dr David Tiplady as their prime representative.

David Tiplady reported that he had received a file referring to a reinsurance scheme for Syndicate 334 and said that Pulbrook's solicitors, Cameron Markby Hewitt, had been most unhelpful in providing him with some files in the last week. As he was also acting for the Syndicate 90 Association, he was aware of a similar scheme for Syndicate 90 that was called Pulbrook Internal Reinsurance Scheme. It operated from 1945 until 1980. Payments to create a catastrophe fund were made to United Standard, a captive insurance company owned by Stewart Wrightson. Immediately prior to closing the syndicate year premiums paid to the catastrophe fund were allowed in the computation of profits of the Syndicate. In the next financial year 97.5% of the premium was repaid to

Syndicate 90 but the payment was neither shown as having been received nor interest charged. This appeared to be window dressing. Matthews Wrightson Pulbrook said D J Freeman was trying to intimidate them. He added that Syndicate 90 may be a victim of fraud in which case they would not be time-barred from legal action. Counsel's view was that something dodgy was going on and had Names been aware of the situation, they would not have joined either Syndicate 90 or Syndicate 334.

In reporting on his letter to David Freeman, Clive said he had confirmed his utmost confidence in David Tiplady. It appeared that Freeman was seriously ill and would not be returning to the business.

David informed the Committee that 'Mr Gaisman and his family had long standing connections with Lloyd's. It could be inferred that his approach to the Opinion was not uncoloured.' Clive was resolute. 'It is clear that to encourage the Association's own troops and striking fear into the enemy the Association must be able to send out a supportive Opinion or else abandon the enterprise.'

The choice of a new counsel would be left to David, who expected to receive an Opinion that would trump Gaisman's Opinion. The new counsel should not be shown Gaisman's Opinion.

David agreed to provide monthly invoices to assist in controlling costs. As queries from Members to him would cost £200 per hour, all queries should be routed via LSS. Funds should be deposited in the Association's bank account at Lloyds Bank.

Cox & Bell, an underwriting agency, had advised their Names on Syndicate 334 not to join the Association. It was speculated that Cox & Bell were attempting to defer things until the Association dropped the matter or they were genuinely attempting some form of settlement. Charles Baron agreed to write to Cox & Bell's Names urging them to join this Association.

Some Names had written to Clive saying that their stop-loss policies covered most of their losses and they were considering not joining the Association. Clive informed them that there was still good reason to join as their losses were likely to increase. He also said that if the Association won the case, they could recover their excess of loss.

Clive passed a thick file of letters from Names round the Committee. Some Names were unable to pay their debts and became Hardship cases. It was agreed that where a Name had applied to the Hardship Committee the Name may join in litigation without paying a subscription to the Association. However, if the case was won such Names would have the subscriptions deducted from the recovered funds.

David said that all defendants would be invited to enter a litigation standstill agreement. The defendants would include Matthews Wrightson Pulbrook, other Names' Agents, such as Fielding & Partners and London Wall Members Agency, plus brokers Winchester Bowring and solicitors Herbert Smith.

Lloyd's Chairman wrote to Clive on 13 March 1991, responding to his lengthy letter of 5 March. He stated there was a clear misunderstanding of the powers, duties and functions of the governing body of the Society. He thought a meeting would be better than continued correspondence, together with, say, four Members of the Committee. The theme of courageous government was raised when Clive accepted the invitation to meet the Chairman, who replied on 22 March that he could not circulate Clive's correspondence to Members of Council, as he had made a comment about Syndicate 90 that was potentially libellous. He wished to arrange a meeting with Clive with the objective of providing an opportunity to explain Lloyd's position. There would be no question of any negotiation.

David's estimated cost of legal action was £1.5 million. He provided details of D J Freeman charge-out rates, saying he would spend the greatest amount of time at £160 per hour. The Association could expect a monthly bill between £4,500 and £9,000 for about six months.

Sir Peter Hordern, MP for Horsham, replied to Keith's letter on 21 March and said he was once a Member of Lloyd's but not now 'au fait' with all the litigation. He did not think that the Government could help and suggested that only the Council of Lloyd's together with the backing of the Membership could reach a solution.

Lloyd's Chairman wrote to Charles Baron on 25 March 1991 explaining that decisions about reinsurance disputes fell to the judgements of

Agents and not at the direction of the Corporation. Everyone was freely entitled to seek legal advice. Charles responded promptly commenting on the critical nature of the reinsurance between Syndicates 418 and 334, and casting grave doubts on Agents' fitness. Self-regulation at Lloyd's should render legal action unnecessary. Incompetent and negligent professionals were not fair to any of the Names.

The *Daily Telegraph* pictured John Redwood, Corporate Affairs Minister, who announced in Parliament that he was investigating large-scale fraud at Lloyd's. A broad-range enquiry was to be made by the Serious Fraud Office about all the problems surrounding the massive losses connected with asbestosis. There was no shortage of disaffected Names who complained that Lloyd's had not been tough enough with insiders. It mentioned the Pulbrook syndicates, in which Names were currently seeking funds for possible legal action. Subsequently it was reported that Lloyd's had protested about the statement in Parliament saying that the Serious Fraud Office was merely looking at the possibility of investigating £200 million of asbestosis claims hitting Outhwaite syndicates.

Keith Lester wrote to David Rowland as Chairman of a Task Force about some constructive comments. At the time Rowland was also Chairman of Sedgewick Group PLC, the largest Lloyd's broker, following a takeover of Matthews Wrightson PLC.

Rowland replied to Keith on 4 April to say he welcomed all the help they could get and that 'all of us participating in Syndicates 90 and 334 are concerned about the future'. He said he would pass the comments through to those whose task was to study the responses.

At Rowland's request, Keith wrote a lengthy letter on 8 April about the Capital Base of Lloyd's. It covered a range of topics starting with 'What is capital?' The fundamental concept of insurance business as being 'of utmost good faith' was discussed together with issues about double counting. There was a problem of double counting through stop-loss recoveries, Estate protection plans and E&O reserves. A few paragraphs followed on skills and experience and the need for Syndicate Annual General Meetings to give an opportunity for Names to meet underwriters.

Keith also commented about Agents' and Members' assets, including an objection to Stephen Merrett being a Task Force member.

Keith mentioned he had been the management accountant for Stewart Wrightson's UK companies and subsequently the joint Managing Director and Finance Director of an innovative and successful Life Assurance Group. He was elected overall for nine years as a Member of the Council of the British Institute of Management (BIM) and was currently Chairman of the Audit Committee. Chairman of the Audit Committee was an honorary office as the de facto non-executive Finance Director of the Institute, who together with the Chairman, Sir Derek Hornby, signed the Institute's Annual Financial Statements. Keith believed that BIM should itself be a paradigm of managerial excellence.

Clive's letter on 16 April 1991 to the Chairman of Lloyd's sought a date for a meeting and requested the discussion to be confined to one topic. The deceived and impoverished Names of Syndicate 334 awaited some courageous government and strong moral leadership, he wrote. He sought some form of conciliation, restitution or redress for the losses occasioned by the false statements he said had been issued by Pulbrook Underwriting Management Ltd. It appeared that the Chairman wished to censor and control that which Council Members may or may not receive. This bore eloquent testimony to the way nominated and elected Members of Council were safely sidelined.

Potential paucity of funds and uncertainties about future costs were the driving force for a tightly controlled, well-managed administration of the Association. The housekeeping letter from LSS Ltd to the Treasurer said weekly bank statements would be provided. Secretarial costs for nine months to March 1991 were £7,000. Circulars to Members cost between £200 and £300 depending on the pages despatched, plus £130 in postage. Correspondence for each instalment subscription request would cost £200. At the end of March 1991 there were 230 Members of the Association and funds totalled £84,365. In the draft budget for the year to 31 March 1992 income came to £473,158 with estimated expenses of £105,347, leaving a balance of £367,811.

Eighth Steering Committee Meeting, 1 May 1991:
Withdrawal from Merrett Syndicates

Eight Committee Members were informed that Michael Jump had not joined the Association and appeared to have resigned from the Steering Committee.

Clive circulated a letter from David Coleridge, Chairman of Lloyd's, indicating that he, Clive, could be guilty of libel against a syndicate. David Tiplady advised:

> Clive could not libel a syndicate. In my experience Names tended to join Action Groups between the issue and serving the writ, particularly if there was a strong chance of winning the case. We have received about £8,250 subscriptions which will be paid to the Association at Louth. All the Names who have read the Gaisman Opinion in our office have joined the Association. Just so that you are aware, I have written off £30,000 of my time to date.

David was keen to continue with the Association, which itself was a positive sign.

Tom Benyon was anxious to help and coordinate action groups. He had requested a fee of £2,000 per month which would be split between six action groups. Adam Raphael said Benyon was a very persuasive lobbyer in the House of Commons. The Treasurer suggested that expenditure be capped to three or four months' fees.

The writ had been issued and a standstill agreement was in place with Winchester Bowring. Unfortunately, no other defendants would enter a standstill agreement. Negotiations showed signs of bearing fruit. Merrett Holdings PLC was prepared to stand behind Pulbrook Underwriting Management and not allow it to go into liquidation. This was regarded as 'good news'.

David Tiplady outlined the stop-loss recovery situation, emphasising that the position provided by the underwriters may not be strictly accurate. Recovered funds went first to stop-loss underwriters to reimburse them for their expenditure. Any excess went to Names. If there was only a partial award, funds went mainly to the stop-loss underwriters which meant that a Name may not recover the policy excess.

The terse letter from David Coleridge to Clive about the proposed meeting indicated he was obviously not prepared to do anything about a negotiated solution. This was confirmed by Roger Elliott, Chairman of Willis Corroon. Committee Members attending the meeting should be mindful that it must not be confrontational.

It was agreed that no Committee Member should profit by reason of his Membership of the Committee. Committee Members should declare their interests in writing, addressed to the Association's Chairman.

Forty Names had been to the Suspension Committee, so Lloyd's was well aware of Names' dissatisfaction. The concept of the preservation of the sanctity of Lloyd's policies had been exposed by Keith at his appearance in late December. Press coverage of Syndicate 334 matters subsided for a while as the Gulf War prevailed.

Roger Elliot arranged for six of eight defendants to agree to discuss the situation. One Members' Agent agreed to assist their Names' cause. D J Freeman was conducting negotiations with solicitors acting for the defendants and gleaning information. A writ issued in April would be served by the middle of August. Collaboration with other Names' Associations was necessary.

Following discussion, the Committee decided that Names should be encouraged to withdraw their support from Merrett Syndicates. Attempts should be made to persuade Coleridge to take some positive action to help Syndicate 334 Names and avoid adverse publicity from litigation. A settlement should be sought in the shortest possible timeframe.

Under the heading 'The Revolt of the Names', Richard Lapper detailed the legal actions by a number of syndicates on 3 May in the *Financial Times*. Names on Syndicates 334 and 90 faced some of the heaviest losses. Some 280 Names on Syndicate 334 lost £30 million while those on Syndicate 90 lost £40 million. Writs had been issued. The *Financial Times* suggested that half the Membership of Lloyd's could be involved in court action before the end of the year. Other examples of action included thirty-three Names of Oakley Vaughan Agency which was in liquidation. The agency had brought a case against the Corporation of Lloyd's alleging that Lloyd's failed to disclose to Names the results of a 1981 enquiry. Also, 800 Names who were Members of the Outhwaite Syndicate in 1982 were suing various Agents to recoup losses of £200 million. Some 570 Names who backed Syndicate 553 managed by Warrilow Agency had issued writs for losses of £80 million. Over a hundred Names who backed Syndicates 106 in 1985 and 108 in 1986 had issued writs against the John Poland Agency. Shortly, 2,000 Names facing potential losses of £300 million were expected to decide to pursue legal action against the Feltrim Agency. It was very apparent that enormous losses were spread across the Market, with many anxious Names in serious financial difficulties, probably facing bankruptcy and emotional stress amongst family members. *Outraged and furious Names were determined to challenge the legality of sums being demanded.*

In the same paper Richard Lapper quoted Alan Lord, that the consequence of losses was dealt with within the family of Lloyd's rather than in a public forum. There would be a procedure to review major insurance losses, but these would be distinct from investigations relating to misconduct. Lloyd's proposed establishing an independent Lloyd's investigation. Clive thought Lloyd's could not be 'truly independent' in this role.

Two days later *The Sunday Times* ran the headline, 'Thousands Risk Ruin as Disasters Hit Lloyd's'. Chatset, an independent consultancy, estimated that losses would be £150 million in 1988, £1 billion in 1989 and a similar deficit in 1990. In the 'Viewpoint' section, Ivan Fallon stated, 'Lloyd's must reform or die.'

On the same day the *Daily Telegraph* headline was, 'The One Big Risk they Can't Insure'. It mentioned disasters of recent years including Hurricane Hugo in 1989, a tropical cyclone that inflicted widespread damage across the northeast Caribbean and southeast United States; the 1988 Piper Alpha explosion, sinking an oil platform in the North Sea, killing 167 people; depression of premiums from competition; slipshod work by underwriters; tax changes that made Membership less worth-while; and notorious frauds that had diminished Lloyd's reputation. It said this year Lloyd's might make a profit but next year it may face a £1 billion loss. The outlook for Lloyd's Names appeared grim, with spec-ulative forecasts indicating that Lloyd's might have to recapitalise 100% as Names might lose all their assets at Lloyd's and more.

There was a further article titled, 'Keep Your Cuff-Links – But Not the Wife', about the Hardship Committee chaired by Dr Mary Archer. Many Names had transferred their assets to their spouse, keeping only the sum necessary for the underwriting deposit. Assets passed within the last five years could be clawed back by Lloyd's. It said some people were divorcing to protect some of their assets from Lloyd's – however, one man lost his money on divorce. Another man bragged to his second wife how he organised his finances to keep his first wife's hands off his cash, only to be clobbered when he was divorced by his second wife. These and similar stories were almost unbelievable, except they were not! Investigative jour-nalists had the 'bit between their teeth'.

W. J. Briggs of London Wall Agencies wrote to Clive saying it was not within their power to intervene in the arbitration. Furthermore, there was no active concealment or deliberate element which led to the avoidance of Syndicate 334's run-off contract.

Ken Lavery, writing from Ontario on 17 May, said he had an under-writing capacity of £1,075,000 on forty-three syndicates. He had five syndicates with open years including 418 and 334. He thought there was enough material for a book! He said he really did not want to spend the rest of his life worrying about Lloyd's next scandal and postulated that if Parkinson was still around, he might have developed a new law. He said he was planning to visit the UK in July and would look forward to meeting Clive.

Keith Lester received estimated results for 1988 with a deficit of £9,733 payable on 30 June 1991. As a live example he was underwriting on twelve syndicates diversely spread across the Market with a base under-writing capacity of £250,000. There were four marine, six non-marine and one each of aviation and motor. The syndicates produced a profit of £3,961 from closed years. There were open-year accounts, one for Syndicate 334 and two for Syndicate 90. The three open-year accounts unexpectedly increased the total capacity by £101,000 to £351,000. The loss was created on the open years amounting to £13,694. The net loss was £9,733 which would be reduced by tax refunds of an undetermined amount at this time. As long as accounts were left open losses could be expected to arise on such syndicates each year.

Her Majesty's Inspector of Taxes responded to Guy Wilson regarding the taxation position. Legal action expenditure in respect of defalcations for negligence would be a tax-deductible trading expense. Costs of discontinuing underwriting might not be incurred wholly and exclusively in earning profits of a trade and could be disallowed. Such claims would be considered on an individual basis.

Chairman Coleridge circulated to Names prior to the Lloyd's Annual General Meeting in June wishing to make three points. He said the Council was keenly aware of the financial hardship being suffered. He was vigorously pursuing all avenues to trade successfully out of the difficulties. He believed the business was now at a point in the trading cycle when all capacity could be put to profitable use. He had been pursuing additional relief with the Government and Names were now able to carry back losses for three years beginning with the 1989 year of account.

Following a headline in *The Times* on 24 May, 'Lloyd's Goes Up the Spout', Bernard Levin declared that underwriting was an elegant form of gambling. He said he was a loyal, even a fervent, supporter of the capitalist system but sometimes wondered why it seemed to be organised, led and operated exclusively by numbskulls, dunces, boobies, dingbats, rattle pates, wallies and jobbernowls.

'Our well organised Association was not being or going to be run by such a fraternity' – the Committee spoke with one voice.

Coleridge's reply was published on 27 May 1991. He said, 'Bernard Levin's article was no more than second-hand regurgitated inaccuracies.' He queried the suggestion that Lloyd's was responsible for the Savings and Loans debacle in the USA. He argued 1988 was the first year of loss since 1967 and in the intervening years profits amounting to £3.6 billion had been paid out. Losses were affected by manmade and natural events in recent years. By comparison losses of North American companies were worse. Previously, in 1969, there had been premature reports of the death of Lloyd's. He confirmed that Lloyd's was not bust. At the end of 1990 the declared assets of the Society amounted to £16 billion.

It was reported that Syndicate 90 had won a $50 million arbitration award against Meacock Underwriting Management. The result was to reduce the amount of loss payable by 75%.

Following Coleridge's letter in *The Times* of 27 May 1991, the newspaper published a response from Mr William P. E. Bennett on 3 June. Bennett said he was an active underwriter at Lloyd's and termed a 'professional'. He explained that there were many different types of insurances written at Lloyd's with vastly different degrees of risk. If a Name had a heavy commitment on catastrophe reinsurance syndicates, he was in gambling terms a 'high roller'. When the smoke cleared those Names remaining would be part of a better, more professional organisation and there would be opportunities to prosper anew.

In the same issue, Tom Benyon wrote as Chairman of Warrilow Names Association and observed that there were three types of syndicate: good, average and poor. Some 70% of losses had avalanched onto around 30% of Names. Lloyd's seems to be descending rapidly through 'caverns measureless to man, down to a sunless sea', he said, quoting Mr Coleridge's forebear, Samuel Taylor Coleridge, the poet.

The Times reported on 8 June 1991 that the Serious Fraud Office had ended their Lloyd's enquiry into the £200 million Outhwaite asbestosis losses. Photographs of Rt Hon Edward Heath, a former Prime Minister, Susan Hampshire, an actress, and Tony Jacklin, a golfer, were on the front page of the 'Business' section. They shared, amongst others, on the Syndicate, in £200 million of asbestosis and pollution claims against the Syndicate.

The Times featured fifty-nine-year-old Coleridge as a family man. The reporter, Gillian Bowditch, described him as slouching on the other side of a vast desk, a large man in red braces and a spotty tie. The Chairman said most people who were bitching and whinging were doing it because they did not like losing – no one had been swindled, and it was nothing to do with unlimited liability, simply pure losses. Coleridge was born in Bombay and educated at Eton and started underwriting in 1955. He had a privileged life, and said he was better educated than most Members of Lloyd's Council. His wife said he was very kind, tolerant, witty and had a roguish charm. Coleridge had built a personal fortune of over £10 million from scratch.

The *Financial Times* headline on 8 June was 'How to Say Goodbye, When the Going Gets Tough'. It listed names of Associations, some of which were taking legal action. The list showing syndicate numbers and the open years included: Oakley Vaughan (1980 and 1982), Outhwaite 317/661 (1982), Warrilow 553 (1984), Pulbrook 90 (1982) and 334 (1985), Poland 106 (1985) and 108 (1986), and Feltrim 540 and 847 (1987–90). The ALM had opened a telephone helpline. Furthermore, Names could apply to Lloyd's Hardship Committee. Hardship was not a generous welfare agency, but it endeavoured to keep roofs over the heads of really stricken Names.

Gervase Tinley received a reply on 10 June to his letter of 20 May 1991 from the Chairman, David Coleridge, in which he had asked about the attribution of losses. Coleridge said he did not see such clear differences in losses as Tinley did. He added that the Council had introduced a review of all loss-making syndicates, and enclosed a copy of an announcement titled 'Council Passes Loss Review Bylaw'. The press release gave details of trigger thresholds which would be subject to review in future years.

Tinley was clearly very worried when he wrote to Mr R. J. Elliott, Chairman of Willis Corroon, saying that he faced a call at Lloyd's of 47.6% of his gross annual pension of £6,000. On 11 June Gervase received a reply from the Chairman's representative, Viscount Chelmsford, who expressed his deep distress at the anxiety and suffering that is the lot of so many pensioners. He was advised to do nothing further for the present.

Tinley responded the next day and elaborated on the distinction between losses attributable to the shortcomings of management and true underwriting losses. He said he felt trapped. He acknowledged that negligence did not apply to Willis Corroon. He observed that his particular concern was that it was grossly inequitable to impose on Names a loss arising from human negligence within Lloyd's. In approaching the Chairman of Willis Corroon, he hoped a way would be found to release him from the trap. In a letter four days later, he said Rowland had invited him to become an Assisted Name as a 'reward and incentive'. It was never suggested to him that the risk might be lessened by participating in syndicates other than those in the Pulbrook stable. By effecting his involuntary retirement, he was obliged to cease underwriting. Viscount Chelmsford informed Tinley that he was familiar with the general terminology used by Stewart Wrightson in their employment contracts. He had seen letters to employees offering them the opportunity to become Names. The warnings given in such letters did not encourage him to consider that any negligence existed from such acts by Stewart Wrightson acting as his employer. He explained that losses could occur through fortuity such as an earthquake or through human negligence. The *Titanic* was quoted as an example; was it fortuitous that the iceberg existed, or that the captain did not see it? Willis Corroon was a public company with obligations to shareholders and employees. Sometimes the obligations could be contradictory and may limit the freedom within which a company may act. The employment letter offering Assisted Membership of Lloyd's to Gervase, including the relevant warnings, did not indicate negligence by the employer. A copy of an item mentioned above in the *Financial Times* of 8 June, 'How to Say Goodbye When the Going Gets Tough', was enclosed.

Ian Taylor MP replied to Keith on 14 June to say he had proposed an amendment to the Finance bill to allow losses to be carried back for three years. The *Daily Telegraph* on 18 June recorded that the Government was prepared to extend emergency tax relief along the lines existing for small businesses. There was criticism in Parliament from Bob Cryer, the left-wing Labour MP, who accused Ministers of pandering to the narrow, selfish interest of the sixty or so Tory Ministers and MPs. In support, Dennis Skinner, 'The Beast of Bolsover', referred to the posh gambling den at Lloyd's. Ian Taylor wrote on 21 June to say his new clause to the Finance bill provoked a five-hour animated debate in the Finance Committee that ended at 2 am. The debate was a constructive one, apart from the discomfiture of the Labour front bench which tried to retract in Dr Jekyll and Mr Hyde fashion the favourable words about Lloyd's it had uttered in Committee only the previous week. The Finance bill had two measures relating to companies being able to set off losses against profits for the past three years, and it would be possible to set off trading losses against capital gains on the sale of assets in the same year. Lloyd's Names' tax position was similar to that of companies. Taylor argued that Names were offered the same entitlement starting with Lloyd's 1989 accounts which could not be closed before December 1991. However, regarding the tough rules for reserving RITC, the Financial Secretary to the Treasury said, 'We have authorised the Revenue to explore with Lloyd's whether there is a case for a new reserve.'

In his speech Taylor said, 'I make no attempt to disguise the fact that Names knew the risks they were taking but there were exceptional reasons for massive losses now being made. I am happy that the debate provides a better basis for relations between Lloyd's and the Treasury and it now seems to be the responsibility of the Council of Lloyd's to take the next initiative.'

Tom Benyon organised a meeting of the chairmen of seven afflicted Names Associations on 18 June to see if there were common strands. The outstanding issue was the capacity of Lloyd's underwriters to delay, obfuscate and escalate costs with money being provided by Names. Estimated legal costs were in the region of £20 million. The meeting decided to form the Society of Names (SoN) to coordinate activities of troubled Syndicate Associations. It was estimated that 25% of Names were in dispute with Lloyd's. A circular was distributed by SoN seeking a subscription of £75. The *Financial Times* of 17 June said that the 985 Outhwaite Names who were facing £200 million losses should not join the SoN chaired by

Benyon. There appeared to be a rift in the ranks of disaffected Names with an implicit criticism of the ALM.

Clive had corresponded with Mr R. A. C. Hewes, Head of Regulatory Services at Lloyd's. There was a technical argument about terms of contract between Names and their Agents. Hewes said he was not able to instruct Clive's Agent on what to implement. He did not think some form of mutualisation would be a practical way to resolve matters as there would have to be a fundamental change in the structure of Lloyd's. Clive asked Hewes if he was trying to convince him that an indirect Name obtained no redress unless an underwriter lifted his hand and said, 'I am to blame, please form a queue for your money.' Very peeved, Clive registered a formal complaint against Hewes on 27 June. He informed Sir Kenneth Clucas, the Lloyd's Members' ombudsman, that Hewes had 'declined to meet a request to protect the interests of an individual Name from established dishonesty on the part of a Lloyd's Agent'. Clive requested help by asking him to investigate the way his complaint had been handled by the Head of Regulatory Services. Clive explained that his Agent, Fielding & Partners, placed him on Pulbrook Underwriting Management Syndicate 334. In 1985 the syndicate was left open and incurred severe losses. Clive claimed that arbitration found dishonesty on the part of Pulbrook Underwriting Management. Pulbrook Underwriting Management had assured Names in the Annual Reports for 1983 and 1984 that reinsurance for 1975 and prior years was unlimited. Expert Opinion said that Pulbrook Underwriting Management actively suppressed information. The result was that his Agent, Fielding & Partners, demanded payment for the loss occasioned by their Sub-Agent Pulbrook Underwriting Management. Clucas eventually replied to Clive on 3 September and agreed to carry out an investigation into the complaint about Mr Hewes. However, he wanted to know details of the alleged maladministration and what injustice Clive had suffered.

Hewes replied to Clive on 17 July, stating it was not within his powers to direct Clive's Agent in a way that would be contrary to the basic obligations of underwriting membership. The successful repudiation of a contract for material nondisclosure did not necessarily imply some deliberate act of concealment. The level of disclosure was a matter of judgement which did not *per se* necessarily constitute dishonesty or cheating. It was therefore incorrect to speak in terms of failure to protect Names from publicly confirmed dishonesty. Clive's reply reiterated and embellished the points of his argument that the Corporation of Lloyd's had failed in its regulatory duties to protect the Names of Syndicate 334. Hewes went on leave, so he did not reply until 16 August.

Newsletter, June 1991

The Association's Chairman's June newsletter gave notice of the AGM to be held on 19 July in Lloyd's Old Library, stating that 264 Names had joined the Association out of a total of 562 on Syndicate 334. Clive reported that the Chairman of Lloyd's refused to meet the Committee despite an earlier promise to do so.

Clive commented to Keith:

> Did you know that certain syndicates were only available to 'Market Men' and their families? These syndicates are more profitable than those of the general run of syndicates with gullible plebs. It seems to me it is 'Merrettocracy'. Huh! Mr Coleridge has complained about whingeing Names. I see it like this, if you place a bet and it goes wrong, don't grumble. However, if the bookie runs off with the money and the stewards look the other way you are entitled to a real bellyache, even more so if the trainer claimed the horse had four legs and it turned out to have only three.

Grinning, Clive jumped three of his fingers a few times across his table.

Keith Lester attended the Annual General Meeting of Lloyd's on 26 June 1991 and, having caught the Chairman's eye, asked him:

> In the Society's Annual Report there was little mention of education and training except in a section stating that education and training was emphasised as being important in Tower Hamlets. Might one

conclude that education and training was good for people in Tower
Hamlets but not for the community of Lloyd's? I would be interested
to know how much the Corporation spent on education and training
and where one might find centres of managerial excellence within the
Lloyd's community. I am ceasing to underwrite on badly managed
syndicates such as those of the Merrett Group. It does not appear to
be good business sense to support syndicates where the Managing
Agents received fees and against whom legal action is proposed.

The Chairman answered:

Twenty-seven people have passed the Lloyd's Market Certificate last
year and over 200 people had registered. The Certificate was now
a requirement for underwriters. The Corporation trained its own
staff, some had degrees. Mr Lester was wrong to think that training
was unimportant and perhaps there should have been a change of
emphasis in the report, but he was right to think that investment
in training and education was seed corn for the future. We treat
training very seriously.

Subsequently Keith sent a copy of his question to Coleridge and
commented that he admired his stamina and patience in answering questions for three hours at the AGM. The Chairman replied, enclosing an
extract from the AGM transcript and thanking him for his kind remarks.

The *Daily Telegraph* reported on 27 June that Lloyd's had announced
a £509 million loss and the Chairman forecast more losses to come.
A fifty-year-old man said he had lost about £200,000 and had already sold
a lot of assets. Adding to his difficulties, unfortunately his life assurance
business had failed this year. *Insurance Age* for the month of June headlined, 'Lloyd's in the Limelight', reporting recent results and predicting
that Names would have to pay £800 million before the end of 1991.

On 1 July *The Times* announced that David Rowland, Chairman
of Sedgewick, was heralded as Lloyd's reformer. He had been invited by

the Chairman of Lloyd's to consider how the Lloyd's Market should be organised and financed to compete in world markets in the next century. Rowland was in bed in Hong Kong when the Chairman's call came to volunteer on army lines. 'You say you are musical. Then move the piano.' The piano was Lloyd's itself – an historic period instrument, ornate, resonant, but increasingly impracticable and out of tune, so that recent performances had been disastrous. There were pressures to make Lloyd's enforce higher standards of competence. Mutualisation was the vogue word at Lloyd's. It would also open a way for corporate Membership by limited liability companies.

Stephen O'Brien, an Association Member, recorded his accidental meeting with Murray Lawrence, the former Lloyd's Chairman, who made it clear that the whole Syndicate 334 affair had been 'one enormous cock-up' and that the wrong arbitration verdict had been reached, against his expectations. He said the Association's tactics were very appropriate and concluded that he was leaving Lloyd's because of the debacle over Syndicate 334 rather than the extent of the losses.

Ninth Steering Committee Meeting, 19 July 1991: Lack of Control at Lloyd's

Five Committee Members attended the Steering Committee plus Tom Benyon, Chairman of SoN. Previously the Association had decided not to join SoN or become involved with other syndicates. Clive was delighted to say that the Lloyd's ombudsman was 'minded to investigate his complaint subject to further information'.

In his absence, the Treasurer's report was presented by the Secretary. Funds at Lloyds Bank amounted to £59,691. A subscription of 3% of line was due at the end of August. D J Freeman had produced a budget indicating that at least £1.5 million would be required to fund legal action. The Committee realised that cash could be dissipated quite quickly as legal and other fees. Careful husbandry of the funds was absolutely essential if sufficient money was available for legal action to be successful. David Tiplady believed that there was a strong case against

Pulbrook Underwriting Management and estimated the total loss for the 1985 account at £26 million. To use and conserve funds effectively he thought the main targets should be Pulbrook Underwriting Management and Winchester Bowring, plus Matthews Wrightson and Willis Faber & Dumas (Agencies).

Tom Benyon advised the Committee on strategy at the forthcoming AGM. He pointed out:

> The Committee should only provide the minimum information about funding at the AGM. I recommend providing a bullish state-ment indicating that if the AGM agreed, the costs would be fully funded. I am sure it is vital not to reveal funding details as it is very likely that Errors & Omissions underwriters' spies will be attending.

The Steering Committee meeting was followed by the first AGM of the Syndicate 334 (1985) Names Association, held in the Old Library at Lloyd's. Forty Members were present. Subsequently, there was criticism about the low attendance. Chairman Clive Francis outlined the history of events and noted that the Association now had 264 Members. In presenting the legal position David Tiplady said, 'Claims had been identified which ranged from extremely strong to worthwhile.' It was resolved unanimously to go ahead with legal action. The writ which had been issued would be served the next week. The Financial Statements were formally adopted, and all Committee Members were re-elected to the Steering Committee.

The June issue of *Maclean's*, Canada's current affairs and news maga-zine, had a picture of the Lloyd's building, headlined, 'Losing it All, Lloyd's of London Investors Cry Foul' and 'Names Have Been Left Hanging Out to Dry', citing that there were 473 Canadian Names. The article was wide-ranging, covering the issues affecting Names and mentioning well-known personalities involved. Warren Hurst, who supplied a copy of the article, featured as a sixty-five-year-old Chartered Accountant who had been Vice-Chairman of a brokerage firm and had also acted as an investment adviser. He also enclosed a copy of his letter of complaint to

John Redwood, Minister of Trade and Industry. Another Name high-lighted, Kenneth Lavery, revealed, 'I am a retired Chartered Accountant helping to organize a group of Names, many of whom may be driven into personal bankruptcy.'

The Association had lodged a complaint with the Lloyd's regulatory authorities about the failure of Members' Agents to protect the financial interests of their Names. The reply from Lloyd's was so wimpish it seemed to be a dereliction of Lloyd's duty to conduct an orderly Market. The Lloyd's ombudsman had taken notice but there was a caveat that the ombudsman could not act because litigation had commenced. The claim was against London Wall Members Agency, Clive's Agent. Clive asked the Steering Committee if they knew of any London Wall Members who were not litigating and if so, would they be prepared to write to the ombudsman.

James Sinclair circularised Names, thanking them for such a magnif-icent response to this year's largely unexpected and unusual cash call, a new and unpleasant experience. Underwriters had thought they had a competitive advantage with a low expense ratio of 6% of net written premiums. However, this had risen to 18% and contributed to the loss. Many underwriters were overpaid, and a review had been taking place regarding Agents' fees and profit commission. The cost of regulation at Lloyd's was also high. Fee income was falling because of the reduction in the number of Names, and Willis Faber & Dumas (Agencies)'s fees were not negotiable. E&O insurance would no longer be a requirement of Lloyd's. This uncontrollable cost since 1980 had ballooned thirty-two times, from £25,000 in 1980 to £800,000 in 1991. Underwriters were reluctant to give Members' Agents cover as there was so much litigation overhanging the Market – reflecting dangerous levels of incompetence that could threaten its survival. As previously, his 1988 forecast was so far out he declined to give a firm forecast for 1989, except to say it would be bad.

Mr R. Hobbs of the DTI wrote to Mr F. Warren Hurst regarding self-regulation at Lloyd's, following his letter to Rt Hon John Redwood, the

Minister. He raised the matter of the modified arbitration procedure, as there was a ceiling of £100,000 proposed in the 1987 Neill report on regulation at Lloyd's. The proposals to streamline the modified arbitration procedure had been issued in a press release, which Hobbs enclosed with his letter. The procedure was not available to Hurst, as the costs of dealing with others were likely to exceed the £100,000 cap. Clive responded to Hurst commenting on his excellent letter to the Minister which neatly summarised the difference between the Minister's illusion and reality. He encouraged Hurst to keep the pressure on Lloyd's.

Newsletter, August 1991
Chairman Clive Francis despatched his August 1991 newsletter to all Syndicate 334 Names, but the enclosures were only sent to paid-up Members of the Association. He confirmed that writs had been served on behalf of the Association.

A complaint had been lodged with R. A. C. Hewes of the Lloyd's Regulatory Authority in July about the failure of Members' Agents and the Corporation of Lloyd's in its regulatory duties to protect the Names of Syndicate 334. Hewes said, 'I am not able to instruct Clive's Agent on what to implement. I agree it would be good to avoid litigation.' This response was so wimpish that it seemed to amount to a dereliction of Lloyd's duty to conduct an orderly Market. Consequently, he asked the Lloyd's ombudsman to investigate.

Association Membership, now 276, was still open for new Members on payment of the appropriate subscription. The newsletter concluded by saying that the Association had a good case and was adequately funded.

A circular arrived from James Sinclair on 6 August. He was looking to the future. In recent years underwriters had taken a beating. Some 100 companies in the USA had gone out of business. He said with so much red ink on balance sheets and interest rates trending down, resulting in loss of interest income on deposits, underwriters would have to increase rates. This was happening now. Confirming his confidence in the future he said he was increasing his capacity to £1 million. He also wrote, following Keith's visit to his office, to say, 'You are wrong to consider all Merrett syndicates in the same way as Syndicate 418. I reiterate that the Market was turning but I can't be sure until the end of the year as it will hinge on the conclusions of the Rowland Task Force.'

John Speirs' letter commented, 'Thank you Clive for your informative newsletter. I have had two bad losses including Syndicate 334 and am retreating from Lloyd's a sadder, considerably poorer and somewhat wiser man. The saddest part of all was the apparent unwillingness of one's Member's Agent to pursue the Managing Agent on behalf of their client.'

Mr Hewes, the Head of Regulatory Services, responded to Clive's proposition that his Members' Agent had a 'duty of care towards their Names', and Clive expressed his wish to bring proceedings against the Managing Agent. Hewes argued that, 'This is highly questionable in the circumstances as the Members' Agency denies any legal liability. It is not for Lloyd's to act in an interfering way.' Clive explained on 23 August:

> If an Agent fails to act to protect his Principal, then he had misrepresented himself by calling himself an Agent and any agreement between such an Agent and Principal is voidable by the Principal. This Association's Committee has formally brought to your attention, a case of wilful nondisclosure of material facts, relating to a contract of insurance by Pulbrook Underwriting Management and Winchester Bowring; I have requested you to investigate this matter on behalf of disadvantaged Names.

Following the Treasurer's request for details of time spent, David Tiplady repeated that he had already written off £30,000 of unrecoverable costs. He said the intensity of work would increase and he would endeavour to stay within budget. The possibility of a settlement was severely prejudiced if it was seen to be conducted in a half-hearted manner. He said he needed the complete support of clients in all that he was endeavouring to do, and agreed to bill his firm's fees monthly.

Clive's postbag was filled with tales of woe and severe distress caused by the failure of the Lloyd's policy. Willis Roxburgh on 20 August 1991 explained, 'I am not joining the Association as I feel it prudent to save every pound. I hope that Syndicate 90 will close in ten years and Syndicate 334 in a reasonably short time. I am also on Syndicate 418 and am going to take legal advice on the matter.' Names on Syndicate 418, the reinsurer of Syndicate 334, would have been caught for the losses had the arbitration favoured Syndicate 334. Either way, Mr Roxburgh would suffer losses.

The next day Mr M. Ceh also explained why he was not joining the Association. He said:

> I have already left Lloyd's. At the age of 73 I have a lot of worry. My substantial stop-loss of £55,000 set against a £20,000 call should easily cover my losses. I would be gambling my comfortable retirement if I continue funding the Association. I am not a gambler and if the action is settled for less than the full losses, I understand that the stop-loss policy may not pay the shortfall. The date of joining may result in different awards according to year, some may win and others might have substantial charges. I prefer not to have the worry as long as I have adequate stop-loss cover.

Mr Ceh was not the only Name to think he had taken out sufficient stop-loss to cover losses and thus decided not to join the Association.

On the same day Mr N. B. Cat of Bridgewater said he was being pursued by his bank and was 'flat broke'. For the present he was unable to pay the Association's subscription.

Lloyd's of London August newsletter reported that John Redwood, Corporate Affairs Minister at the DTI, reaffirmed Government support for Lloyd's and its concept of unlimited liability. Lloyd's deserved a tribute as every penny and cent of legitimate claims had been paid, which was the advantage to clients of substantial resources at Lloyd's, backed by unlimited liability. Gervase Tinley wrote to John Redwood on 21 August giving vent to his views, emphasising that an Agent had a duty of care. He enclosed a copy of the above-mentioned Lloyd's newsletter. He said Lloyd's Chairman had confirmed that Lloyd's made no distinction between internal insurance policies and those external to Lloyd's. On the same day he corresponded similarly with his Member of Parliament, Sir Peter Hordern. Mr R. H. Hobbs of the DTI replied on 16 September, mentioning that the dispute was being litigated and it was inappropriate for him to comment. The Council was given wide powers under the Lloyd's Act 1982 and other matters referred to by Gervase were not regulatory. He also said that underwriting rates were hardening, giving rise to more profitable business, and noted the current dissatisfaction may abate from that source alone. Whilst the Council pursued market-related issues with such vigour, he doubted there was anything to be gained from overt Government intervention. In reply Gervase speculated that the whole letter could have been written by the Lloyd's secretariat.

Charles Baron reported on his visit to Stephen Merrett on 22 September, saying he had a most pleasant and courteous discussion. Merrett had said that during the arbitration he had offered a 50% compromise through Herbert Smith, solicitors. This was turned down. He stated he was very unhappy with the style of campaign adopted by Syndicate 334. Clive wrote to congratulate Charles on an excellent piece of diplomacy and hoped future negotiations would be conducted without acrimony. Jasper Salisbury-Jones wrote to Charles about his visit, remarking that activity and publicity were 'friends'. He said that he entirely supported the policy of 'stirring up as much trouble as we could as we have nothing to lose'.

On 22 August Charles Maskens, an Association Member, wrote to Clive from Brussels to express thanks for the work of the Association. However, he was critical of the low attendance at the AGM. He said his English was not very fluent and he had little understanding of the British legal system. He hoped a passive presence was not seen as disinterest, because he strongly supported the action.

On 28 August the *Financial Times* published an article by Richard Lapper titled, 'Names Welcome Lloyd's Pay Study'. It said the ALM was concerned because underwriters received a high salary but committed only a small amount of their own funds to their syndicate. The survey also showed sharp differences in performance between two Members' Agencies. Gooda Walker Names made 8% profit in 1988 while those with Gooda Walker Partners made an average loss of 45.5%.

Tom Benyon's consultancy services for the Association were invoiced for three months to July at £1,000 per month plus expenses. There was a detailed list of his activities. This included David Tiplady and Clive Francis meeting with the Finance Director of Sedgewick to discuss troubled syndicates; speaking on the BBC's *Today* programme; meeting Duncan Hughes of the *Daily Telegraph*; also *European Business Today*; Gillian Bowditch of *The Times*; and Rebecca Smithers and Tony McAllister, both of the *Guardian*. These contacts produced extensive coverage in UK and overseas media. Additionally, he had met the Association's Committee and arranged for all nonpayers to be individually telephoned, urging them to pay.

On 2 September Benyon was in trouble from Clive. He had been complaining by correspondence to all Committee Members that he had not been paid his consultancy fee. Clive had clearly set out the procedure for payment in his letter of 17 May which had been ignored. Clive enquired:

> As you have not yet clarified the matter, should payments be made to you or your Company, Handplume Ltd? A formal invoice should be addressed to Syndicate 334 (1985) Names Association and sent to Louth Secretarial Services who would forward a cheque to the Treasurer for signature. Please reconcile the two earlier submissions with the current one. I am not at all happy that you have circulated 'this trivia' to all Members of the Committee. Kindly do not speak to me about this on the phone or in conversation again. We need to minimise concomitant copying and postage costs.

The Association was like a business where efficient collection of revenue and control of expenditure was vital to furthering its objectives. Clive was very supportive of the responsibilities of the Treasurer.

Business Insurance reported on 16 and 30 August that 'Lloyd's Faces Litigation to Void Members' Losses'. Many North American Names were heading to court to avoid paying losses. They were charging Lloyd's with fraudulent misrepresentation, fraudulent conduct and practices, and infringement of US and Canadian securities laws. The US Securities Exchange Commission conducted an 'informal' investigation to determine whether Lloyd's had infringed securities law as alleged. Subsequently, on 30 September *Business Insurance* reported that two US Lloyd's Names had persuaded a federal magistrate to recommend the issuance of an injunction. The effect was to bar Lloyd's from calling on letters of credit until alleged securities law violations were heard in a federal court. The result would prevent Lloyd's from doing business in the USA.

Tenth Steering Committee Meeting, 18 September 1991: Unfair Distribution of Losses

Ten Committee Members, including the newly coopted Adam Raphael, that met at D J Freeman's offices were joined by Tom Benyon, who stayed for half an hour. Tom said press coverage had helped successfully to heighten Syndicate 334's profile. As 70% of losses had fallen on 30% of Names, Lloyd's must aim for retroactive mutualisation and arrange more fairly the distribution of losses across all syndicates. He was organising a 'Troubled Names Conference' on 23 September and had met Dr Mary Archer who chaired the Hardship Committee. Clive mentioned that he was aware that twenty-four Working Names were with the Hardship Committee.

The Treasurer indicated that 4% of line, being £400 for every £10,000 of underwriting capacity, as subscription to the Association was past due. It had raised £250,000. Some ninety-four Members had not yet paid. The nonpayers were to be followed up with a polite letter.

David Tiplady's fee rate had risen from £160 to £180 per hour. He was asked to approach his partners requesting them to retain the budgeted rate of £160 until 30 June 1992. A high inflation rate would inevitably increase the costs of legal action. To partially offset increased costs, bank deposits with a duration of less than a year were earning 9% per annum interest.

David reported that no further Opinion had been received from counsel because the chosen counsel had a conflict of interest having acted for Winchester Bowring. The solicitors acting for Winchester Bowring had 'screamed down the phone' at him, signifying that counsel knew more about Winchester Bowring than was good for him.

It was agreed to pay expenses to Committee Members retrospectively and to pay Clive a sum of £4,000 for the past and £5,000 per annum in future.

Alasdair Ferguson analysed funds received by the Association. He reported on 19 September that D J Freeman's fees had increased by 13% plus another 2.5% for the recent VAT increase. He estimated that the war chest needed to be £2 million. He was very concerned whether the Association had sufficient funds to conduct *any* legal action. Considering both syndicate 334 and 90, he proposed that there should be different levies for three different groups of Names. He suggested Names on Syndicates 334 and 90 only pay 10% while Names on both syndicates pay 7.5%. There had to be enough funds to cover the legal costs and those of the other side if the action was lost. If the first action was successful, then the chances of the second action would be improved. He questioned whether both Syndicates 90 and 334 needed £2 million. He did not think David would lose Names £2 million. By reducing the levy for Names on both syndicates it might entice more Members to join the Associations. The proposal was not accepted.

To ensure that Syndicate 334 issues received wider publicity, Keith decided to stand again for election to Lloyd's Council and wrote letters seeking nomination. Michael Jump was prepared to nominate him. Although Michael was an original founder of the Action Group, he had decided not to join the Association as he was dubious about the chances of success. Furthermore, he thought he had enough stop-loss not to benefit from legal action success. Another individual wrote to say he was not prepared to sponsor Keith's nomination as he was not active at Lloyd's and 'just an old fogey sitting on his farm'. One of the original sponsors agreeing was Michael Goold, a leather manufacturer in Walsall. He and

Keith were old boys of Queen Mary's Grammar School, Walsall, and first met at the opening of the 1986 Building by Queen Elizabeth II.

Kenneth Lavery wrote to Mr J. R. M. Foster, Secretary, Investigations Committee, on 24 September amending the complaint in his letter of May 13. He was underwriting on Syndicates 418 and 334 with losses of £47,419. The detailed, carefully argued letter had an extensive schedule of twenty-six exhibits. He made claims against Stephen Merrett and Ernst & Whinney, the auditors, on the basis that they had falsely stated that the books had been properly kept. The audit report for Syndicate 418 in 1982 did not give a 'true and fair view', he wrote. The 1984 Annual Report of the Syndicate was wrong and deceptive. Annual Reports served both as an invitation for existing Names to continue and a prospectus for new Names. Many Names had joined syndicates induced by fraudulent misrepresentations and material nondisclosures, he contended. He had analysed the financial results and membership in detail, pointing out how key people were involved and the difficulty of finding disinterested individuals to deal objectively and fairly with the issues.

Kenneth said:

I accuse the underwriters of Pulbrook Underwriting Management Ltd of publishing false Annual Syndicate Reports for Syndicate 334 stating that in June 1984 they had affected reinsurance for 1975 and prior years on an unlimited basis. In my view the Directors wilfully concealed a substantial amount of long-tail business. The underwriters, Messrs Turner and Verrall, broker Winchester Bowring and the Directors of Pulbrook Underwriting Management failed to act in utmost good faith regarding the run-off policy with Syndicate 418. I see that Merrett and Pulbrook Syndicates were all the same Group and underwrote the Errors and Omissions policies. It smells, even across the Atlantic! I judge the arbitration outcome was a rogue result. Last but not least I make a claim against Lloyd's, for not conducting insurance business in accordance with the Lloyd's Act 1982 and failing to stop fraudulent practices. I have requested many times that the agreements between me and Syndicates 418 and 334 be declared void ab initio. I sent a sterling draft on July 25 with instructions that it be retained in my personal reserve until I receive satisfactory replies to my questions and have given written approval to pay the cash call. Ken's analysis illustrated an affair riddled with personal conflicts of interest resulting in substantial pecuniary advantage to Merrett and others. His examination of the status report file showed the only clear-cut victory by Syndicate 418 was if the Merrett Group sued itself.

Several times Adam Raphael had commented to Clive that, according to Market rumours, the Association lacked combat readiness. On 25 July Clive addressed Adam Raphael's repeated perception that the Association lacked combat readiness in both funds and determination. He sought Adam's advice on how to counter this perception. He was puzzled, as writs had been issued and served. The legal action was fully funded. Moreover, he said the view given by Adam did not coincide with David Tiplady's account of the E&O insurers being astonished and angered by the virulence of the Association's campaign. Furthermore, the Association now had the Head of Lloyd's Regulatory Services being investigated by the ombudsman for his lack of action. Clive had a letter from the Chairman of Lloyd's pleading confidentiality because of the marshalled facts and the cogency of the arguments presented. Clive wondered if he had been remiss in not providing all the back copies of relevant correspondence to Adam at the time he joined the Committee.

Clive received a very depressing letter from Mrs T. Den of Cannock. She said she had signed a letter dictated by her husband, once a relatively wealthy man, which informed the Chairman, 'I cannot pay £900 subscription to the Association as I have no money and am being kept by my wife on an old-age pension. I am over eighty years old. Lloyd's was paid £200,000 cash calls and I have been suspended from underwriting. I can't sign my name as I have had a cancer taken off my hand.' Clive responded promptly saying he was very sorry to learn of Mr

Den's predicament and hoped the injured hand recovered quickly. He explained that the Rules of the Association allowed contributions to be waived if the Name had applied to the Lloyd's Hardship Committee and recommended Mr Den make such an application.

Clive wrote to Committee Members saying that it had been agreed to send a polite reminder that the second subscription was due, to those who had not paid the latest tranche. The Treasurer quickly concocted such a letter but Clive thought it required a little beefing up. In consultation with the Treasurer a little more beef was introduced, reminding certain Members that the second subscription was due and required prompt replies 'without more ado'. Clive confessed that he had erred in that the beefing-up was a little too robust and resulted in some complaints and explanations for delay in payment.

The Treasurer received a letter from Major W. H. Edwards of Chudleigh complaining about the unfriendly tone of the letter requesting the latest payment and would have preferred a timely reminder. He said all his papers were in New Zealand. He also asked for a copy of the audited balance sheet of the Association 'without more ado', repeating the form of words in the Treasurer's demand letter. Sir John Barraclough of Bath also sent in his subscription, saying it was late because he had been absent abroad. Mr R. Viner of Sheffield expressed his concern that if only half those affected subscribed to the Association it would mean the costs would be a very heavy burden on those that had. David Greig of Sydney, Australia, was unable to ascertain the whereabouts of his initial contribution to the Association, although subsequently his first instalment had been received. Daniel Bennett writing from Miami said all his funds were in the BCCI and he was in the process of opening new accounts. On 7 July 1991, the Hong Kong Office was ordered to close, claiming BCCI had problem loans and the Sheikh of Abu Dhabi, the major shareholder of BCCI, refused to provide funds. The bank was liquidated on 17 July 1991. Some delay was attributed to the need to send letters by mail as the efficiency of postal services in some countries was less than desirable.

On 7 October 1991, Clive wrote to John Chappell, an actuary in Australia, about the relationship between stop-loss underwriters and any award received by Names from legal action. He said an award would be paid to the Name personally and he would be in a good position to negotiate any refund to the stop-loss underwriters.

Frank Wright of Washington, DC sent newspaper clippings of articles from *Business Insurance* on 25 October covering activities at Lloyd's. A US court had dismissed a suit by a Name against Lloyd's; articles included detailed litigation facing Lloyd's to void Names' losses. About 100 US Names were preparing to sue Lloyd's in the Federal Court of New York. They had collected $250,000 towards funding the litigation. Lloyd's was seeking an injunction against one of the New York Names, Dale Jenkins, to prevent a suit in the US courts. Had Lloyd's registered under the securities law, it was alleged, Lloyd's would have been more closely regulated in the United States. Other topics included the Task Force investigation, legal cases barring letters of credit, loss of underwriting Names and the plague of long-tail liability claims.

Names resided in many foreign countries, particularly the United States of America, Canada, Continental Europe, Australia and New Zealand. About 15% of Association Members lived abroad. The Association was able to recover the VAT on a proportion of expenses paid on behalf of Members resident outside the UK.

The ALM October briefing featured Lloyd's major loss syndicates. It detailed and commented on Names Associations such as Outhwaite 1982, Warrilow 1984, Pulbrook 334 (1985), Syndicate 90 (1982), Rose Thomson Young 355, Poland (1985), Feltrim and the Gooda Walker Action Group. There were eight other syndicates with large losses and this included Syndicate 418. It reported that a letter from Canadian Name Kenneth Lavery regarding Merrett Syndicate 418 had been circulated in early August and a Syndicate 418 General Meeting had been arranged for 4 November. Subsequently, 1,050 Members of Feltrim Names' Association had assented to the issue of a protective writ.

The financial position of the Association at 31 October 1991 was summarised as follows:

	£
Subscriptions	327,961
Expenses	(66,183)
Bank Balance	**261,778**
Creditors	(13,588)

Keith Lester received notification from Mr A. P. Barber, the Secretary to the Council, that ten candidates had been nominated for election to Council. A postal ballot would be held and a notice posted in the under-writing room on 13 November.

On 1 November 1991 Alasdair Ferguson wrote to Clive enclosing extracts from the year ending 31 December 1990 audited financial statements of Winchester Bowring and Pulbrook Underwriting Management. Clive sought Alasdair's views on these businesses with a view to recovering losses. They showed the value of the two companies were not worth 'powder and shot', in other words, they were valueless, having minimal net assets. Alasdair pointed out that Winchester Bowring Limited had made £3.9 million profit. Cash in the bank amounted to £39 million but after liabilities there was only £5.9 million free cash. Pulbrook Underwriting Management was a relatively small company with a turnover of £700,000 and profits of £400,000 before tax. Generally, profit had been paid as corporation tax or distributed as dividends. Capital and reserves amounted to £209,000 but subject to contingent liabilities. Protection was provided 'under Merrett Group Professional Indemnity Policy' which appeared to be the company's only major asset.

Alasdair Ferguson requested through Clive written confirmation from David about the funding for the Association's claims and its source, and referred to a possible conflict of interest as David acted for the two Syndicates, 334 and 90. Success rewards may not be sufficiently ample to remunerate both plaintiffs, he argued. He asked for details showing where certainty existed and where doubt should properly be entertained.

David replied on 5 November that it would not be worth suing for the assets declared in Pulbrook Underwriting Management's annual accounts. However, the target was the E&O policy. He *believed* the Managing Agent carried £25 million cover for the 1985 year of account. Winchester Bowring would also have E&O cover of an unknown amount. David was satisfied that Pulbrook Underwriting Management, had enough cumulative assets for the Association's legal action potentially to achieve a substantial recovery and any doubts should be laid aside.

Syndicate 90 was different, as the year of account was an earlier one. Even though it may be primarily insured into the same Lloyd's syndicate or syndicates, the reinsurance would be so arranged as to be capable of responding fully up to the level of cover for that particular year. In other words, Pulbrook Underwriting Management's insurers for Syndicate 334 1985 year could pay £25 million and this should not impede the ability of Syndicate 90 insurers to pay an equivalent sum for 1982. Therefore Syndicates 334 and 90 were not in competition and their actions were complementary. The only area of doubt was the willingness of parent companies to support their subsidiaries. Willis Corroon, the UK holding company, had indicated they would support Willis Faber & Dumas (Agencies) and Pulbrook Underwriting Management. However, so far the ultimate holding company, Marsh & McLennan, had not commented. The E&O alone may not be sufficient to recompense fully Syndicate 90 Names and it may be resolved by being insured into CentreWrite, the corporation's reinsurance company, using any award of damages, or settlement sum, as a premium.

Clive sought clarification from David Tiplady by way of a categoric statement of the *actuality*, rather than *belief*, that Pulbrook Underwriting Management had a £25 million E&O policy in 1995. Regarding Winchester Bowring, David should make sure that each defendant was equally able to provide the restitution the Association sought, should it only win against one. He requested David to provide him with copies of Willis Corroon and Merrett Holdings, indications of support, and to make enquiries of Marsh & McLennan as to their stance on the matter.

Charles Baron, monitoring the Association's bank balance at Louth, advised the Treasurer on 7 November that the Association's funds at Lloyds Bank were being credited to his personal account and not to the Association's account. This caused considerable embarrassment at the next Committee Meeting. It also destroyed account confidentiality. Funds were moved to a new account at Barclays in Sevenoaks. In addition, it came to light that Lloyd's Bank had been deducting tax from the Association's interest income, whereas Barclays said the income should be paid gross.

The results of election to Lloyd's Council were announced on 14 November. The winner received 3,204 votes and Lester 911.

A list of Association Members and their first and second instalments was distributed by LSS on 2 December 1991. Including US dollar balances the cash at bank amounted to approximately £320,000. Some twenty-eight Members had not paid the second instalment, totalling £26,700. Clive drafted a letter for the Treasurer to send to nonpayers, which is worth replicating:

> Dear...
>
> I can only apologise for the infelicitous wording of the reminder you recently received. In endeavouring to reconcile the opposing needs of strength of expression to obviate the cost of another reminder and those of diplomatic politeness I obviously erred towards the former. This I much regret and send my apologies. At the same time, I would ask you to bear in mind that we are all amateurs in precisely the same boat as yourself and giving freely of our own free time on your behalf. I hope you will continue to give your support.
>
> Keith Lester, Treasurer

Eleventh Steering Committee Meeting, 3 December 1991

Eleven Committee Members attending were informed that ninety 'late joiners' as Names from 1983 onwards had an average loss of £80,000 and may be subject to misrepresentation. Names' rights associated with different joining dates were too complicated for discussion and decision and the subject was carried forward for future consideration.

It was speculated that Syndicate 334 losses might be £32 million but could rise to £50 million. The total would not be known until the 1985 year was closed. It was believed that Matthews Wrightson Pulbrook had a £25 million E&O policy and Winchester Bowring no more than £8 million. Merrett would stand behind Matthews Wrightson Pulbrook. However, for 1992 the Merrett Group underwriting capacity had been reduced by £100 million. This would seriously affect underwriting income. The Committee thought there were sufficient funds for legal action. Syndicate 334 had a simpler legal case and was slightly more advanced than Syndicate 90, so that it might well come to court sooner.

D J Freeman & Co had not agreed to reduce David Tiplady's fee from £180 to the £160 per hour budgeted rate. He did not confirm that he had addressed the matter with the partners, as requested at the last meeting.

On 5 December the Treasurer copied an article in 'Listing Particulars' about Willis Corroon to Clive commenting that it was important not to close off possible claims for misrepresentation. Misrepresentation claims should only be dropped when claims against the Managing Agents were successful and it could be seen that there were adequate financial resources to pay the amount being claimed in full.

Keith and his wife had lunch with Ernest Moore, the underwriter of Syndicate 90, at Lloyd's. Rather unexpectedly, Ernest said he did not drink alcoholic beverages at lunch time and that he sent inebriated staff home in the afternoon. Keith concurred with such a view, as on one occasion his staff had been informed that at lunch time they should not exceed alcohol levels permitted to drive a car if they were to return to work in the afternoon. It seemed to be a tradition at Lloyd's to have long, boozy lunches. On 11 December, Keith wrote to Ernest and thanked him for his help and guidance, informing him that he was leaving all the Merrett Group syndicates. He was in the process of taking legal action as he was dismayed at the failure of Lloyd's policies. Surprisingly, in an interview on

25 April 2024, John Neal, Lloyd's CEO, was reported in *City AM* saying that booziness was still a problem at Lloyd's.

Newsletter, December 1991

The Association's strong position derived from the simplicity of the issues that were clear and difficult to refute. They were summarised in the newsletter. A trial date would be sought next April. Clive explained:

> It is my privilege to chair a united, harmonious and highly qualified Committee. The Committee Members included a barrister, the Executive Editor of the *Observer*, four Chartered Accountants, one of whom was both a JP and an ex-Lloyd's broker, and two businessmen. The Committee was advised carefully and constructively by a solicitor, Dr David Tiplady.

Most of the 283 Members had paid the second tranche. It was not too late for additional Names to join the Association and with this in mind the newsletter was being distributed to 545 surviving Syndicate 334 Names.

There was information about correspondence between a Name and the Agent Cox & Bell. It pursued the concept that an Agent at Lloyd's had a duty in law to protect the interests of the Principal and recover losses occasioned by the negligent actions of a Sub-Agent. Cox & Bell maintained they had taken legal advice; the concept was not correct and therefore they could take no action (see correspondence dated 14 February 1992).

The Steering Committee needed to appoint an auditor. Charles Baron suggested Forrester Boyd & Co, Wayneflete House, Louth, a branch of a largish regional firm. He said that Sir John Grenside, a former President of the Institute of Chartered Accountants in England and Wales, was well satisfied with their service. As accounting records were held in Louth this might be a suitable appointment. They were also auditors to the Syndicate 90 Names Association. The Treasurer received quotes from two audit firms in Louth. Forrester Boyd gave a lower quote at £450 plus VAT, and this was approved by the Committee.

David Tiplady firmed up the Association's claims. Syndicate 418 reinsurance contract's failure was caused by negligence in placing the reinsurance by Pulbrook Underwriting Management and/or Winchester Bowring. Pulbrook Underwriting Management was negligent in closing certain years by relying upon Syndicate 418 reinsurance. The earliest year they might have kept open was 1979. This benefited those joining after 1979, however, 1979, 1980 and 1981 joiners were time-barred. Statements made to Names by Pulbrook Underwriting Management and Matthews Wrightson Pulbrook agency may well have been negligent. Time-bar, preventing legal action as a result of the passage of time, became a recurring theme as potential legal cases were discussed and sometimes dropped.

Mr J. H. of Ontario wrote on 5 January 1992 saying he was unemployed and his pension would not be available until September. After a review with his bank manager, he hoped to be able to pay the second tranche on 1 March.

Mr A. G. D. of Totnes wrote to say that his liabilities exceeded his total assets and he had no money to pay the Association's subscription. However, he fully approved of the Association's actions.

Clive replied to Major W. H. (Bill) Edwards MC who had requested a copy of the Association's accounts. Clive explained that these details were not normally distributed with newsletters. One of the tactics was to convince the opposition that the Association was well funded. If the opposition thought it was underfunded, they would prolong litigation by trying to exhaust the funds and any hope of settlement would fly out of the window. However, the Association's accounts would have to be published later in the year.

Willis Faber & Dumas (Agencies) distributed a copy of David Rowland's Task Force Proposals. The letter said rapid implementation of the proposals offered Lloyd's a real prospect of returning to what everyone wanted, soundly based growth, hard-nosed underwriting, reasonable costs, producing long-term worthwhile sustainable profits for Names.

On 2 February 1992 Adam Raphael, recently appointed as Chairman of Syndicate 90 Association, responded to Clive about the differing interests of those who joined pre-1980 and those joining later. There may be a possibility of two causes of action. He explained that Syndicate 90 had a similar situation and decided to restrict action to the failure of the reinsurance contract because of Pulbrook Underwriting Management negligence. He reasoned that combining differing causes of action would have added so much to the cost that the Syndicate 90 Association could not have funded it within the budget. There would be considerable added delay in getting the case to court. It would be very difficult if not impossible to amalgamate the differing financial interests following either settlement or court action. He thought the above applied with even more force to Syndicate 334. If the reinsurance action succeeded there would be 100% recovery of losses. Consequently, there would be no advantage to the majority of Names financing subsidiary causes of action. He did not think the financial backing was enough, except for the most direct and simplest of cases. Nothing was more likely, nay, guaranteed, to produce delay, he said, than 'to complicate our case'.

Adam stated, 'The Association is at a crucial stage. Without impugning the motives of D J Freeman in any way, it is natural that they should want to preserve as many causes of action as possible. The Committee's job is to pursue the strongest case within the resources of the Association.'

The February issue of *Lloyd's Log* published a letter from Keith Lester, stating that risk capital for Lloyd's syndicates was a scarce commodity and Names must be treated as highly valued customers. Information from his Agent indicated that Merrett syndicates had lost over £100 million of capacity. In contrast the *Financial Times* reported that Hayter Brockbank had increased capacity by 70%. Using published statistics and assuming a £10,000 line on each of Lloyd's Chairman David Coleridge's syndicates in his 1991 portfolio, Keith calculated average return amounted to 12% per year over seven years. He suggested that Names should join syndicates which were paradigms of managerial excellence, with competent well-motivated staff. Quality should be preferred to quantity.

Charles Baron expressed to Clive his concerns on 4 February regarding eighty Names who joined Syndicate 334 in 1983 and onwards. This group had a strong case which would be expensive to prosecute and had no advantage for other Association Members. Greater funds would be needed incurring a delay to the main action, which had a reasonably good chance of success of benefiting each Member up to 100% of loss. If the main case failed and the minority succeeded it would be difficult to persuade the minority group to share their award.

Clive received some *good* news at last. Outhwaite Names Association, that had been in contention in the High Court, had won a settlement of £135 million. This was very encouraging and gave impetus for other Names' Associations to pursue their claims ardently. Clive became excited by the prospect of taking the Association's case to court as soon as possible and obtained a copy of the report in *The Times* on 10 February which detailed the settlement.

Neville Lumb of Huddersfield said to Clive:

Cox & Bell has failed to act in my best interests or in a satisfactory manner and I am entitled to seek redress through other media. Nothing that has been copied to you was marked 'confidential'. They related primarily to the Gooda Walker underwriting and reflected examples of dissatisfaction with their attitude as Agents. I confirm that all copies of correspondence held by you between Cox & Bell and me are genuine photostats. You can use them to further the interests of the Association as you think fit

Mr J. R. W. Ling, FCA of Cox & Bell underwriting Agents, wrote to the Treasurer on 17 January, who suggested he may have noticed that the December 1991 newsletter contained some very disparaging comments about Cox & Bell Ltd, implying that it had deliberately misled at least one of its Names. He was writing to all Syndicate 334 Names stating that Cox & Bell had done all in its power to look after the interests of Names. A copy of a letter was enclosed from Fishburn Boxer, Cox & Bell's solicitor, dated 14 January 1992. Fishburn Boxer wrote to say that one of their client's Names had asserted that an Agent at Lloyd's had a duty in law to protect the interests of a Principal and asserted that an Agent had a duty in law to recover losses occasioned by the negligent action of a Sub-Agent. Their client, Cox & Bell, had obtained legal advice they said stated that it had no duty to protect the interests of its Principal and had no duty to recover losses occasioned by any negligent action of a Sub-Agent. For that reason, their client Cox & Bell maintained it could take no further action. For many months the Name had sought a copy of the legal advice. The newsletter said that Cox & Bell had admitted that it had not received legal advice. Fishburn Boxer complained that the December newsletter used an extremely distasteful metaphor which was clearly intended to suggest that the client was dishonest and untruthful in its dealings with its Names. The solicitor said the assertions were defamatory, damaging and untrue. It was clear that it was libellous and malicious. There could be no justification for publishing untruthful and defamatory matter to anyone, especially to such a wide readership. A lengthy detailed account of steps taken by Cox & Bell to assist Names was provided.

Cox & Bell's solicitors required that Mr Francis and the Association promptly publish a retraction of the inaccurate and damaging allegations made against their client – who reserved the right to issue proceedings without further notice – in terms to be seen and approved by them. In addition, other points were raised involving imputations against their client's integrity. Fishburn Boxer were taking further instructions from their client regarding these matters.

Clive found it necessary to apologise to a Mr Gradon of London for being troubled with Cox & Bell's 14 February letter. He complained that Cox & Bell had failed to extend the courtesy of sending him a copy. He assured Mr Gradon that there was no possibility that the Association would be attacked. Stressing that he was writing in confidence, Clive said that part of the tactics in achieving the Association's goal was to exert unremitting pressure on the Corporation of Lloyd's, the Council of Lloyd's, Matthews Wrightson Pulbrook and all Members' Agents to produce a settlement. The fact that Cox & Bell had become agitated could be taken as a sign that the tactics were working. Clive was at the receiving end of an astonishing number of letters outlining the shortcomings of Names' Agents. The name of Cox & Bell had cropped up in complaints more often than most, which may have been fortuitous. The Committee was advised on tactics by two or three Market Men and it was deemed that pressure and antagonism win much more than soft words. He mentioned the recent public attempt at conciliation with Stephen Merrett that got nowhere. In conclusion Clive said if a retraction was considered to be a better tactical move, he would issue one.

The *Daily Telegraph* on 21 February 1992 headlined, 'Lloyd's Problems Laid at Revenue's Door.' It said Lloyd's was caught in a double ambush. As the 1980s wore on the Revenue's policy progressively limited syndicates' ability to reserve for potentially extraordinary losses. Furthermore, the American courts had appointed the insurance industry as a surrogate social security system. Michael Freeman & Co, solicitors, alleged that cash calls were so 'flawed' that Names were not liable.

On the same day, the paper pointed out that 'Valuable time is ticking away for Lloyd's', elaborating that the first of solicitor Michael Freeman's injunctions would be heard in the High Court. Mr M. Freeman's clients were trying to escape their obligations. Freeman was seeking to bar Lloyd's syndicates from access to funds which Names had pledged to them. If this and other cases were upheld, then Lloyd's could run out of cash to pay claims. The object was to get the Market to pay losses on his syndicates by some form of mutualisation, when there might then be a glimmer of hope for loss-making syndicates.

Newsletter, February 1992

The victory of Outhwaite Names and the settlement of a Warrilow action was regarded as a great boost to those Names suffering severe losses. The Outhwaite settlement was nearly 90% of the amount claimed. Of this, the eighty-nine Members' Agents involved contributed some 80%. Mark Connoley, the solicitor advising Outhwaite Names, maintained that the figures suggested a de facto admission of responsibility.

However, for Syndicate 334 (1985) Names there was disappointment in that the principle of vicarious responsibility of the Members' Agents was not established by judgement as a legal precedent. Vicarious liability is the holding of a person or entity responsible for damages or harm caused by someone else. It applies in situations in which a person or entity holds a superior position to an Agent.

This legal disappointment was in no way matched by the bitter one for those Outhwaite Names who were persuaded for one reason or another not to join their Names' Association. They had lost out completely and now needed to overcome a time-bar. Thus, they had been severely penalised by acceding to pressure not to litigate brought by Members' Agents. Moreover, they appeared not to have been informed of the Opinion of leading counsel that any recoveries in litigation go first to pay off all the losses and expenses incurred by Names, before any stop-loss insurer is reimbursed. Recoveries were payable directly to the Name. There was a salutary lesson for Names on Syndicate 334 who had not yet subscribed to the Association. Clive was keen to promote this lesson to such Names.

Suddenly settlement seemed to be the flavour of the month at Lloyd's. The Committee would be sad to think that any Syndicate 334 Names had failed to take advantage of the strength of its litigation position through the Association. There was still time to join this strong and assertive Names' Association.

Many Agents including Cox & Bell initially sought to dissuade Syndicate 334 Names from joining the Association and then revised their advice and left the matter to the Names. Cox & Bell, somewhat stung by observations in the last newsletter, had issued a lengthy contradiction and sent it to some Members of the Association. However, Clive continued to say in the newsletter that 'my informant', a doughty Member of this Association, resolutely maintained that he considered himself to have been misled by his Agent.

In addition, Cox & Bell's solicitors made an observation that might startle their Members who nurtured the concept that an Agent must act in his Principal's best interests. They said that it would normally be imprudent for Cox & Bell to issue proceedings on behalf of Names. It appeared they were suggesting that a Members' Agent at Lloyd's was in some peculiar way immune from the general laws of agency. Clive questioned whether the word 'imprudent' was an open admission of a conflict of interest. By inactivity and refusal to protect their Principal's interests, he maintained, they had wrongfully subordinated their Principal's interests to their own and those of their insurers. Clive suggested that in the circumstances of such a conflict they do not look after their clients' best interests they should resign and refund the commissions paid to them. Mrs Milling-Smith was a twenty-six-year-old widow with young children (see 20 June 1990). Her sad tale was one of the nastiest of the current crop of Lloyd's horror stories. Resulting from her introduction to Cox & Bell her life was in ruins. The forced sale of her house was imminent and the welfare of her handicapped child hopelessly jeopardised.

Cox & Bell distributed a memorandum regarding the Association's February newsletter. It said there were incorrect statements about the late Brian Bell. It was understood that the Steering Committee had agreed that no further comment was to be made about Cox & Bell as such comments were not in the interests of Members of the Association. It continued that if no further allegations were made against the company, in the interests of all concerned they would let the matter rest, so that the Association could get on with its proper task of attempting to obtain recompense for Names. Clive's high-risk strategy had forced a climb-down by Cox & Bell. For the Treasurer's response to Mr Ling of Cox & Bell, Clive gave some suggested wording. He said he would be grateful if the Treasurer could spare the time to reply, as it would serve to worry not only Cox & Bell but their solicitors. Replying on 13 March the Treasurer said he was very pleased to see that Ling expressed the view that there would be no purpose in a libel action and he accepted the view that the vendetta was not that of the Syndicate 334 (1985) Names Association. Mr Francis had, they said, posed some very relevant questions to his firm's solicitors and it would be interesting to know the answers.

Ling wrote to the Treasurer thanking him for his letter and agreed that it was to no one's benefit to engage in legal action except for lawyers. He added that he had been unpleasantly surprised that Clive's February newsletter continued the personal vendetta against Cox & Bell Ltd and at somewhat greater length.

There was a Channel 4 programme about Lloyd's before Christmas. Coleridge denied on television that he was a Member of a very small and profitable syndicate. The camera swept over relevant documents and showed the contrary to be the case.

Twelfth Steering Committee Meeting, 25 February 1992:
Shocking Increase in Losses

While seated comfortably in the offices of D J Freeman, the Steering Committee became aware that the underwriter of Syndicate 334, Mr Gray, was forecasting losses of £55 million to £60 million, a large increase on previous forecasts. Suddenly, serious disquiet was expressed, giving rise to distinctly uncomfortable feelings. More information would be sought most urgently.

David Tiplady explained that according to counsel for Michael Freeman & Co, litigants were entitled to keep enough recoveries to cover all losses, including the uninsured excess, expenses and legal fees, from stop-loss and legal action. The concept was that the Names should not be left with a profit. David did not dissent from counsel's Opinion. Holman Wade, the stop-loss insurers, did not necessarily agree with this, as they thought recoveries should first of all be paid to them as stop-loss underwriters.

Since the Outhwaite settlement, David said several Names had joined the Association. However, Syndicate 334's contractual claims were now time-barred. Only a court decision would allow settlement. The claim against Matthews Wrightson Pulbrook would be for £60 million, and uncapped as the liability could continue to grow. He confirmed Syndicate 90's claim would be lodged in a different year to that of Syndicate 334, thus not attacking the same pool of reinsurance.

Currently there were 314 Association Members and the more Members and funds, the greater the chance of ultimate success. Late joiners to the Association had a dilution effect, giving rise to suggestions for an increased subscription. There was also a potential class action for eighty late joiners to Syndicate 334, but it was not advisable to start a separate action. Clive produced the *fourth* file of correspondence from Names and made it available for inspection.

Further to recent correspondence Clive said that Cox & Bell in a change of heart recommended their Names to join the Association. Adam Raphael pointed out the dangers of this kind of exchange of correspondence and the Chairman agreed that the risk he had run was too great and no more communications would be sent to Cox & Bell.

The Association's financial year end would be 31 January. Funds could be deposited for a month at an interest rate of 10.125% per annum and slightly less for six months. The retail price index was at 4.3%, and the Bank of England base rate stood at 10.38% with a forecast for the base rate to fall.

Alasdair Ferguson wrote about Clive's poor undisclosed financial situation on 27 February. While Clive would not agree to receive a payment, he might consider accepting a success fee. This was unquantified. On another matter, the Association's doughty legal expert Dr David Tiplady was getting married shortly and the question arose about a suitable wedding present.

John Darby of Leicestershire wrote on 27 February to Clive about his daughter Louise's involvement with Lloyd's, complaining of false promises, serious incompetence, excessive risk-taking, sharp practice and a general lack of consideration for legal restrictions, resulting in a substantial unnecessary loss or, more positively, an extraordinary lack of profit.

Darby wrote that Louise joined Lloyd's through Brian Bell, who promised to put her on the *safest* syndicates and arrange stop-loss. Brian Bell *failed* to arrange a stop-loss policy for three years. When the Syndicate 90 loss arose, he agreed to pay the cash calls from his own pocket as his E&O policy started at much too high a point. In fact, he set up a bank account in her name and *guaranteed* the loan balance plus interest to pay her calls. He persuaded her to *double* her underwriting. He told her that as she was embarking on marriage, she could get married *debt-free* and her problems would be over. Brian Bell died. The agency moved to Cox & Bell and they continued to pay the interest charges on the calls. However, Louise's affairs got progressively worse and she had to cease underwriting. Cox & Bell *withdrew the arrangement*, causing her to pay off the bank. Louise became *time-barred* from suing the restructured business, now named Osborne Bell. John Darby wondered if Cox & Bell had realised this.

Considering the shocking accounts of Louise and Bridget Milling-Smith as clients, it seemed likely they were not the only Names of Cox & Bell to suffer incompetence or sharp practice. There had been no requirement for a detailed 'know your client' review assessing the level of risk the client should take.

The Treasurer wrote to the Editor of *Accountancy* congratulating Alan Purkiss on an informed and balanced article about Lloyd's in the March 1992 issue. Purkiss had commented on the failure of the Syndicate 334 reinsurance policy and queried the prospective low return to Names, quoted at 5%, as inadequate to attract new Names, particularly with the risk of unlimited liability.

A letter was received from the court receivership of the Estate of the late Ian Robert Maxwell seeking information about Maxwell's involvement in the Association and the nature of the claims. A copy of the judgement of 16 December 1991 was enclosed. On 3 March 1992, it was reported that Ian Robert Maxwell MC (born 10 June 1923, died 5 November 1991) was a British media proprietor, former elected Member of Parliament, suspected spy and fraudster. Originally from Czechoslovakia, Maxwell rose from poverty to create an extensive publishing empire, building up Pergamon Press to a major publishing house. After six years as a Labour MP during the 1960s, Maxwell again put all his energy into business, successively buying the British Printing Corporation, Mirror Group Newspapers and Macmillan Publishers, among other publishing companies. In 1991, his body was discovered floating in the Atlantic Ocean, having apparently fallen overboard from his yacht the *Lady Ghislaine*. He was buried in Jerusalem. After his death, huge discrepancies in his companies' finances were revealed, including his fraudulent misappropriation of the Mirror Group pension fund. Maxwell had stolen hundreds of millions of pounds from his own companies' pension funds. The Association could give no assistance regarding Maxwell's involvement with Lloyd's other than those he was entitled to as a Member of Syndicate 334 in 1985.

The previous September three Names won a judgement in a US court against Lloyd's but it was overturned on 2 March 1992 in a Chicago District court. The Names alleged that agreements signed with Lloyd's and the Agents who handle their affairs should not be enforced because of Names' rights to protection by the US securities laws that take precedence. Lloyd's contended that any dispute should be heard in an English court. In the *Financial Times* of 3 March, Richard Lapper summarised fourteen legal actions including Syndicate 334 settled or underway or proposed to recover losses. The previous autumn a federal judge in Denver found that US courts had no jurisdiction over a similar plaintiff's claims. An appeal had been launched. The US courts had still to hear a third case brought against Lloyd's.

In the same issue of the *Financial Times* there was a report that Michael Freeman, solicitor, was coordinating the action of 600 Names relating to cash deposits. Lloyd's Chairman, David Coleridge, had warned Names that the actions would fail and add legal costs to the bills they already faced. Another firm of solicitors, Norton Rose, rated in the top three for commercial litigation, was coordinating 150 Names. They had joined the litigation against Lloyd's launched the previous November by New York lawyers Proskauer Rose under a 'no win, no pay' contingent fee system.

A UK High Court judge heard a motion by Lloyd's to have litigation between it, Members' Agents and Names transferred to the Commercial Court. Several hundred Names were seeking an injunction to prevent Lloyd's drawing down their deposits to meet cash calls. Agents had agreed to freeze the deposits temporarily pending a full court hearing later in the month.

Sir Jeremy Morse wrote to Keith's client Coralie Bell. He said he was the Chairman of the Lloyd's Task Force Working Party and sought views in writing to be sent to Mr A. P. Barber, the Secretary of the Working Party. Coralie said that if Keith sent her a typewritten letter, she would submit it as from her. Bell's letter to Morse was about governance in the Lloyd's Market and she enclosed a copy of Keith's comments to David Rowland.

Underwriter Robert Hiscox's memorandum of 12 March announced to all Names and supporting Agents of Syndicate 33 that he had reached a settlement agreement with the Outhwaite Syndicate. The Outhwaite Syndicate would be liable to all future claims without limit for the years in dispute. They were pleased to stop paying legal fees. Going to court or arbitration was exactly like going to the races. Everyone knew that a horse could run faster than another, but that didn't mean that it would necessarily win. However good the case at law, one was at the mercy of the frailty of lawyers which was a desire to be intellectual or legalistic, with total disregard to common sense or the fundamental business issues concerned. Keith Lester congratulated Hiscox, as an admirer of his rumbustious, innovative and common-sense approach to the management of his syndicates. On the same day Keith sent congratulatory letters to Ian Taylor MP and Sir Peter Hordern MP on being re-elected to the House of Commons, and enclosed a letter he had sent to James Sinclair of Willis Faber & Dumas (Agencies) about Lloyd's.

Clive wrote to thank Keith for a very pleasant lunch last Thursday, 12 March, saying it was most convivial, informative and much appreciated. Clive's dire predicament with Lloyd's had been discussed and he said he was proposing to underwrite with a capacity of £1 million. His extreme financial difficulties were something that he had never foreseen. It seemed to Keith that it was not the time to increase risk by increasing underwriting capacity, but Clive was a risk-taker!

One dissatisfied Name complained there were consistently well-performing syndicates to which only Working Names could have access. Lloyd's released syndicates' performance tables to demonstrate that insiders were not benefiting unfairly at the expense of External Names. These were revealed in the *Financial Times* of 18 March. Over the three years to 1988 there was no significant difference in the proportion of Working to External Names on the top twenty and bottom twenty syndicates. The percentage of capital provided by Working Names was in line with their share of the total Market capital and the Market had not been fraudulently distorted.

Clive received a letter from Richard Micklethwaite of Wellington Syndicates Action Group, requesting that it was circulated to the Associations' Members. David Tiplady commented on 6 April, saying:

> The letter is misleading as it suggests that all its questions contained a legal justification for refusing to pay cash calls. I would not like it to be circulated without a substantial caveat attached. I prefer that Members received the direct guidance of their own Committee rather than advice from sources that was often badly expressed and poorly thought-through.

Serious irregularities were reported in the press regarding the administration of one of the Gooda Walker syndicates. Lloyd's was forced to disclose the findings, following legal action started on behalf of some 800 Lloyd's Names by solicitor Michael Freeman. The revelations would cause serious repercussions across the whole of the London excess of loss reinsurance market.

Thirteenth Steering Committee Meeting, 13 April 1992

Eight Committee Members heard that the Association had 331 Members.

James Sinclair of Willis Faber & (Dumas) Agencies had confirmed that the excess of loss underwriters had reserved at least £40 million. The perception in the Market was that the Association had a very strong case. Mr Justice Saville had recently amended the rules relating to legal process so that Discovery had to precede the request for a court hearing date. David Tiplady said this might delay the Association's case. The Committee agreed that the Association should proceed as far as possible, with a view to a court hearing before the end of the year. David commented that the E&O insurers had taken the view that they would probably 'lose the Syndicate 334 case' and this phrase should feature in the next newsletter.

Alasdair Ferguson had seen Martin Gray, the Syndicate 334 underwriter, who expressed serious concern about the potential collapse of Lloyd's, although he had seen some positive signs regarding pollution claims. Underwriters had won the Diamond Shamrock chemical pollution case in the New Jersey Court of Appeal, and the Rocky Mountain Arsenal Case relating to a chemical manufacturing site was due to be heard in the US Supreme Court within a month.

David confirmed that Members who had not paid the Association's subscriptions could be taken off the writ. It was resolved not to do this but to send out a letter by recorded delivery pointing out the Rules of the Association and requesting payment. There was also continuing uncertainty about the order in which recoveries should be paid, as it depended on the strict wording of each stop-loss policy. Some older policies did not state that the stop-loss insurer should be paid out first. Consequently, payment could initially be made to the insured.

David reported that the defence to the writ had been received requiring further and better particulars and mentioning time restraints on Discovery. Mr Justice Saville was now a dedicated judge on Lloyd's matters and the Association had a priority on his time. He said there were 820 Names on Syndicate 418 and they were wondering if they had cause of action against Stephen Merrett. Clive said there was a Committee of Committees chaired by Peter Nutting that might well become a negotiating body without legal advisers and very few expenses.

A copy of Feltrim Names' Association Chairman's Report stated that the number of Members assenting to a protective writ was 1,050.

The time taken to create a functioning Committee, collect subscriptions from Members and formally launch the Association may have appeared to be very long. However, this was nothing compared with the delays and frustrations in bringing the case to court. The next chapter deals with judiciary issues and Names forced into Hardship.

Summary of Key Issues

1. Loss mitigation; stop-loss, taxation and Hardship were considered.
2. Indications were given of the extent of Syndicate 334 losses and publicity.
3. There were concerns about Lloyd's solvency, viability and Lloyd's Chairman Coleridge's views.
4. Information given about relations with Ministers and Members of Parliament.
5. Lloyd's establishment was challenged and the Members' ombudsman contacted.
6. How much could the Association recover?
7. Numerous stories were received from distressed Names.
8. Cox & Bell clients made complaints.

CHAPTER 5

Getting in Front of a Judge

Once more unto the breach, dear friends, once more
Or close up the wall with our English dead.

Henry V, Act 3 Scene 1

To inform Names and other interested parties, one-day courses were organised, for example, by Westminster Management Consultants Ltd. Courses were wide-ranging including the immediate outlook for Lloyd's, the open-year problem, reinsurance arrangements, a litigation update, tax considerations and benefits for Names following the Rowland report. A view from Westminster was provided by Ian Taylor MBE MP, a Member of the Conservative Backbench Finance Committee.

Keith Lester wrote to James Sinclair of Willis Faber & Dumas (Agencies) on 16 April about economic pressures, quoting Robert Hiscox's strong desire to cease paying legal fees. It was observed that for litigious organisations growth was stunted and they may disintegrate. It was difficult in the present circumstances to justify recommending Lloyd's Membership to prospective Names. Economic pressure could have sufficient impact on the group to induce reconsideration of the wisdom of litigation. Merrett Holdings was affecting economic pressure adversely on individuals and other enterprises. The Council of Lloyd's was powerless to act. Keith asked if his company had considered withdrawing all support from Merrett Group syndicates. Thanking James Sinclair for the help and advice Keith looked forward to a constructively useful reply which would render obsolete Hiscox's perceptive and succinct observations about litigation. James responded, agreeing that it was sad that so many Names felt obliged to go to the High Court to put the discipline and control back into the Market. This was what happened with Outhwaite. The E&O underwriters appeared to be blind and confident right up to the time of their stunning defeat in court. It brought Lloyd's into line with all other professional organisations, as underwriters could be negligent. Regarding the withdrawal from Merrett syndicates, he expected Syndicate 418 to perform ahead of the Market in the years 1986 to 1993. If this was the case, why withdraw support from well-performing syndicates? A mass resignation of Members would force syndicates across the board to stay open, which would trap Names in perpetuity. This was not an exciting prospect.

David Coleridge responded to Guy Wilson's letter of 14 April, to say that he was sorry Guy was disillusioned with Lloyd's. He asserted that Lloyd's had no legal liability for losses which might be regarded as 'hard luck'. Current losses were truly exceptional, were spread across the Market and should be mitigated in some way by the Society as a whole. He had received hundreds and hundreds of letters and together with comments made to the Task Force, any proposed solution must have a fair level of support. There would also be a fair number of opponents. All he could say was that he had ideas on his desk for how a market-wide solution could be arranged and was considering every possibility. He assured Guy that Lloyd's was not going bust in any way, shape or form.

A. P. Barber replied to Keith Lester's letter of 21 April on behalf of Sir Jeremy Morse's Working Party. The Working Party had received written responses from approximately 1,000 Names. He had not been able to respond as promptly as he would have wished and expressed that no discourtesy was intended. He had communicated Keith's views to the Working Party.

Sir Peter Hordern did not think the Government could do much to help. It was up to the Council of Lloyd's with the backing of the Membership to reach a solution. Replying to subsequent correspondence including a copy of James Sinclair's recent letter, he indicated it was a tangled web too complex for him to unravel. He was a Name at Lloyd's in the past but not now *au fait* with all the various movements and litigation. However, it seemed that the Association had a good man in Sinclair on its side.

On 4 May 1992 Keith wrote to Clive recommending that Syndicate 334 Names cease dealing with the Merrett Group. Merrett, as the Association's Agent, was abusing the system and mismanaging the business. Could the Association find alternative Agents to replace the Merrett Group? With the support of the Committee would Clive be prepared to stand for election to Lloyd's Council?

In response to a 'direction' from the Chairman of Lloyd's, Willis Faber & Dumas (Agencies) sent a form to Keith on 21 May asking his consent for stop-loss recoveries to be paid to them. They would hold any stop-loss recoveries, for the time being, as Trustees of the Premiums Trust Deed. No funds would be released until any outstanding cash calls and losses were funded and the Name's annual solvency test satisfied. This was an attempt by Lloyd's to stop a leakage of funds from the Society.

On 1 June 1992 David Tiplady wrote to Association Members stating that pleadings were about to close and explaining the obligation in litigation to give Discovery of documents. The rules of the Supreme Court required the claimants to inform defendants of the relevant documents that they had in their possession or custody or had power over. David requested that any documents not already submitted should to be sent to him, including correspondence, personal memoranda, records of meetings and copies of information received from Members' Agents and the Syndicate 334 Managing Agent.

Fourteenth Steering Committee Meeting, 2 June 1992:
Standard & Poor's Downgrade

Clive attended the Super Group where the Members are the Chairmen of most Action Groups. He informed the Committee:

> About 10,000 Names are already insolvent and probably a further 8,000 will follow. Pollution and asbestosis claims were gathering pace rather than diminishing. The Americans were doing their best

to resuscitate old policies using insurance archaeologists to discover any possible claims. The Standard and Poor's Rating Agency has downgraded Lloyd's recommending careful scrutiny of syndicates' ability to pay claims. The seriousness of this downgrade precipitated consultations with the Bank of England as Lloyd's may need a cash boost of £2.5 billion this year. Syndicate 334 losses to date had increased to £47.5 million.

David Tiplady emphasised that it was crucial to get to court as soon as possible. Many Names were in very serious financial difficulty, and it was obvious the situation was still deteriorating with no end in sight.

Clive signified his willingness to stand for election to Lloyd's Council in November. There was no elected Council Member representing Names who had been forced to cease underwriting. This would be an issue in his campaign.

Michael Turner, the active underwriter for Syndicate 334, had applied to join the Association. This would be a politically sensitive application requiring careful consideration and discussion with Clive.

The Steering Committee approved the audited annual financial statements for the period 14 February 1991 to 31 January 1992 showing net assets of £264,652. Subscriptions and income receivable from 1 February to 31 May amounted to £637,140 and £507,656 cash remained after expenses. Some cash could be placed on a six-month deposit. D J Freeman's costs were currently running below budget but expenses were expected to increase in the Discovery phase.

The *Independent* reported the Chairman of Lloyd's on 3 June 1992 had said that Names must be given help. It was patently clear to him and the Council that some amelioration of past years' losses was essential to secure future capacity at a time of sharply improving Market conditions. A fall of up to 20% of the 28,000 Members would reduce Membership to its lowest number since 1980. Lloyd's overall capacity was dropping from £10 billion to £9 billion. The Chairman could not guarantee the success of any scheme through a referendum. Fears were expressed that underwriting Names who were suing Lloyd's in the courts may cause grave damage to Lloyd's reputation and its unique chain of security.

On the same day James Sinclair invited Syndicate 334 Names to the 1992 Names meeting with a reception afterwards in the Captain's Dining Room. This would be an opportunity to meet underwriters, directors and staff.

Mr R. W. Snell of Ascot was retired, and said he had not suffered to the same degree as many other Members. Apparently, he had no idea that he could underwrite on syndicates outside the Pulbrook stable and considered this was a gross failure by his Agent. Much of his thought was occupied with Lloyd's and he feared for his and his family's future, and that of Lloyd's. He implored Sinclair to do everything possible to achieve a degree of justice for all. Enclosed with the letter was a press picture of Stephen Merrett. The article was headlined, 'Underwriter Earns More than £1m'. Income details reported were: £247,536 as Chairman of Merrett Holdings, £225,000 salary and profit commission, £675,000 dividends on shares in Merrett Holdings. However, Syndicate 418 was left open for 1985 because of heavy asbestosis and pollution claims, and his personal underwriting losses amounted to more than £132,000. He had increased his line on Syndicate 418 from £393,000 to £1,000,000. Clive commented that the press cutting would provide an idea of the strength of the financial interests against which the Association was trying to operate.

In his reply to Mr Snell, Clive said in his view Lloyd's ran as a small central clique where the take-home pay defied description and which seemed to have no moral qualms about the damage they inflicted on their Names. He quoted one Managing Agent: 'If the good Lord hadn't made Names to be shorn, he wouldn't have made them sheep.' Clive added a note of personal history, saying that he had served in the Royal Air Force for twenty years after the Second World War in Cyprus, Borneo, Malaya, Egypt et cetera, in fact helping to supervise the demise of the Empire. He was therefore ill-equipped to discern the depth and extent of any chicanery at Lloyd's. He said:

We have been remarkably fortunate in the way in which we have retreated from our Empire and as far as many of us are concerned the only remaining torch of illusory decadence is carried by Lloyd's. I am only now beginning to understand the moral turpitude of those who have posed in the past as our 'Agents at Lloyd's'. The ineffectiveness of our Parliament was beyond farcical in granting self-regulation to Lloyd's. Lloyd's had become the insurance hooligans of Europe, if not the world.

On 15 June Clive received a letter of appreciation and thanks to the Members of the Committee from Michael W. Goold, and his apologies for being unable to attend the AGM. Goold hoped an appropriate resolution would be moved during the meeting as he would like to be associated with the enthusiastic acclamation with which such a proposal would be greeted. Clive circulated the letter to the Committee and informed Mr Goold of his kindness in writing in such terms. Clive suggested that they might care to reflect thankfully on the simplicity and strength of their case and the cohesion of the Committee.

Coopers & Lybrand, the accounting firm, issued an article around 8 June 1992, titled, 'All is Not Losses at Lloyd's'. It commented upon the unprecedented level of cash calls on the 1989 and 1990 accounts. Cash calls had needed settlement far more quickly than in the past as there was a move towards earlier claims settlements, aiming to improve services from Lloyd's. There were instances of reinsurance syndicates experiencing significant delays in making reinsurance recoveries or situations where they had exhausted their reinsurance and had to resort to borrowing. The number of syndicates involved and consequently the substantial sums of money at stake had caused concern throughout the banking community. It was probable that certain banks had been close to their lending ceiling in terms of their overall exposure. Underwriting Agents were giving notice that they would not support syndicates likely to be unprofitable. Consequently, there would be fewer syndicates in 1992 with a greater probability of profits for those remaining. The 1991 account should return to profit. Those Names able to continue underwriting may reap the profits which the Market indicated were available. Lloyd's had poor years following the 1906 San Francisco earthquake and Hurricane Betsy in 1965. In subsequent years Lloyd's became extremely profitable. A reduction in capacity should push rates up and the future of Lloyd's may be looking brighter.

At a General Meeting of Lloyd's Names on 24 June 1992, Chairman David Coleridge made a statement about 'A leaner and fitter Lloyd's'. The results for the 1989 year of account were delayed by a small number of syndicates and their new Managing Agents. Coleridge announced that the losses amounted to £2.063 billion, an appalling result. Some £398 million was accounted for by deterioration in old years. Some comfort was drawn from the change in trend resulting in a reduction of the provisions. This in part reflected the success that insurers had had in recent pollution cases in the US. An absolute priority was to demonstrate that Lloyd's continued to offer the very best security to all those who bought Lloyd's policies. He pointed out that heavy losses in the US had caused over 200 insurance companies to become insolvent. The very extensive publicity given by a minority of Names unwilling to fund losses damaged the reputation of all Names. It was especially important that Lloyd's gave an unqualified guarantee that all valid claims would be met. Realising the potential size of the year's losses, Council decided to boost the Central Fund by a special levy. Furthermore, from next year CentreWrite would provide a scheme to cover each Name's losses in excess of 80% of their premium income.

First Annual General Meeting of Syndicate 334 (1985) Names Association, 3 July 1992

The First Annual General Meeting of the Association was on 3 July 1992 at D J Freeman's offices and some forty Association Members attended. After the Chairman's report, David Tiplady explained that the Discovery phase required a list of all the documents that parties might want to rely upon. The lists would be exchanged and he would call for specific documents to be disclosed so they could be examined, and the defend-

ants would do the same. On completion of Discovery, he would go to
court for a trial date and the earliest date would be at the beginning of
1993. It was the intention to accelerate this case and the dedicated judge,
Mr Justice Saville, would have a long list of cases, and the sooner the
Association appeared in front of him, the better. David Tiplady thought
the Syndicate 334 case was the first in the queue. In litigation cases it
was general practice that there were discussions about a settlement whilst
the formal stages were being conducted. The number of Members of the
Association was 356 and the total Names on Syndicate 334 was 562. The
increase in Membership of the Association might have been partly due
to the Outhwaite settlement and the inability of Names who had not
joined the Outhwaite Association to recover any funds when the settlement was reached. The total subscription to the Association would be in
the region of £1.1 million and should be ample to pay the Association's
costs and the defendant's costs should the case fail. Overdue subscriptions
had reduced to £19,083. Membership of the Association was still open
but new Members would be charged an amount to bring them into line
with those who had already paid.

During questions David explained:

> I think Syndicate 334 1979 year should have been left open. If
> the main case failed then those who joined after 1979 could have
> a second shot at the target. The arbitration was finished and could
> not be reopened with the result that Syndicate 418 Names had
> escaped liability. Syndicate 418 almost certainly formed part of
> the Errors and Omissions insurance and would subscribe to any
> Syndicate 334 settlement. I believe there is sufficient cover in the
> Errors and Omissions policies to fully reimburse Members but
> the detailed composition of insurers or the amount of cover is not
> known. Stop-loss insurers argue that in any settlement they should
> be reimbursed first. However, I *think* the reverse is correct, so that
> Names should be paid first, which was a case recently upheld by
> Mr Justice Saville.

In answer to a question, Clive informed a Hardship Case member, 'Names in Hardship are allowed to retain a modest dwelling and an income of £14,000 per annum. Any settlement pay out will be used to reduce the amount due to Lloyd's.'

The financial statements to 31 January 1992 were approved, and nine Steering Committee Members were re-elected.

Sir David Walker's July 1992 report, commissioned by the Government and the Bank of England, had reported on the London Market excess of loss (LMX) spiral in the Lloyd's Insurance Market. The spiral was named because the high risks were reinsured in the Market with appropriate underwriters who then reinsured the reinsurance in the Market, and the procedure when repeated turned into a 'spiral' as it was the same syndicates involved in the transactions.

Sir David stated that there was laxity in working standards at Lloyd's as well as a problem with professionalism, care and diligence. Clive wrote a commentary titled 'Lloyd's Dodgiest Hour' and had a list of 'Nine Questions' originating from Walker's report, to illustrate why 6,000 burnt Names felt so strongly over apparent lack of probity and morality in the way the Market had been run and regulated. He mentioned that through his participation in dustbin syndicates, his Lloyd's losses exceeded his assets by £1.7 million, and he was only a medium player. John Rew, Chairman of Chatset, had calculated that the shortfall from those who couldn't or wouldn't pay approached £1 billion. Walker showed that for the years 1983 to 1990, Lloyd's Committee Members' results were 761% greater than the average profit of all External Names. Profits of Directors of Managing and Members' Agencies were 464% greater than External Names. It was pointed out that Council had abandoned the bylaw requiring Agents to carry E&O cover. However, the Association's claim was notified when the E&O policies were in force. Clive said that the defendants had reserved £40 million against the success of the Association's case, but did not disclose the source of his knowledge.

Clive complained about the 'Big Five'. He said:

Five key very influential Names reinsured their own syndicates with other syndicates which could never pay. The only way the Big Five could make their questionable reinsurance programmes respond was by forcing a levy on the hapless Names to boost the Central Fund. The fund in turn then paid to cover the enormous loss left uncovered by the ruined Names, to settle claims on the Five's ill-judged reinsurances. I doubt whether any Names will enjoy paying the Central Fund levy to cover up the mistakes of Mr Stephen Merrett, of Syndicate 481 and the Merrett Group, who reportedly took home £1 million in pay and dividends. Nor would they relish stumping up knowing that David Coleridge recently built a house in St Moritz according to a Swiss informant costing more than £6 million. Many thousands of Names saw their gallant Chairman on television being positively parsimonious with the truth over his Membership of a profitable baby syndicate which contained only six Names. Five of these had 'left Lloyd's' and the sixth was Chairman Coleridge. For such activity in a public company, the Board would have demanded his resignation. Lloyd's only reaction was a knowing giggle! The valedictory message of the Queen's solicitor to the Association of Lloyd's Members was, 'many Names now face horrendous difficulties as a result of a decade of commercial indiscipline at Lloyd's'. Indiscipline quaintly exemplified by a report of a recent past Chairman of Lloyd's, Sir Peter Green, shamefacedly handing back £13 million, exclaiming, 'I'm told I shouldn't have taken this money from my Names.' The best synopsis of Sir David Walker's report was in the *Sunday Times* Business Comment on 5 July 1992. The commentator referred to the professionals at Lloyd's not being fit to regulate a flea circus.

Clive quoted the old market aphorism ascribed to a Lloyd's Managing Agent, saying, 'If the Good Lord hadn't meant the sheep to be shorn, He wouldn't have made them sheep. There were now 6,000 killer sheep waiting to bite the legs off Lloyd's, articulate, desperate and determined.'

Charles Baron wrote to Clive as he was concerned about Members who had not paid the subscription instalments. He said that the Association must not be seen to be throwing away money in terms of a settlement, which belonged to fully paid-up Members or those who had applied to the Hardship Committee. He complained that of the Committee, only he, Guy Wilson and Clive attended the Association's AGM, and thought a record of attendees ought to be made.

The Secretary of Lloyd's Council circulated information about an Extraordinary General Meeting (EGM) on 27 July and postal ballot regarding the proposed resolutions for the reform of Lloyd's. The ALM provided comments on the resolutions but they were not adopted.

Julia Barkworth of LSS sent demands for payment of outstanding subscriptions due to the Association. She also wrote on 7 August to the accounting firm KPMG, Dublin, regarding the subscriptions for Mr T. K. Laidlaw who was proposing to join the Association. He was also a Name on Syndicate 90. A 15% late joiner's fee was mentioned.

Sir Gerard Vaughan MP wrote in the *House Magazine* of Parliament, 'There does appear to have been negligence and fraud. Nobody attending a Lloyd's meeting could fail to notice the air of complacency, the unwillingness to change and the sense that there was no need to be frank over what had happened.' Would people be happy to be called an apparent fraudster in public by a Member of Parliament and a Member of Lloyd's? The commercial need was for leadership by borrowing a quarter of a billion pounds now to enable as many damaged Names as possible to trade out.

Clive wrote to the Governor of the Bank of England, Sir Robin Leigh-Pemberton, on 22 July saying that Lloyd's had imposed a levy on its Names to bring the Central Fund up to £1 billion, to reassure the world of the substance backing a Lloyd's policy. Lloyd's Chairman had recently announced that of the £1 billion, £800 million was earmarked for existing losses. Clive enclosed papers which suggested that Lloyd's was unlikely to survive if it followed its present commercial bent. He noted that in 1968 Lord Cromer tartly observed that if Lloyd's followed its policy of *sauve qui peut*, being a state of panic or disorder, it was bound to end in disaster.

Clive suggested that the disaster was nearly upon the Society and that strong remedial action needed to be taken. An Associate Director of the Bank of England, Mr P. H. Kent, replied on 29 July. The point of the levy, he said, was to double the size of the Central Fund to ensure that obligations to Lloyd's policyholders could be met. Without the levy the Market's solvency would be at greater risk. Lloyd's had said that the level of £800 million would fall during the summer as Names restored the required levels of funds at Lloyd's. He mentioned Sir David Walker's report that found there was no evidence of systematic fraud, but underwriting standards fell below best Market practice. The key question for Names facing serious difficulties was their ability to trade out of current and previous losses. Lloyd's was making progress in implementing the Rowland Task Force proposals which would improve the likelihood of the Market remaining viable and return-ing to profitability in the near future. 'We at The Bank,' he said, 'believed that a satisfactory resolution to the current problems was vital to maintain London's position as a leading international insurance centre.'

Clive replied to Kent quoting Sir David Walker's report that '*the advantage taken by the insider Working Names of the External Names was not immodest*'. The importance of Lloyd's to the City of London was well known and it was vital to maintain London's position as a leading international insurance centre. However, the Bank of England had appeared to be wrong-footed in the past over the Barlow Clowes affair in which gilt-edged Government bonds were traded in order to create tax advantages, and which was wound up in 1988, owing £190 million to victims; the scandal of the BCCI which was an authorised UK bank with head offices in London and Karachi and was involved in massive money laundering; and Robert Maxwell, where the Bank of England was criticised for allowing Maxwell to take over Robert Fraser, a merchant bank. It was understood there was weakness in regulatory authorities and the buck ultimately stopped at the Bank of England. Clive antici-pated that Mr Kent would have been apprised of the utterly damning Feltrim and Gooda Walker reports. On each of the previous occasions it appeared that the Bank entirely ignored the plight of the little investor cheated and defenceless. Clive stated he was the Chairman of a Names Association with Members from all over Canada, the USA, Australia and New Zealand, some of them insurance brokers. Their repugnance at what was happening at Lloyd's resulted in their avowal to reduce business with and dependence on Lloyd's. Clive challenged Kent's statement that the Market would remain viable. The 'can't pay and won't pay' amounted to £1 billion. With shrinking premium income limits there was no way the decreasing numbers of remaining Names could shoulder the burden from the past. Mathematically Lloyd's was about to subside under the weight of a decade of commercial indiscipline. It was estimated that £2 billion was needed as an injection of capital. Clive wondered if Kent felt there was a need for action on both moral and commercial grounds. He suggested that Lloyd's was a significant national asset both in reputation and earning power and wanted to know if the bank was content to watch it founder.

A Lloyd's EGM was held on 27 July and as a ballot had taken place the meeting was expected to last half an hour – but it lasted four hours. The Chairman announced that he would not be standing for re-election and that he was nominating his own successor. This came in for fierce criticism as the 'old boy' network was handing the crown from one old boy to another. Voices were raised in unparalleled criticism of the institution of Lloyd's and its governance. Names stood up repeatedly to catch the Chairman's eye. Once caught, the Name vehemently expressed his dismay and anger at the catastrophe taking place, saying, 'It is a betrayal, an abandonment of managerial duties effecting sophisticated legalised theft resulting in financial indiscipline and an inability to regulate even a "flea circus".' The vehemence and passion surprised even the fiercest critics of Lloyd's. The Chairman was seen to flinch physically, whilst the first three rows, reserved for the dutiful and the obsequious, supported faces that grew longer and longer, becoming more visibly agitated. At one stage the intervention by Sir Peter Miller, a past Chairman, on behalf of the 'old guard' suffered the indignity of being slow-handclapped. It got louder and louder and he was unceremoniously booed off the rostrum with cries of 'Shame' and 'GO!' John Rew, of Chatset, gave a masterly dissertation, with ironic references to the *Titanic*, but demonstrated how near to collapse Lloyd's had been. It was a mathematical certainty that Lloyd's would collapse unless there was an injection of capital. The fundamental cause of the problem resulted from so-called dustbin LMX Syndicates. There were five large organisations headed by five Members or ex-Members of Council including Messrs Coleridge, Merrett and Jackson. Of £700 million sustained by the dustbin LMX Syndicates, £623 million was caused by the Big Five. The Big Five reinsured themselves with the underwriters of the dustbin syndicates. These syndicates owed £800 million which they could not pay. In the end the hapless Names had to pay. The direct result of commercial incompetence of the Big Five was the ruin of 6,000 Names and a levy on the rest of the Society. The Society would have an overhang from those who could not pay. The question was 'When will the next levy be?' For those remaining in the Market it was not a question of future profits but whether they would be bankrupted in the next three or four years. The faces of the great, the good and the insulated in attendance looked agitated, incredulous and distressed. The guilty did not look the least bit guilty.

Clive was working voluntarily very long hours on behalf of the Association and had a weak personal financial situation. Following a discussion with Charles and Alasdair, on 11 August 1992 Jasper Salisbury-Jones enquired about a possible honorarium for Clive. He suggested a figure of £20,000. As there was no provision in the Association's Rules for payment to officers, the proposal needed to be put to a General Meeting. Charles expressed the cautious view, 'Unless the legal action succeeds there might not be money available to pay Clive. We are still admitting new Members and need to collect future subscriptions. We have no firm idea of the ultimate costs. However, there is a strong case for recognising Clive's outstanding efforts.'

Dudley Fishburn MP wrote saying he had written to Rt Hon Michael Heseltine adding a handwritten note saying that he had many Lloyd's Names in his constituency. He suspected that Lloyd's reinsurance was there in name alone and not a reality. If Lloyd's was insolvent the Government must be more aware and more active.

Two Members of the Association wished to resign. Clive informed Messrs Viner and Clark that there was no entitlement to a return of subscriptions. A copy of the relevant Rules of the Association was enclosed.

Unexpectedly, Keith received a kind letter from Michael Goold on 26 August offering support should he decide to stand for election to Council again. He replied that he had just taken over an accountancy practice with Guy Wilson and was now extremely busy and could not justify the time away from work. He mentioned that Clive Francis was planning to stand for election to Lloyd's Council and asked if he would be prepared to nominate Clive. Michael gave a prompt positive response.

On 10 September, Anthony Boswood QC and Stephen Moriarty provided advice to the Feltrim Names Association. They were asked to consider the difficult question of how to handle 'individual' as opposed to 'collective' claims by Names against their Members' Agents arising from their participation in one or more of the stricken LMX syndicates. They concluded that a Names' Individual Action Group should be formed. Names would irrevocably delegate conduct of their individual claims to the Names' Individual Action Group. It was believed that the pooling of resources would achieve massive savings in time and lawyers' fees. The Names' Individual Action Group would be an independent body but work in close harmony with the four existing Names' Associations. With such a structure there would be at least a reasonable chance of agreement on timing and prosecution of various claims both individual and collective. The court would prefer to deal with at least one of the collective claims before tackling thousands of individual claims. This may have become impossible if individual claims proceeded in a random uncoordinated fashion. They urged those involved to do their utmost to reach agreement on the establishment of a Names' Individual Action Group.

Fifteenth Steering Committee Meeting, 22 September 1992

Adam Raphael reported on his and Charles Baron's meeting with Stephen Merrett and Malcolm Cox, the lead E&O underwriter. The underwriter did not want to go to court and an offer of £10 million was suggested in settlement. They thought estimated losses totalling £100 million was too high. A figure of £20 million settlement was then discussed although losses to date were over £40 million. An essential part of any settlement would be capping of losses. Merrett maintained there were insufficient funds and when he was asked the amount of his E&O cover, he declined to comment. Charles suggested Merrett purchase a stop-loss policy on behalf of the Names to cap the loss, otherwise Syndicate 334 1985 year might remain open for many years. It might be that £20 million was the extent of the E&O policy and if so, there were not any more funds.

A subscription of 2% of line would be due in February 1993. Some defaulters had not paid the 2% of line due in August 1992. The Committee decided to close applications from prospective joiners from the date of the meeting.

David Tiplady confirmed, 'The Discovery process is virtually at an end. An exchange of documents will take place shortly with a view to a court hearing around Easter 1993. I have informed underwriters that the Association was only suing for uninsured losses. I think that this might provoke stop-loss underwriters to join the Association's action. My choice of counsel is Mr Manse QC with Jonathan Gaisman as his junior.'

Harry Purchase informed the Committee that asbestosis problems were still deteriorating with as many as 15 million Americans being affected. The State Compensation funds had already run out of money. Many American insurers had gone into liquidation. It only left the Federal Government and Lloyd's to pay claims. Some European insurers had no confidence in Lloyd's. They had ceased to place their business with Lloyd's.

Clive commented on Lloyd's AGM and EGM and said that Lloyd's Chairman David Coleridge was to be admired for his performance but not for the contents of his utterances. Clive was nominated to stand for Council.

In a written response, David explained to Clive that it was not possible to review the E&O cover of the various defendants as they would not make the information available. For them to do so might invalidate the cover. Clive asked, firstly, if adequate notice was given on behalf of each individual plaintiff so that the E&O cover of the respective Members' Agents was triggered. David believed that some if not all E&O policies had been triggered by a single general notification. Secondly, as far as could be ascertained, whether the E&O cover was sufficient. If a particular agency had inadequate cover, it may well be that other E&O insurers would make good the deficit. This was what happened in the Outhwaite case. It was clearly in the interests of E&O underwriters to obfuscate matters as much as possible. Insurance cover would be consumed on a first come, first served basis. Consequently, he believed it was essential that the Association's case was progressed with all possible speed.

In reply to Alasdair Ferguson's query, David said that their Lordships would confirm the Court of Appeal's decision about the terms of settlement for stop-loss policies. Even in the worst case any recovery that fed back to stop-loss underwriters would serve to increase the level of protection for future losses. The primary objective was to cap future losses. He assumed that any quotation that could be obtained would be on an individual Name's basis, either through CentreWrite or elsewhere. It would be useful to have any such quotations regarding an out-of-court settlement. Lloyd's CentreWrite quotations would not be available for some considerable time.

On 14 November 1992 Alasdair Ferguson produced a thoughtful paper on the subject of 'Litigation or Negotiation?' The table below gave a statistical background.

	Syndicate 334	Names Association
Total number of Names	562	366
Total Line £m	17.6	11.6
Loss to date £m	37.5	24.7
Average line per Name £	31,700	
Average loss per Name £	67,500	
Loss as a % of line	212.8	

The table showed the number of Names on Syndicate 334 and 65% were Members of the Association. The total line was the maximum capacity of the Syndicate and 66% of capacity was held by Members. Losses to date were estimates. Based on the estimates the loss per line was calculated at over 212.8%, i.e., for every £10,000 of capital provided by Names the loss was £21,280, hence the average loss per Name on the Syndicate was £67,500 to date. The Syndicate's total loss had been speculated to rise to £50 million when calls per Name could rise to almost £90,000. As Members had losses arising on other syndicates, such as Syndicate 90, the crucial importance of taking urgent legal action to address the excessive unreasonable losses was clear.

The paper discussed the future of both the Syndicate and of Lloyd's querying whether a negotiated or court settlement would be preferable, and their associated risks. Discussion about fund distribution in the case of an award in cash, or capping of potential liabilities, and consequences of failure were considered. There was also mention of the composition of the negotiating team. One thing that could really scupper the Association's case was for some solo effort by a Name to start legal proceedings, or overlap the Association's case. Such an event might cause the whole matter to be considered in a consolidated action which might take years and prove too unwieldy to mount. The paper was circulated by Clive on 16 November to the Committee together with a proposal for a Names' Individual Action Group (see 10 September 1992).

Clive Boxer, in the November issue of *Corporate Cover* titled 'Bottoms Up, Top Down', considered the order in which parties to a claim should be paid from legal action recoveries. The Court of Appeal held that the deductible was the first to pay out and the last to recoup. One of the examples illustrated the point, also shown in the table below, of an insured arranged stop-loss cover of £100,000 in excess of £25,000. The insured suffered a loss of £160,000. Consequently, the first £25,000 – the excess – would be borne by the insured. The next £100,000 would be charged to the stop-loss underwriter, and the last £35,000, unrecovered by the insured (£160,000 less £25,000 less £100,000, leaving £35,000).

The Name would not recover £60,000 (£25,000 plus £35,000). Some stop-loss underwriters set out this method of distribution of a claim in the policy.

Details	Name	Underwriter	Total
Initial excess £	25,000	0	25,000
Insurance claim £		100,000	100,000
Remainder £	35,000	0	35,000
Total £	60,000	100,000	160,000
	Unrecovered by Name	Paid to insured	Total loss incurred

The case was being appealed to the House of Lords with judgement early next year. It was considered important for wider insurance cover, such as professional indemnity policies.

Sixteenth Steering Committee Meeting, 2 December 1992: Inklings of Hope

The Steering Committee held at D J Freeman's offices was attended by Christopher Stockwell, the Chairman of the 'Super Group of Names' Action Groups' (LNAWP), who spoke about current events. He said that the cover-up of asbestosis in the 1970s might result in a claim against Lloyd's. There might be a deal to close all the open years next year, provided it could be sold to all Lloyd's Names. Some Names were facing unrealistic losses and some stop-loss underwriters were thinking it was better to settle claims rather than dragging the issues through the courts for many years. He concurred that litigation should be a matter of last resort and claims should be settled as quickly as possible.

It came to Clive's attention that the Governor of the Bank of England, Robin Leigh-Pemberton, and Lord Hanson the industrialist both thought they had been successfully extricated from Lloyd's. They were fortunate. It might not be the case for Names unable to resign as they owed money to Lloyd's. This created implications for their heirs, as the debts remained with their Estates which could not be finalised and wound up until the debts were settled.

Current reserving for pollution was about £4 billion which was at the lower end of a range which rose to £120 billion. Only lawyers' fees had been paid on pollution cases so far. The Bank of England had given a 'nod and a wink' to suggest that they would be prepared to assist in funding a deal over several years. Action Groups would cease legal actions if the E&O insurers could agree terms. A deal should cap all future losses which was likely to be in place by February or March 1993. It was rumoured that some £600 million had been double counted in reserves, in effect reducing the net liabilities by such an amount.

Lloyd's may well lose the 'Order 14 Summary Judgement' case, in that a court may say that there was a defence to be heard. If a defendant could satisfy a judge that there was a case to be heard and no Order 14 Summary Judgement, there could be delays of two, three or four years waiting for the court to hear the case. This would hasten the end of Lloyd's. Lloyd's auditors had a problem determining the solvency required by the DTI in 1992 and providing the certificate of solvency. They may well have a bigger problem in 1993.

David Tiplady observed that an individual could bring an action which, if it was defeated, would create a precedent and act against the Association's interests.

The Times had reported on 24 November that there was a backlog in the Commercial Court. Mr Justice Saville, who was responsible for the Commercial Court list, was unable to hear a case for longer than four weeks until twelve months' time. The Association's case would be ready for the Commercial Court by April. Using a deputy judge, David could immediately apply for a court date.

Membership of the Association had closed, but not pleadings. David said he required an Opinion from an accountant. He would also like to appoint Jonathan Manse QC as the Association's counsel. The Committee emphatically agreed that there should be no further dealings with Merrett until the Association received an approach from him. Clive said, 'Under no circumstances is any Member of the Committee empowered to approach Mr Merrett.'

The Treasurer had prepared a draft letter to be sent to defaulting Names stating that they would be removed from the writ if they failed to pay by 31 December 1992. The executors of the late Mr E. K. Robarts responded saying that they had decided to continue with the action and were waiting for grant of probate to release funds for the Association's subscription.

The LNAWP had met Peter Middleton, Lloyd's CEO, and Clive gave some background information about him. Middleton was a Yorkshire man who had entered a monastery, training to become a monk. However, he left to read philosophy at the Sorbonne but gave that up after a year to attend Hull University, taking a course in economics and social science. He joined the Foreign Office as a diplomat with overseas postings. He moved to Midland Bank where he was appointed to Thomas Cook and turned round the troubled business that was eventually sold very profitably. This led to his appointment at Lloyd's where he considered that most underwriters were 'dumbos'. He gave the Super Group two quotations, saying, 'Firstly, without sorting out the problems, Lloyd's had no future and secondly, without protecting Lloyd's Names as shareholders, Lloyd's had no future.' There was considerable astonishment at these utterances. They indicated a complete change of direction and gave considerable grounds for hope of an overall settlement. In January 1993 Middleton wanted to close all open years and was proposing to provide a scheme by the end of the month. Doubts arose because of resistance from reinsurance underwriters to settle claims that had not arisen from legal decisions. Collecting £3 billion and distributing the sum in a way acceptable to Names exposed complexities. There was an urgent need for a solution.

Newsletter, January 1993

Clive stated in the newsletter that it was the greatest personal disappointment that there was no firm court date. The Association's case was ready and well-funded. Judges were in short supply in the Commercial Court.

This court was set up to resolve mercantile disputes expeditiously in the principles and practice of English law, by judges of exceptional reputation and expertise. There was a current lack of Commercial Court judges as two had recently been promoted to the Court of Appeal and had not been replaced. Only one judge remained, Mr Justice Saville, who was also responsible for the commercial list. No case that might last for a substantial period could expect to be listed until further judges became available. Would this world-renowned tribunal maintain its reputation for providing the best dispute resolution for international trade and commerce? Losing this reputation and the very substantial benefits the service brought to the country meant a loss in terms of money and international prestige. The Committee had written to the Lord Chancellor expressing their concerns in cogent terms.

Asbestosis claims were escalating spectacularly right across the market and were at the bottom of all 'our', the Names', sorrows. In *Keene v INA* in 1985 the 'trigger' approach was proposed. Under this theory insurance coverage was triggered by the initial exposure, continuing damage from asbestos already inhaled and by manifestations of asbestosis disease. The US Supreme Court allowed the 'triple trigger' approach to stand, whereby a company that had written a policy for a period of one year might be liable to claims for forty years. V. B. Levit of San Francisco, solicitors, spoke of the tremendous potential liability of Lloyd's from selling huge amounts of excess of loss coverage since the 1930s to leading American asbestos insulation manufacturers. There was evidence that the insurance industry, including Lloyd's, concealed information about the excess mortality in asbestos workers. In 1980 the upward spirals of asbestos verdicts continued, for example, $3 million damages compensation was awarded to the widow of an asbestos insulator. In 1981 Johns Manville's corporate counsel informed the auditors, Coopers & Lybrand, that the eventual outcome of the asbestos litigation could not be predicted, and the ultimate liability could not be estimated with any degree of certainty. Accordingly, Coopers & Lybrand qualified the audit reports of Johns Manville for the years 1979 and 1980.

It was recorded that several people saw the asbestos situation arising. In 1973 Ralph Rokeby-Johnson of Sturge Syndicate 210 said to another underwriter, 'I hope Peter Green has got all his asbestosis reinsurance in place. He is going to need every bit that he can get. You mark my words, asbestosis is going to change the wealth of nations and certainly bankrupt Lloyd's.' Fifteen million Americans had been exposed to asbestos. By 1979 Lloyd's was so concerned about the asbestosis situation that the Asbestos Working Party (AWP) was set up. There is documentary evidence that every affected underwriter with asbestosis liability on the books knew that disaster was inevitable. In the late 1970s and early 1980s, Lloyd's recruited thousands and thousands of new Names in the almost certain knowledge they were going to lose their shirts. It was calculated that 142 syndicates ought not to have closed their 1979 accounts because of the huge liabilities to come. The severity of this failure to keep 1979 open was now being felt.

Clive questioned the professional qualifications and intellectual quality of Agents who did not give advice to further their Principals' well-being. He commented that a former Chairman of Lloyd's, Sir Peter Green, was disciplined regarding money that went walkabout in Bermuda and the Cayman Islands, politely termed 'off-balance-sheet rollover funds'. He wondered what happened to the interest and was it and the capital credited to a Name's account? Another senior person spirited away some $40 million. Finally, he said, unless the Syndicate 334 case was won there would be a slow bleed for many years. The Association was well funded and all that was needed was a judge.

Executors of E. K. Robarts decided to continue with the action and were waiting for grant of probate to release funds for the subscription to the Association. John Munford of Twickenham on 26 January wanted to know if the next subscription to the Association was necessary and if the case would ever get to court. He had paid £39,962 above the stop-loss excess for 1985, suffered losses of more than £300,000 on the 1989 account and a similar figure for 1990, of which £47,000 had already been paid. He asked for a copy of the Association's accounts and if there was a case for him to continue with the Syndicate 334 Association. In reply, Clive informed him that he was a Feltrim and Gooda Walker victim himself and fully appreciated the suffering and misery caused by Lloyd's losses. He had received many long and unhappy telephone calls. His house was now let and he was living in digs. Firstly, the time scale of litigation subscriptions was fixed by the Rules of the Association. Those who have already paid would not be happy to see any blurring of the edges. Secondly, there was a continuing expenditure on solicitors' activities in the run-up to the trial. The Committee felt it was vital that the war chest was ready in case the Committee's determined pressure to obtain a judge fructified. The Committee was very conscious that asbestosis claims were rising across the market and the situation was deteriorating. This state of affairs looked very gloomy indeed. A judgement or settlement resulting in some protection against future losses was urgently needed. This newsletter was a grim warning. No one had any idea of just how long the syndicates' losses may continue and the size of the losses to come.

John Bennett of Hartfield said he was a Member of Rose Thompson & Young, Feltrim and Wellington Syndicates, and his wife underwrote through Poland Agencies. His living had slipped from comfortable to embarrassing. He suggested the newsletter should find its way into the press. He was now aged seventy-two, and had been a Name since 1951. He had never received a big profit from Lloyd's and was now completely disillusioned and even more disgusted with Lloyd's than before.

Mr C. G. M. Lumsden of Chaffe Street, solicitors in Manchester, wrote to Clive on 29 January regarding a recent memorandum from Osborne Bell that indicated it had no assets and that the directors would consider liquidation if they received any writs. Lumsden wrote, 'My parents have already issued writs! A winding-up petition is being considered and a possible writ for a declaration that the "new" Cox & Bell company remained liable for the "old" Osborne Bell liabilities. A court would be justified in lifting the corporate veil.' Clive replied to Lumsden on 4 February, enquiring if Osborne Bell had complied with the Lloyd's bylaws and had obtained E&O cover for the relevant years. Lumsden's

letter was forwarded to David Tiplady with a request to ensure that no
Association Members were endangered by this manoeuvre in any way.

From Farnham, Simon Harrap confirmed his opinion that the case
for Syndicate 334 was as strong as ever but was distressed that there
was no court date fixed, as judges were in short supply. However, what
saddened him was the embittered tone of the remainder of the January
newsletter, as he did not see why Clive should see it as an opportunity to unburden his thoughts about the whole Lloyd's community,
mentioning golf course gossip, disciplinary proceedings and duping
of innocent potential Members of Lloyd's by unqualified Members'
Agents. This would seem to have little to do with updating Members
of the Association on progress or lack of it, in presenting their case to
court. Whilst he thanked Clive for chairing the Association, he suggested
that in future if there was no news to report, comments were made to
that effect, without airing irrelevant personal views. Clive responded on
3 February and thanked Harrap for the detailed feedback. He said he was
unrepentant. He sat on several Names' Committees including the Super
Group and the Asbestosis Working Party. In the latter the Association
was being assisted by a few brokers and ex-Lloyd's underwriters. Clive
emphasised in his reply that theft was what was now unfolding. To a
non-Lloyd's man, it was startlingly repulsive duplicity, tax evasion and
External-Name-soaking. There were a number of names for it: misappropriation of funds, fraudulent conversion, fraud and false accounting,
but the simple name which covered all was *theft*. He continued, 'I have
just received my Gooda Walker interim report. The attention of all was
drawn to the purchase and running of some nineteen cars, with money
taken from the Syndicate Premiums Trust Funds. This was stealing!'

Clive elaborated:

I'm sorry Simon that you mistook my expressions of disgust and
anger for bitterness. Bitterness is a wholly unproductive emotion,
which generally devoured its own begetter. Anger is followed by a
desire for retribution and in this case, for the multitude of cheated

External Names. I have received many letters of pitiful distress from ruined Names and those facing ruin. There have been five suicides to date. I have had literally hundreds of telephone conversations with Names regaling me with tales of irresponsible utterances from their unknowledgeable Agents. One phone call with the Managing Director of a Members' Agency told me that his wife was not joining a particular Action Group. After four minutes' conversation he changed his mind. What was a man like that doing advising Names? I am unashamedly angry at the way Names have been treated. I never sought the appointment as Chairman. I feel I would be failing in my duty if I did not give encouragement to the faint-hearted and pass on to the duped that knowledge gleaned from the conflict. Without strong motivation there would be no Chairman or Association. Whilst my views may be deemed personal, a better term is 'synoptic', views common to Committee Members of the 27 Action Groups now litigating or contemplating litigation against their Agents. I enclose a copy I have received of an unnamed underwriter's notes written at the time, who felt a frission of disgust, by way of illustration:

Underwriter's Notes of a Discussion about Asbestosis in the Coffee Room at Lloyd's One Morning in 1981

One morning in 1981 I went up to the Coffee Room for a daily brokers' meeting with Chris Rome, Brian Roddick, Brian Evans and Ivor Gibson. Ivor Gibson, cargo underwriting Syndicate 448 (Wellington), was already there, sipping coffee, in tremendous form. 'Oh, I must tell you, we've just got rid of our Incidental Non-Marine Portfolio. We placed an unlimited reinsurance with a pooling excess for 1979 and all back years, for $900,000. All that bloody crap that Jim Bailey was writing, it's all gone now. Thank God for that. Now I shall probably stay on the Syndicate when I retire. We know that asbestosis is a killer.' 'Do you know who has written it?' he was asked. 'That bloody clever xxxx Outhwaite. That'll teach him to be so clever. My God, he does not

know what's going to hit him. He is going to be blown out of the water,
that'll teach him not to be so superior, that'll teach him a lesson.' Ivor
was bubbling with joy

I felt a frission of disgust and sympathy for the RHM Outhwaite
Names especially if Rokeby-Johnson was going to be right.

Rokeby-Johnson had been warning about impending liabilities since 1973. The notes had come to Clive's attention probably at some meeting he attended. It was clear that in 1981 underwriters were carrying on the normal procedure of laying off risk and reinsuring earlier years, as Syndicate 334 had also done. Some underwriters were more aware than others of the oncoming asbestosis crisis as market intelligence was not homogeneous. Others may have assumed that market intelligence was incorrect and were prepared to arrange a suitable premium for the risk being presented.

Clive urged Harrap to write to his MP immediately, voicing great concern at the lack of judges.

Mr P. J. Aiken of Dorchester said he had written to his MP, Sir James Spicer, and asked him to put pressure on the Lord Chancellor's Department concerning the lack of judges. He was so pleased to see that Clive's aggression and his interest remained undiminished. He looked forward to the day when he could meet and celebrate the success of a case won.

On 31 January LSS advised that five subscribers to the Association had not paid the subscriptions in full. Reasons for nonpayment included: business bankrupt, losses with BCCI, no funds, no contact and no reason. The amount they had not subscribed totalled £11,500.

Mr E. M. Wrisdale, on 3 February 1993, queried the necessity to pay the latest subscription to the Association. The following day Clive replied with thanks for Wrisdale's supportive action in writing to his MP Sir Peter Tapsell. He said that the Committee sympathised with his view, but all Members were bound by the same rules regarding subscriptions. Those Members who have already paid might cavil at any blurring of the issue.

Keith Lester wrote to Ian Taylor MBE MP on 6 February and sent him a copy of the January newsletter. He mentioned the shortage of judges and wondered if he, Ian, could assist. Keith pointed out that an alternative to court action would be to settle out of court. Ian responded saying that he had taken note of the enclosures about Lloyd's and was delighted that Keith was continuing his Membership of his organisation, the Esher Enterprise Club.

Colonel Michael Cobb from Devon asked if he could continue Membership of the Association on a reduced basis, stating Lloyd's was cleaning him out and he could not pay the subscription. He was concerned that if he was bankrupt and paid up, the court would consider he had denuded the creditors of some funds. He thought the January newsletter was both horrifying and informative.

Chatset, a consulting firm for measuring syndicate performance, produced an estimate of probable future losses and the cost of capping the losses in a report dated 22 December 1992. In summary, the result depended partly on the rate of exchange of the pound sterling to the US dollar as US losses were paid in dollars. Original run-off calculations for Syndicate 334 were at £1 to $1.87. Subsequently the rate was £1 to $1.56, creating a substantial increase in sterling costs. The Chatset calculation for outstanding claims including IBNR amounted to £97,181,000 using a sterling exchange rate of $1.60. This came to 549% of line. It was estimated that pollution claims were 84% of the total and would be paid over twenty-five to thirty-five years. A time and distance policy investment interest rate was 7.5% and $1 million invested currently should return about $2 million in nine years or $4 million in eighteen years. It was reasonable to assume that monies put up at the time to fund future losses should only be some 40% of the final losses paid. Thus, the cost per £10,000 line would be £21,960 or 219.6% (40% of 549%). The Association's Members' total claim would be £25.25 million. This held good only if the settlement was capped.

Chatset also reported a recent House of Lords ruling, where recoveries would be top-sliced so that a Name would receive nothing until the stop-loss underwriter had been reimbursed in full. Chatset considered that any quotation from CentreWrite would assume losses 50% higher than the Chatset estimate of 549%, increasing to 800% of line. CentreWrite was charging a Risk Premium because of the preponderance of pollution claims, and it may be difficult to obtain a quotation from them.

The Chatset report concluded with three suggested scenarios for finalising the actions.

1. The Association accepted the losses so far and sought damages equal to the time and distance policy estimated at £30 million. The Association formed a limited-liability company with Members becoming shareholders, which purchased the time and distance policy. The Company may run for twenty-five years. Each year the Name would be given funds (as dividends?) to pay the losses. This flexible arrangement would allow for negotiations with underwriters.

2. The Association accepted the losses so far and sought damages for estimated future losses at £65 million. This sum would be distributed to Association Members or underwriters, where Names had stop-loss policies. Names with stop-loss policies would benefit by having their indemnity increased. If the defendants accepted the estimated future losses, they would almost certainly seek a reduction on the basis the sum should be discounted.

3. The Association accepted the losses so far and sought damages equal to the time and distance policy estimated at £30 million. This would provide a flow of funds to cover the estimated future losses. The Association passed the benefit of the policy to each Member (could this be done?). The Syndicate might remain open for, say, twenty-five years. Names would be personally liable for paying losses each year. There should be enough funds to pay the losses.

Solutions 1 and 3 were flawed as they needed the approval of Association Members and complexities would arise regarding the length of time the proposed solution would be active, say, twenty-five years. Solution 2 was not dissimilar to the legal action presently being sought.

Mindful of importance of getting to court quickly to improve the tactical position and understanding the severity of the situation, Jasper Salisbury-Jones wrote to the Committee on 11 February. He commented that Chatset used conventional methods to estimate the outcome based on reduced 'over-optimism'. The calculations included more emphasis on potential pollution claims. The final answer could be very different from the estimates and suggested a quote from CentreWrite would represent a proper measure of the damage. Alternatively, a court may have to estimate future losses and return annually to detail the actual losses. Pessimistically, the defendants might run out of money resulting from paying other claims. Charles Barron did not like the Chatset suggestion about accepting losses already paid (Solution 1) for he was concerned about his ultimate Estate. He was not keen to assume acceptance of such losses. It was imperative that the Association's case got to court as soon as practicable… or possibly sooner!

John P. Ryan, an actuary with Tillinghast, a firm of actuaries, suggested that Alasdair Ferguson acquired a copy and further information about a recent Coopers & Lybrand report on Syndicate 334, and independent advice on the amount of damages for additional uncertainty, as Coopers & Lybrand would have made no provision for this. The Association should also obtain independent advice on the likely payout pattern of future claims with an evaluation of the time and distance; and on determining the actual arrangements required to enter into an agreement with a reinsurer. Fees for a review of the actuarial report would cost £12,000 to £17,000 plus VAT and a full independent actuarial review and report would be in the region of £30,000 to £50,000. It might take eight weeks to prepare the reports following receipt of Coopers & Lybrand information.

On 26 February KPMG actuarial services wrote to Alasdair. To put a claim into court for damages the Association needed to know the quantum of losses that would be incurred and would have been covered by the reinsurance agreement. The partner, Richard C. Wilkinson, indicated that fees for producing a report assessing the quantum of losses would be of the order of £75,000 to £100,000.

Alasdair Ferguson summarised the task of assessing future losses in a circular to the Committee on 25 February including the above quotations from KPMG. Pulbrook Underwriting Management had commissioned a detailed actuarial investigation and Names were entitled to receive a copy and they had not responded to David Tiplady's request for one. The Chatset estimate had been circulated but it was unlikely to be accepted by the defendants. Alasdair provided a schedule of his assessment of damages and accepted the Chatset estimate of the total loss being $197.6 million, of which the Association's share would be $128 million. He used an exchange rate of £1 = $1.436 and wondered if this rate would be applicable for twenty-five years. He said past and future losses would come to some £65 million, amounting to an average of 550% per Member. Consequently, any claim for damages must be supported by organisations with relevant experience and reputation.

Mr Malcolm from Solihull wrote to the Parliamentary Secretary at the Lord Chancellor's Department as he was sorry there was no date for the case to be heard. He had already been taken for £500,000. He said in retrospect he should not have joined Lloyd's but at the time he had confidence in the abilities and honesty of those carrying on the business. One Name said at a recent meeting, 'I despair. The only way I can get relief is to die.' This was not correct as liabilities transferred to the Name's Estate. Perhaps he meant that when he died, he did not have the worry. Clive's observation was, 'Make no mistake, the misery would continue, shouldered by the Russon Estate's executors and trustees!'

On 26 February the Lord Chancellor, the Rt Hon James Mackay, replied to Sir Peter Horden's letter of 15 February dealing with Gervase Tinley's concerns. He explained that he nominated High Court judges who may be deployed to sit in the Commercial Court. The commercial judge oversees the list that determines the dates of hearings and sits full-time in the Commercial Court. Others who sit there are drawn from the pool of nominated judges according to need and availability. Recent promotions to the Court of Appeal had a temporary effect on planning Commercial Court lists. At the beginning of last term only five judges were available to sit. Other difficulties were caused by long cases overrunning and the expedition of urgent ones. It was not possible to secure immediate replacements from a relatively small number of suitable practitioners. Full-time appointments of new High Court judges suitable for nomination to the Commercial Court pool were difficult to arrange. Since 30 November 1992 three further judges had been added to the pool. Mr Justice Saville, the commercial judge, and Lord Taylor, the Lord Chief Justice, now had eleven nominated judges. It was important to adhere to fixtures arranged several months in advance in the Commercial Court. The Lord Chief Justice must also consider the needs of the Crown Court, the Queen's Bench Division, the Court of Appeal (Criminal Division) and the Divisional Court. The Lord Chancellor said the Lord Chief Justice considered a reduction of waiting times in the latter two courts to be of utmost importance. Difficult questions of priority would need to be resolved in allocating judges. They had asked a group of senior judges and officials to advise them on the work, deployment and numbers of High Court judges. This was a complex matter given the wide variety of jurisdictions in which these judges sat. The advice would help identify any problem areas and, if these existed, to clarify what needed to be done to resolve any difficulties. The Lord Chancellor concluded by saying that he had enclosed a copy of the letter for Sir Peter's constituent and mentioned that he had received similar letters from a number of other Members of Parliament, and he had replied in similar terms.

Sir Peter Hordern forwarded the Lord Chancellor's letter to Gervase Tinley. When thanking Sir Peter, Gervase wondered if he had correctly interpreted the somewhat opaque response and that the position was somewhat better than hitherto. He trusted that justice would prevail ultimately and as a senior, hoped he was not being too selfish in wanting to be around when that happened.

The Willis Faber & Dumas (Agencies) newsletter of 26 February 1993 by James Sinclair stated that there had been an explosion of growth in paper, due to regulatory requirements. Syndicates wanted to identify more closely with Names and Agents found it necessary to write frequently on topics of which Names should be appraised. The paper flow had become an unacceptable burden to Names. To reduce this, the newsletter included a second section of the report that related to syndicate movements and technicalities of the business that previously was sent separately. Losses for 1990 would be similar to 1989 at £1.8 to £2 billion. The whole loss cycle for the years 1988 to 1991 would aggregate at a loss figure of £5.5 billion and included recapitalising the Central Guarantee Fund (CGF). At 31 December 1991, Names' funds at Lloyd's stood at £4.7 billion. Thus, over the loss-cycle Names had needed to recapitalise the entire business to allow Lloyd's to continue trading. Lloyd's capacity had shrunk from a high point in 1988 of £11.3 billion to £8.5 billion in 1993. The UK retail price index had increased by 35% since 1988. Adjusting for inflation in real terms the 1994 capacity should be £15.3 billion. Names would not, or could not, recapitalise to the 1988 position. Lloyd's Central had advised that syndicates would be charged interest at 5% over the Bank of England prime rate for any outstanding cash balances unpaid at 31 July 1993. The purpose of the 5% penalty was to encourage timely payment and preserve equity between Names.

Over the past five years the Lloyd's turnover had been static at £4 billion while expenses had risen from £494 million to £1.1 billion. The parabolic trajectory of the Lloyd's expense line compounded mathematically would have been remarkable even to Sir Isaac Newton! Costs were to be attacked by Lloyd's Central. The elimination of excess expenditure would no doubt be painful to many sections of the Lloyd's community, such as the Lloyd's bureaucracy or collaterals.

Some good news was given. The discipline of a contracting Market would be quite profound, forcing underwriters to review their entire underwriting book of business. For the first time in twenty years, they would be able to charge high rates and harsh terms for business. Another good discipline in 1992 was the requirement to underwrite and retain risk for profit. Lloyd's was not too exposed to US reinsurance programmes. Benefit from this would be demonstrated when loss figures for Hurricane

Andrew in September 1992 were finally calculated reflecting better discipline in terms of syndicate net retentions and better restructuring of reinsurance without relying on risks dumped into the LMX spiral.

In the newsletter Sinclair concluded by approving key senior staff changes, David Rowland, Chairman of Lloyd's, Peter Middleton, Chief Executive and Brian Garraway heading up the Regulatory Board. They would be seeking ways to reduce costs, settling the growing cancer of litigation and closing run-off accounts.

Seventeenth Steering Committee Meeting, 4 March 1993: Impending Meltdown of Lloyd's

Clive informed the eight Committee Members how delighted he was with the response to his January newsletter but expressed dismay at the lack of a court date, which might happen in the coming October. David Tiplady should now proceed towards the Summons for Directions by the end of April 1993.

Four applications for Membership of the Association had been received in the last week. Of a total Syndicate 334 membership of 562, there were 265 Association Members, plus 11 in Hardship. Overdue subscriptions from individuals should be given until 30 April to pay their remaining instalments. Failure to pay would mean removal from the writ and forfeiture of funds paid to date. The writ should not be opened for additional Members. Congratulations were expressed as Jasper Salisbury-Jones and Alasdair Ferguson had been elected to the Syndicate 90 Names' Association Committee.

The meltdown of Lloyd's looked on the cards with a grim fear pervading the Market that jobs and businesses would be lost. Capacity was down to £6 billion as this equated to 1% of the world's insurance business – whereas the Munich Re had approximately 17%. Lloyd's was losing not only business, thus reducing its contribution to the Treasury, but international influence. Municipal Mutual, which was the ninth-largest insurer, had just gone into liquidation. Other insurers in the US and UK companies' market and elsewhere were collapsing or in a weak, financially precarious position. Lloyd's cash flow, critical for paying valid claims, was under pressure from unpaid cash calls.

Financial statements for the year to 31 January 1993 were approved and signed. The interest rate receivable on Bank deposits was at 5.5% overnight or fixed at 9%. Mailings cost £500 to £650 each. Income was £592,458 and funds available amounted to £679,504. The Treasurer proposed that legal action and associated costs ceased until a court date had been fixed as he was very concerned that funds would dribble away in solicitors' fees. Dr Tiplady agreed to prepare a budget for work to October 1993.

'The Lord Chief Justice Wins Fight for Extra High Court Judges', was the headline in the press. It was reported that Lord Taylor, the Lord Chief Justice, had won his battle for the appointment of more judges to help reduce the backlog of cases in the High Court and the Criminal Division of the Court of Appeal. Lord Mackay, the Lord Chancellor, was to recommend the appointment of ten additional judges, bringing the number of High Court judges to ninety-five.

It had been rumoured that 1990 losses could exceed £2.6 billion. The loss for 1990 and 1991 might be £5 billion. Keith Lester wrote to David Rowland as Chairman of Lloyd's, wondering if there was some double counting. The double counting example related to Names on Syndicate 334 having to pay losses whilst E&O underwriters were reserving for the same losses. In addition, the Names Association had over £1 million to spend with solicitors instead of funding Lloyd's business. A letter dated 10 July 1981 from David Carrington of Willis Faber & Dumas (Agencies) was enclosed, telling Keith that the 'Special Reinsurance' referred to in the marine underwriters' report had been placed – either the policy was valid, or the policy was placed by an incompetent management, who should recompense Names. Finally, he asked if the Chairman could force a rapid solution to some of the simpler cases to enable some reserves to be released within the Market. Many Names were financially stretched and may be unable to pay. This could give rise to a possible lack of confidence and precipitate nonpayment by those who otherwise had the means. 'Dare we contemplate the ultimate conclusion of this logic?' Rowland replied, saying, 'We are very much exercised in the issue of double counting and doing a great deal of work to see how this can best be handled, both in terms of presentation of results and Names' positions.' He thanked Keith very much for raising the issue.

Subsequently, Keith sent some further thoughts on double counting to Rowland. Firstly, he suggested that each syndicate should calculate the reserves it had set aside in case it lost litigation. Perhaps 50% of these reserves could be released to Names. While this release would drain down Lloyd's resources, the element of double counting could be quantified. Secondly, Lloyd's Central should seek a long-term facility against the value of the central assets. Names could be offered loans up to the value of 50% of the litigation reserves. The idea of a central loan facility was analogous to arrangements some Members had made to obtain long-term finance to fund losses during a very difficult period. On 22 March, Rowland replied to Keith saying he was interested to read these thoughts and thanked him for taking trouble to elaborate on his ideas.

Ian Taylor copied Keith with a letter he had received from Lloyd's Chairman David Rowland, thanking him for all the time and effort he had put in during the last two years, strongly supporting Lloyd's in the Houses of Parliament, and for very recent comments on a vital issue for Lloyd's. This was good progress towards a proper reserving regime which would greatly simplify matters for Lloyd's Names in dealing with HM Inspector of Taxes. The Society, he said, would become stronger and more stable with improved reserving opportunities. The terms in which the Chancellor referred to Lloyd's gave him an especial pleasure.

Jasper Salisbury-Jones wrote on 15 March to Robin A. J. Jackson, Chairman of CentreWrite Ltd. The Association's Committee thought its case was almost certainly the next one of Lloyd's actions to get a full hearing, at trial around October 1993. If the plaintiffs won, the quantum of damages could be considered by the court towards the end of the year or early in 1994. A CentreWrite quote to close the 1985 account would be the best measurement of future loss. In the absence of such a quote, both sides would have to call actuarial and other expert witnesses. They would have to debate the very matters which CentreWrite would have to decide within the next couple of years. Even after expert evidence a court might not necessarily make an accurate estimate of the future loss. A CentreWrite quote would be correct, by definition, because it would enable a plaintiff to buy out his future liability.

If the CentreWrite quote for closing 1985 year of account for Syndicate 334 could be available by the beginning of 1994 it would save cost and reduce uncertainty. The difficulties of calculating a definite figure for a syndicate with a substantial element of long-tail business was a problem common to many syndicates with open years for 1988 and earlier. The purpose was to ask Robin Jackson of CentreWrite to give a high priority to a quotation for Syndicate 334. It was believed he had the resources, and it was merely a question of him and his colleagues deciding to tackle Syndicate 334 before other similar syndicates. Jasper said he was aware of his potential conflict of interest but he suggested that there would be nothing improper in using his influence with the management of Syndicate 334 to speed up the flow of key information from them to CentreWrite. Jasper requested that a quote was produced within nine months to close the 1985 year of Syndicate 334. Jackson replied to Jasper promptly and he would see that the letter was brought to the attention of the Board and Management of CentreWrite. Once the 1990 accounts of all open years had been received, they would be going through the whole list to identify targets and allocate resources for the next two years. CentreWrite had sent questionnaires to all the relevant Managing Agents which should provide the raw material for the calculation of quotations. While he made no promises, he said that CentreWrite had no desire to become involved in litigation. Jasper copied the CentreWrite letter to David Tiplady pointing out that CentreWrite had not received the requested completed questionnaire from Syndicate 334!

Harry Hyams of London copied correspondence to Clive from Lord Goodman and the Lord Chancellor. The Lord Chancellor suggested to Lord Goodman the names of three retired judges. Clive replied to Harry

Purchase on 1 April saying that he had received fourteen almost identical responses from the Lord Chancellor to various MPs and a helpful peer. Yet there was no date for a hearing. David commented that he was not happy with the judges' names already mentioned. He said he was half-expecting a call from Lord Goodman to whisper a few more names of judges.

Following the distribution of the Lloyd's business plan, Clive wrote to Lloyd's CEO Peter Middleton on 10 April. He said that he had sat with twenty-four other Chairmen of Names' Action Groups (the Super Group) which represented 16,000 Names, and confirmed that the groups were resolutely behind Christopher Stockwell's proposals put to him for the solution of Lloyd's problems. If it was true that he was going to leave many cheated and impoverished Names stranded, then he may count on a bitter, articulate and monumental fight.

The Super Group was adamant in refusing to accept a proposal which left many burnt Names in penury without restitution. The forecast losses were now such that all Names would come to realise that they were related to each other via the Central Fund. This meant that the levy on the less afflicted would be paying for the grievously afflicted. Clive threatened to ensure a rejection of the business plan at the forthcoming EGM if this countenanced the sacrifice of any group of severely hit Names.

The Lloyd's Names AWP had amassed a wealth of historical documents and compiled a lengthy record of evidence, for use of all Names' Action Groups in their legal actions. Clive's summary of this historical documentation was titled 'Fiddlentia'. The report stated that losses for Lloyd's 1990 and 1991 accounts were forecast to exceed £3.4 billion. Lloyd's would have lost more money than it had ever made since Edward Lloyd started his coffeehouse in 1688. For the first time in history Lloyd's was not paying out on valid claims. Six Canadian banks had refused to honour letters of credit and guarantees in respect of Canadian Names until evidence of fraud had been disproved. Lloyd's had been crippled by the greed, complacency and moral turpitude of those who led and regulated Lloyd's in the 1970s and 1980s. One guilty Chairman of Lloyd's was disciplined for knowingly and wilfully having his hands in his Names' till. Another Chairman of Lloyd's attempted to pretend in a television interview that he had never been an insider dealing in a baby syndicate. The interviewer proved him to be untruthful. In 1973, the Sturge underwriter Rokeby-Johnson said, 'Asbestosis is going to bankrupt Lloyd's.' He had reinsured all his asbestosis problems in 1976 with the Fireman's Fund of San Francisco.

Continuing Clive's 'Fiddlentia' summary, he explained that in 1979 eleven Lloyd's underwriters met in New York. The Citibank manager of Lloyd's American Trust Fund said that asbestosis was going to swamp Lloyd's. 'You have got to recruit 250,000 new Names if you want to see this thing through, little men who can be broken.' Lloyd's subsequently set up the AWP to monitor asbestos claims. The Chairman, Mr E. E. Nelson, was later found guilty of discreditable conduct. On 10 November 1981 the advisory panel auditors met under the Chairmanship of Mr R. J. Kiln. Kiln issued specific instructions that any reference to projections of asbestosis claims for the next three to five years should be omitted from the audit instructions. This appeared to be concealment and material nondisclosure.

Three years later, in February 1982, some syndicates were notified of outstanding claims and Neville Russell, Chartered Accountants, wrote to Lloyd's Audit Department on behalf of five other firms of auditors. They were unable to determine the final liability. Asbestosis fell into this category and they asked for instructions. Randall replied on behalf of the Audit Committee and seemingly gave no firm or direct answer. It was thought that some 142 asbestos-liable syndicates should not have closed the 1979 account because of the huge unquantifiable losses pointed out by Neville Russell. In March 1982 Murray Lawrence, Deputy Chairman of Lloyd's, wrote to all Managing Agents leaving it to them to inform their Names about the breaking asbestosis storm. One Agent's Board Meeting minutes recorded, 'We dare not tell the Names otherwise they will desert in droves.' It appeared there were commercial connections between the auditors and the Managing Agents whose syndicates they audited. The auditors presented to unsuspecting Names a true and fair picture, perhaps disarmed by their detailed knowledge of 'offshore off-balance-sheet roll-over funds', parked overseas against a rainy day. Off-balance-sheet funds made a mockery of equity between Names, and verged on false accounting. Managing Agents had enjoyed an extra income in managing these funds. In consequence the Inland Revenue attacked the rollover funds as improper, costing the syndicates involved some £44 million in restitution. The funds were repatriated just in time to present an entirely false picture of syndicate profits to Names and would-be Names, for the years from 1982 to 1985. Without repatriation many syndicates would have reported a wholly different picture in those years. The Committee of Lloyd's recruited some 19,000 Names in 1980, 1981 and 1982, and existing Names increased their underwriting just in time for the inundation forecast by Rokeby-Johnson in 1973.

Frank Wright said he would not acknowledge his indebtedness to Lloyd's as he thought the indebtedness was the responsibility of Lloyd's. He refused to confirm that he was willing but unable to meet underwriting commitments as it assumed the liabilities existed. The Hardship Committee had informed him that it did not deal with Names by meeting them for a discussion and the only way forward was by written exchanges. Alan Turner of Willis Faber & Dumas (Agencies) said the Hardship Committee needed a full disclosure of his and his wife's assets. At the time when prospective Names were initially considering Membership they were informed that a spouse's assets were not liable to be seized by Lloyd's in the event that the Name was unable to pay debts to Lloyd's. Frank said his wife had never been a Name at Lloyd's and had no legal responsibility for his debts. Many Names made sure that some assets were held solely by their wives. A wife's financial affairs were confidential. Risks of unlimited liability were potentially too high for many individuals to be prepared to put all the family's assets at risk on joining Lloyd's. It was a way for a family to diversify and spread an unimaginable and unlikely risk. This was sensible and equivalent to a back-stop insurance policy.

George Aldrich of Evesham contacted Clive:

I have been swindled. My nightmare scenario is that Lloyd's new business plan will spend Names' money covering over professional negligence, greed and criminal activity. I fear that Mr Rowland et al will bring in fresh money to look after the ongoing business. A settlement won't bring justice for those worse off than me. The Action Groups suffer from of a lack of resolve to bring justice to those who have caused the problems and to fight vigorously for full and comprehensive compensation. However, I was relieved to read your letter of hard-hitting words to Peter Middleton dated 10 April.

The Commercial Court listing office advised David Tiplady that Mr Justice Saville would be allocated to a six-month fraud trial beginning in October 1993. In the light of this unexpected and unexplained development, David suggested that the Association proceed to have the case listed as soon as possible before the first available Commercial Court judge.

Two days later, following receipt of the budget for the year to 31 January 1994, David provided his proposed legal costs. As the case had been put back from February to October concern was expressed about the funds dwindling away while preparing for the hearing. He recorded his views of the impossibility of the Treasurer's suggestion that legal expenditure should be stopped until a date for a court hearing was fixed. He said he was working with two objects in mind, firstly, to bring the case to court as quickly as possible and, secondly, to present the case in court as strongly as possible. Work necessary to achieve these objects must carry on. He asked that if there were any detailed suggestions or proposals for ways in which costs may be reduced, consistent with the above objects, he would be delighted to hear them. Strategy and funding came to the fore.

David Tiplady's note of 10 March 1993 estimated that his firm's costs might amount to £941,000 including VAT should the Association lose the case but did not include the other side's costs. However, he still maintained there would be sufficient funds available within the Association to meet the worst-case position. David's original estimate, dated 15 March

1991, was for total costs of £1.5 million and there appeared to be a shortfall of £600,000. Alasdair Ferguson thought it was best to raise cash before the case was heard rather than afterwards. Annual interest income on deposits was estimated at £28,000 per annum.

Lloyd's Chairman David Rowland wrote to all Names enclosing a copy of the Lloyd's business plan and the corporation's annual report and accounts. He said that a presentation had been arranged for Members and Market practitioners on 25 May at 2 pm at the Royal Albert Hall. He and Peter Middleton would like the opportunity to explain and discuss the issues and to answer questions. The plan outlined the programme for the next three years and included setting up a Company called NewCo. Arrangements had also been made to broadcast a programme on BBC One on 30 April at 5.45 am, which could be watched or recorded.

David Springbett of Taplow commented on the Lloyd's business plan. He said that unless the 'old years' and the 'solvency issue' could be resolved then Lloyd's had no future. Meltdown would be preferred by the vast majority of Names, rather than total financial ruin confronting them under the business plan scenario. A 'ring fence' was the correct way to handle the old-year problem but the business plan had to cap every Name's exposure 'NOW'. The plan should not permit a RITC in a few years' time, becoming so large that Names would find it unaffordable. This would produce another round of litigation. The business plan hinted that Names were distancing their assets from Lloyd's. Overseas Names could not or would not pay and the cost would fall upon the CGF. The business plan stated that Names on 1996 underwriting years onwards would have no liabilities for the past. Lloyd's would not call more than a maximum levy 'to be announced later' as a contribution to the CGF. The maximum should have been in the business plan. It was probably omitted for one of two reasons – either nobody had a clue what might be required or they were too terrified to announce it. It was proposed to introduce corporate limited-liability capital using a limited liability company. Corporate subscribers and new Names would not be interested in contributing additional amounts to the CGF. NewCo should obtain all the capital it needed at the outset, but there may not be enough money to satisfy the demand. Lloyd's had to be guilty of a massive deception.

In summary Springbett estimated the total of losses per year. The 1989 loss shown was £2.1 billion. However, closing the sixty-eight open syndicates would possibly cost another £3 billion thus totalling £5 billion. The 1990 loss was estimated at £2.8 billion. The number of open syndicates may exceed sixty-eight in 1990 and it was speculated that to close those might require another £2.2 billion. Thus 1989 and 1990 losses might total £10 billion. Speculating about additional specific losses might require another £15 billion coming to a total £25 billion overall.

Meltdown would cause problems for Estates of the deceased. The Estates would have to be reopened as RITC was not an excuse for nonpayment. There would be mass litigation against those solicitors who had closed Estates without drawing attention to the contingent liability should the RITC fail. The CGF must borrow £5 billion from banks now. Half could be deposited with the banks on a long-term basis. All litigation should be compromised immediately and the Lloyd's share mutualised into the CGF. Ravaged Names, those most severely damaged or devastated, should continue to underwrite under supervision and should be protected by an Estate protection plan. It was better to spread this liability over a longer period than having an unpayable call now. There was speculation as to whether CGF levies were legal. The Lloyd's Act 1982 stated that 'Names were liable for their own losses and could not be mutualised'. The CGF had no liability to pay losses. To succeed, Lloyd's must develop a proper marketing strategy. It needed a realistic procedure for payment of premiums and for lapsing of policies where premiums were not paid. In conclusion Springbett emphasised that the business plan needed modification along the lines suggested, otherwise it would fail. Trust between Names and Lloyd's needed to be rebuilt.

Clive responded to Springbett the following day. He called the business plan 'Middleton's Mouse', quoting the Roman poet Horace: 'The Mountains went into labour and all that came forth was a mouse.' Clive suddenly realised that the vital statistics omitted were increases in the old years' losses. It seemed most Names were being misled by the bare pure-year results where old-year deteriorations were somehow decoupled. The only practical solution appeared to be major loan scheme.

Alasdair Ferguson felt that Clive's role had changed. He was not only Chairman of the Association but also the driving force on many other organisations. These included Syndicate 418 Names' Association, the LNAWP (the Super Group), Lloyd's Names AWP and the SoN. Rumour had it that no Lloyd's organisation could be registered without Clive's name on the letter heading. Not all Super Group Members held identical opinions. The Super Group supported much of the business plan and aimed to concentrate on the LMX spiral problems initially. Many Names were recruited on a false prospectus which had led to financial distress. The Group proposed that these 'burnt Names' should receive restitution through an impost on future profits and a substantial contribution from central resources. Lloyd's did not have the necessary funds as it was in a very parlous financial state and must raise money to rescue the 'burnt Names'. The business plan dismissed the possibility of raising capital as impracticable and undesirable. This led to the observation, 'Who would lend money to a loss-making organisation which was not credit-worthy and did not know whether the requested amount would be enough?' An article in the *Financial Times* implied that Middleton believed that any action by one group of Names was only going to be settled at the expense of another group of Names. This was only partly true as insurance brokers and Lloyd's auditors had considerable financial resources.

The Treasurer prepared some notes on 18 May expressing his concern about the increasing costs of legal activity. Whilst there were funds the solicitors would seek to obtain them and funds would dwindle away. Once the money had gone the Association would be in a very weak position. David Tiplady's charge-out rate had increased from £160 to £220 per hour since the beginning in 1990, an increase of 38%. There was no squeeze on solicitors to ensure a performance-orientated payment, i.e., obtaining an offer or getting a hearing.

Eighteenth Steering Committee Meeting, 26 May 1993:
Nineteen Judges Required – Really?

The day after the presentation at the Royal Albert Hall of the Lloyd's business plan and the corporation's annual report and accounts, the Steering Committee met at D J Freeman's offices.

A few days before, Mr Justice Saville had met David Tiplady and other lawyers at the offices, stating that he had to take a global view of all the Lloyd's cases. The Commercial Court would be occupied for between five and ten years. Nineteen judges would be needed for the first five years and ten judges for the next five years. Lawyers acting for defendants were delighted with this news. David thought the matter had been to the Lord Chancellor and probably as far as the Cabinet. He said there was only one way forward for the Association, namely to issue a summons, go for a listing and apply for directions. He said Saville should be forced to carry out his duties even if it meant issuing a writ of mandamus, which is a judicial writ issued as a command to an inferior court or ordering a person to perform a public or statutory duty.

David said that Lord Justice Carr was to head a legal panel to be set up by Lloyd's. Lord Justice Carr was said not to be very sympathetic towards or in favour of Names at Lloyd's. It looked as though he was specially chosen as a stitch-up. Saville requested details of all the claims from Action Groups in time for a meeting on 21 and 22 June. Dr Tiplady would represent the Association and commented that offers had been made to ten lawyers to act as judges and all refused. Ultimately this would result in an order of mandamus.

Clive outlined his views on the business plan and proposed ring-fencing liabilities. He mentioned that Lloyd's reserves were estimated at £23 billion whereas the asbestosis and pollution claims could be £40 billion. The Committee agreed to write to Peter Middleton, David Rowland and the Lord Chancellor about potential claims and how urgent it was to bring the Association's case to be heard in court.

Harry Purchase mentioned that a substantial amount of reinsurance was laid off outside Lloyd's in the company market. Thus, it was not a

foregone conclusion that an overall settlement of disputes would necessarily be met by effective mutualisation within the Lloyd's community.
Mutualisation meant spreading the collective syndicate assets and claims
across all syndicates.

There was an informal meeting on 27 May to discuss financial
worries with Clive, David and Alasdair. David said the legal expenses
had been running at some £8,000 per month for the last six months. He
predicted that the next six months' total would not exceed £40,000 and
concluded there might be a shortfall of between £150,000 and £250,000.
On 21 April the Treasurer had predicted a shortfall of £400,000. They
were very reluctant to decide against taking legal action. It was thought
that Members would not be prepared to pay more money. A suggestion
was to ask the richer Names to act as guarantors. No one knew any
richer Names apart from Harry Hyams. Finally, Clive undertook to see
if there was a suitable insurance policy should costs be awarded against
the Association.

On 30 May, Clive wrote to Peter Middleton conveying the admiration and thanks of the Committee for his efforts in launching the business
plan. He added that the Syndicate 334 Association's case was ready for
trial. It was a simple case involving a relatively small sum of £50 million.
Clive suggested that a negotiated settlement may prove a catalyst for his
movement towards a non-litigious resolution.

Keith Lester wrote to James Sinclair on 15 June regarding his underwriting results and seeking advice stating the magnitude of losses on
Syndicates 334 and 90. The Syndicate 90 (1982) loss was near to 1,000%.
Projected calls would soon leave him without funds. He wanted to know
when he would have to cease underwriting and if he could draw down on
his guarantee. He did not expect to be able to provide further funds in
November. Sinclair replied promptly, saying Keith could draw down on
his guarantee and it may mean underwriting at lower premium allocation in 1994. He did not foresee Keith as a Hardship case, adding, 'The
Syndicate 90 loss "took my breath away", I am waiting for the accounts to
identify the reason for the rapid deterioration. I think Errors & Omissions

insurers will have to make a substantial offer. Leadership on litigation issues will have to come from Lloyd's Chairman.'

The June issue of the SoN said the asbestos-related liabilities were estimated between £20 billion and £60 billion. There was roughly a one-third and two-thirds split between Lloyd's and the London insurance companies. At £20 billion total liabilities, Lloyd's would need to reserve £8 billion. Additional reserves would be required for loss of hearing and lead poisoning, as well as toxicity and other pollution-related losses. The Lloyd's business plan envisaged £4 billion of reserves being transferred to NewCo, the reinsurance company owned by Lloyd's. NewCo would reinsure all 1985 and prior years' liabilities. At £4 billion, it seemed unlikely that Names would be able to fully fund the reserves necessary to establish NewCo. NewCo may ultimately prove to be insolvent. However, this was not a story of unremitting doom and gloom. A window of opportunity had opened for settlement of 'old-year' policies.

Ralph B. Bunje Jr said the Lloyd's business plan was an outstanding effort and was 70% of the solution. However, the NewCo idea fell short. The plan was not a means of settling the E&O litigation, as it appeared to erode the existing capital base and relied too heavily on corporate capital to protect the 1994 and 1995 accounts. Lastly, it was too general for Names to understand how it affected them individually, leading to confusion and uncertainty. Bunje's proposal for improving upon the business plan and to make it 100% effective started with closing all the open years up to 1992 into NewCo. The 1992 syndicates could begin from scratch with no prior-year liabilities. Names had failed to protect their position because they focused on recovering losses through litigation, rather than proposing constructive solutions to the problems.

David Tiplady wrote about a meeting on 28 June with lawyers and Mr Justice Saville. The whole matter of litigation at Lloyd's was under the close control of the Commercial Court. The main question was the responsibility of Members' Agents for the wrongdoing of Managing Agents. This was thought to be a matter of general importance and should be tried as a preliminary issue. The defendants were anxious to find and exploit every means possible to delay all actions. They were challenging the Association's Discovery, claiming Members had not disclosed all the documentation they were holding, and seeking further and better particulars on the points of claim. Saville said he would not be able to rule on any summons for directions until he had formulated and put in place his own overall strategy. He believed there were two issues as far as Syndicate 334 was concerned – firstly, whether Members' Agents were responsible in law for the misdeeds of Managing Agents and, secondly, whether certain claims were time-barred.

Nineteenth Steering Committee Meeting, 15 July 1993: No Excuses

Mr Justice Saville had said that he was not interested in receiving excuses from lawyers to the effect they want to delay matters regarding Discovery. He had agreed to try preliminary issues in September regarding Members' Agents' liability and/or responsibility for the misdeeds of Managing Agents. The limitation of claims and the Latent Damage Act would also be tried. It had been decided not to try the auditors on a preliminary issue. David Tiplady said, 'I will seek a trial date in the next few days. The preliminary hearings will not hold up the Association's trial and the points established will save the Association costs.'

Under the Lloyd's business plan, two panels would be set up in an attempt to obviate or settle the threatened avalanche of litigation. A legal one would be headed by Sir Michael Kerr and a financial one under Sir Jeremy Morse. The Kerr Panel was to assess the relative strengths of each Action Group's case. The Morse Panel was to assess what monies were available for settlement. The claims had to be quantified as to what had been paid, outstanding calls and estimated future amounts. For Syndicate 334, 214% of line had already been called. Chatset guessed a total call of 450% for the syndicate in 1992, although this may be much higher in view of ongoing receipt of pollution advices.

The procedure was outlined. The Association had to submit its case. There were fourteen days for the respondents to respond, followed by a further few days to respond to their response. The Kerr Panel would review and rank the findings. Matters would then be passed to the Morse Panel for review. Some reinsurance companies might not respond, but E&O insurers were willing to cooperate. Offers would be made to all Names on the syndicate, not just to Association Members.

The ALM's conference was held in Boston, USA, and attended by David Tiplady. Names made it clear that the business plan took no account of burnt Names and Lloyd's would not go forward on the back of burnt Names. Clive decided not to join the new long-tail Action Group as the Association's cause of action was not founded on long-tail problems but on negligence.

David Tiplady's detailed submission to the review panel was circulated. It said the underlying cause of the problems was the long-tail exposure to US liability, particularly asbestos and pollution, which resulted in the 1985 year being left open. After studying the information Clive thanked David for his clarity of exposition. It was the first time any Committee Member had seen a detailed synopsis of the Association's case and everyone was greatly encouraged.

Claud Gurney of Penshurst complained that the Lloyd's business plan was drawn up in the narrow interests of those who ran Lloyd's, as it proposed to ring-fence the current Names who would be left with all the liabilities of the past. The business plan had superficial attractions – capping and partial settlement of losses as well as transfers of reserves created for one purpose to be used for another. There would be two classes of Names, Future Names and Present Names. The Council reserved the right to levy Central Fund contributions upon the latter. It had never been concerned about equity between Names. In conclusion the ring fence must be run in the interests of those Names trapped inside.

On 23 July, Keith Lester wrote to Charles Hulbert-Powell of Willis Faber & Dumas (Agencies) and told him that asbestosis and pollution losses were escalating at 11% and this compared, for example, with the UK gross domestic product increasing only at 4% per annum. If this trend continued, he could not contain such losses into the future, suggesting that he drew down on his guarantee and underwrote a lower

stamp. Once that was exhausted an application would have to be made
to the Hardship Committee. This was an unexpected and appalling
conclusion to arrive at.

Subsequently, Alasdair Ferguson's paper on 6 October 1993 was
a précis of the submission to the review panels. Claims were being
brought against the Names' Agent, Matthews Wrightson Pulbrook Ltd,
and Underwriting Agent Pulbrook Underwriting Management Ltd, and
other relevant Members' Agents.

The first claim arose from the successful avoidance of reinsurance
placed with Syndicate 418 and the second claim from failure to leave
open the years 1979 to 1985. Names alleged that avoidance was caused
by breaches of contract and negligence. The Association, as plaintiffs, had
had no Discovery from Pulbrook Underwriting Management. The plaintiffs claimed the loss amounted to £81.2 million.

Extracts were included from the Merrett Holdings PLC audited
financial statements dated 30 September 1992. After deduction of tax
and an extraordinary item there was a loss of £935,000. Capacity had
reduced from £498 million in 1992 to £385 million in 1993 and uncertainty was expressed about 1994. The balance sheet showed shareholders'
funds of about £4.4 million, but with fixed assets at £6.1 million there
was a deficit of current assets of £1.7 million. Stephen Merrett owned just
over half of the issued share capital. He paid himself a salary of £250,000.
Alasdair concluded that Merrett Holdings PLC would be unable to pay
any damages arising from a successful legal action.

There was insurance for each of three underwriting divisions with
an excess of £1 million. There was one automatic reinstatement of cover
except for the policy commencing 26 August 1992 that had no provision.
Thus, notifications of actions after that date were uninsured.

The paper gave threatened legal actions against the Merrett Group by
policy year, ones with relevance to the Association included:

1987/88	Outhwaite dispute, Syndicates 90 and 418
1989/90	Syndicates 90 and 334
1990/91	Syndicate 105/108
1991/92	US Names' Action

Clive asked Alasdair to circulate his paper to the Committee. He said, 'At this vital moment I have no means of copying or promulgating this information.' Having sold his house and living in digs without office facilities, Clive was having severe administrative and financial difficulties. He was heading into Hardship.

John Burrows' letter said that US legislation no longer expressed the will of its citizens for upholding the principles of liberty, justice and freedom. The horrifying thing was to see the enormous number of policies issued by Lloyd's from 1945 to 1985 in the USA. Asbestosis claims were estimated between £14 billion and £20 billion. Burrows had received a letter from Glenn W. Bailey, Chairman of Keene Corporation of New York, containing a speech given to the International Defence Council in London on 13 July. Glenn said he started the Keene Corporation twenty-six years earlier, costing $800,000. He bought Baldwin-Ehret-Hill (BEH) for $8 million. BEH had a small asbestos product that was loss-making and shut down in the early 1970s. Bailey was now spending $800,000 per week on litigation. Some lawyers were charging $10,000 per hour. This asbestosis litigation was just the leading edge of legalised extortion.

For the sake of fairness American lawyers should work towards improving the American system and he made some suggestions.

1. The loser pays to be retained, as it will minimise the number of frivolous lawsuits.
2. The lawsuit lottery mentality resulting from contingency fees causing irresponsible jury awards should be resisted.
3. Ban nonconsensual mass consolidation of entirely diverse cases. This was an innovation resorted to by trial judges to reduce their case

load. It was impossible for an individual defendant or plaintiff to get fair treatment.

4. Set standards for evidence, especially where expert testimony is introduced that was sharply at odds with the scientific opinion.

5. Punitive damages should be awarded only for the most malevolent motive and gross negligence.

6. Several liability rather than joint and several liability. In the latter case it could force all co-defendants into bankruptcy because the last one standing picks up the tab for the total verdicts.

7. No litigation in American history had:

    • created as much panic
    • involved as many individual claimants
    • consumed as many judicial resources
    • resulted in as much compensation to as many non-sick claimants
    • compelled the number of defendants' bankruptcy

Bailey concluded by saying no litigation had been as lucrative to lawyers as asbestos litigation, adding that he was planning to write a standard handbook on litigation titled *Extortion: How To Do It Legally*.

On 3 August the *Financial Times* ran the headline, 'Pressure Grows on Lloyd's Executive', referring to calls for Stephen Merrett to resign as Deputy Chairman. Merrett said he believed the loss review had been conducted incorrectly, but supported loss reviews so that Names received information about major losses. Senior Market figures believed that Merrett's decision to criticise the findings of the loss review was quite incompatible with his position as Deputy Chairman. On 25 August, the *Daily Telegraph* ran the headline 'Merrett Loses More Names'. One of the biggest agencies, Willis Faber & Dumas (Agencies), was withdrawing Names from Merrett syndicates. Some Names said they were unhappy with Merrett's reinsurance joint venture with Marsh & McLennan in Bermuda. There were fears of a 194% deterioration of the Syndicate 90 1982 open year.

On 9 August Clive asked David Tiplady about the pooling of recoveries following the intention to change the Association's Rule 9 about remunerating the Association's officers. He also enquired if Discovery had yielded the precise E&O cover by each of the target Members' Agents. The Committee had not yet discussed the action it would take if any Members' Agent was unable to meet obligations over and above the E&O cover. It was Clive's view that such agencies should be forced into liquidation. He asked if it was right to broadcast such a decision to increase pressure on the Council and encourage Merrett to come up with an acceptable settlement. He was not sure how the Association could obtain the benefit of capping against future losses from those Agents with inadequate cover. These were serious and important questions as the Committee faced uncertainties about the amount available from E&O policies, net assets on liquidation of companies, as well as unknown liabilities and guarantees held by target businesses.

Newsletter, August 1993
Mr Justice Saville had agreed a trial date in December to hear questions of limitation and the whole of March 1994 for the substantive issues. There were twenty-nine Names' Actions Groups in process or contemplating litigation. Some three weeks had passed while conferring informally with legal representatives, aimed at avoiding the Commercial Court being bogged down with Lloyd's affairs. There were two major issues common to all Action Groups which should be tried first. The Association's only issue was whether the actions of Members' Agents were responsible for the actions of Managing Agents of those syndicates on which Names were placed. If Members' Agents were found to be responsible a sizeable proportion of the Association's case would be won, and the Association's costs reduced.

The Association's submission to the Kerr–Morse Panel had been made. In the absence of a formidable settlement offer the Association would continue pursuing its case through the courts. There were those who held that the panels were smokescreens to reassure prospective corporate capital investors that the threat of long-running litigation was being resolved. However, the Morse offer was likely to be very small and no money would leave Lloyd's. Corporate investors were highly nervous as Standard and Poor's rating agency had already issued a condemning credit rating.

Each Member's Agent carried a finite amount of E&O cover and when that was exhausted the Agency and possibly the Directors would be in line for bankruptcy. It was not surprising that Working Names had fervently embraced the business plan. They hoped that through the panels' offers the rebellious Names could be quelled. Their hopes were likely to be sadly dashed. One cynic put it that the term 'ring fence' had hitherto been reserved to describe an enclosure for sheep prior to shearing and an accountant observed that, 'All Lloyd's Names are now bust but most don't realise it yet.'

The weakness of the Middleton–Rowland business plan was that it did nothing for the injured Names. However, it created NewCo in an attempt to manage existing reserves more efficiently. The protective connotation of 'ring fence' was to be applied purely to protect the new Corporate Lloyd's of 1994 onwards and not to protect those consigned to it. The best protection for Names was offered by the David Springbett Plan (also known as the Lysold Plan). Each Name could see what the liabilities would be and that they were capped. It imposed a tax on future turnover to pay for the mistakes of the past. Market practitioners were rubbishing the Springbett Plan. Litigation threatened the whole future of the Lloyd's business plan unless the problem of injured Names was addressed. In his circular the previous week, Chairman David Rowland said the 1989 and 1990 years were properly reserved. If that was truly the case all open years should have been closed.

The real cause of the damage was the myriad of 'no aggregate limit' liability policies, issued by many syndicates since World War II. There were repeated claims going back to 1947. Insurance archaeologists were having a field-day unearthing Lloyd's policies. Whilst there were finite limits for each claim there was no aggregate, meaning that the number of claims was limitless. The claims for asbestosis, repetitive strain injury

(RSI), Agent Orange and DES showed little sign of abating. Just so long as Lloyd's was perceived as a limitless milch cow it would be milked for every penny. It was now accepted that 80% of payments made on asbestosis claims was going to American lawyers and 50% of claims for RSI were asbestosis clients under the same lawyer. If claims money dried up so would claims.

Rowland, in his preamble, tried to frighten Names into believing that if Lloyd's went bust they would be pursued by American lawyers. He omitted to mention that because each policy was underwritten by several thousand Names on different syndicates the risk had been spread widely. No American lawyer was going to pursue thousands of Names through the courts. It was becoming more and more apparent that the Lloyd's business plan as it stood was badly flawed. It was clear that those entrusted with the governance of the Market were only too aware of the overwhelming magnitude of the asbestosis debacle. The problem was concealed and in most cases Market people safeguarded their own interests without regard to Names.

From 1980 to 1989 not one Chairman of Lloyd's made any mention of asbestosis in the Annual Report. In 1981, Mr Kiln, whilst chairing the Lloyd's Audit Advisory Panel, after a discussion about asbestosis, directed that the minutes of the meeting make no mention of asbestosis claims. Some 18,000 new Names were recruited and were victims of material nondisclosure. Capacity soared with virtually no increase in business. Victims of the spiral paid for the excess capacity with their life savings, their marriages and their homes, and in some cases their lives.

Newsletter, August 1993: Part Two
Part Two of the August newsletter was an excerpt from the Gresham 321 Names' Group report. It set out the present state of Lloyd's with great clarity. One E&O underwriter calculated that without reinsurance cover his loss would be 100%. As a result, he would be sued by his Names and be out of business. The Kerr Panel was attempting to address the problem. Ensuring that no Name came out insolvent would

require a cap on losses. The Super Group said that Lloyd's would have to borrow. In 1993 only 58% of the previous number of Names were underwriting 19,537 out of 33,630 on the electoral roll. Next year there may only be 15,000 Names underwriting. On resignation few would escape from having no liabilities to Lloyd's and less than 45% of those remaining would be underwriting. If insolvency of Lloyd's loomed, the Super Group advised Names to make a voluntary drawdown of their Lloyd's deposit. Distancing of assets was illegal. However, any person from whom a Name might inherit could be asked to change their will and leave the bequest in trust or to children or spouse for as long as there was a liability to Lloyd's.

On 27 August the *Daily Telegraph* ran the headline 'The Smart Money Will Wait'. Lloyd's corporate capital may have been one of the catchier propositions for 1994. With interest rates low, the prospect of boosting income from a share portfolio would be highly attractive especially if the insurance cycle was turning up. This presumed that the Lloyd's business plan would work well enough. Ring-fencing the old claims from the new capital was likely to be easier in theory than practice. There was a strong argument that the new capital should contribute to the goodwill it would be exploiting.

Second Annual General Meeting, 9 September 1993
The Second AGM of the Syndicate 334 (1985) Names Association was held at D J Freeman's offices. Nine Committee and forty-three other Members attended.

Clive Francis welcomed Members and said:

> When we started on this road, I had no idea it would take this long.
> It has been a complex process and I understand the anxiety caused.
> I expect losses for Members on Syndicate 90 will be even worse than
> for Syndicate 334. No one knows when claims for asbestosis and
> general American liability problems will cease.

Clive continued:

Stephen Merrett resigned as Deputy Chairman of Lloyd's yesterday, Wednesday, 8 September, as his position had become untenable. It was hoped that Lloyd's did not embitter him too much because the Association had to deal with a personality. The damage caused by Mr Outhwaite and Mr Merrett taking so much asbestosis and general liability was regrettable especially when one considered that Mr Rokeby-Johnson of Sturge Syndicate 210 had foreseen this in 1974. I have a chart going back several years showing that Lloyd's policies had no aggregate limit. It was not until 1979/80 that Lloyd's realised the situation and by then claims were soaring, many of which went back forty years. Lloyd's reserves in the past decade had gone from £1 billion to £11 billion now in 1993. In 1982, Neville Russell, a firm of Chartered Accountants, gave a warning that the asbestosis claims to come were unquantifiable. It seems the warnings were not broadcast to the Market.

Clive reported:

The timetable for the court is set out. The preliminary issue as to whether Members' Agents were responsible for the actions of Managing Agents will be heard by Mr Justice Saville on 29 September followed by the Association's hearing on limitation. The main issue as to whether the Association got paid or not would be heard in March 1994. Once liability had been assessed, the question of quantum arose followed by the very difficult matter of capping the amount. Without a cap, Names could be paying for many years. The preliminary trial would last two weeks. The Association's case would go ahead in December for a week and then for the whole of March. Winnings will be used firstly to settle costs, and then the first tranche will go to the Name who had paid in excess of the stop-loss. The second tranche will go to the stop-loss underwriter. If there is any money left it will be paid to the Name towards the excess before stop-loss.

David Tiplady explained that the Association was one of thirty that had made a submission to Sir Michael Kerr. The other side had replied, and the Association had submitted its right of response. The strength of the Association's case was its simplicity. He emphasised the very short deadlines given for initial submissions, Members' Agents replies and the final right of response. The panel consisted of three eminent lawyers who had half a day for each case. Thirty minutes would be available for oral submission by the Association's counsel. Claims would be graded: very strong, reasonable, poor and no hope. The Morse Panel would announce the amount of money available to settle and the Association would have to decide whether to accept.

Jasper Salisbury-Jones spoke of the necessity of changing the Association's Rule 9 regarding remuneration of officers. The purpose was to formalise the situation should the Association get an offer or win in court. After paying costs, recoveries would be distributed according to Members' lines. It was essential to avoid a challenge to the distribution process. There were 562 Names on the Syndicate, of whom 382 were Association Members. The total estimated losses were around £84 million without capping.

Members of the Committee were proposed for re-election and elected en bloc. The Treasurer added that part of the vigour of the Committee was because it was so well led by Clive Francis.

Christopher Stockwell of the Super Group felt it wrong that Names were being asked to vote on the admission of corporate capital before more was known about the terms of the Morse settlement. There were concerns about the burden NewCo may impose on present Names and the very substantial number of years likely to be left open, which might generate jobs for life for Agents who might otherwise have no job. There should be a limit to corporate capital and subject to a vote by existing Names. Existing Names should have pre-emption rights on capacity.

On 13 September 1993, Geoffrey Lawson of Godalming said that for a number of years he was Chairman of the PCW Names Steering Committee. In the absence of a judgement for the full amount claimed, he said the Committee would have to consider carefully the merit of accepting a compromise. Individual Names would have different financial positions. The amount lost by each Name depended on the amount of personal stop-loss, if any. If a Name had a stop-loss policy that had not defaulted, the net loss suffered was less than it otherwise would be, leaving more money to be spread amongst those less fortunate.

John Holder of Ellesmere wrote to Clive and raised the issue of common links between Managing Agents and Members' Agents, as with Syndicates 90 and 334. He said there would be some Names with Agents other than Pulbrook and he wondered where the duty of care lay. He found it inconceivable that the duty of care that had previously existed was destroyed by the 1982 Lloyd's Act.

Newsletter, September 1993

Lloyd's would be sending a proxy form about the proposed Lloyd's EGM for the purpose of approving bylaws related to corporate capital. Corporate capital may well be in the interest of the Society in the longer term, while in the short term it could be premature and to the disadvantage of Members in Action Groups. If the bylaws were voted through a successful resolution of Action Groups' claims may become less critical to the future of the Society. This could seriously prejudice the Committee's chances of reaching an acceptable settlement for Association Members. Clive asked Members not to give the proxy to Lloyd's but instead either to him or Christopher Stockwell.

Clive accepted the Chairmanship of Lloyd's Action Group for Restitution and Deposit Defence, which sought to represent the hardest-hit or bottom 3,000 Names. The Action Group had retained an unusual barrister, Gordon Apsion, who had a highly individualistic and aggressive style. He intended to arraign the Council for failure to regulate certain Members of Council and for the nondisclosure of material facts, and the auditors for breach of duty. He had no great standing in the City but had won a number of public body and regulatory cases. Clive advised the Committee, 'I have thought carefully before accepting this appointment as I am concerned whether it would have an adverse effect on the Association. The hardest hit is a group of Names about to lose everything because of the now-revealed chicanery at Lloyd's. They most certainly need my help.'

David Rowland wrote to all Names on 21 September enclosing a notice of an EGM on 20 October to consider the bylaws adopted by Council on 8 September. The changes were of such importance that the Membership should approve them, urging Names to vote and not to be complacent. Names should not use the vote as an attempt to interfere with the dispute resolution process as it would not succeed. Very demanding timetables had been set for the legal and financial advisory panels to complete their work and could not be brought forward. The legal panel had less than nine weeks to reach conclusions on claims relating to more than 130 syndicate years. The letter continued with Council's advice on how to vote.

The October issue of SoN headlined, 'The Bum of the Flightle Bee'. It stated that Names would only recover a percentage, say, 40%, of their losses. Names may be offered a high cap on future losses. The mood of despair was universal six months ago but was already moderating. A substantial number of Names would consider any settlement attractive. However, without a special deal for ruined Names, the New Year would see fights between the Action Group Committees, the marginal Names, who could trade on, and the ruined Names, who would be hostile. Then there would be disputes amongst the Action Groups, between those who wanted to settle with the least good cases, or had the mildest Chairmen, or no money with no court date in sight, and those Group Committees who did not want to settle but had the power to deal on their Members' behalf. The latter would be fully funded and have good cases with imminent court dates. Lawyers would advise that litigation should proceed.

SoN also published a short item titled, 'Quick Justice'. Timing was critical. Judge Sir Michael Kerr had agreed to evaluate thirty-two cases in three months. SoN stated that he said he would not break the record. At Devonport Assizes in 1779, Judge Hunter tried twenty-nine prisoners in a day. He began by saying, 'There is nothing of much concern in any of these cases', and finished up sentencing them all to death by hanging. However, he was merciful and spared one of them, transporting him to Australia for life for stealing a handkerchief. Judge Hunter got on with his job with celerity – would Sir Michael Kerr be as successful?

Neil Shaw, Chairman of the ALM, wrote to Members about corporate capital. The ALM agreed with the Super Group that proposals to admit corporate capital would be beneficial. Names would not be denied access because capacity had been reserved for corporate Members. Names would also have the right to maintain their 1993 underwriting participations. The ALM said Names should vote personally at the EGM on these very important issues or give their proxy with instructions on how to vote.

Initially published in the *New Yorker* on 10 October 1993, the *Night & Day* newspaper published a long article by Julian Barnes about Lloyd's titled 'Safe as Houses'. He said, 'that's what an investment with Lloyd's is meant to be', but as they say in San Francisco, houses can go down as well as up. Some of Britain's poshest people were destitute. Dr Mary Archer, Chair of the Hardship Committee, was there to help them out. The article gave examples of Names' underwriting situations. A photograph showed Clive's typical meditative smile of disbelief in what he was hearing. The caption said, 'I spent 20 years in the RAF. You know – Trust and Honour. Then to find in such an august body like Lloyd's a bunch of craven crooks.' He owed Lloyd's £2 million. In contrast, Melvyn Bragg, the television executive, said he was 'doing very well'. One anonymous Name handed over a *Daily Mail* picture of Dr Archer in a cocktail dress saying, 'It probably cost more than she'll give me to live on for a year'.

On 13 October, Richard Spooner, a distressed Name, circulated a paper reviewing a prospective settlement offer. He said the Council showed no sign of being willing to take on external borrowing or to borrow from the Trust Funds. Peter Middleton was looking to the finance panel to determine how much money would be available and where it would come from. An offer would be made, together with a calculation sent directly to Names and not via Action Groups. The date was set so that there would be enough time for corporate capital to raise funds before the end of the year. There was no mention that a Kerr–Morse offer would provide a cap for future losses. The EGM date was set so that new Members, individual or corporate, could join Lloyd's at the beginning of the New Year.

On 20 October 1993 Lloyd's held an EGM in the Underwriting Room at 4.30 pm. Clive's subsequent commentary about the EGM stated some 6,600 votes were mandated to the Action Group chairmen. Prior to EGM it was realised that the Super Group did not have enough votes to affect the outcome of the election and some thirty-seven members of the Super Group held a two-hour debate on how best to wield 6,600 votes. It was finally agreed to abstain in the belief that this would carry more weight with the executives in their suite of offices on the twelfth floor of the Lloyd's building. Clive considered the intellectual pressure of the conversation was somewhat above him, especially when it was discussed that the Super Group should support the Council. They postulated that this would enable them to exert a greater influence on the Council. This was a process of reasoning he found difficult to comprehend or accept. Clive's 'Munich' protest went unheeded and he was one of only five who voted against the motion to abstain the proxies in the resulting ballot. A newsletter on 25 October from Colin Hook, the Chairman of the Feltrim Names' Association, recorded that a Super Group motion to adjourn the Lloyd's EGM was lost, with 13,297 votes against and only 6,579 in favour. Lloyd's EGM motions were carried by 12,000 votes to some 650 votes against. Consequently, the bylaws adopted by Council on 8 September were passed, allowing corporate vehicles to subscribe underwriting capital to Lloyd's.

Mr Justice Saville's recent judgement on 12 October was that Members' Agents were contractually responsible to their Names for the misdeeds of Managing Agents. He also confirmed that Managing Agents were themselves liable in tort. On 20 October, in a further judgement on an Outhwaite case, he decided that the exception to the normal six-year rule of limitation based upon deliberate concealment could apply where the acts of deliberate concealment arose after the acts allegedly constituting the breach of duty.

The finance panel had agreed to reimburse the expenses of Action Groups in the proposed settlement. To achieve commonality, the Working Party wanted estimated information about outstanding legal and professional liabilities, as well as administration costs. A provision of £20 per head for the Super Group to cover newsletters, ongoing monitoring and costs of winding up the Action Group should be included. Add in also the cost of a 'thank you' dinner for the Committee and key persons. Some Committees had been purely voluntary and some provision for an honorarium should be calculated. However, success fees were not allowable.

The Association's new leading counsel, Nicholas Strauss QC, was of the view that there was no advantage in hearing questions of time-bar separately from other Association issues. Counsel for the defendants took the same view. The trial would commence on 21 February 1994. In an article in the *Independent* on 2 November the defendants designated the Association's case as 'weak'. This was based on the defendants' assumption that the claims were time-barred. But for this assumption the case would be 'strong'. David Tiplady believed that the Association would have the sympathy of the court when seeking to establish that the defendants' assumption was ill-founded.

David Tiplady wrote to Clive about Michael Turner, the former deputy and principal underwriter of Syndicate 334 and an Association Member. As such he was a plaintiff. Pulbrook Underwriting Management had indicated that they would be seeking to recover from him all their loss should they be found liable for damages. If he withdrew from litigation, it was anticipated, they would not take this step. He had given a witness statement to the Association and his evidence could be very important. David's view was that Michael Turner should be allowed to resign. He also thought the Association should not sign the Super Group memorandum of agreement seeking a negotiating period up to 15 January. Only five weeks later the Association would be in court. If the Kerr–Morse Panel offer was rejected, negotiations may be taking place in advance of the trial. David explained that the Association's interests were not the same as some in big Action Groups in the Super Group. Unsurprisingly, Clive wrote on 15 November indicating that the Kerr–Morse Panel conclusions may be subject to slippage.

Alasdair Ferguson circulated his paper on future losses of the downward spiral of Merrett Holdings PLC, using Chatset predictions. The increased predicted losses were derived from a telephone call with Charles Sturge, the joint Editor of Chatset.

Numbers of Names

Syndicates	90/82	334/85
Names in both Action Groups	200	200
Names in one Action Group	138	166
Total number of Action Group Names	**338**	**366**
Names not in Action Group	140	196
Total number of Names on syndicate	**478**	**562**

Past and Future Losses

Syndicates	90 (including 82)		334 (including 85)	
	Syndicate	Action Group	Syndicate	Action Group
Stamp £m	17.0	12.0	17.7	11.6
Losses to date £m	(77.5)	(54.7)	(42.8)	(28.1)
Loss as a % of line	456	456	242	242
Predicted future loss £m	(289)	(204)	(106)	(70)
Future loss as a % of line	1,700	1,700	600	600
Predicted total loss £m	**(366)**	**(259)**	**(149)**	**(98)**
As a % of line	2,156	2,156	842	842

The table clearly showed extreme losses, with 842% loss on Syndicate 334 escalating to 2,156% loss for Syndicate 90. The Association had a 65% Membership of the syndicate, whilst that for Syndicate 90 was 70%. The high percentage of Members taking action reflected the dire circumstances of many and the desperate urgency to achieve an acceptable, fair settlement cannot be overstressed.

Legal action by the Association was summarised. The first claim arose from the successful arbitration and avoidance by Syndicate 418 of an unlimited run-off reinsurance. The second claim was a failure to leave open 1979 and later years prior to 1985. The defendants were Matthews Wrightson Pulbrook and Pulbrook Underwriting Management Ltd and other Members' Agents. The first claim was for quantum, £81.2 million less any increase in the premium or excess. There was no estimated value of the second claim. A schedule showed the Names on Syndicate 334 by the different Names' Agencies and an analysis by Members of the Association. Of the 562 Names on the syndicate, 420 were with Matthews Wrightson Pulbrook which had been renamed Willis Faber & Dumas (Agencies) and of these 298 were Association Members. The total Association Membership was 366. Information about Members' Agents revealed that some were subsidiaries of large groups while four were inactive or not trading. None of the Agents had significant reserves according to their recent financial statements.

Newsletter, November 1993

Clive drew attention to an article in the *Independent* which classed the Association's case as 'weak' based on the views of the defendant's solicitors which were influenced by the effect of the statute of limitations. Were it not for that assumption, the case would have been classified as 'strong'? The erstwhile leading counsel, Jonathan Mance QC, had become a judge, and the new leading counsel was Nicholas Strauss QC. The Commercial Court had given directions that time-bar and other issues should be tried together.

The Lloyd's settlement offer (LSO) was to be posted to each Name separately. The Super Group believed the first offer would be unsatisfactory. Lloyd's needed a high acceptance level to demonstrate to corporate capital that it had the old-year litigation under control. If an Association Member accepted the offer, it may be a breach of contract with other Association Members. The Association's litigation would commence on 21 February 1994 in the Commercial Court and if the Association won there would be a cash settlement.

Mr C. A. Coward of London thought that pressure was being applied by a veiled threat regarding a potential breach of contract on Members who may not concur with Clive's views. Clive informed him that this was a risk the Committee took to state unambiguously the correct legal position. Had it not done so the Committee could well have been accused of failing in its duty. The offending paragraph in the newsletter had been carefully drafted by the Association's legal advisers. Furthermore, it was clear that Lloyd's would deliver a global settlement of greatest advantage to the Market and may be divisive as far as External Names were concerned. Mr J. A. Kalms pointed out that the Association was suing for damages which would be paid free of tax whereas any settlement receipt would be taxable. John Munford thought the disgraceful practices of some syndicates should be aired through the courts. He expressed appreciation for the Committee's efforts and would accept its decision regarding any offer.

Michael Goold of West Hagley said he would not sign anything until he heard from Clive. He stated his requirements, including, most importantly, a cap for protection against future losses. In addition, the 1986 and prior years insured into NewCo should be ring-fenced and subsequent years reinsured into a suitable vehicle, such as CentreWrite. An offer somewhere between 40p and 50p in the pound subject to the limitation of future losses would be acceptable. Although suffering large losses as a Member of Syndicates 90, 418, 540 and 847 as well as some other semiduds, he was fortunate in having some means and a business to sustain him. He would not shed any tears for Stephen Merrett and indeed had a feeling of schadenfreude uppermost in his mind.

Dr John Maxwell, a London physician, was not prepared to accept credits; it should be cash or nothing. He thought Feltrim would go bust and this would prevent him accepting any 'all in' offer. He said he was ready to go bankrupt and could not see any other reasonable solution. Do not be too soft on Merrett, he advised, as leopards do not change their spots. He said Clive was doing a great job and suggested Clive should 'hang Merrett by his balls before he grabbed Clive's'. Clive replied, informing John that his views would be circulated to Committee Members. Hardship seemed to Clive to be a more attractive option than going bankrupt.

Mr D. H. Crisp of Poole had applied to Hardship two years before but no agreement had yet been signed. The agreement would strip him of his remaining assets, including half his house, and kill virtually all his income. He would welcome any settlement that would give some hope of ending this seemingly endless sorry business. Clive responded that in his view the term 'settlement' was a bit of a euphemism implying finality which LSO did not give.

Mr M. R. Pitt said: 'I have been a Name for fifteen years and had a record of constantly increasing losses which were now unquantified. I am also a Member of Syndicate 418 (1985) Names Association having written £70,000 line in 1985. Departments at Lloyd's are not replying to my letters about interest on late payments.' It seems Mr Pitt was corresponding with the wrong department at Lloyd's. As a Name he should have given instructions to his Agent on what payments to make. If they failed to comply and he suffered loss or damage, he would be entitled to reclaim the loss from his Agents.

Clive reported on 8 December 1993 that the Super Group chairmen voted overwhelmingly to recommend that the LSO was rejected. Christopher Stockwell said he had been misled by Peter Middleton who had promised negotiations that had not taken place prior to release of the offer. The Morse Panel had five dissenting members whose views had been ignored. The prospect of taking Lloyd's to the European court was hotting up. This would mean that Lloyd's would be unlikely to get any properly advised Name to court for a debt hearing for years to come. A letter from the Super Group gave several reasons for refusing the settlement offer particularly as the offer did not cap losses and meant surrendering the right to sue Lloyd's. The offer was less than the Errors & Omissions underwriters' liability and the method of payment was unfair as Errors & Omissions underwriters had finality, but the Names did not. The Super Group's belief was that Names had been the innocent victims of one of the greatest confidence tricks the country had ever seen and recommended that Names should not pay money to Lloyd's without a court order against them.

On 9 December Charles Baron wrote to Sir Peter Tapsell MP about some Canadian Names who were in the UK court, with a number of preliminary issues on writs issued against Lloyd's. Lloyd's response was that it had *no obligation to act in good faith* in respect of its relationship with Names. Astonishingly, this demolished Lloyd's unique selling point that insurance is about acting in good faith which implied good faith towards insured employees and Names. Charles said it was remarkable that a major City institution stated that it was not bound to tell the truth to, nor behave honestly with, its investors. Could the country afford a drain on its balance of payments which placed continuing employment of its insiders so far above its external investors? The losses also depleted the Exchequer resulting from the clawback by loss-making Names from the Inland Revenue.

Clive was bombarded by letters and phone calls expressing severe disappointment and dismay at the terms of the LSO. He could not help circulating the following unattributed copy letter he received describing a recycling use for the documentation.

*A **Nameless Name of The Old Vicarage, Stoneybroke, Bankrupts, SH1T 4Q2**, wrote to the Chairman, David Rowland, to thank him for the settlement offer. He said it was document for which he and his wife had found a domestic use. He had two objections, the paper was too thick and shiny, and there were no perforations where the pages joined the spine. He asked if the omissions could be rectified in future offers. It would not only save costs but contribute further amenity to his hard-pressed household.*

Clive said he knew it was from a Member of the Association. Some recipients thought it was extremely rude while others thought it was supremely apposite.

The *Sunday Telegraph* of 12 December reported that the Chairmen of Lloyd's Action Groups that rejected Lloyd's £900 million offer would be sued. Chairmen of the biggest claimants including Gooda Walker and Feltrim Syndicates had rejected the LSO. Clive Francis was offered £700,000 to set against a claim of £2 million and spoke for many in rejecting the offer. E&O underwriters had had their losses capped but the LSO did not cap Names' losses. Companies, market reinsurers, such as Munich Re, said they would meet claims determined by the settlement offer if the settlement went through.

Clive wrote to the Committee on 13 December saying that all Committee Members thought the settlement offer should be rejected and should consider whether the Association should hold a Special General Meeting (SGM). The Association's Rules did not require an SGM, however, it could be argued that the cogency of the decision might be greater if taken by an SGM. Dissenters would find it more difficult to complain about the consequences of their dissent. Jasper Salisbury-Jones suggested that any Association Members wishing to accept the LSO could buy themselves out of the Association by making a contribution in cash. The following day David Tiplady needed the Committee's approval to the agreed facts prepared by counsel for the High Court of Justice by 15 – that's tomorrow! Of *concern* was a requirement to agree a paragraph that '*all Names are taken to know the customs and practices of the Lloyd's Market at all material times*'. No Name could sign it truthfully. It was suspected to be a bit of bureaucratic legalese and probably could not be upheld if tested in court.

Lord Wrenbury, a retired solicitor, said there were two ways of drawing a contract – firstly, one with solicitors acting on both sides able to debate and cut out anything that was unacceptable to their client, and, secondly, sometimes the document was to be signed by laymen whom one knew would either not fully understand it or have no opportunity of altering the document before signing it. The LSO fell between two stools. It was addressed to laymen but on the other hand it constituted one of the most brilliantly one-sided documents it had ever been his privilege to read. It was extremely competently drawn, which made it even more dangerous. Paraphrasing the Book of Genesis, chapter 25, it was *'The birth right which you give up.'* Lord Wrenbury concluded that a Lloyd's special credit would be given, over which Names would have no control and whose amount could be varied after acceptance. Every 'vulture' in Lloyd's would be entitled to first pick. Names would give up the right to continue litigation or to sue Lloyd's. It would also give up the best chance of forcing Lloyd's to reconsider the necessity for a cap on future liabilities. Subsequently, a Name would not be able to claim having been induced to accept the LSO based on incorrect information. Everything would be done on a confidential basis and no one owed any 'accepting Name' a duty of care or was responsible to him for their actions.

Newsletter, December 1993

The December 1993 newsletter informed the Association that five Members of the Morse Panel refused to endorse its findings. The arguments for rejection of the LSO were admirably set out by Lord Wrenbury, Deputy Chairman of Merrett Syndicate 418 Names Association. Total E&O reserves were much greater than the £400 million indicated in the LSO which was all that could be afforded, according to David Rowland. The Committee unanimously recommended rejection. The future position was complicated by those who 'can't pay/won't pay' and the remaining Names would also need to fund those losses as well. There were 3,000 angry American Names litigating and Lloyd's was unlikely to receive more than their deposits. There were likely to be increasing levies to be paid to the Central Fund. Lloyd's had said that anyone considering applying for Hardship should accept the LSO, otherwise they would be unlikely to receive a Hardship proposal. This might be considered as immoral blackmail and wholly improper, indicating the desperation of Lloyd's for the acceptance of its inequitable offer. Clive indicated that a formula would be devised so that those Members wishing to leave the Association could do so but not to the disadvantage of those remaining. A questionnaire was included with the newsletter requesting information about the way Members proposed to vote.

Twentieth Steering Committee Meeting, 22 December 1993

David Tiplady said that counsel Nicholas Strauss QC would be willing to meet the Committee. The court hearing would commence on 21 February 1994. Most of the work had been completed. In a recent judgement Mr Justice Saville decided that Members' Agents were responsible for the deeds of Managing Agents and Managing Agents were responsible to Names. *Hansard* reports could be read to determine what Parliament intended when proposing legislation, such as the Lloyd's Act 1982. Saville had handed over his responsibilities to Mr Justice Cresswell. David Tiplady said Cresswell had ruled in favour of his D J Freeman clients in every case. While Cresswell hinted that he would not permit a dash for cash, Syndicate 334 Association was not targeting the same E&O pot as other Action Groups. A cash payment on winning the case would be paid to the Name concerned. In Hardship cases Lloyd's would have to extract the money from the Name.

Some £910,000 of the Association's cash had been placed on deposit over the festive period until 4 January 1994 at an interest rate of 5.19% per annum. Two invoices had been received from D J Freeman totalling £115,000 and were returned to be adjusted for the VAT recovery on overseas Members. About 15% of Members were from overseas. David Tiplady indicated that the brief fee for the silk would be £75,000 – £37,500 for a junior and £2,000 per day for the court hearing. Expert witnesses might amount to £50,000. He confirmed that the court would not order any individual or subgroup to pay the shortfall of costs if the Association were to lose the case. Michael Jump had left the Committee for fear of such an outcome.

Clive mentioned that he had received an offer from Lloyd's addressed to him personally as well as one as Chairman of the Association. Lloyd's was attempting to receive as many proxies as possible to lessen the impact of Action Groups. Clive mentioned that the response received from Names were twelve to one for rejecting the Lloyd's settlement offer and continuing with litigation. Guy Wilson stated that 299 of 300 Names on the Janson Green Action Group (a member of LNAWP) voted in favour of rejection.

David Tiplady wrote to the Committee on 23 December with details of fees that he had negotiated including lead counsel from £75,000 to £55,000 and junior counsel from £35,000 to £30,000. When the defendants' costs were taken into account, he estimated a possible saving of £55,000. A few days later Alasdair Ferguson suggested a possible additional levy from Association Members. He thought that if a levy was made after the case was lost it was probable many would not pay. If there was a shortfall, the defendants would show no mercy and might seek payment from Committee Members. He concluded that the Association must have enough funds to cover all costs in fighting and losing the case. Subsequently, David proposed a 5% levy.

On 3 January 1994 Clive explained to the Committee that there were diverse views about the financial position. Some said David set the budget and he was stuck with it, while others thought that more money should be raised now, up to 5% of line. Over the Christmas break newspaper perception was that Lloyd's had made a 'right old shambles of the numerical element' of the LSO with mistakes as to 'quantum', being the amount, for practically every personal offer. David thought this may lead to an extension to the acceptance date deadline and had drafted a post-deadline newsletter for comment. The Association had received only twenty-nine requests for an EGM, and it was proposed not to hold one. Doubts had been raised about the classification of the Association's case in the LSO.

Clive wrote to Association Members to thank them for their rapid response to the last newsletter and return of the questionnaire. There was overwhelming support for rejection of the LSO. Clive realised some Members felt isolated and lonely and may be only too glad to discuss matters other than with the Agent who many suspected of talking their own book. He would be pleased to discuss matters, preferring weekdays before 5 pm.

John Charnley of Shedfield, in a letter in *The Times*, queried why those applying for Hardship must accept the LSO. By not accepting the LSO the Names were not doing all they could to reduce their losses according to Lloyd's, but this was a false argument. Accepting the offer would still leave many Names insolvent several times over. Litigation offered a better prospect, suggesting that Lloyd's and the Hardship Committee would benefit in four ways: the amount gained may be greater, none of the money would have come from the Central Fund, new funds would come to Lloyd's after a successful action against the E&O insurers and only by a court decision would the E&O insurers be obliged to meet their liabilities in full. A commentary in the same paper said cracks were beginning to appear in the corporate capital veneer of the Lloyd's Insurance Market. Abtrust, one of a new breed of limited-liability investors, was forced to scale back its underwriting from £50 million of premiums to £38.3 million. There were two points of view, firstly, to congratulate the management in holding back from joining some of the poorer-quality syndicates or, secondly, to take umbrage on the failure to win adequate capacity on the Markets' best syndicates. 'City Diary' in the same paper reported the average age of a Lloyd's Name was fifty-eight years. In ten years, 50% would be dead and the Market would be in the hands of corporate capital companies. It promulgated that it was time to buy shares – received wisdom suggested that it was time to buy shares when share prices were low with prospects of an increased return. As the insurance premiums were rising with a turning Market, Lloyd's could be a good bet for corporate capital. It was doubtful that 50% of Names would be dead in ten years as males could have a life expectancy possibly for another twenty years and females slightly longer.

Alasdair Ferguson circulated a paper on 7 January titled, 'Finance for Legal Action', quoting the Association's Rules which stated, *'subject to directions by resolution in General Meeting the affairs shall be controlled and directed by the Committee which shall have absolute discretion vested in it. However, the Committee shall not commence any authorised proceedings unless satisfied that the funds are sufficient to defray the costs.'* He predicted that costs of the action for a four-week trial, and defendants' costs if the case was lost, were £1,040,000, and for a seven-week trial £1,170,000. Non-legal costs may amount to £10,745 and interest receivable at £28,000. He indicated that a levy of 3% would raise £348,000 and a 5% levy £580,000. He argued that if the case was won the money could be refunded within three months. He proposed to threaten that failure to pay the levy would mean that a Member would not benefit if the case was won. The procedure for realising the levy was set out.

The timing of the Kerr–Morse offer resulted in a dilemma. The Association should either seek to postpone the date of the hearing from 21 February or call a General Meeting and resolve to increase subscriptions as soon as possible by giving three weeks' notice. The earliest date for a meeting would be 4 February 1994.

Twenty-first Steering Committee Meeting, 13 January 1994: Strengthening Funding

The Steering Committee met at D J Freeman's Offices and discussed legal costs. The budget had been set when David Tiplady's hourly rate was £160 per hour and that had increased to £220 per hour plus VAT. It had been agreed that D J Freeman's fees would be rendered monthly, but this had not occurred since May 1993.

Alasdair argued the case for a levy and provided a timetable with a timeline for the fund-raising procedure. It was resolved to raise 6% of line forthwith. A postal ballot would be required. David said that the defendants had privately admitted that the Association's case was strong subject to the limitation argument and reported that the QC was tremendously bullish. The judge hearing the case had changed to Mr Justice Potter. It was agreed to inform the press that the Committee had recommended rejection of the LSO. Fifty-nine Members had indicated they would go into Hardship.

Newsletter, January 1994

Clive wrote to Association Members on 13 January stating that the assessment of the Association's case as weak by the Kerr Panel was a curious one. The Committee was entirely convinced of its merit but concluded that the Association's coffers should be strengthened. It was concerned that the defendants might be tempted to run the Association out of money by filibustering tactics in the courtroom. A further subscription of 6% of line should be called. The Association's rules required an endorsement by ballot and a ballot paper was enclosed with the letter.

A doggerel, which is a comic verse with an irregular rhythm, was circulated:

The Man from Lloyd's or The Lay of the Last Name

The Duke, the Knight, the country gent
inherited their wealth
their lands, their farms, their country seats,
quite openly, no stealth.

'I'll show you how to make much more',
he said, 'and help old England too,
just pledge the ruddy lot to me.
You'll see what I can do',
said the man from Lloyd's.

Young Ginny was a tennis player,
my goodness she could play.
She did us proud at Wimbledon
that great and glorious day.

I see you've made a bob or two
he said 'Don't give it all away
in tax or whatever else you do.
Give it me. Hooray, hooray',
said the man from Lloyd's.

Henry was a fighter
the best that England sired
he fought his way right to the top
and cleanly, too, not mired.

'I hear you've got some surplus cash',
he said, 'just let me show
what I can do, you'll see,
I'll make it grow and grow',
said the man from Lloyd's.

John had worked hard all his life
and left Jane well provided.
At least she'd have no money strife
After he decided

To shuffle off this mortal coil.
He said, 'Now don't you fret,
my dear, you needn't toil,
trust me, see what you'll get',
said the man from Lloyd's.

Charlie's dad had never earned
above four quid a week,
so, when Charles sold his business
for a million, he could scarcely speak;

but how to keep it safe
and not to get too fat,
'Just give it all to me
and I'll take care of that',
said the man from Lloyd's.

The Duke, the Knight, the country gent,
brave Ginny, Henry* too,
the widow Jane and Charlie,
their millions went down the loo.

And thousands more, some rich, now poor
all taken for a ride,
So many who could take no more
with some driven to suicide
by the man from Lloyd's.

So many who could take no more
just signed their settlement offers
and queued at Hardship's stony door
so empty were their coffers.

'My powers of attornee – hee,'
he said, 'I'll wave at you
I am your new Committee – hee,
I've got your lawful funds too',
said the man from Lloyd's.

Epilogue
'If the Lord hadn't wanted them shorn,
he wouldn't have made them sheep,'
said the man from Lloyd's.

by Charles Baron (son of Cassandra)

---

* This might refer to Virginia Wade and Henry Cooper, who were Names.

Summary of Key Issues

1. Continued pressure on MPs and Ministers.

2. Comments made about Sir David Walker's 1992 report.

3. Open year and finalisation issues were considered.

4. The Association Rules changed to allow payment to Committee Members.

5. Communications streamed from Names expressing frustration and stress at delays in getting to Court.

6. Bailey of Keene Corporation detailed his experiences.

7. Concerns were expressed about the shortage of judges, the commercial list and trial date.

8. Estimates, double counting and speculations on losses resulted in fears of Lloyd's collapse.

9. Commentaries received on Lloyd's business plan and Springbett suggestions.

10. Submissions made to the Kerr & Morse Panels.

11. Lloyd's EGM approved Corporate Capital.

12. Lloyd's settlement offer was rejected.

13. E&O and asset were considered for funding recoveries.

CHAPTER 6

Action in Her Majesty's High Court of Justice

English Camp
Of fighting men they have full three score thousand
There's five to one; besides they all are fresh.
God's arm strike with us! 'tis a fearful odds.

Henry V, Act 4 Scene 3

Adam Raphael, the Association's Committee Member and the Chairman of Syndicate 90 (1982) Names Association, wrote to his Members on 19 January 1994 that there was an overwhelming majority in favour of rejecting the Lloyd's settlement offer following the SGM of the Syndicate 90 Association. He said that his Association would be pressing ahead with litigation and there would be a need for further funding to cover defendants' costs should the case be lost.

John Rosser FCA, a retired Senior Partner of a firm of Chartered Accountants and a Devonshire Committee Member, had been appointed to enquire into insolvency or impending insolvency of Members' Agents, and to protect the interests of Names in liquidation proceedings. A meeting was proposed to explore the possible appointment of a specialist liquidator.

The Syndicate 334 Association received a fee note from Simon Morgan Associates regarding the issue of a press release on 20 January. The firm had contacted eight representatives of the press including *The Times*, *Daily Telegraph*, *Guardian*, *Financial Times*, the Press Association, Reuters, the *Wall Street Journal* and *Lloyd's List*. Press coverage was very important in getting the message out about Names' difficulties and the serious circumstances affecting them at Lloyd's.

Clive said in a letter on 28 January to the Association's Membership that ninety-seven Members voted in favour of raising more money and ten against. Thus, there would be a cash call of 6% of line on or before 17 February. The result of the Gooda Walker and Feltrim meetings echoed the Association's ballot in rejecting the Lloyd's offer. One Gooda Walker Member described the offer as 'having more strings attached to it than a parachute and none of the lifesaving qualities'. Clive commented that the use of the word 'settlement' in the Lloyd's offer without capping was nothing of the sort. It was the duty of the Committee to point out that those Association Members whose own circumstances dictated that they should accept the offer would breach the undertaking they gave on joining the Association. Lloyd's may seek to use accepting Names' powers of attorney and thwart the wishes of the Association. To protect the litigating interests of all the non-accepting Association Members, those who accepted the offer in breach of the Association's Rules would be deemed defaulters. The defaulters would lose the right to vote.

The January edition of *Inside Eye* published an extended article titled, 'The Long-tails of Woe'. Cash calls were being made on new generations of Names who joined after 1995 due to chronic under-reserving in earlier years. There were no short-cuts on long-tail claims and this tail was long. Heidi Hutter, director of project NewCo for Lloyd's old and open years, said the difficulty right now was to offer a cap when she had no basis to back it. The American courts were holding that asbestosis was a continuing injury to a person's body. All insurers who provided coverage from the time of the initial exposure to the time of manifestation of the disease were jointly and severally liable to defend and indemnify the insured, if liability was established. There was little public sympathy for polluters and insurers in America, where insurers were held in low esteem. In addition, punitive damages or clean-up costs may be awarded where there were perceptions of deceit or deliberate misfeasance.

Clive circulated a paper on 9 February 1994 on topics for discussion prepared by the Association's counsel, Nicholas Strauss QC.

The issues for decision were:

1. whether the Managing Agents owed Names a duty of care
2. whether Managing Agents were negligent:
   (a) in describing £540,000 long-tail liabilities as short-tail such as cargo
   (b) in failing to disclose certain or likely liabilities on Johns Manville lines totalling $895,000
   (c) in failing to disclose 'block reserves' for asbestosis and DES of $450,000 and $600,000 respectively
3. whether, if these matters were disclosed, there would have been reinsurance and, if so, on what terms
4. whether, if the Managing Agents were liable, the Members' Agents (who were not personally negligent) were also liable

Issues not being dealt with at the forthcoming hearing were the claims in respect of the closing of 1978–84 years of account and associated amount of loss.

Twenty-Second Steering Committee Meeting, 10 February 1994

At a Meeting of the Steering Committee which was held in D J Freeman's offices, Nicholas Strauss QC said the Association needed to win on all four points. He was reasonably confident of winning them and if so, an interim payment would be requested. Post-1981 Names could only succeed against Managing Agents. Chairman Clive said it was the first time that he realised that post-1981 Names could not go against Members' Agents, only against underwriting Managing Agents as they were not time-barred.

Clive wrote to David Tiplady on 16 February that the Association had received sustained advice that the case was strong and unlikely to be time-barred. He was dismayed and astonished, almost amounting to disbelief, as he read and listened to Mr Strauss's dissertation about the

Association's case. As the law was unclear with difficulties outlined by Mr Strauss it appeared that the only cause for redress was tort. The case might have to go to the House of Lords. Apart from fifteen Members of the Association whose agreements were under seal, some 207 Members of the Association of the syndicate in 1981 were time-barred and, despite having a strong case, they had no hope of restitution under contract. The remainder of the Association had no case at all. Clive wanted to know how David reconciled his advice with Mr Strauss's paper.

David replied that from the Strauss presentation it would be extremely difficult to tell the wood from the trees, unless one was an expert in this area of the law. Nevertheless, subject to emphasis and style of presentation, Mr Strauss's advice was substantially the same as his.

David said there were two obstacles to progress; the first obstacle was the time-bar. It would be necessary to prove that Members' Agents owed a duty in tort. This point should have been determined in the Merrett/Gooda Walker/Feltrim preliminary issue hearing last year. The Agents were unable to agree the necessary basic facts and the point was left open. It was now up to the Association to settle the point. Mr Strauss pointed out that whole area of Lloyd's litigation was one where very few direct precedents had been established. Those who joined after 1981 could hardly blame their Members' Agents for events which occurred during 1981, when the Agency relationship had yet to be established.

The second obstacle identified at the outset concerned the three grounds of nondisclosure on which the arbitration panel found in favour of Merrett Syndicate 418. It would be necessary to show that Pulbrook Underwriting Management was negligent in all three. He was confident of two and the Association's experts' opinions gave him great encouragement regarding the third. The Association must also satisfy the court that Syndicate 418 would have written the policy albeit on somewhat different terms. David said there were circumstances where close links between Matthews Wrightson Pulbrook Names Agency and Pulbrook Underwriting Management would be legally relevant. The Association was asserting that each Members' Agent owed a nondelegable duty of care to their Names. This was broken when the Sub-Agent Matthews Wrightson Pulbrook failed to place the reinsurance properly.

However, David said the fact that Matthews Wrightson Pulbrook Underwriting Management had common directors with the Matthews Wrightson Names Agency was highly significant in connection with Syndicate 90 No. 2 claims to which Salisbury-Jones and Charles Baron were parties, but common directorships were irrelevant to the Syndicate 334 claim. The whole area of Lloyd's litigation was fraught with difficulty and the Association's case was no exception.

The Association's Financial Accounts for the year ended 31 January 1993 showed total subscriptions received to date were £1,118,500, of which funds available were £679,504. There were concerns that the funding was insufficient should the case be lost and an additional 6% subscription had been agreed, totalling 16% of line amounting to some £1.7 million.

Financial Accounts for the Year Ended 31 January 1993

Details	£	£
Subscriptions at 10% of line		1,118,500
Net receipts during year		539,850
Interest and recoveries		52,608
Total receipts		592,458
Less expenses		
D J Freeman	-136,786	
Other	-40,820	
Total expenses		-177,606
Excess of income over expenses		414,852
Add balance from 1992		264,652
Funds available 31 January 1993		**679,504**

Clive circulated highly confidential information to the Committee on 19 February 1994 saying the Association received an offer of £11 million. It was similar to one whispered some months ago. On the principle of not accepting the first offer the new offer was politely rejected with the message that the Committee was prepared to listen. It was stressed that the offer must be kept confidential at this stage as tactically it was wiser not to exploit in public that an offer had been made. Receiving an offer highlighted two problems, firstly, to assess the value of the offer and, secondly, dealing with the nonpayers of the 6% levy. The Committee needed to consider how to ensure any cash by settlement, offer or judgement could safely be consigned into the intended hands without being intercepted or delayed in any way by Lloyd's.

Newsletter, February 1994

Clive announced that the court case would commence at 10 am on Thursday, 24 February in the Royal Courts of Justice, the Strand, London, in front of Mr Justice Potter. The hearing would last some four weeks and be heard on Mondays to Thursdays. The judgements of Mr Justice Saville on vicarious responsibility of Members' Agents and the rights of Names to sue their Agents both in contract and in tort were subsequently robustly upheld in the Court of Appeal.

Clive said:

> Few of us meeting to form the Association in July 1990 would have believed that it would take more than three and a half years to get to court. Nor did many of us fully comprehend the severity of the Lloyd's debacle. The Committee was greatly encouraged by the immediate response to the additional levy of 6% of line. The Committee hoped that the results of the case would alleviate the financial distress of an increasing number of Names in considerable measure.

Chairman Clive faxed the Committee on 22 February to say that twenty-six of the Association's Members had died although their Estates were maintaining an interest in Membership.

Providing two tables of detailed calculations Alasdair Ferguson faxed Clive concerning the amounts that might be received by the Association's Members. He said:

> For me, an acceptable offer to the Association would total over £20 million or 200% of line. My view is, those Association Members in Hardship or proposing to apply for Hardship, should not receive any offer or award. For Names in Hardship any award would be paid directly to Lloyd's and not have any direct benefit to the individual. Consequently, excluding Hardship Names from the award would give a larger sum to the remainder.

A very important contrary point was made, that if the award was very substantial it might remove some Hardship Names from Hardship, which would be grossly unfair.

On 22 Adam Raphael had raised a condition of the Members' Hardship Committee that all litigation recoveries must be turned over by the Name to the Members' Hardship Committee. He asked, what was the point of 6% defaulters claiming Hardship to remain on board without paying the Association's levy? Any recovery would be of no net benefit to an Association Member in Hardship. Should the Association not be rigid in the application of its Rules, thus enabling the pot to be shared out between fewer Members? This in turn could allow the Association to accept a lower figure should a further offer be made.

There was a countervailing argument that the Association's Committee had a duty to do its best for its Members. It was not the business of the Association to inquire into the destination of litigation recoveries.

David Tiplady rang Clive on Friday, 23 February to say the offer had been increased to £20 million. The Association's legal advisers were recommending acceptance of the offer. Clive phoned Jasper who very kindly left his billet to hotfoot to Tiplady's office, where he acted as anchor man for the afternoon and evening. John Rew of Chatset thought the net present value of future losses was in the region of £30 million to

£45 million. If the Association obtained a sum in the region of £21 million
to £28 million it would have obtained 75% of the objective without a
shot. The Committee agreed to propose a counter-offer of £24 million,
although Harry Purchase said this was not enough and Charles Baron
suggested £35 million. Of 362 Members there were 104 who had not paid
the final levy and could shortly be declared defaulters. Some of these had
resigned and some may be so deeply in Hardship, like Clive, that there
was no point in carrying them. However, Clive had paid the 6% subscription. If defaulters were excluded there would be a bigger pot to share
amongst those remaining. The fact an offer was made to the Association
was broadcast all over the Market.

Clive informed the Committee on Wednesday, 28 February, 'All offers
have been withdrawn without explanation. However, the Association
had a good day in court with the judge making sympathetic noises. The
Association won an order to obtain documents from Winchester Bowring,
which they were appealing. In the meantime, the Association's representatives had access to the documents.' It was reported in the *Daily Telegraph*
on 4 March that 'Talks to Settle Names Case Fail'. Negotiations to settle
the Lloyd's Pulbrook case were thought to have collapsed on Monday.
Insurers acting for Managing Agents refused Names' demands over
£20 million. Market insiders suggested the insurers were reluctant to
settle for fear of sending signals of weakness to other litigants. The House
of Lords would hear an appeal on whether Members' Agents were liable
for Managing Agents' alleged negligence on 15 March.

John Rew of Chatset had provided a formal Opinion on 23 February
1994 that the total present value of the loss would be in the region of
£70 million to £80 million for the 362 Association Members. He provided
Clive with detailed Chatset workings on 3 March. In the Chatset reports
he had standardised the IBNR. For Syndicate 334 there was a heavy
element of outstandings relating to pollution and little was known about
the cash flow. However, his calculations compared favourably with the
CentreWrite quotations. The Treasurer wrote to John Rew to thank him
for the fax to Clive with the workings and asked him what sum should

be made available today to cover his calculated £94.9 million shortfall. Also, he asked for the probable timing for payment of claims. It was difficult to reconcile his net present value of £21 million to £28 million with potential losses indicated in the 4 March *Daily Telegraph* story of £152 million. The hawkish majority of the Association's Committee thought every penny should be claimed.

Clive wrote to the Committee with his agenda items for a Committee Meeting that could be long and contentious, including dealing with Hardship cases, considering the size of an acceptable offer as Lloyd's appeared to be failing, and the possibility of forming a trust to distribute the funds, or to buy a run-off policy.

Following a strongly worded letter on 7 March demanding the final tranche of 6%, a second rather mollifying letter was sent to Association Members experiencing genuine financial distress. The Committee was concerned that no Member of the Association should suffer from the right to recover any damages through an inability to pay the final 6% tranche due to genuine financial hardship. It was proposed form a 'genuine distress subcommittee' to examine the merits of each waiver application.

Clive had attended court for three of the six days of the hearing and was greatly encouraged by Judge Potter's grasp of Lloyd's affairs. He noted that each clarification or elucidation requested by the judge seemed to point in the Association's favour. Clive said he was a little surprised that Judge Potter had booked a holiday starting the next weekend and that the hearing would finish on Friday, 11 March. He was concerned about those who had failed to pay the 6% tranche. Fifteen applications for waiver had been received. Twenty-eight Members had failed to respond. A letter was sent to defaulting Members.

Information was circularised that subscriptions to the Association were tax-deductible from underwriting profits and would not give rise to any tax liability of the Association. The amounts of any award would be taxable on Names by reference to the date on which the Names became unconditionally entitled to the monies.

Newsletter, March 1994: Judgement Expected after About Six Weeks
On Friday, 11 March 1994 Judge Potter had retired to consider his
judgement which was expected after about six weeks. Members' Agents
had appealed the judgement by Mr Justice Saville that Members'
Agents had vicarious responsibility for the actions of Managing Agents.
Initially, leave to appeal to the House of Lords was refused and the
Members' Agents had to petition the Lords to get a hearing. The Court
of Appeal robustly upheld Mr Justice Saville's judgement. The impact
of the Lords' judgement on the Association's case would be heard at a
further one-day hearing.

The newsletter explained that the Committee had calculated the net
present value for the sum necessary to cover 75% of the Association's
claim and it was not too distant from the £20 million hinted by the
Defence. News of an offer, mentioned above on 23 February, had swept
the Lloyd's Market on the Friday afternoon and by Monday morning
the excitement was intense. Suddenly, mid-morning all offers were
withdrawn. The circumstances surrounding the offer and its abrupt withdrawal remained a mystery.

The response to the levy of 6% contribution was most impressive and
funds should be adequate to withstand an appeal to the Appeal Court and
up to the House of Lords if necessary.

The Treasurer reported the financial position on 9 March 1994 was:

6% call received	£521,103
D J Freeman Fees outstanding	£192,346
Cash balance	£1,454,429

On 15 March Charles Baron suggested that those Names who had
only paid a proportion of the subscription should receive an allocation
of any award in proportion to the amount paid of the total due. The
letter requested a receipt from all Names indicating they understood the
proposed arrangement.

Jasper Salisbury-Jones gave his views:

> It is a serious matter to declare someone a defaulter. I think the
> Committee is vulnerable to attack for not giving twenty-one days
> plus seven days' notice of an SGM. This was the sort of irregularity
> that might be pounced upon by an aggrieved Member. However, in
> view of the overwhelming vote in favour it would be held that any
> defects could be cured by proceeding as if proper notice had been
> given. I recommend that suitable letters are sent out to individual
> nonresponders by recorded delivery, as a final letter giving them a
> fixed time to reply such as, in seven days. Once the time has elapsed
> then the Committee should pass a resolution, by correspondence with
> the Committee Members, declaring the defaulter by name. If a Name
> has applied to Hardship Committee, the Name is entitled to receive
> all litigation awards up until the Hardship Agreement was signed.

He continued, 'I have applied to the Hardship Committee unfortunately.
I would like to request a waiver for the payment of the Association's calls
for subscriptions.'

The Chairman wrote to the Treasurer on 21 March about the nonpayment of the 6% tranche and the resolution passed by the Committee to
apportion an award to the nonpayers in the ratio of amount paid to total
due. A suitable letter to the defaulters was drafted so that no liability
for the decision could be attributed to individual Committee Members.
Consequently, monies should be retained by the Association until a
disclaimer had been received from the relevant Member. There was a list
of sixty-one nonpayers including twelve original Hardship applications
and fifteen new ones, seventeen Members who had not replied, and seventeen who had various reasons for not paying. Three Members had died.
Some of those in genuine distress had written to say how pleased they
were with the decision about Hardship.

Concern had been expressed about the payment of costs should the
Association have insufficient funds. The usual rules regarding liability

would entitle successful defendants to demand payment from any Member or group of Members. This was because responsibility for costs was 'joint and several'. Potentially each plaintiff was responsible for the whole of the costs awarded to the other side, which could be very onerous.

David Tiplady said he had been to see the Chief Taxing Master on 16 March who at first was inclined to endorse the above traditional approach. However, David brought to his attention the 'Guide for Use in Group Actions', produced by the Supreme Court Procedure Committee in May 1991. This was not designed with Lloyd's in mind but would appear applicable. The section on 'Common Liability Costs' described those costs and disbursements incurred in relation to all matters arising from the investigation, pleading, preparation for trial and trial of the common liability issues. Any 'common liability costs' ordered to be paid by the plaintiffs to the defendants should be 'several and limited to that plaintiff's own portion'. The Chief Taxing Master immediately agreed that it should be applied to Lloyd's litigation. He suggested that the Association made an application for the appropriate Order. He added that if the judge had difficulty with the point, he would inevitably bring it to the attention of the Chief Taxing Master who would advise accordingly. He was concerned that the information was not disseminated beyond the Syndicate 334 and 90 Committees. If the defendants got wind of the knowledge, they would do their best to pre-empt or forestall the Association as it might reduce the amount the defendant would receive.

On 12 April 1994 a copy of a letter to Peter Middleton from LNAWP was circulated. Catherine Mackenzie-Smith, an international lawyer, had been investigating conflicts between the American and British legal systems. Supported by counsel, she had formed the view that it was unnecessary to pay many of the claims for asbestosis that were being paid because there was protection by the Protection of Trading Interests Act 1980. Section 5 of the Act prevented the enforcement of 'multiple damages' in their entirety. No court in the United Kingdom could entertain proceedings at common law for the recovery of any sum paid under a judgement awarding multiple damages. Multiple damages were defined as amounts awarded by doubling, trebling or otherwise multiplying a sum assessed as compensation for loss or damage sustained by the person in whose favour the judgement was given. There was little doubt that damages awarded by American state courts against insured producers of asbestos and pollutants fell into the category of 'multiple damages'. Names could see no reason why Lloyd's should go on paying when British law seemed to offer them protection.

Paul Turner, the Managing Director of James Hallam Ltd, wrote to Clive on 19 April regarding Judicial Delay (Judge) Indemnities insurance. The insurance was against the possibility a judge may not be able to hand down their decision, for instance, if the judge died. In that event the case may have to be heard again and result in significant extra costs. The Committee declined the insurance proposal. Additionally, Mr H. Verney FCA also asked if anyone thought the Association should pay insurance should Judge Potter drop dead. No one agreed with the idea.

Lloyd's issued a proposal for Financing Reinsurance Recoveries on 20 April 1994. The aim was to bring liquidity into the Market, reduce Market costs, capture reinsurance debt centrally and speed up the recovery process. The main points included issuing up to $500 million to $1,000 million, five- to seven-year bonds, in sterling, US dollars and Canadian dollars. Finance would be provided to Premiums Trust Funds. Funding would be available at a syndicate level, collateralised by reinsurance recovery collection notes for paid claims. It was planned to implement the proposal in the third quarter of 1994.

The *Daily Telegraph* on 25 April reported an asbestosis shortfall at Lloyd's of £11 billion. Peter Middleton had denied claims that Lloyd's planned to let NewCo go bust. Lloyd's consistently denied that it had a solvency problem. In Lloyd's Annual Report, £661 million had been provided to cover debts owed by insolvent Names. The 1991 losses were forecast at £2.4 to £3 billion. Middleton was reported as earning £324,000 the previous year and David Rowland £472,000. In the same paper there was a headline, 'Names Claim that Lloyd's Could Face Insolvency'.

Judge Potter had said that the judgement on the Syndicate 334 case would not be promulgated until after the Lords had pronounced on the remainder of the vicarious responsibility case. Judgement could be expected in June. David Tiplady said the Lords were unlikely to go against the judgement of two eminent brains in the Appeal Court. However, Jasper Salisbury-Jones concluded that the case had made the judges think, which was a bad sign.

Several Members were applying for Hardship. Amongst them was Michael Cobb, who was rather despondent, writing on 28 April to say he would have to apply to the Hardship Committee or go bust. The £500 subscription to the Association was a better spend than giving it to Lloyd's. Frank Wright's broker sent details of his application to the Hardship Committee with a request that the Association continued legal action on his behalf without paying further subscriptions as agreed by the Committee.

Mr N. D. Pilbrow FCA ATII sought information about Names' affairs, stating there were three options. These were to pay up and trade out, apply to Hardship, or pursue recoveries through Action groups. He promoted the idea of selling an interest in the proceeds of recoveries from successful litigation and had designed a scheme to achieve this outcome for a cost in the region of £800. The Committee rejected this idea.

On 5 May 1994 Stuart Kettle of D J Freeman wrote to LSS regarding five Names who were on the writ but were not Association Members. He sent a statement of monies received by D J Freeman for these Names and would credit the next invoice to the Association with £15,742.17. LSS could then seek payment of additional tranches. Subsequently Clive confirmed that the number of subscription defaulters had reduced to three.

There was a meeting on 13 May between a senior DTI official and Super Group members, Alan Porter and Christopher Stockwell. Some of the DTI responses to questions expressed confidence that Lloyd's would pass the solvency test. The regulatory role as required by Parliament was to protect the interests of policyholders. However, protection of Names was a matter solely for the Council of Lloyd's which had failed the task woefully. There were major problems of quantifying liabilities and no actuary could obtain a premium for cover for an E&O insurance.

Newsletter, May 1994: Power Politics

Clive reminded the readers that he had been at this project for four years. The first meeting was on 6 June 1990.

Mr Justice Potter was awaiting the decision of the House of Lords regarding the Gooda Walker Action Group on Members' Agents vicarious responsibility in contract and the Merrett Syndicate 418 seeking the same in tort. The judgement was expected in late June. Judge Potter's judgement on the Association's case may not be delivered until mid-July. An SGM would be convened to empower the Committee to conduct or resist Appeal proceedings.

The 1993 Syndicate 334 underwriting accounts for 1985 showed that the Syndicate had ceased to trade. In consequence no one had an interest in the future of Syndicate 334 except as a comfortable niche for run-off. The Committee would look very carefully at the management of the run-off with a view to minimising cost to Names. The report gave a very different view of future Syndicate 334 losses, much lower than Chatset estimates which had indicated that 75% of losses were to come. It transpired that if the syndicate received an advice of a claim from United States attorneys which was described as unquantifiable, it was entered in the syndicate books as a zero liability. Hence the discrepancy with Chatset.

Clive said that Michael Deeny had attempted a palace coup at the Super Group to remove Christopher Stockwell as Chairman. For sheer impressive delivery coupled with cogent meaning conveyed per minute of speech, Stockwell far outshone his detractors. He resolutely declined to take any of the procedural lifelines thrown at him by his supporters and insisted on his would-be deposers being allowed to make their case in full. Not only was this a courageous line to take but also a politically astute one. In the end the palace plotters were defeated. The Deeny cabal had seriously misjudged the situation in its election. Speaker after speaker, some shouting with their voices quaking in anger, denounced Deeny's attempt to hijack the meeting for the purpose of deposing Stockwell. Some Super Group Members had been given only a few hours' notice of Deeny's attempt to remove Stockwell as Chairman. Anyone who saw the photograph in the *Daily Telegraph* and the description of Stockwell's supposed resignation from the Chairmanship could not fail to conclude this was a press plant by the Deeny cabal. The plant deliberately sought to present a *fait accompli* to the Chairmen constituents of the Super Group. The report indicated that Stockwell had resigned and this 'unsettled the Market' being detrimental to those trading on at Lloyd's. Deeny claimed to have consulted thirty-seven Chairmen of the Super Group Action Groups' Members but only persuaded twelve to endorse his motion.

Clive noted that another Lloyd's suicide was reported last Friday. He suggested that the Super Group, rather than engaging in constitutional wrangling, should be looking after burnt Names and ignoring those trading on like Deeny, who cheerfully proposed to wave them goodbye.

Although Clive had chided Stockwell for his over-conciliatory approach, he had done a marvellous job. Clive concluded that Stockwell's intellect, character and knowledge coupled with his ability to present a cogent case with great articulation in both written and spoken word made him an outstanding candidate to represent the injured Names on the Council of Lloyd's.

On 1 June, Ms Sheila Glaser of Weybridge contacted Clive, 'May I congratulate you and the Committee for your enthusiasm and tenacity?' Clive replied appreciatively, 'Thank you very much Sheila for your kind words. Committee work is usually a pretty thankless task.'

Stuart Kettle of D J Freeman responded to the Treasurer's enquiry of 9 June about fees and future costs. Estimated future costs came to £300,000. He said appeals to the Appeal Court and House of Lords would not exceed £100,000 resulting in a maximum total estimated future costs of £400,000. Should the Association lose, then usually 75% of the other side's costs would be due, estimated at a maximum of £450,000, making future costs total £850,000 plus provisions for expenses already incurred of £300,000, which came to £1,150,000. The Treasurer reported the cash balances at 16 June 1994 as £1,583,756. This left net funds including interest on deposits of approximately £500,000. This should be sufficient to see the Association through to the end of the legal action. Stuart had provided a list of Names who were on the writ for LSS to check their records.

Arrangements for the planned Committee meeting on 22 June had to be changed because of the prospect of a disruptive rail strike.

Shenton's illustrated cartoon in the *Solicitors Journal* showed a book being read to a child in bed titled '101 Financial Horror Stories', the reader saying 'with losses SO LARGE as to be unquantified'.

The *Solicitors Journal* featured the headline, 'To Pay or Not to Pay? That Is *The* Question for Victim Names.' Solicitors were used to talking to victim Names at Lloyd's and by a combination of tax allowances for losses and recoveries from stop-loss, bankruptcy might be avoided. Names were advised to join Action Groups.

Harry Purchase was strike-bound. However, as planned Clive and Jasper Salisbury-Jones had met Matthews Wrightson Pulbrook officers, John Winter the Managing Director and Donald Chilvers the Non-Executive Chairman, who pointed out that they were new imports and did not represent the 'old order'. However, they appeared to pay out Names' money at Lloyd's say-so, without so much as a question. It was agreed to invite them to the Association's AGM and their proposed presentation should be restricted to explaining the difference between their forecasting and that of Chatset. The Association was not a business but several co-plaintiffs joining together to pursue an action for compensation. The Committee acted on behalf of the whole group for ease of administration. It was not considered to be subject to value-added tax (VAT).

A copy of the private and confidential note of a meeting with Christopher Stockwell and the DTI on 13 May was circulated to a very limited number of Action Group Chairmen. One copy had found its way to the senior DTI official who attended the meeting and upset the senior official who said the Department would have to send a letter rebutting some of the points made. It appeared that the DTI had no concern for the ruined Names or the failure of regulation at Lloyd's but was solely interested in the protection of policyholders. The DTI was accepting Lloyd's figures without a detailed enquiry. The cause of the debate was not served by leaking information.

In a letter to Super Group Members on 21 June, Clive said there was a formidable case to be argued about the Neville Russell letter and the two subsequent Randall drafted letters dated 18 March 1982, which had been sent out under Lloyd's Chairman Murray Lawrence's signature. Roger Bradley was reported to say, 'The wheels came off Lloyd's in 1979 and Lloyd's spent the next seven years trying to cover this up.' Clive suggested that the Super Group should address itself to what was a question of equity and morality. Implicit in this was some form of restitution for ruined Names.

In the House of Lords' debate on 27 June as reported in *Hansard*, Lord Williams of Elvel stressed the importance of Lloyd's. He said Lloyd's had contributed £15 billion to the UK invisible earnings since 1983, averaging 31% of total invisibles. Lloyd's led two-thirds of the insurance written in the London insurance market and employed 60,000 people directly or indirectly. In support of Lord Williams of Elvel, Lord Marlsford said he was a victim of Lloyd's and suggested he shared this situation with over 200 members of the House of Lords. Furthermore, he stated that Lloyd's had a 'public voice' where David Rowland was mentioned in the *Daily Telegraph* of 13 May, stating that 'the solvency situation is good'. However, the 'private voice' stated that the Central Fund had provided £400 million and the greater the delay in recovery proceedings, the greater the risk to Lloyd's solvency and its ability to pay policyholders' valid claims. He added there was a fundamental conflict of interest between the interests of Working Names and External Names.

Following the report in the May newsletter, Clive perceived a continuing political power battle between Christopher Stockwell and Michael Deeny and complained to Stockwell about the direction of the Super Group. He said it was quite wrong that the Super Group's time at this juncture should be consumed in debating the niceties of a neo-trade union charter reminiscent of the last century. Even the Labour Party had got rid of the block vote and this was hardly the time to introduce such an anachronism into the Super Group debate. On 1 July Clive reported to the Committee that Stockwell had been severely attacked by Deeny in what appeared to be a little more than a clash of personalities.

On the same day Clive received a phone call from an Irish accountant saying that his two clients had not heard from the Association for a long time. The Names were not on the Association's list of Members and it transpired that eight Names on the Writ were not Members of the Association. LSS asked D J Freeman to forward the original subscriptions. D J Freeman declined to provide the subscriptions on the grounds they were their private clients. However, they had been added to the writ without consulting the Committee. Subsidising D J Freeman private clients could be very serious for the Association. It could gravely inhibit any action the Association might wish to take, in directing how litigation recoveries could be properly kept out of the clutches of Lloyd's and others. The amount involved was £44,000 and had led to a delay in producing the Association's audited financial statements.

Mr J. L. Finlay, Chairman of the Names Defence Association, wrote to the Chairman of Citibank on 8 August 1994. He expressed concern that Lloyd's was worried that some syndicates were now approaching insolvency in real life rather than in the DTI's theoretical accountancy tests. His letter concerned the validity of the legal authorities for the proposed bank borrowing facilities issued in April 1994 for Lloyd's managers and run-off managers of Lloyd's syndicates. The loan being negotiated was between $500,000,000 and £1,000,000,000. Peter Middleton had also received a letter on the topic to which he replied that the lawyers had taken the greatest care to ensure that all the legal points had been fully researched and answered, particularly in view of the size and innovative nature of the facility. Citibank replied on 21 July that specific financial arrangements were confidential.

Clive faxed on 25 August that the House of Lords decision had been announced. A Managing Agent owed a duty of care in tort to indirect Names. The Members' Agents were vicariously liable for the mismanagement of a syndicate by the Managing Agent. Judge Potter's judgement was now awaited on whether a Members' Agent owed a duty in tort to its Names.

Historical Loss Development

On 28 July Lloyd's of London Press held a conference on 'The Management of Long-Tail Risks' and provided a copy of the presentations giving up-to-date information about the asbestosis and pollution claims from the USA. Heidi Hutter, Director of NewCo, discussed the development of losses from asbestosis and environmental claims demonstrating a surge in claims after twenty-four years (see graph on next page).

The planned Association's AGM and SGM on 28 July were postponed because of a rail strike. The meeting would be reconvened once a judgement had been announced, probably in October.

Clive wrote to the Committee on 31 July that it had occurred to his untutored brain that if the Association had lost its case, then Judge Potter would have already pronounced. He suggested that the Association could derive some encouragement from the delay. These musings followed a call from the Chairman of Pulbrook Underwriting Management, Donald Chilvers, announcing that shortly the Syndicate 334 (1985) run-off would be leaving the Merrett stable and going under the wing of Whittington.

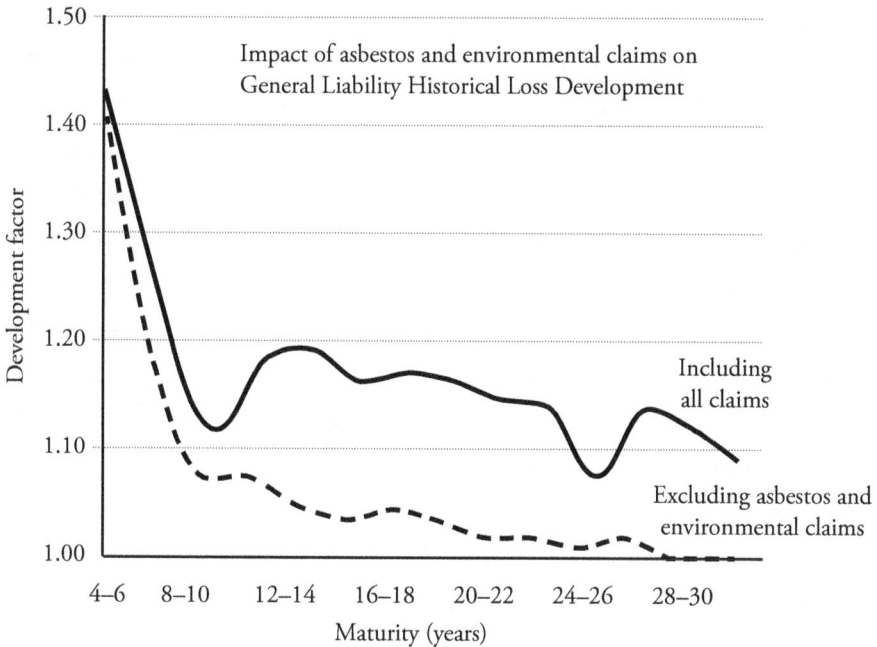

Impact of asbestos and environmental claims on
General Liability Historical Loss Development

Including
all claims

Excluding asbestos and
environmental claims

Development factor

Maturity (years)

Based on the Historical Loss Study, Reinsurance Association
of America and Milliman & Robertson Inc., (1991).

Clive wondered if there was a good judgement for the Association and, if the award exceeded the amount of Pulbrook Underwriting Management E&O cover, could the Association put Pulbrook Underwriting Management into liquidation? Thinking circumspectly about a major failure at Lloyd's he considered what terms might be extracted by the Association.

It was reported that Lloyd's would propose employing debt collectors and on 30 July the *Daily Telegraph*'s headline said, 'Lloyd's Casts Net For Defaulters'. Then on 2 August 1994 the same paper reported that two-thirds of Names had unpaid cash calls. Some £500 million had been paid of £1.7 billion due. It reported that £600 million of the Lloyd's Central Fund had been set aside for shortfalls and Peter Middleton would apply to Lloyd's Council to pursue some 16,000 nonpaying Names.

Clive wrote to Sydney Chapman MP on the same day about the questionable solvency at Lloyd's, as Lloyd's Central Fund was nearly exhausted before the 1991 year of account had been taken into consideration. Lloyd's

Statutory Statement of Business (SSOB) included provisions for 347 open years where an actuary had certified that the syndicates' liabilities could not be quantified. This was possibly an unmanageable burden on the remaining 179 syndicates still trading. There was no statutory requirement to audit SSOB. Clive contended that assets declared may no longer be in existence or had been accurately valued. He asked his MP to provide him with assurance that the figures presented by Lloyd's to support its solvency were properly and fully investigated. This was an incredibly serious situation with 347 open syndicates having unquantifiable liabilities and gave rise to speculation that Lloyd's would not survive. Liquidation would result in an enormous mess that would take years for solicitors to sort out. Ruined and burnt Names would receive no benefit. Clive considered that the basic dilemma related to Lloyd's solvency. If Lloyd's sued against Names' debts that were uncollectible then assets backing the policies would have to be written off. Then as a possible result Lloyd's might become insolvent and the Government might become liable for the losses of Names and policyholders.

Clive's fax said the reason for the next Committee meeting was to discuss an award following a judgement. Consequently, if no judgement had been announced by the week preceding the date for a Committee meeting, he suggested postponing the meeting on a week-by-week basis. David Tiplady had told him that a joint approach should be made to Judge Potter by the Association's counsel and the defendant's counsel asking for a decision sooner rather than later. Words should be couched in terms of exquisite legal politeness.

Of 368 Members of the Association twelve were resident in Europe and forty-one in the rest of the world.

During Keith's conversation with James Sinclair on 11 August, Sinclair said that the Merrett Group was going into liquidation and hinted that there may be a takeover of the Managing Agents with his own people on the Committee together with a representative of the Association. There was £1.2 billion of assets to run-off the claims. Names had big problems from inflated claims that had not reduced. There were big fees for screwing Names and the

Americans loved it. For the run-off Committee, the 'Managing Agent' would need 'true and fair' men. Five or six parties might tender. The office would cost around £150,000 and the box £60,000. There would be a comfortable fee. The Association should sponsor a candidate.

Newsletter, August 1994

Clive said that the Association had been waiting anxiously for Mr Justice Potter to pronounce on the Association's case. However, the wheels of justice grind exceedingly slowly and could actually go into reverse. Consequent on the House of Lords decision, the defendants had seized on a particular point in those rulings and demanded that the Association returns to court for further arguments to be heard. This meant that the Association would have to wait until the judge and all counsel had returned from their various vacations. It was likely that this further hearing would be sometime in September. There was no guarantee that judgement would be immediately forthcoming.

Clive provided some background information through Membership of the Super Group and the Lloyd's Names AWP. It had been observed that there was a culture of heavy drinking by some people at one time and this might have affected underwriting judgements.

A story had unfolded during conversations with Roger Bradley, the ex-Janson Green underwriter. Both Stephen Merrett and Dick Outhwaite were brought up as rival siblings in the box of Stephen's father, Roy Merrett. The box was the underwriter's desk at Lloyd's and large enough to seat a few people. There was understood to be animosity and intense rivalry between the two. Robin Jackson was Merrett's chief non-marine underwriter and a Member of the Lloyd's Names AWP since its inception in 1980. It was not unreasonable to conclude that Merrett was fully aware of the looming disaster of asbestosis. Outhwaite was spectacularly tarred with the taint of imprudence for the conduct of his own competing run-off policies. Why Outhwaite and Merrett engaged in their ludicrous contest to see who could lose the greatest amount of money was not fully understood but was germane to this story.

As the Association's arbitration showed, Merrett was deemed to have been grossly negligent in failing to make proper enquiries. It was not clear who was the underwriter of Syndicate 418, however, John Emney was fired by the board of Merrett Underwriting Management in March 1985. He was immediately reinstated by Merrett. The Board of Merrett Underwriting Management overruled Merrett and confirmed the dismissal of Emney in June 1985. The common view was that Merrett Underwriting Management needed a scapegoat. It appeared that Emney had agreed the risks on the long-tail contracts with the brokers concerned who provided a slip for initialling. The slip was the document prepared by a broker describing the risks to be covered and presented to the syndicate underwriter to initial the percentage of risk the syndicate was prepared to accept. Slips were not signed when the deal was done as they were taken late each afternoon to be agreed by Merrett. It was common Market knowledge that in the war with Outhwaite, Emney was often reported as telling brokers to see what Outhwaite was quoting and he would go lower. However, it was certain that Emney was fired or was made a scapegoat for imprudent underwriting and Merrett was castigated for imprudence in the arbitration award.

David Tiplady wrote that the law had changed since the time of the arbitration as the House of Lords decision in *Pan Atlantic Insurance Co v Pine Top Insurance Co Ltd* (1994) overruled *Container Transport International Inc. (CTI) v Oceanus Mutual Underwriting Association (Bermuda) Ltd*. Firstly, it must now be established that any nondisclosure was material and, secondly, it must be established that it did affect the judgement of the underwriter. If the law at the time of the arbitration had been understood to be as the House of Lords now said it was, then Syndicate 334 Names may well have been successful.

It should not be difficult to show that any prudent underwriter would make proper enquiries, the outcome of which would undeniably have affected the underwriter's judgement. It was a clear indication that had Merrett known of the nondisclosed material he would not have written the policy, or not on the terms concluded. This nondisclosure did in fact affect his judgement but only as to the size of the premium he would have quoted. Charles suggested that the strongest argument appeared to be that Pulbrook Underwriting Management's nondisclosure was material, because it enabled Syndicate 418 to avoid the reinsurance on a technicality accepted by the arbitrators. Clive said he thought the *Pine Top* decision did not disadvantage the Association's case and might even become an advantage. Names joining after 1981 would have believed the Pulbrook Underwriting Management statement that the syndicate held the vital long-tail insurance protection.

On 9 September Clive wrote to John Winter, the Managing Director of Pulbrook Underwriting Management, regarding the consultative document on run-off companies. Clive said that the use of a specialist claims unit (SCU) was persuasive. However, he thought there might be occasions where what was conceived as claims policy for all Names could conflict with what was best for particular claims presented to Syndicate 334 for payment. In his reply Winter said that he had been negotiating a delegation agreement with the SCU for the past month. Although it was very useful to have a central coordinating function, the ultimate authority must remain with the syndicates. They would be pursuing this matter with much vigor.

Newsletter, September 1994: Still Waiting for Judgement, Still Fairly Imminent!

The Chairman's September newsletter reported that the defendants had now abandoned their request for an extra day in court. Final arguments based on two recent House of Lords decisions would be entered by written submissions only. There would no longer be a need to wait in a queue for a court date and Mr Justice Potter should be able to announce his judgement much earlier. The question of vicarious responsibility of the Members' Agents for the actions of Managing Agents in tort was still to be decided. If the Association received a favourable judgement on the negligence aspect, it was likely to be appealed ultimately to the House of Lords. As the basis of the Association's claim was negligence by Pulbrook

Underwriting Management in not disclosing material facts and if the Association had failed in this, it was thought that the judgement would have been announced months ago. The ways of the law are unamenable to this form of logic and it would be wrong to entertain more than a glimmer of hope.

The date for the AGM and SGM were dependant on the date of the announcement of the judgement. On the assumption that this would occur in the next month, planning for the meetings would be in late October or early November.

Two deceased Names with Estate protection plans (EPPs) were found to be on the writ but not Members of the Association. It was agreed to accept the subscriptions to the Association from the EPPs on the grounds that the executors might otherwise pursue the Association for any winnings. Clive asked for the funds from D J Freeman for the ghost Members.

Clive wrote to Committee Members about his litigation subscriptions. He felt as Chairman impelled to contribute to the last tranche of 6%. Although treating for Lloyd's Hardship, he was not required to pay under the Rules of the Association. Now on the point of signing a Hardship agreement he was required to hand over all litigation recoveries. After discussion with the Treasurer, it seemed to be to the advantage of the Association's funds if he were to revert to his original stake and factor down. This would decrease the amount of any possible recovery due to Lloyd's and increase the residual funds of the Association, in the event of a win. The healthy state of the Associations' finances was considered. Clive said the returned tranche amounting to £2,400 would accrue to him. He confessed that he needed the money and Committee Members should discuss the matter with the Treasurer without reference to him. Charles Baron wrote to all Committee Members saying the only person making the most difficult decision to repay the 6% to Clive was Clive himself. Alasdair Ferguson wrote to Committee Members regarding a possible payment to Clive for his services to the Association. He attached notes for reviewing the matter including an amendment to the Rules of the Association.

Charles Baron felt compelled to put his own financial circumstances before the Committee. In the four years of the life of the Association his Lloyd's deposit had been wiped out. He had two unpaid calls. His solvency requirement was a joke. His current income was a matter approaching derision and he was seriously contemplating selling his house. He had three open syndicates and stop-loss for two of them. Syndicate 334 was the most likely to be successful. Syndicate 90 was the main reason for his severe financial position where he had no stop-loss. Sums up to £100,000 would go to replenish the stop-loss underwriters. He was wondering if he too should ask for a repayment of his 6% subscription. He said he was in an agony of indecision as to whether to apply for Hardship before the shutters came down in December. He said he would resign from the Committee.

Clive had thought it was in his own best interests to have the 6% tranche repaid. He did not think it would do the Association any harm. Likewise, it was also for Charles Baron to judge his own best interests. Jasper Salisbury-Jones, also applying for Hardship, wrote on 27 September 1994 that he did not see how it would be a good idea for the Association to repay Charles part of the Association's fees, as stop-loss complicated the position. There was a fair chance of enough recoveries from the various Action Groups during the next twelve months to override the stop-loss. Jasper was also unclear as to why Charles thought it necessary to resign from the Committee.

Clive wrote to David Tiplady on 10 October as a layman, pointing out that as a Name did not delegate his underwriting, he surrendered all rights to have any say whatsoever in underwriting. A Name empowered his Agent and if a Sub-Agent made a muck of things the Agent must take responsibility. A Lloyd's Members' Agent performed a task more akin to that of a partner or quasi-Principal than an Agent. If an Agent was granted such absolute and irrevocable powers, then he must be held to account if things went wrong.

Jason Wheeler of CentreWrite wrote to Clive about EPPs taken out by Names who were deceased. The EPPs provided funds for claims by deceased Names in litigation. He enquired as to whether Clive was in a position to tell them the likely settlement of the litigation and the future deterioration of Syndicate 334 1985 account. He looked forward to Clive's reply as soon as possible. Clive's response to John Winter on 16 October expressed astonishment about the CentreWrite request for information needed for EPPs. He asked questions which Winter answered on 30 September. He said it was a responsibility of Pulbrook Underwriting Management to pay claims. Most of the outstanding claims arose on policies that were contentious. These were largely based upon an interpretation of US legislation enacted well after the date of the policy. The policyholders were mainly large American companies who were plaintiffs in litigation against the insurance market. Pulbrook Underwriting Management's job as fiduciary agent for Names was to resist and minimise the exposure.

Christopher Stockwell's Super Group Strategy and Programme was circulated. Stockwell explained to Clive:

> The Super Group objectives are to provide a forum for the exchange of views and information between Action Groups, undertake research, investigations, provide a lobby and a platform for advancing the collective views of Action Groups to the media, the authorities and to Lloyd's. The 'rottweiler' campaign by Lloyd's to recover funds should be resisted as Lloyd's is not being honest with the Names. Lloyd's says it will pay all claims, such a policy is impossible as claims are infinite and Names resources are finite. NewCo could not succeed without a massive commutation of US liability policies that are producing asbestos and pollution claims. Also, Lloyd's cannot quantify Names' debts and is not able to seek judgements for agreed amounts. Every Name has a distinct and separate defence. Stop-loss credits are not adequately backed by reserves and not all liabilities have been properly reserved. The Central Fund will not have enough cash. Sometimes I feel swamped, particularly as some people criticised the Super Group for not being sufficiently focused.

Newsletter, October 1994 Newsletter

The October newsletter informed Members that the Committee had just learnt the timetable and that the deadline for defendants' submissions would be Wednesday, 5 October and the Association's replies were required by 14 October. Judgement might be reasonably expected by 28 October and would almost certainly be appealed. However, the Association was well funded for this eventuality.

Clive commented on the astonishing size of a recent award to Gooda Walker and the forceful condemnations in the judgement. He assured Association Members that there was an undisputed amount in the E&O insurers' reserves, and that the offer made by the Association's defendants that was rapidly withdrawn indicated resources were present. It was important to be clear that the Association's case related to entirely different years of account to that of Gooda Walker.

Pulbrook Underwriting Management appeared to be clinging to the argument that it could not be held liable to those Names who joined Syndicate 334 after 1979. Clive's view was that it was liable by virtue of continuously holding out in several subsequent Syndicate 334 Annual Reports that Pulbrook Underwriting Management was covered for all liabilities of 1976 and prior years. Without this defective assertion who would have joined the syndicate?

Articles in the press on 21 October were headlined, 'Names Fume at Wildly Inaccurate Debt Letter' and 'Syndicates in Risks Data Row'. The first article was a complaint by Michael Becket that Lloyd's had made major errors in writing to Names inviting them to discuss their outstanding debts. The complaints arose because some angry Names had settled their debts. One Name said his letter showed a debt of £0. Another was for £50,000 when the correct amount was £300. Lloyd's said it was not a demand for payment, merely the opportunity to deal with a problem. The second article, by Claire Sambrook, said that syndicates had come under fire for failing to provide the Insurance Market with the information it needed to manage its multibillion-pound exposure to pollution-, health hazard- and asbestos-related claims. Some Agents complained that

NewCo was setting impossible deadlines for returning information and claimed the Market's strong tradition of haphazard record-keeping was holding up the task. Brokers had to go through documents in their basements to find policy cover notes that may be forty years old. Heidi Hutter of NewCo said the problem was not getting returns back but 'difficulty in understanding what we've got'.

Alasdair had met Clive to discuss the refunding of his subscriptions. His lingering fear was that if the Association started repaying a tranche, other Committee or Association Members might follow suit. He now understood that this repayment would apply to circumstances which were unique to Clive. Consequently, he had no objection to the proposal.

The Super Group issued a press release on 20 October about David Rowland's proposal to change the Premiums Trust Deeds (PTD). There appeared to be no advantage to the majority of Names who would have ceased to trade by the end of the year. Most Names were victims of a failure of self-regulation that had greatly added to their losses. The Super Group questioned how this initiative showed good faith to the ruined Names or how it fitted with the statutory duty of the Society to protect Names. It was unlikely that Names would agree to a retrospective amendment to the PTD even if it could be done legally. The Super Group Chairman, Christopher Stockwell, commented that Lloyd's was proposing to effect change by a resolution of the Council approved by the Secretary of State. This they believed would not require ratification by the Names and would circumvent the normal bylaw approval procedures. The Super Group had decided to seek counsel's Opinion on the legality of what was proposed. The Executive of the ALM issued a press release welcoming the Lloyd's initiative, without consulting the ALM Committee or its Members, However, some Members of the ALM were pushing for the withdrawal of the press release. Stockwell said he hoped to reach an agreement with the ALM to seek counsel's Opinion together and, if possible, to issue a joint letter to all Names. He had made a similar proposal to the SoN.

Lloyd's decided to take strong-arm tactics against Names who refused to pay. Lloyd's said, 'If we do not take draconian measures our very future is at stake.' The idea was to change the PTD that covered the financial relationship with Names. It would allow Lloyd's to get its hands on compensation awards to Names. Since the 1982 Lloyd's Act's emphasis was on the welfare of the customer rather than the providers of capital, it would be hard for Rt Hon Michael Heseltine, Secretary of State, to refuse the request. Either way he could win. If Heseltine refused, he would be blamed for driving the Market out of business; by accepting, a horde of angry Names would blame him for taking the side of the Market that robbed them. Lloyd's must grasp the nettle and devise a settlement with all the aggrieved Names. Tom Benyon, SoN Chairman, commented that many Names felt 'it's tails they lose, heads Lloyd's wins'. He explained that the Premiums Trust Funds (PTF) had traditionally supported the Market. These funds were used for receiving premiums on behalf of Names and paying out claims and profits. A 1992 court case made clear that compensation payments for negligence did not have to be paid into the Trust Funds. Lloyd's future intention was that compensation payments should be paid to the level required to cover Names' outstanding liabilities.

The press had a field day covering the matter. On 21 October the *Financial Times'* headline was 'Lloyd's May Change Debt Recovery Rule'. The *Guardian* commented that Lloyd's sought to claw back pay-outs awarded by courts from Names. The article said the announcement of debt recovery triggered an outcry from Names' representatives, 22,000 of whom were suing over their vast losses. The *Guardian* article also quoted Tom Benyon saying, 'The burnt Names are going to be ballistic with anger. The *Times* headline was 'Lloyd's Moves to Seize Awards' in which Rowland was quoted as saying that Lloyd's was owed a total of £1.2 billion by more than 10,000 Names, a debt that was being funded by other Names. Those that had paid their debts were angry that others might not have done so. The *Independent* headline was 'Stakes Raised to Danger Level' and in the Business Section, 'Lloyd's Needs Rule Change to Survive'. It was in the interests of the Society of Lloyd's to keep as much cash in the business as possible and not to let it leak out to Names' bank accounts. The rule changes proposed preserved cash in the Lloyd's business and were very unpopular with Names.

On 22 October Clive wrote to the Committee about the quaintly titled 'consultation document' sent to Names which he thought had disturbing implications for the Association's Members particularly regarding the pursuit of appeals. Enclosed with the letter was a document from Christopher Thomas Everard graphically demonstrating the 'Law of Lloyd's losses', i.e., the size of a Name's losses was directly proportional to his distance from the twelfth (top) floor in the Lloyd's building. This was extracted from pages 30 and 31 of Sir David Walker's report showing Lloyd's total results for eight years from 1983 to 1990, disclosing that LMX losses fell almost entirely on the External Members and North Americans. Some Names on four syndicates were landed with demands for over £1 million. An analysis of Lloyd's results showed the distribution of profits and losses to different categories of Names.

Lloyd's Results 1983–90

Profits (losses)	£
Lloyd's Council and Committee Members	72,400
Underwriters	64,000
Directors of brokers	60,400
Other Working Names	58,800
Agencies' shareholders + some External Names	41,200
Directors of managing and Members' Agents	40,800
Retired Working Names	24,400
Relations of Working Names	(5,600)
All External Names	(11,200)
Names in USA, Canada and Mexico	(35,200)

Lloyd's Council and Committee Members were at or near the top floor and Names from the USA, Canada and Mexico were furthest away. Australia and New Zealand Names were not shown separately.

Clive suggested that the Council's proposals were abhorrent. They seemed to move the goalposts by introducing retrospective legislation altering the contracts into which Names entered many years ago. They would favour most those who had least to lose, i.e., those in power who grew rich from their own abysmal failure to regulate Lloyd's except to their own advantage. They would further penalise those very people who were cynically recruited after the full implications of the unlimited losses occurring from the asbestosis debacle were known by Council. He said he could not amplify or verify the rumour voiced at the last Super Group meeting about doubts regarding Lloyd's solvency recently. Clive understood that this was overridden by Michael Heseltine, the President of the Board of Trade, and Prime Minister John Major. The political will was that Lloyd's would survive. Lloyd's appeared to be going out on a plank by saying it would not survive if Names got their hands on their litigation winnings.

Clive proposed various ways for Association Members to respond including commenting on the consultation as provided in the consultation document and to organise direct representation to David Rowland. Additionally, to put pressure on the Secretary of State through each Name's MP, mount a challenge in the courts to the legality of the proposal and stimulate coordinated press action. Clive asked the Committee if there was any dissent from his view as he wished the Committee to present a united front. He wanted to write to the Membership in robust terms. No one objected.

Newletter No. 2, October 1994: Disappointment, Anxiety and Irritation

In the second October newsletter on the 25th, Clive stated his disappointment in the slippage of the judgement date to 11 November and was waiting with some anxiety and irritation.

He quoted examples of suppression of information from External Names, such as the Cromer report and the Chester report regarding the Oakley Vaughan debacle as evidence of rampant insider dealing. He provided information about the meaning and implications of 'offshore and off-balance-sheet rollover funds' of the 1960s and 1970s. These illegal funds had to be repatriated in the early 1980s and falsified the syndicate profits. The repayments allayed worries of existing External Names and induced 18,000 gullible new Names to join. Clive's view of Rowland's proposed retrospective alteration of Names' contracts was that he was really saying that for the sake of Market jobs, and related pensions, the Market was happy to ruin or bankrupt many External Names. The prospect was of thousands of External Names being denied the fruits of litigation against insiders, who would continue enjoying the standards of living to which they had become accustomed on the back of the Association's Members' money.

The loss was stated as £8 billion in the last four years with another £4 billion in the next four. Uncollected cash exceeded the Central Fund. Too many people were burying their heads in the sand and the most commonly used word associated with NewCo was 'if'. Clive suggested that some 27,000 Names would be towed out to the mid-Atlantic on a barge called NewCo and sunk without trace.

The Financial Recovery Department (FRD) had sent out 14,000 debt collecting letters, many containing wholly inaccurate figures clearly indicating that Lloyd's was getting more and more unreliable. Advice was to consult a legal adviser who should attend any meeting with officials. For those contemplating a voluntary drawdown, the wording of the draw-down request for 1994 had been radically changed from earlier years and could be a dangerous trap. A draft letter to the Names' Agent was attached to the newsletter together with a draft letter for those wishing to question the calculation of their solvency statement.

Keith wrote to Ian Taylor MP on 31 October about the retrospective empowerment sought by Lloyd's from the Secretary of State. He asked various questions, including, was he content to see a contract in English law altered arbitrarily and retrospectively against the wishes of the party concerned? Was he prepared to countenance this challenge by Lloyd's to Parliament's will in seeking to evade the provisions of the Bankruptcy Acts by Lloyd's, usurping the position of a Name's preferential creditor? Did he realise that the passage of this measure would effectively stifle any attempt by an injured Name to seek redress at law for the woeful catalogue of incompetence and dishonesty partially revealed by the due process of law? Did he realise that Names were effectively denied the remedies of the courts by this empowerment? An Appeal Lord recently remarked that 'administrative convenience can never be allowed to transcend British justice'. Was he going to endorse or refute this dictum? He requested that his MP conveyed his queries vehemently to the President of the Board of Trade and his staff.

Ian Taylor replied, sending Keith a letter from Jonathan Evans, Parliamentary Under secretary of State for Corporate Affairs, on 28 November about the proposal to amend Lloyd's Premiums Trust Deeds (PTD). Mr Evans said it was not envisaged that that the Secretary of State would make a decision until Lloyd's had supplied a comprehensive account of the responses it had received. Trust Funds were established by a Trust Deed approved by the Secretary of State as a condition of Lloyd's underwriters being exempted from Part II of the Insurance Companies Act 1982. When considering the variation proposed by Lloyd's, the Secretary of State's primary concern would be the protection of policyholders.

John Winter said Pulbrook Underwriting Management was in the final stages of moving the run-off to Whittington and he looked forward to meeting Clive and his colleagues on 6 December at a conference of Merrett Group-managed syndicates.

Lloyd's bylaws made the protection of Names' interests Pulbrook Underwriting Management's prime fiduciary duty. 'NewCo' had been renamed 'Equitas' and would not have its initial reserve figures until the Association's Names received the Syndicate's accounts in April rather than December. This would be a Pulbrook Underwriting Management responsibility rather than that of Equitas. All Equitas returns had been professionally completed and submitted. There was little comfort for Names in the Opinion of Mr Kenneth Rokison QC from the Protection of Trading Interests Act 1980.

On 1 November 1994 Alasdair Ferguson wrote to the Treasurer about possible remuneration for Clive. He had spoken to all Committee

Members who were full of admiration for the work done by Clive. Everyone was sympathetic to Clive's financial difficulties. However, concern was expressed that any use of the 'war chest' other than for financing legal action was undesirable. He spoke to Clive that the balance of opinion on the Committee was against altering the rule by which Committee Members served without remuneration. Clive accepted this with very good grace and said he would work with undiminished vigour towards the success of the Association's cause.

The same day James Sinclair sent a letter to all Syndicate 334 Names in run-off. He said that competing schemes and products would be announced to take Names out of unlimited liability to that of limited liability. It was a requirement that all Names should have completed setting up their funds at Lloyd's by now for 1995. He advised caution in being sure that the limited-liability vehicles to be used were efficient, reliable, inexpensive to operate and the tax implications fully understood. Willis Faber & Dumas (Agencies) had already created Lomond Underwriting PLC which awaited flotation on the London Stock Exchange.

Stuart Kettle enclosed his firm's fee note for £3,953.23 and time sheet for the attention of the Treasurer on 3 November. There was also a suggested additional fee note for £23,000 plus VAT from the clerk to Nicholas Strauss QC. Once brief fees were agreed in the form of staged payments, as in this case, all work by counsel for the trial preparation should be covered from the date of the first staged payment. The first staged payment became due on Wednesday, 29 December 1993. There was a risk that any payments made to counsel on a voluntary basis may not be recovered as properly taxed costs if the Names' claims were successful. Stuart said he normally opposed making any additional payments to counsel. However, lengthy and detailed submissions were prepared by senior counsel at the request of the judge. The greater number of these submissions was prepared by Mr Strauss himself, comprising two large lever arch files of written material based on an enormous amount of research. Consequently, Stuart would consider an amount of £8,000 plus VAT as reasonable in the circumstances. He stressed that such a sum was considered unnecessary concerning remuneration of senior counsel. If he was instructed to allow no such payment, then such a position was justified and appropriate.

Deborah Banasiak of D J Freeman wrote about payment of damages to the EPP open to claims from either the executors or EPP insurers that any damages were wrongly distributed. Clive responded to her letter on 22 November suggesting it was a little premature to incur expense in obtaining such advice at the present juncture and thanked her for pointing out the dangers. He said he hoped that the expense of this correspondence had not fallen on the Association and would be grateful if she would affirm the point to the Treasurer. The instructions the Committee gave to D J Freeman were not to deal with any individual enquiries but confine their instructions solely to the pursuit of litigation for the recovery of damages from Pulbrook Underwriting Management. All Association Members had surrendered to the Committee their rights to the allocation of any such recoveries under the Association's rules.

The slippage of the judgement date was causing great problems in the Association's diary. The Committee was being nut-crackered between the events and the need to hold the AGM in 1994. The situation was further complicated by the PTD drama. The legal challenge was in process and the outcome would have a profound effect on deliberations at the AGM.

Alan Porter, Treasurer of the Litigating Names Committee, informed Clive that Michael Deeny would be Chairman of a committee aimed at stopping Lloyd's from amending the PTD by action in the High Court. Lloyd's action was illegal in the Opinions of a trio of QCs. A £250,000 litigation fund would be enough and a subscription of £12 per Name was requested. Clive said he supported such litigation as it was emphatically in the Association's interest.

Clive discussed with the Committee on 11 November:

To my utter dismay and concern, according to the judge's clerk, judgement is not to be expected for at least another three weeks. The troops are getting very restive. However, overaggressive approaches to the judge at this juncture could possibly be counterproductive. I think the only thing which could be profitably kicked at the moment is the cat, which has sensed the situation and is over half-way up a chestnut tree!

His lack of amusement at this appalling situation was audible on the phone line.

The Appeal Court ruling on 11 November, as reported in the *Daily Telegraph*, that Lloyd's was subject to European competition laws enabled Names to take the battle to the national press. The case revolved round the Lloyd's Central Fund which meets policyholders' insurance claims when Names fail to pay. The £806 million Central Fund was standing in for £1.2 billion of Names' losses. The Writs Response Group (WRG) claimed that the Central Fund arrangements were anti-competitive under European law. It was claimed that Names who had lost money on the notorious LMX spiral, where syndicates laid off loss with each other, might now be able to sue Lloyd's. Lawyers in the *Daily Telegraph* claimed that thousands of Names could sue Lloyd's for damages and avoid paying their losses. Solicitors for the WRG claimed that the Lloyd's steamroller had stopped and Lloyd's must call off the debt collectors in their attempts to recover money from Names. The Appeal Court's ruling overturned Mr Justice Saville's decision in December 1993. Lloyd's said it would appeal the ruling to the House of Lords that the Central Fund arrangements were anti-competitive under European law, and that Lloyd's may not recover money paid out on their account.

The Court upheld Mr Justice Saville's view that the contract between Lloyd's and Names implied no duty of care.

On the same day Ralph Atkins, the insurance correspondent in another newspaper, reported 'Court of Appeal Setback for Lloyd's'. The ruling created confusion about the legal status of some of the Insurance Market's practices. The Court raised a question mark over whether Lloyd's practice of encouraging the reinsurance of its policies within the Market might have breached European competition laws. Lloyd's was applying to Brussels for the necessary exemption from European law to clarify the position. The WRG argued that the Market comprised an 'association of undertakings'. Arrangements made centrally could amount to a cartel agreement under the Treaty of Rome. The offering of Lloyd's policies within the Market may have given the syndicates an unfair advantage over outside reinsurance companies. The same day, *The Times* featured, 'Court Halts Lloyd's Debt Collection'. Granting the appeal, Sir Thomas Bingham, Master of the Rolls, said he was overturning the original ruling 'with diffidence, reluctance and regret'. Handing down the judgement, he said, 'We know this affects a very large sum of money and a very large number of Names.'

The *Independent* called it 'Another Hole'. It said the underwriting cycle was nearing its peak and Lloyd's should be making big money. However, the incompetence of the past still threatened to sink the Market. The Appeal Court judges agreed that since Lloyd's had failed to apply for exemption to European Community competition law it was possible for Names to argue that the Central Fund distorted competition between Lloyd's and other insurers. Another newspaper headline said, 'Court Casts Doubt over Lloyd's Debt Collection'. Christopher Stockwell, as Chairman of the Super Group, said no Names should be asked for any further payment until the issues were resolved. The court was at pains to point out that Lloyd's was wrong on the European law matter simply because it did not have the facts to decide on the issue at this stage. Lloyd's said it would continue its debt recovery operation. However, the judgement cast further serious doubt on whether Lloyd's should continue to trade.

Lloyd's was reported to have no solvency problem, as recoveries from Names were contingent assets which would be taken into account for solvency purposes.

Under the headline, 'Princes, Bishops, Crooks; Insure with Them in London', Christopher Fildes in the *Daily Telegraph* on 14 November reported that Carlos Miro enjoyed doing business in London. Carlos Miro had not been over lately because he was in prison in America

having pleaded guilty to sixteen charges of insurance fraud. He helped
to sink the Transit Casualty Company of Missouri, described by its liquidators as the *Titanic* of American insurance, and its sister ship called
London United Investments (LUI). LUI with Prince Michael of Kent
on its Board was the biggest insurance failure in the London market's
history. An investigative Committee of the US House of Representatives
learned from Miro how the Lloyd's professionals taught him to churn
commissions as the retail broker and again by arranging the reinsurers' own insurance programme. Consequently, they could work their
commissions up to 25% of the gross premiums. Miro became a Name
at Lloyd's. When he asked his Agent about the Lloyd's means test, he got
an affronted reply, 'Well we presume you're a gentleman or we wouldn't
have asked you to join us.' Seven years of Membership cost him $60,000
in losses and thus he had another chance to learn about insurance business from professionals at Lloyd's.

Prince Michael was introduced by 'Ronnie' Driver, Chairman of
LUI. The company's business was coming from America and a royal
connection always went down well there. The Prince's family was full of
high-ranking Freemasons as was the Council of Lloyd's. LUI's subsidiary, H. S. Weavers, was outside Lloyd's and managed a pool of insurance
on behalf of a dozen companies and was said to 'hold the pen' for them.
That meant to write business on their behalf. It arranged cover for
makers of chemicals, hazardous building materials, medical malpractice risks, directors' liability and professional indemnity for lawyers and
accountants. Business came rolling in. As Weavers' operations got out
of hand it ignored proper bookkeeping and sensible internal controls.
When Congressmen went to look at the records, they were invited to
take their pick from amongst six million pieces of paper. In the end they
were shown some pencilled notes in loose-leaf binders. The pages were
sometimes lengthened with the aid of sticky tape. The Board of C. R.
Driver, another LUI subsidiary, was graced for nine years by Mervyn
Stockwood, the flamboyant Anglican Bishop. Neither Church nor state
could save LUI from its doom.

Early in the relationship Transit Company and LUI established two jointly owned agencies, Russell Re in Michigan and National Underwriting Agency in Chicago. National Underwriting Agency went boldly for policies on pharmaceuticals, asbestos, toxic wastes and generated losses estimated at $1.6 billion. Its fortunes declined and it went under owing $4 billion. When Russell Re was founded, shares were issued to its management, Transit and to an American lawyer called Robert Schloeb who was acting as a nominee. Money had accumulated in Schloeb's trustee account. He was suddenly ordered to send $210,000 to Liechtenstein. Schloeb told Congressmen that he was acting for three of LUI's directors. This had come as news to the other LUI directors causing detonations in the board-room and at a shareholders' meeting but no substantive change of control before LUI went into administration in May 1990. The DTI inspectors found that some £35 million had been diverted from C. R. Driver and Weavers to Liechtenstein.

When the US Congressmen first tried to question Carlos Miro, they wrote to the British Ambassador in Washington and told him that Miro was in London using a fraudulent Mexican passport and doing business to match. The Ambassador coolly replied that Miro was not in Great Britain and no investigations were planned. Miro subsequently told Congressmen that it was 'somewhat humorous' to read that he was not in Great Britain when he was sitting in his London office. The Congressmen found it less amusing as the LUI failure cost its American customers fortunes, saying in print that UK insurance supervisors were unhelpful and inept. It was clear to see why Miro liked it.

The November issue of *Reactions* said that the consultative document on run-off companies for Lloyd's syndicates had prompted plenty of crit-icism. In the Lloyd's business plan last year, 1993, it had indicated its intention to regulate companies that carry out run-off services for syndi-cates by a licensing system. Concern was raised over the requirements for getting a licence, the tendering process, length of the licence and mechan-ics of switching to the new regime. However, short-term run-offs were to be managed by the Managing Agent.

Newsletter, November 1994

In the November newsletter Clive stated that Mr Justice Potter would be taking over the Commercial Court. Judgement could not now be expected before the end of the law term on 21 December 1994. It would still be impossible to fix a date for the AGM.

Mr Strauss's clerk wrote to Stuart Kettle of D J Freeman saying he was surprised by the terms of Stuart's letter to the Association's Treasurer of 3 November. His impression from phone conversations was that the grounds for charging additional fees were reasonable although the client might question the amount. It was correct to say that the brief fee covered trial preparation. However, it did not cover the work of preparing expert evidence virtually from scratch. The crucial evidence of the main expert in the original form was inadequate to deal with the issues. Mr Strauss spent a very considerable additional time preparing notes and questions for the expert. There were three long consultations, some 50% of the total of forty-three hours spent dealing with this, which was not covered by the brief fee. Excluding this work, the total time spent in preparing for trial up to the end of the first day was 187 hours, appreciably more than the 120 to 150 hours estimated at the time the brief fee was agreed. The additional fees related to work over the weekends of 26 and 27 February and 5 and 6 March 1994 to put the plaintiff's final submissions in writing more than was normal. The Court had allowed appreciably less time than the parties had signified was necessary. The judge indicated that if the trial was not finished in time, it would be adjourned for a considerable period. Mr Strauss spent the whole of the weekend of 26 and 27 February and most of the following weekend preparing extensive written submissions to reduce the time spent in court and avoid adjournment. It was requested that the letter be placed before the Committee.

Mr M. E. Henderson of London wrote to Clive on 15 November 1994 that through the Association, he did not wish to contribute to the Litigating Names Committee High Court action. Clive responded on 17 November, stating that the Committee had expressed unanimous opposition to the changes to the Premiums Trust Deeds. He wondered if

Mr Henderson agreed that his litigation award should be paid to the PTF and be mindful of the subsequent taxation implications. Clive said the subscription amount involved was £4,392 and Mr Henderson could raise the matter at the AGM.

Clive wrote to Rowland on 15 November saying that 366 Members of this Association were injured Lloyd's Names and opposing his proposals to alter retrospectively the Lloyd's PTD contracts with Names. An analysis of reserving ratios indicated a consistent overstatement of profits for the past three decades. Those who stood to gain from the false declarations were those who regulated the Market. Legions of old policies, with an escalating number of claims under policy wording which bore no relation to the premiums received.

Both the *Financial Times* and the *Guardian* published an article on 18 November stating, 'Lloyd's to Raise Pot for Names as the Litigation Threat Forces a £1.1 Billion Offer'. The increase was an effort to halt the litigation which was threatening to engulf the stricken Market. The previous £900 million was voted down by the Names and rumours of a fresh offer had been gaining strength in recent weeks. Many Action Groups were realising that even if they were given a court award there may be no money to pay it. It suggested an offer could be made to Names before Christmas. It was said that Lloyd's Chief Executive, Peter Middleton, had got the backing of Michael Deeny, the charismatic and influential Chairman of the 3,000-strong Gooda Walker Names Action Group. John Rew of Chatset said, 'I think you've got to give people something tangible. I lost £100,000 on one syndicate and the last offer gave me £1,000 which is neither here nor there.' Lloyd's survival depended on its ability to continue to convince the world that it was solvent and would always pay valid claims.

On 28 November Christopher Stockwell wrote to Rt Hon Michael Heseltine PC MP, President of the Board of Trade, setting out the belief that the proposed amendment of the Trust Deed of Lloyd's Premiums Trust Fund (PTF) was objectionable as a matter of European Community law under the European Community Treaty. If the amendment to the

PTD was approved there would be no answer to a resulting claim against the British Government by injured Names. The Secretary of State's remit so far as Trust Deeds were concerned was limited to Insurance Company Act considerations. He quoted Article 5 of the European Community Treaty that requires the UK to '*abstain from any measure which could jeopardise the attainment of the objective of the Treaty*'. The PTD expressly required the prior approval of the Secretary of State's remit to any variation of the original PTD. Approval for a variation must meet the requirements of the European Convention on Human Rights (EHCR). The principles contained in the EHCR form fundamental principles of European Community law. A restricted remit in reviewing the PTD would result in an infringement. The Super Group believed it applied to insurance, a field covered by Community law. On the same day, the Super Group wrote to the Secretary to Lloyd's Council drawing attention to counsel's advice for the Super Group, firstly, that it was against the bylaws to capture funds from litigation to reduce liabilities to the Name's PTF and, secondly, the Name may have a case for damages against Lloyd's.

Clive circulated a copy of a letter dated 29 November from the Names Defence Association addressed to Mr W. A. Proctor, Clerk of the Treasury and Civil Service Select Committee. The Names Defence Association letter demonstrated the progress of what might be called the fraud case against Lloyd's. There was a certain rivalry between the Names Defence Association, Global Defence Association and the Writs Response Group. The situation was compounded with personal animosities between the leaderships of the three groupings, aided by the legal firms assisting each group. This was an idiotic situation as much of the evidence so jealously guarded by each group was common to all of them. Clive thought that Christopher Stockwell of the Super Group was doing his best to unify the disparate forces and unite the three groups under one umbrella.

A detailed paper was prepared and circulated on 6 December by the Global Defence Association regarding allegations of misconduct and fraud at Lloyd's in three parts. Firstly, under the heading of misrepresentation, secondly, considering the quality of accounting and consequently the creation of a false market, and thirdly, breaches in European law. There was a commentary on the implications of Lloyd's solvency. There was good business to be done at Lloyd's but the paper suggested that this could not happen within the structure of the Society of Lloyd's based on a Central Fund. It then mentioned the father of Lloyd's, Julius Angerstein, who in the nineteenth century forbade the creation of a Central Fund as it would make everyone vulnerable to the incompetent and crooked. This was exactly what had happened. The mistake was to make the Society solvency dependant on a Central Fund without ensuring a tough enough regulatory regime to avoid the inevitable consequences.

Peter Middleton wrote to all Action Group Chairmen and Chairmen of the E&O Underwriters Steering Group on 7 December, saying that it was right to take a first step towards a settlement and investigate the extent of E&O cover and validation of the computer model on which the calculations would be made. The aim was to achieve a fair solution grounded in reality to spiral and long-tail disputes, achieving consensus step by step.

Lloyd's Chairman David Rowland's letter to all Names was about changes to the PTD. The consultation period had ended. Nothing had arisen that should cause Lloyd's to change its strategy of amending the PTD enabling the benefits of litigation awards to flow through them. The Council had decided to postpone implementation of its PTD strategy for a period, to allow the best chance for a negotiated settlement to be achieved. A report on the consultation regarding the proposed amendments to the PTD was enclosed with the Chairman's letter. Some 1,892 responses had been received from individual Names by the deadline of 18 November and over 300 responses after the deadline. Strong views were conveyed by many Names, both by those who, having paid their own losses were not willing to bear those of other Names who chose not to, and by those who believed that the Council's proposal was illegal and immoral. Some 6% of the total number of Names responded – 53% of those responding were still underwriting in 1994 and 65% supported the proposed amendments. Most concern regarded the apparent retrospective nature of the amendment. It was described as 'moving the goal posts', 'dishonourable' and 'not even the Government stoops so low'. It was suggested that all losses should be mutualised.

In the Super Group circular to Action Groups on 11 December, Christopher Stockwell said the Council's decision to back down followed an indication from the Secretary of State that the proposal to amend the PTD was unlikely to be agreed by him. Before getting drawn into a web of potential failure again, the Super Group Members should consider the preconditions for success. A discussion paper on terms for a settlement was attached, together with a press release titled, 'Lloyd's Settlement Initiative'. All parties in the Lloyd's litigation claimed to want a settlement and on their own terms described below.

The E&O underwriters wanted:
- to pay as little as possible as slowly as possible with the maximum recovery from their reinsurers.

Lloyd's wanted:
- an end to litigation and attendant publicity.
- the unwinding of the double counting with the proceeds enhancing Names' solvency.
- capacity for trading.

Names wanted:
- finality for all their underwriting obligations.
- cash in their pockets, not settlement credits or funny money within the Lloyd's Premiums Trust Fund.
- acknowledgement of the incompetence and wrongdoing that has ruined Lloyd's Names.
- judgements against Agents which would allow them to pursue auditors for further compensation.
- judgements to 'set off' against Lloyd's claims on Names.

Names of the Merrett Group Managed Syndicates were invited to a conference on 6 December to receive a progress report. Topics included the run-off, structure and objective, developments in claims, Superfund reform, Equitas and transfer to Whittington Syndicate Management Ltd.

On 14 December the Clerk to Mr Justice Potter informed D J Freeman that delivery of the judgement would have to wait until early next term on a date to be notified.

Newsletter, December 1994

It seemed almost incomprehensible being forced to write a newsletter about another deferment for the Association's judgement date. Mr Justice Potter said pressure of work caused the delay and made a vague commitment to the delivery early in the next law term. This delay increased the worry and anxiety of those in deep financial trouble who may be depending on the result, to formulate Hardship matters. A new settlement was being suggested that Names' greatest asset was the trading name of Lloyd's and apart from litigation the only hope was from future participation in the ongoing trading of that name. There was great political will to preserve Lloyd's and it should capitalise on that will with the desire of Market men to preserve their jobs and pensions. Now was the time for Names to impose their terms rather than accepting what crumbs may be offered.

Clive wrote to Michael Deeny, Chairman of the Litigating Names Committee, thanking him for his letter of 12 December and thought it reflected a very encouraging position. Lloyd's had agreed to pay the costs of Names in determining the legality of the PTD proposals. He requested that the Association's subscriptions were returned. Clive pointed out that the Association had entrusted the conduct of litigation action in opposing alterations to the PTD to his care but had not empowered him in any way to negotiate on any other matters with Lloyd's, nor empowered him to consult or instruct any solicitors on behalf of the Association except in opposing the PTD proposals.

Another circular to the Committee was about one of the Association's Members, Elizabeth Anstey. D J Freeman had received a letter from the Society of Lloyd's that Anstey, their client, had signed a Hardship Agreement and assigned absolutely to Lloyd's her beneficial interest in any damages or award to which she became entitled following judgement or determination. It made a request to the Association to undertake to Lloyd's to pay over all such awards. Clive responded saying that his first reaction was considerably more than irritation that the solicitors for the Association should be acting for what might be termed the opposition. It may well be that Anstey might decide unilaterally to vary the terms of her agreement. D J Freeman could ultimately be acting not only in conflict with but against the best interests of one of the Association's litigants. It was the Committee's duty to do its best for its Members and it had no power to give the undertaking requested. It was Mrs Anstey's business if she had given an undertaking to hand over her litigation recoveries and not the Association's business. He did not believe the Committee should get involved in any subsequent arguments between the two other parties. Subsequently, Jasper Salisbury-Jones pointed out on 3 January 1995 that the Rules of the Association did not provide for wide discretionary powers. Recoveries should be held upon trust. Consequently, the Association had been put on notice that a payment should not be made to Mrs Anstey without further enquiries.

In a letter to D J Freeman, Clive commented on the adverse effects delay in the judgement could have on many litigating Members of the Association. The Hardship Committee had set some stringent timetables for those who may be contemplating Hardship. Clive asked that D J Freeman express to Mr Justice Potter in suitable terms just how much hung not upon the decision itself but the swift delivery of the decision.

The WRG sent a letter seeking Members by explaining the legal action it had taken. It considered that Lloyd's did not comply with European law. There was a detailed consideration of legal technicalities and the letter concluded quoting Article 6 of European Convention on Human Rights which provides *'in the determination of his civil rights and obligations ... everyone is entitled to a fair public hearing by an independent and impartial tribunal established by law...* The proposed amendment would deny the right to a judicial procedure and hence infringe Article 6 of the European Convention on Human Rights. This was followed up by Christopher Stockwell who wrote on 6 December to Jonathan Evans MP summarising the main allegations made by various groups against Lloyd's.

WRG planned to close its Membership list on 10 February.

Clive wrote to Action Group Chairmen on 28 December to express his concern that the Super Group was already dancing to Peter Middleton's music down a dangerous path, when the Super Group could itself be calling the tune. He said the Super Group was in a far stronger position than it had ever been to negotiate not only capping but also some form of restitution. Roughly 6% of the Membership replied to the PTD proposals. Rowland could well have gone to the Secretary of State claiming that 94% of the Membership had not objected. Clive concluded that Rowland had been soundly beaten on a political front, as a result of the pressure generated by ministerial meetings and Members of Parliament in response to their postbags. London still wrote half the world's marine insurance and remained the reinsurance centre of the world. The value of Lloyd's to the City of London and to invisible exports should not be underestimated. This was reflected by the political will to see Lloyd's survive. There were very different agenda for different categories of Name such as litigants, non-litigants, those who were trading on or just surviving, and the truly wiped-out. The great danger was that many Names may be unwilling to take any form of gamble and as a result emasculate their Action Groups. Such Names may allow themselves to be spoofed into accepting much less than may be possible in a united action. The propaganda effect of the PTD was far more serious than the reality. Clive insisted it was imperative to settle the matter in court, without delay, both to call the bluff and to demonstrate the strength of the Super Group position. He said a better deal should be demanded.

Jasper expressed his wish to have a Committee meeting as it was over nine months since the hearing was concluded and ten months at the earliest before a judgement could be handed down. Any judgement would be appealed but nobody could appeal until a judgement had been received.

He favoured a letter to *The Times* denouncing the delay, by an Association Member who was not on the Committee. On 2 January 1995, Clive faxed the Committee about the lack of a Committee Meeting as it had not met since June. There were several issues needing discussion. These included payment of counsel's extra fees, Elizabeth Anstey, the role of the Super Group, the new settlement initiative, the basis of claims on E&O cover and prodding the eponymous judge. The backlog should be cleared before discussing a judgement.

Clive prepared a letter on 4 January 1995 to Peter Middleton thanking him for his letter of 7 December. It said five Members of the Morse Panel refused to sign the financial report as they felt they had been misled by the E&O underwriters. Clive concluded that no offer was likely to be acceptable without a finite cap on future liabilities and some form of restitution derived from the future trading of Lloyd's. Nothing less would satisfy his angry and cheated Names. At present litigation seemed to hold far more promise than the current suggestion.

Clive and Charles Baron met Peter Middleton (P. M.) on 5 January and reported that it was a most conciliatory meeting and suspected that it was more for Middleton to get the cut of the people he was dealing with, rather than a consultation. The settlement would be on an Action Group-by-Action Group basis. Clive handed his letter of 4 January to Middleton. The tone was deliberately aggressive and hostile and was grateful to the Committee for endorsing the approach. Middleton went fairly swiftly through Clive's letter. When he came to the question of fraud P. M.'s response was emphatic and affirmative and volunteered, 'Not only fraud but some very terrible things have happened in this Market.' Clive felt disarmed by the openness of his position and candour of his demeanour. Middleton thanked Clive for the frankness of the letter saying he needed to be constantly reminded of the terrible events that had happened to Names and the suffering that many were enduring. Clive wondered what was producing this ultra-conciliatory and frank approach. What was Middleton's agenda and – surely he had an eye on life after Lloyd's? Middleton looked strained, harassed and several times referred to having to convince the Council of where their best interests lay and the real danger of failing to find a settlement. He said to Clive:

> I came to Lloyd's thinking it was just another company problem to clear up. Something I had done previously at Midland Bank and Thomas Cook, the travel company. I was quite unprepared for the size of the mess. The staff is of low-calibre market personnel. There is a total absence of training other than being taken on at a box and shuffling papers until in time rising to the position of a Nabob, a person of conspicuous wealth or high status.

Middleton continued, 'Lloyd's carries 10% of the asbestosis problem leaving 90% with other companies but I do not know whether some of the external companies reinsured into Lloyd's. Many external insurance companies are in trouble.' Clive, changing the subject and looking intently at Peter Middleton, commented, 'Our Association does not care to negotiate under the threat of amendments to the Premiums Trust Deeds. We need urgently to discuss restitution from future earnings.' Middleton had found much to commend in David Springbett's plan of May 1994.

Clive had taken the lift to the Twelfth Floor where Middleton occupied one of the finest rooms with unrivalled views of London, looking towards St Paul's. He seemed rather isolated from the other big wheels in Lloyd's. Although surrounded by his secretariat there was no evidence of sitting side-by-side with Rowland. He gave the impression of being an honest broker. Clive reflected on the meeting into the small hours. He remained unsure of Middleton's motives and personal agenda. Middleton was certainly not left with the impression that the Committee would be a pushover.

Middleton was working on a cap on losses at syndicate level only. He had asked the Equitas team to concentrate on establishing the ultimate liability of litigating syndicates and report by early February. It was not clear if this would include LMX syndicates and some other liabilities. Equitas would not be authorised until October or ready to start business until

January 1996. Some 5,000 Names were being supported by the Central
Fund and by the end of the year there were likely to be 10,000. Middleton
wanted to be in a position by February to put to Council the possible costs
of a settlement versus not having a settlement. The E&O project conducted
by Allen & Overy regarding the extent of E&O cover should produce some
results by the end of the month. The investigation should show not only the
level of cover but also the notifications. Until Equitas had been established
there was no mechanism for an overall cap. Insolvent Names would need
some incentive if they were to accept an offer. The offer may be for litigating
Names only. Council must consider what should be done for non-litigating
Names. Middleton revealed that he had met the outgoing Commissioner of
Insurance for New York State who admitted that, 'We recognise that these
liabilities cannot be met.' Middleton had suggested it would be helpful if he
would say that outside his office, but the Commissioner said he could not.

The record of another Action Group meeting showed that Middleton
saw the settlement process proceeding as a series of discussions with Action
Group Chairmen. He could not envisage an offer proceeding unless it was
agreed by them. He was uncertain whether one overall deal or thirty-eight
separate deals should be the way forward. He would have no problem
making the offer to Action Groups and leaving it to them to decide how
the distribution should take place rather than make an offer to Names.

Harry Purchase, as a former Managing Director of a subsidiary of
Stewart Wrightson, had strong negative views of his former boss David
Rowland that exhibited tensions in his relationship. He also reported
company gossip at a senior level.

Harry faxed Clive on 5 January giving his congratulations on the
report of the visit to Peter Middleton and confirmed his view that the
Association must take a firm stand. Rumours in the Market were that
Middleton actually wanted out of Lloyd's, he was tired and had enough
and may not stay for the full contract. Secretly and perhaps now more
publicly, he was distressed at the way Names had been fleeced. His flir-
tations with a much younger girl would have caused a stir on the twelfth
floor. Rowland, though divorced and now remarried, was a 'pious little

prig' when it came to office romances and public glare. It might tarnish his chances of the knighthood he so desperately wanted. Harry did not believe that the Committee had any part to play in saving the Market. The Committee was there to do the utmost to obtain full restitution for those who elected it and, of course, for Committee Members. He could not agree, however, that settlement was at whatever terms the Council might throw at the Committee. One assumes that before any Action Group moves forward on the settlement route, there will be considerable liaison between Action Group Chairmen. Presumably he would attempt the first settlements with those designated 'a weak case'.

On 5 January Clive wrote to Alasdair Ferguson thanking him for his letter of 2 January which had caused him to think and reflect upon his draft letter to Peter Middleton, prior to the visit on 4 January. The draft had received unqualified support and had another purpose, which was to suggest to all other Action Group Chairmen that the negotiating position might be considerably stronger than hitherto thought. Clive had noted Alasdair's views with particular care out of respect he held for them and strongly objected that the Committee and Association were being asked to 'negotiate' under the shadow of the Premiums Trust Deed threat. Clive stressed that his job was to do the best for the Association's Members and he would be failing in his duty if he did not press for more at this juncture. He said the Association was yet in the opening dance and there was much to be gained from a resolute stance, which could be softened later.

Clive wrote to the Treasurer on 5 January enclosing his expenses for the quarter and mentioned two extra items, rent and depreciation. As he no longer had a house his landlady has expressed her resentment at having a dining room being permanently used and turned into an office. She blew her top at Alasdair's visit and was now demanding rent of £250 per month. She explained that she had no mission to subsidise the Association's work. Her dining room was littered with computers, fax machines, telephones, dictating machines, answering machines and filing cabinets. As his phone went from early morning to late at night, and sometimes he worked a fifteen-hour day plus weekends, one might concede she had a point. Regarding the depreciation charge, Clive said he had purchased all the equipment out of his own pocket which for the past four years has been devoted to the Association's work.

Newsletter, January 1995

The Chairman's January newsletter commented on the lack of a judgement. Clive thought that it had to do with Mr Justice Phillips who approved the 'first past-the-post principle' following the Gooda Walker Action Group claim. Mr Justice Potter delayed his judgement to harmonise with Mr Justice Phillips as the Gooda Walker Action Group had won a right to an interim payment. Nevertheless, Mr Justice Phillips made it plain that a limited pot should be shared out between all litigation Action Groups. He regretted that he could not do that, although the 'first-past the-post principle' would have little or no effect on the monies eventually available to the Association as it was a different pot in a different year.

The proposals to amend the PTD were roundly defeated on two fronts, firstly, by presentation to Rowland and Middleton of cogent, almost irrefutable legal arguments against the success of these proposals should the matter come to court and, secondly, through very strong political opposition marshalled by Names. Many of the Action Group Chairmen believed the proposals were 'dead ducks'.

Clive was puzzled and deplored the disarray within and amongst the various defence groups. Some declined to cooperate with the Super Group citing personality differences with the Chairman, Christopher Stockwell. It was the Committee's view that this cacophony of squabble was very far from the injured Names' best interests. An umbrella organisation sponsored by the Super Group had been formed called Lloyd's Defence Shield. Much of the evidence needed in defence of Names and utilised by various approaches was common to all.

Clive addressed the matter of 'where the money went'. He cited Names' losses of £8.1 billion while brokers, Members' and Managing Agents took out £11.3 billion and supported the statement by circulating a schedule prepared from Chatset records.

Delay to the Association's AGM was a result of the delayed handing down of the judgement. The AGM was now outside the period prescribed in the Rules and approval and endorsement would be required. He pointed out the real hardship and anxiety experienced by Members. Many of them had difficult and unhappy decisions pressing upon them in negotiations with the Lloyd's Financial Recovery Department.

A circular from Michael Deeny of the Litigating Names Committee on 15 January stated that the DTI had approved the changes to the PTD which took much longer than Lloyd's had expected, requiring three Council meetings. He believed the Litigating Names Committee campaign had led the DTI telling Lloyd's privately but emphatically that they must try to deliver an acceptable settlement offer before August to avoid the DTI having to make some controversial and very difficult decision on Lloyd's solvency.

Twenty-Third Steering Committee Meeting, 19 January 1995: No Decision Yet – Should the Judge Be Approached?

Clive informed the eight Committee Members present that if there had been no judgement by 14 February, he should write to Mr Justice Potter, after clearance with David Tiplady, who should also make a joint approach with other interested solicitors.

The Treasurer reported financial information for the period 1 February 1994 to 31 December 1994. Subscriptions amounted to £601,833, plus interest received of £31,056. Expenses totalled £487,486 and of these D J Freeman's costs were £435,244.

Nicholas Strauss's additional fee of £23,000 plus VAT was discussed, including a letter dated 14 November from his clerk. The brief fee had been agreed with Mr Strauss, who had no claim on the Association's funds resulting from his under-budgeting of time. Charles Baron considered that the Association should only pay what was agreed at the outset and defer the matter until judgement had been given.

Whittington had taken on the Syndicate 334 run-off and the new Monitoring Committee included Charles. Charles asked, 'As Whittington have so far refused to pay my expenses, truly a trivial sum, would the Committee agree to pay them should the situation continue? I would like to mention that Clive will be invited to join the Monitoring Committee.'

Clive observed, 'I think the Super Group is really in considerable disarray. Christopher Stockwell is attempting to form an umbrella group called the Lloyd's Defence Shield. The subscription to the Super Group will be due in December 1995 and we should review it at that time, as it may not be needed.' David Tiplady thought that the case of fraud by the WRG against Lloyd's was unlikely to be proved. The Association's case, with appeals going to Court of Appeal and the House of Lords, was likely to result in any damages being paid in 1997 at the earliest.

Jasper Salisbury-Jones raised the possibility of a change of counsel and wondered who should represent the Association on appeal. David considered that Mr Strauss was thorough and conscientious but need not necessarily be used as an appellate lawyer. Further discussion was deferred.

On 24 January D J Freeman forwarded a copy of Mr Justice Phillips' judgement of 16 January regarding *Cox v Bankside Members' Agency* which established the 'first-past-the-post principle'. He said a number of E&O policies had automatic reinstatement. If an initial claim exceeded the limit of E&O cover the claimant could not claim against the reinstated cover. Consequently, policies carrying reinstatement could not be exhausted by a single claimant. *The Times Law Report* on 27 January stated that Lloyd's claims were to be met in the order following Mr Justice Phillips's judgement of 16 January.

Peter Purchon of Haslemere was a former Managing Director of a subsidiary of Stewart Wrightson who expressed disquiet in his letter of 1 February 1995 at the manner of Clive's approach in the newsletter (not recorded here in detail), and he thought that E&O underwriters would be willing to participate in discussions about an overall settlement. He considered the Association's cause would be promoted more successfully if Clive's remarks concentrated on the redress required by the Association and if he had not written to Peter Middleton in such offensive terms. He thought Clive's comments about David Rowland were inaccurate and vindictive as Rowland was a man of unimpeachable integrity. Continuing legal action for years ahead would be expensive in legal costs and thus likely to diminish the amount of money available to Names. He urged Clive and Members of the Committee to negotiate with utmost vigour for a just and equitable settlement.

Clive replied on 5 February confirming distribution of Peter Purchon's letter to the Committee together with his reply. Until a judgement was obtained no meaningful discussions could take place. An overall settlement involving nothing but Premiums Trust Fund (PTF) credits may suit some but be anathema to others, especially to burnt Names. Until a firm offer was made to the Association, and Members had voted to accept it, in preference to the proceeds of a judgement, he thought Purchon's view was very much open to debate. Clive felt it was better for Lloyd's to continue trading, however, it was inequitable that Names had unlimited liability whereas Members' Agents and Managing Agents were protected by limited-liability companies. All Lloyd's Agents should carry enough E&O cover in respect of negligence and mismanagement allegations. Lloyd's had introduced compulsory E&O cover in 1982 but it reduced the requirement by 60% in 1985. In 1990 the Council abolished the requirement in defiance of undertakings to Parliament. Ian Hay Davison, as prospective Chief Executive of Lloyd's (a post he then held, 1983–86), was asked by the Governor of the Bank of England to go to Lloyd's and pluck out a few rotten apples. To his horror he discovered the whole barrel to be tainted. Those still underwriting may care to reflect on how much of their survival had been due to superb judgement in their choice of syndicates. Alternatively, how much was due to their successful underwriters being able to offload fearsome problems to more gullible underwriters of less-fortunate Names? The Association's robust stance was the opening round in a complex negotiation. There had been several messages of support for this stance. Clive was sorry that Purchon was the sole dissenter as he considered it inappropriate for extracting the best deal for the Association. Clive suggested Purchon put his views forward at the forthcoming AGM.

Tony Levene in *The Sunday Times* on 2 September 1984, stated that Ian Hay Davison had written to the Prime Minister protesting the failure to bring criminal actions against insurers who made secret profits in offshore reinsurance companies. However, the Department of Prosecutions believed that any case brought would be so complicated that it would be impossible to explain the facts adequately to a jury. Most of the money was capable of being repaid so no one would have suffered. There were fears that many of the Lloyd's men implicated in the scandals had left Britain and extradition proceedings would be expensive in time and money. Ian Hay Davison was also quoted in the Names Defence Association March 1995 newssheet saying, 'The job to be done was daunting, but it would involve things I knew about: the unravelling of fraud and the development of accounting rules.'

Several items of correspondence arrived on 1 February relating to proposed changes to the Association's Rule 11.7 about remuneration of Committee Members. Rules could only be changed at a SGM with twenty-one days' notice. A fax indicated that Michael Deeny might receive £1 million for the Gooda Walker victory. The Super Group had deliberated at length and were of the firm opinion that Action Group officers should receive a reasonable fee for success and suggested £25 per hour. Guy Wilson had been charging this rate as Secretary of the Association, as he was not a Member of Syndicate 334.

The Treasurer faxed Charles on 3 February to say that in principle he was opposed to making remuneration payments to the Committee as it was vital to conserve cash resources to settle the undetermined costs of legal action. However, taking account of the extended period of time the Association had lasted and should the legal action be successful, he would change his mind. He agreed that Clive should put an enabling motion to the SGM.

David Rowland wrote on 3 February to all Names about recent developments, as he believed a negotiated settlement offered the best chance of a fair resolution of the disputes. Council had concluded that circumstances affecting litigation recoveries had changed in the past two months.

It was necessary to seek the consent of the Secretary of State for Trade and Industry to alter the PTD. Mr Justice Phillips recently established the principle of 'first past the post'. He had also ruled that E&O was available to cover interim awards of damages. A hearing was fixed for 6 February for Gooda Walker Names to apply for an interim award. The hearing was much earlier than expected and the amounts at issue were very large. Because of that hearing, sums becoming payable to Names would escape the PTF unless the amendments were made promptly. Proposed amendments would only apply to damages awarded after the date the amendments were made. Delay would create unfairness as Names awarded would receive damages before the amendments, whereas those awarded damages after the date would only receive credits in the PTF. Some Names had said openly that they would not use the proceeds of litigation or settlement to meet their outstanding liabilities to Lloyd's. Failure to make such payments could mean their debts falling upon the Central Fund. The Central Fund was financed by all Names and its principal purpose was to ensure all valid claims by Lloyd's policyholders were paid in full. The Council was striving to avoid asking Names to contribute more, whilst covering the debts of defaulters. To be fair to the great majority of Names who had settled their losses, Council believed that compensation received by Names should be used to settle their obligations. The issue of solvency at the end of 1994 had resulted in changes agreed with the DTI in the rules around the valuation of liabilities. The Council was convinced that the Market's return to substantial profits, now apparent, was the best way forward for all Lloyd's Names. It was very important that Lloyd's expertise, negotiating power and the management of very large assets that were put aside to meet old-year liabilities were concentrated in Equitas. Equitas aimed to lift from Names the uncertainty surrounding these assets. Agents were advised not to close 1985 and prior liabilities years of account unless they were completely satisfied that they were adequately reserved.

Clive circulated a note to the Committee that the judgement was imminent, probably next Friday, 10 February. Whether there would be a decision in the coming week would be known by Thursday. Clive had booked the Royal Geographical Society for the AGM and the SGM for 15 March 1995 at 2 pm.

Clive had been working all over the weekend until 4.30 on Sunday afternoon when he sat and looked at his computer for a few moments and then stared round the room. He started muttering to himself, 'I'm pissed off, I'm *really* pissed off!' He held his head as he had a slight headache. Getting up, he walked round the room stressed and frustrated. He had been working on the Association's stuff all the week, including Saturday, and now it was Sunday: typing, researching, copying, stapling and filling festering envelopes. Looking at the piles of files he counted fourteen of Committee work, eight of correspondence and must have saved the Association many thousands of pounds in dealing with professionals alone. There were four full files of the Super Group correspondence with other Chairmen, and filing cabinets stuffed with associated paperwork. He was constantly on the telephone helping Members, counselling, advising and putting people in touch. He was running a business, dedicated to producing a profit of £25 million over five years! Fortunately, the finances of the Association were sound and perhaps the Association should have made proper provision for a secretariat from the beginning, but no one foresaw that it would take five years. It could last another two! The work was more than full-time. He asked himself, 'What business could possibly operate in this way? Bugger it! It would be nice to have some time off.' He sat down again at his computer, 'Sod the plaudits, I'm totally broke, tied to this desk and would like to be able to eat out occasionally, by earning the equivalent of an audio typist. God! I wish I had a secretary!' He started typing an email to the Committee, 'Sorry boys, but I'm pissed off', and detailed his frustrations. He had no intention of battening on other Names' miseries but at least he was working full-time to alleviate them.

Clive faxed to say five Committee Members were in favour of a Rule change regarding payments to Committee Members, two against and with one abstention. The changes would be proposed at the SGM. Twenty-one days' notice was required.

Clive advised the Committee by fax on 6 February that judgement would be handed down at 9.45am on Friday, 10 March 1995. D J Freeman would receive an advance copy the evening before, but Clive would not be able to see it until one hour before handing down. He understood it was a very long judgement. Should the Association win, Clive thought some research was required as to whether or not the defendants were capable of responding and how many of the defendants were in liquidation.

Mr Justice Potter's judgement in the case of *P J Aiken & Others v Stewart Wrightson Members Agency Limited and Others* (Syndicate 334 (1985) Names Association case) is summarised as follows.

1. The Members' Agents owed a duty in contract (but not in tort) to all the plaintiffs, whether by themselves or Pulbrook Underwriting Management, to act with reasonable skill and care in relation to the placing of run-off reinsurance in September 1981.

2. Pulbrook Underwriting Management owed a duty in tort to all the plaintiffs to act with reasonable skill and care in relation to the placing of run-off reinsurance in September 1981.

3. The Members' Agents and Pulbrook Underwriting Management were each in breach of their respective duties by reason of Pulbrook Underwriting Management's failure to disclose three matters which it was held in the interim (arbitration) award should have been disclosed.

4. If the three matters which should have been disclosed had been disclosed, run-off reinsurance would have been placed on the same terms as it was placed, save that the premium would have been $750,000.

5. Save for the eleven plaintiffs whose underwriting agency agreements were under seal all the plaintiffs' claims in contract against the Members' Agents in relation to the run-off reinsurance were statute-barred.

Therefore, Pulbrook Underwriting Management was found to be in breach of their duty in tort and would be liable for claimed losses. The Members' Agents succeeded in the main, in avoiding liability on the basis they were only liable in contract and any contractual claims were statute-barred. It was the intention to apply for an interim payment. However, the defendants were expected to appeal the judgement.

D J Freeman's letter recording the judgement reported that in their view the result was a good one especially as the case was rated 'weak' by the Kerr Panel in the first Lloyd's business plan. The successful outcome had to a large extent been influenced by the faith in the Association's case and commitment of their abilities to it shown by Nicholas Strauss QC and Adam Fenton of counsel.

Newsletter, February 1995: Fantastic News!
The Association had won against both the Managing and Members' Agents although the case against the Members' Agents was time-barred.

Lloyd's Chairman had resiled from his undertaking to suspend the proposals to alter the PTD. The abandoned proposals were originally put on hold to allow the new settlement initiative to get under way in an atmosphere of trust. Clive said the short-term expediency at Lloyd's triumphed over moral scruple and clear strategy. He thought the omens did not look good especially as Lloyd's might be committing commercial suicide by advertising to the world that it was so desperate for cash that it had to resort to this breach of faith.

Initial reports indicated that the 1992 losses to be announced would again exceed £2 billion. The announcement would be before the bill for Equitas was made public. Cash sums demanded for a Name's liabilities to be assumed into Equitas were rising to unmanageable proportions, despite a claim that discounting would be allowed.

Clive urged Members to attend and/or vote at the forthcoming AGM and SGMs. He also pressed the Litigating Names Committee to take immediate action to counter the PTD proposals and not to wait for a *fait accompli*. He was concerned about delay by Lloyd's seeking court approval. If the PTD proposals were passed there would be great anxiety caused to the Association's successful litigants.

Leonard Black of Leonard Black Associates and the Names Defense Association issued a paper on 14 February 1995 titled, 'Basic Self-Preservation for Names'. He stated that the underwriting Name now had to be responsible for the purported claims and reserves that had been written on their behalf, but also for prepayments of future syndicate and claim handling charges expensed against them by specific Managing Agents and run-off operators. He gave a list of examples from the 1993 Annual Reports and Accounts and reproduced relevant bylaws. The list included the Wellington Agency which was responsible for the Syndicate 334 (1985) run-off. It showed expenditure totalling £4,172,000 and Black questioned the figures and wanted to know the legality and construction of the amounts.

Jasper Salisbury-Jones commented on 16 February about the proposed change of Association rules. The Committee had always shied away from paying the Chairman an honorarium because it was feared funds needed for legal action would be dissipated. He said there was now an overwhelming case for considering an honorarium for the Chairman. He also raised the position of the Treasurer and asked if the number of hours spent on the Association's behalf could be determined. He provided an outline of remuneration possibilities for consideration backdated to 1 January 1993. He suggested that payment for past work was staged over eight months at a rate of £20 per hour.

Clive wrote to Peter Middleton on 17 February that the Association had established the liability of Pulbrook Underwriting Management in front of Mr Justice Potter, but quantum had not yet been agreed. Full satisfaction would be in the region of £80 million. Clive said he would welcome any proposals by Middleton leading the Association to discontinue litigation.

Clive circulated a letter from Michael Deeny, Chairman of the Litigating Names Committee, on 16 February, regarding the new proposals for changing the PTD. A significant change was that the litigation recoveries would not be paid into the PTF until the courts had ruled it was lawful to do so. Lloyd's had agreed to test the matter in court. Middleton assured Deeny that Lloyd's was totally committed to finding an acceptable settlement. The effect of changes to the PTD appeared to be a holding operation to prevent cash leaving the system. The Litigating Names Committee was very conscious that Lloyd's might conduct litigation in a leisurely fashion. However, once proceedings began the timetable was not under Lloyd's exclusive control. Middleton indicated that Lloyd's was prepared to pay the Litigating Names Committee the costs of litigation and was totally committed to defeating the iniquitous proposals in court, thus protecting the litigation recoveries which so many had worked so hard to obtain.

Jasper's thoughtful letter concluded that the syndicate's losses to the end of 1993 were £39,455,000, about 223% of line, and expected the Association to receive an award of about £26 million at net present value. It was guessed that Pulbrook Underwriting Management E&O cover was £20 million, indicating a probable unfunded shortfall of £6 million.

On 20 February, Clive faxed a summary of issues prepared by Alasdair for consideration by the Committee including the substance of an Appeal, interests of other Action Groups, scooping the pool, and defendant's financial resources including E&O cover. He also provided information about Members' Agents and estimated their net worth. The final schedule was a list of 562 Syndicate 334 Names by Agency identifying 366 Members of the Association. He finished his summary with a well-known nursery rhyme:

Old Mother Hubbard went to the cupboard to get her poor dog a bone
When she got there, the cupboard was bare
And so, the poor doggie got none.

Clive said that only four of the twelve Members' Agents listed were still trading. If any of the eleven Members under seal were with a liquidating Members' Agent then it might be possible to start to unravel the E&O

mystery. In response to Alasdair's doggerel, Clive concluded that Lloyd's had no proprietary rights over rottweilers as the Association could get its own.

Clive wrote to David Tiplady on 20 February enquiring about the warranties given at the time of the purchase of Pulbrook Underwriting Management by Merrett Group. He pointed out that if warranties were given the considerable liabilities may have remained with Stewart Wrightson which was subsequently absorbed by Willis Corroon PLC. He thought that if the E&O cover was insufficient the responsibility could be tracked to the ample coffers of Willis Corroon.

Twenty-Fourth Steering Committee Meeting, 24 February 1995

At 31 January 1995 funds amounted to £1,069,771. During the year subscriptions and interest came to £677,245 and expenses were £344,876. The Committee agreed by a majority of five to one with one abstention to make a recommendation to the AGM that an *ex-gratia* payment of £40,000 be made to the Chairman.

The counsel to be used for an appeal was discussed. David observed that Mr Strauss was well spoken of in the Potter judgement. He had won on every point in the trial. Mr Strauss had handled matters successfully to date and knew the case thoroughly. It was agreed to retain him without the need for a second silk (the term 'silk' is the legal slang for counsel whose ability and expertise has been recognised by appointment as Queen's Counsel or, since the accession, King's Counsel). David endorsed the excellent work of Mr Strauss.

Clive announced in the Syndicate 334 (1985) Names Association Chairman's newsletters of 27 and 28 February 1995 that the AGM and SGMs were to be held on the 15 March and his letter provided the Committee's recommendations on future legal tactics for consideration at the meetings.

Mr Justice Potter ruled that the claims against the Members' Agents were time-barred since proceedings had commenced more than six years after the relevant events. With the contract claim stymied by the six-year

time-bar, to establish liability against the Members Agents, it was necessary to show they were liable in tort: basically that they were in breach of
a duty of care owed to the plaintiffs, as a result of which negligence the
plaintiffs had suffered financial loss or other harm. The issue involved
complex points of law and the learned judge had decided in favour of
the Agents. It was the Committee's preliminary recommendation that
an appeal against this part of Judge Potter's ruling should be initiated.
Because of the limited timescale for launching appeals the Association
would need to endorse the action at the SGM.

As the Association won its case against both the Managing and
Members' Agents, a summons had been issued for an interim payment.
This should be heard within some six weeks.

Lloyd's had admitted that there was uncertainty over whether it
could use the power of variation to incorporate the litigation recoveries as
assets of the Premiums Trust Deeds (PTD). On 28 February, Katherine
Rimell of Theodore Goddard wrote to the Rose Thomson Young Action
Group about the proposed amendments to the PTD. There were several
conclusions.

1. The PTD had no definition of receivables and referred to reinsurance
    proceeds. Until a claim was made under a policy of reinsurance the
    right of those funds was a 'chose in action'. A chose is a right that can
    be enforced by legal action and the Name's right to receive proceeds
    under an insurance policy.

2. It was not clear whether a chose in action was an asset specifically
    invested in a Name and should be referred to specifically or by infer-
    ence in the definition of the Trust Deed. It was proposed to raise
    loans secured on part or all of the PTF.

3. If, contrary to the view of Theodore Goddard, choses in action were
    part of the PTF, borrowings could be secured on them.

4. If not, the Trustees of the PTF were acting outside their powers.
    Amendments allowing loans to be raised on assets liable in the future
    become comprised within the PTF.

Summary of Key Issues

1. Additional funds were raised to cover the cost of possible failure.

2. Data shows the development of asbestosis claims.

3. NewCo was renamed Equitas.

4. Concerns were expressed about Lloyd's solvency and its survival, and there was concealment of vitally important information from the Market.

5. Nicholas Strauss QC prepared papers for court on 24 February 1994.

6. The Association's case appeared in front of Judge Potter.

7. There were frustrations and anxieties caused by the delays in handing down the judgement.

8. The Association won its legal case.

9. Syndicate 334 ceased trading and was transferred to Whittington Syndicate Management Ltd.

10. Changes to the Premiums Trust Deeds were debated.

CHAPTER 7

Continuing Uncertainties about Cash and Lloyd's Solvency Concerns

King Henry: I tell thee truly Herald
I know not if the day is ours or no;
French Herald: The day is yours.
King Henry: What is this castle call'd that stands hard by?
French Herald: They call it Agincourt.

Henry V, Act 4 Scene 7

On 1 March 1995 Christopher Stockwell of the Super Group wrote to David Rowland saying the most important responsibility of the Council of Lloyd's was the protection of Names' interests. The Super Group believed a majority of those currently underwriting were only doing so because they were trapped in open years. The overwhelming majority of Names did not consider they had legal or moral responsibilities to the American policyholders that were producing most claims. He suggested that there should be a change of policy in the USA and not to pay all the claims presented. Ceasing to trade in America would not be against the interests of the majority of Names although most would welcome the Market continuing.

The Super Group was also aware that the Lloyd's American Premium Trust Fund (LAPTF) had not been administered correctly in the past. With the right management to protect the interests of Names there was a real possibility that substantial funds in the LAPTF could accrue to existing Names. LAPTF believed that Council should initiate a review of the business options for Lloyd's including Names that had ceased trading.

Stockwell's letter to Rowland including a paper titled 'Supplementary Submission to the Treasury Select Committee' was circulated. The paper discussed background information about Lloyd's. It included losses from asbestos and pollution, misrepresentation, inadequate reserving, profitability of non-marine and others, regulation, capital adequacy, risk weighting, solvency margins and concealment. It concluded that the regulatory system was still not satisfactory. The paper asked, who benefitted from the failures? Stockwell urged Rowland to ensure scrutiny of the paper by the Department of Trade & Industry Select Committee.

The Lloyd's Names Information Network produced a paper titled 'Phoenix or Armageddon'. Criteria for a new structure for the Society were detailed including limited liability for all participants. All business activity should be regulated by the Securities and Futures Authority and the DTI. There should be no special exemptions, creation of appropriate catastrophe reserving or ending of annual ventures. It also suggested abandoning the unlimited undertaking to pay all valid claims, which was a marketing ploy used by brokers to bring business to London. Lloyd's had continued to assert that it was in the interests of the Names for the Society to continue trading. At no time had it produced any evidence for this assertion. There were substantial reasons for believing that Names would be much better off by the Society ceasing to trade and substantial advantages to the Exchequer.

Continuing the Society, as distinct from the business, would appear to operate principally for a small minority of insider Names, American policyholders and lawyers, motivated by seeking a share in any damages awarded.

Mounting cash calls for losses forced Keith Lester to apply for Hardship on 2 March 1995 assisted by Saida Saddiqui, a solicitor. There was a gruelling discussion at Lloyd's Chatham office. Keith felt outrage, depression and dismay on arriving at such a low point in his business life which he did not believe resulted from his wrongdoing. He was certainly down, but not out, thanks to the Hardship arrangement, which was of great practical value. Technically he was bankrupt, something he had never envisaged; neither had his wife. Stress from Keith's dreadful circumstances had taken a huge toll on his marriage. The Hardship agreement was certainly not conducive to marital harmony.

John M. Donner of Crowcombe, with forty years' experience at Lloyd's, and who as Chairman of Donner Underwriting Agencies was awarded the Queen's Award for Export, circulated a lengthy, very detailed open letter to Rowland accusing him of a conspiracy of silence.

Donner wrote that Rowland, as a former Chairman of Stewart Wrightson Holdings of which Pulbrook Underwriting Management was a subsidiary, should have been aware of any fraud, deliberate concealment, negligence and cover-up. There was a failure of regulation. Donner said it was time for the Chairman of Lloyd's to reveal the truth.

Andrew Duguid, Secretary of Lloyd's Council, wrote to Names about the Premiums Trust Deed (PTD) explaining that amendments to the PTD were to ensure compensation received by Names for their losses was used to settle their obligations in respect of cash calls and Central Fund drawdowns. The Secretary of State, Michael Heseltine, approved the amendments on 2 March and Council passed a resolution bringing them into effect. Lloyd's would take steps to test the legality of the change in court. Pending the outcome of such proceedings, litigation recoveries caught by the amendment must not be paid or distributed to the Name, their solicitor or Action Group otherwise than to the Trustees of the Name's Premiums Trust Fund (PTF).

Circulated on 10 March was David Tiplady's review of action and his advice as to the merits of an appeal. He said the action addressed issues resulting from the successful avoidance by Merrett Syndicate 418 of a contract of insurance placed by Pulbrook Underwriting Management on behalf of Syndicate 334. Mr Justice Potter held that the duty owed to Names was a duty in tort. There was no contract between Pulbrook Underwriting Management and any Name on the Syndicate 334 1985 account. Mr Justice Potter held that the duty owed to Names by the Members' Agents arose solely by virtue of the contract between the Names and them. In his opinion there was no parallel duty imposed by the law of tort. The cause of action for a breach of contractual or tortuous duty must be instigated within six years of the cause of the action arising. The critical events in this case occurred in late 1981. The first writ was served in early 1991. If the six-year rule applied to all claims they would have been time-barred, even though the syndicate was not aware of them until the successful arbitration in early 1990.

However, there was an exception to the six-year-rule designed to cover situations in which the victim of a breach of duty only learnt belatedly of the information which would enable appropriate legal action. The exception arose under the Latent Damage Act 1986. The wording of the statute was far from clear. In an earlier case the Court of Appeal interpreted it not to apply to claims under contract but only to claims in tort. This enabled the Association to succeed in the claim against the Managing Agent, but that against the Member's Agent was time-barred, except for a few Names whose contracts were under seal. It was possible to appeal the judgement on two counts.

First, seek to establish the Latent Damage Act 1986 applied to claims in contract as well as tort, as the same facts applied to both claims. In all probability it would be necessary to take the Appeal to the House of Lords. At least one Member of the House of Lords, Lord Goff, had already expressed the view (in *Henderson v Merrett*) that the Latent Damage Act 1986 did not apply to claims in contract. There would be considerable difficulty in persuading the House of Lords that this view was incorrect.

Second, the Association could Appeal Mr Justice Potter's decision that the Members' Agents owed Names no duty in the law of tort. Consequently, the Latent Damage Act 1986 would apply and there would be no time-bar. The Association's counsel had made a very valiant attempt to pick his way through a mass of highly complicated cases. David said neither he nor counsel was sanguine about the prospect of success. This ruling also affected many other Action Groups.

David faxed the Joint Advice of Nicholas Strauss QC and Adam Fenton on the question of an appeal which was very discouraging. Essentially, they believed Mr Justice Potter was correct. He wondered if the Association may wish to take a second Opinion from a more robust leader or decide not to appeal at all.

Twenty-Fifth Steering Committee Meeting, Third AGM and SGM, 15 March 1995

The Steering Committee met on 15 March 1995 at noon at the prestigious Royal Geographical Society, Kensington Gore, SW7. All Committee Members were present except for Adam Raphael and they dealt largely with administrative matters for the AGM and SGM.

The AGM and SGM were held at 2 pm in the same building. The Chairman addressed the AGM meeting, saying:

> There are ninety-two Association Members present and I would like to thank you for all for coming. Firstly, I would like to pay tribute to Dr David Tiplady, the Association's legal adviser, who has guided the Association through nearly five years of preparation for litigation and in conducting the litigation to such good effect. Secondly, I also thank the 'extraordinary' Committee which has kept together virtually without a bicker. It has been a very, very good, supportive and generous Committee and it has worked extremely well. However, there is still quite a long path to tread and obstacles to be overcome. Lloyd's seems to be throwing hurdle after hurdle to prevent Names receiving restitution. I do not think it is in Names' interests to engineer the downfall of Lloyd's. There are two virtually opposing groups of Names: those trading on, possibly because their deposit is in hock, and those who are hopelessly burnt. The former have a very different outlook from the latter, who have been dispossessed, chewed up and spat out. This is something very difficult to reconcile with the word 'Society'. You might have noticed recently, the magazine *One Lime Street* expressed great joy that Michael Heseltine, the Secretary of State, has agreed to the alteration of the PTD. The whole message was 'Ah, well, Rowland had triumphed and burnt Names can get lost.' The Association has lost £26 million to date and over the next fifteen years Chatset forecast another £58 million, totalling £84 million. Syndicate 334 Names would lose £128 million overall. You can see in the Financial Statements that the Association is well funded with over a million pounds in the kitty.

Audited Financial Statements Year, Ending 31 January 1995

		1995		1994
	£	£	£	£
Subscriptions		622,267		221,510
Interest and other income		54,978		62,516
Total income		677,245		284,026
Less expenses				
D J Freeman	-294,439		-179,437	
Other expenses	-50,437		-46,691	
Total expenses	-344,876	-344,876	-226,128	-226,128
Excess of income over expenses		332,369		57,898
Balance brought forward		737,402		679,504
Funds available		1,069,771		737,402

David Tiplady informed the meeting that the Association was completely successful in law against both the Managing and Members' Agents. Unfortunately, the claims against the Members' Agents were held to be time-barred. To prevent time running out again, the intention to lodge an appeal had been given but he and counsel were not confident of success. Costs of the appeal would be relatively small. The Association had sought an interim payment and had asked for £85 million. Tiplady suspected £20 million-plus might be received.

He mentioned a recent case giving winnings to the 'first past the post'. This case favoured the Association as it was one of the 'first past the post'. The changes to the PTD would be challenged in court and even if expedited a final ruling would be unlikely for twelve months.

The AGM was closed and the SGM opened. The resolution to initiate an appeal was passed. Clive said that the Association should resist any appeal by the defendants and also launch an appeal against the time-bar. While the defendants had not indicated that they wished to appeal, their solicitors had enquired how much it would take to settle.

They were probably mindful that they would not escape liability and he had asked them to make a proposal in preference to further litigation. Putting Pulbrook Underwriting Management into liquidation was a way of finding out the value of the E&O policy. There was an extended discussion about the costs of an appeal estimated at £200,000 for the Association's and other side's costs, if the case was lost. There may be an additional £100,000 for an appeal to the House of Lords which would only relate to a point of law.

Jasper Salisbury-Jones explained the Special Resolution remunerating Committee Members for services, saying:

> The Association has lasted nearly five years, much longer than one or two years as originally envisaged. Committee Members have been giving their time voluntarily. Recently Action Groups had realised they need greater professionalism with offices and staff. The Association has come to the point fortunately, when it no longer needs to worry about running out of money. The Committee feel very strongly that Clive should be compensated as he has been working more or less full-time and is no longer able to provide financial support. His assets have been shattered mainly by other syndicates. To prevent outrageous payments being made an aggregate total per calendar year for the Committee to be in force from 1 January 1991 was proposed.

The Special Resolutions were passed.

Judge Potter had said that Pulbrook was negligent and the Association would seek full recompense for the losses. There were very few Names for whom Syndicate 334 was the sole cause of grief and therefore it was necessary to look across the Market as a whole to obtain the best possible settlement for the largest number of Names.

A question was whether changes to the PTD were within the objectives of the Association. Clive responded:

The effect of the changes was to catch the litigation recoveries which would become payable to the PTD. It would also allow Agents to borrow on Names' accounts, borrow in between syndicates and to borrow on funds from the 1986, 1987 and 1988 accounts. The borrowing process was very, very sloppy and dangerous. They would be in knots when the money ran out.

Equitas aimed to have quotations for premiums in September. Prior to 1982 brokers kept written insurance policies and no one now knew what policies were in existence. Many brokers had amalgamated, merged or disappeared. Names were paying out on policies from the 1950s and 1960s with no aggregate limit. Clive expected a settlement offer in the autumn but the additional premium to cap the losses would not be known until April 1996. The losses would be discounted to take account of time, which was good news, equivalent to a time and distance policy premium.

Clive and Alasdair Ferguson were immensely impressed with Heidi Hutter, the Chief Executive of Equitas, when they met her recently and had tremendous confidence in the progress she was making.

In conclusion Harry Purchase spoke passionately:

I would like to propose a vote of thanks to Clive. We know him as a man of indomitable spirit. Committee Members return home in the evenings to be greeted by something like 15 metres of fax spewing out of their machines, full of that particular persuasive eloquence that only Clive can muster. Not only did we have that but there was a constant stream of letters, briefs and 'can we get back to him today with our answers?' He has conducted meetings with the sort of aplomb with which he has conducted today's meetings; and he is a *star* of television. At times he is unbearable! Having said that, a vote of thanks is due to him for conducting the meeting and the Association's affairs as well as he has.

There was resounding applause. Subsequently, Clive reported that he had received several messages of thanks for his conduct of the Association and its meetings.

Paul Box, the Manager of Lloyd's Members' Agency Services, considered that any Action Group involved with the years prior to 1986 would not require their recoveries to be paid into the PTF. This appeared to be contrary to Council's policy.

Nicholas Warren QC prepared a standard response to Andrew Duguid's letter of 3 March for use by Action Groups, stating:

> We make no admission as to the validity or effect of the notice thereby given or as to Lloyd's rights in respect of any monies coming into our hands. In particular, we do not admit that the amendments to the PTD are effective to give Lloyd's priority over any earlier assignee or over any Names' Action Group of which he is a Member.

Action Groups were trying to leave their options open. Solicitors for the Managing Agents had twice enquired what figure would be acceptable to settle. They were told either to make an offer or produce the relevant E&O policies for inspection. They had given notice of an appeal, as expected.

Mr A. C. Pollard, Managing Director of Syndicate Underwriting Management Ltd (SUM), wrote to Alan Porter of the Litigating Names Committee. SUM handled run-off syndicates. The correspondence regarded centralisation of claims handling within Lloyd's. He said Lloyd's had two claims areas, the Special Claims Unit (SCU) handling all asbestosis, pollution and health-hazard claims and, secondly, the Lloyd's Claims Scheme handling all other types of claims. The SCU view was that more and more run-off business would be centralised in the agency and one or two other major companies.

It seemed appropriate that the interest of Names on run-off syndicates should be concentrated within run-off companies and not within Lloyd's centrally. He did not think Names on SUM's syndicates were compromised by the current arrangements. However, if claims handling authority were removed from SUM's syndicates and passed to on-going syndicates with different commercial interests, the Names may be at a disadvantage.

The Super Group circulated to Action Group Chairmen on 27 March regarding the intermingling of funds. The practice of inter-syndicate lending had been gradually stopped but the dubious practice of inter-Name and inter-year borrowing within the same syndicate continued. It would be a breach of responsibility as trustees of the PTF for the intermingling of funds and liabilities to continue. Managing Agents had been unwinding inter-syndicate lending due to fears over their trusteeship responsibilities and should unwind inter-Name, inter-year unsecured lending within a syndicate. One syndicate run-off manager admitted that an average solvent Name was lending £11,000 to insolvent Names. Clive used a draft letter about intermingling from the Super Group to send to Whittington Syndicate Management Ltd, the agency running off Syndicate 334.

The conduct of the run-off by Whittington Syndicate Management Ltd was probably as important as the fructification of the litigation. Charles Baron was appointed to monitor the run-off and reported an intermingling of funds of different years, an unwelcome aspect of the run-off. For instance, 1985 funds were used to pay claims on the 1990 account. The latter were a different syndicate of Names compared to the former. It was apparent that Managing Agents were finding it very difficult to obtain money from the Lloyd's Central Fund. The Equitas premium would not be known until September 1995. A settlement offer could not be properly evaluated without Names knowing the amount of the Equitas invoices. Clive issued a warning about Lloyd's potential insolvency as solvent Names were lending to insolvent Names to settle claims. Over half the Names had ceased to trade with the proportion expected to increase because of the current year's losses.

On 28 March, Charles thanked John Winter for providing Syndicate 334 figures of the surplus cash and investments for 1985 at £34,986,000 *surplus* and for 1990 £3,992,000 *deficit*. Charles asked if part of the 1985 surplus consisted of a loan to the 1990 year and the amount. As Names had several but not joint liability, he asked that Winter confirm that such

loans would be repaid immediately and no further loans would be made
from the 1985 year to any other syndicate. In the Whittington figures
cash calls received from Names were assumed to be less than 100%. The
balance would be receivable from the Central Fund for those who 'can't
pay or won't pay'. Relating this to the sanctity of the Lloyd's policy, 100%
of an agreed claim should not be paid until the deficit had been made
good from the Central Fund. He asked how much was due from the
Central Fund and how long such a debt had been outstanding and if
claims were being paid in full ahead of such receipts.

Mike Wells of Whittington Syndicate Management telephoned
Charles that IBNR had shot up from 62% to 82% between September
and the December year end. The reason was the London Market Claims
Service was unable to provide up-to-date figures of net outstandings. As
IBNR was pure guesswork, Clive thought it most unfair that such figures
were used to assess Names' individual solvency requirements.

Reactions Special Report on the London Company market appeared
in the April issue as, 'How to Leave London'. It said too many insurance companies were entering run-off and were doomed to insolvency. Six
companies were in run-off in 1992 and 1993. The only winners were the
company's own staff, lawyers and run-off operators.

Clive wrote to Whittington Syndicate Management Ltd as trustees of
the Names' PTF saying that each year of account was an annual venture.
The Association had been informed that some £4 million from the 1985
account of Syndicate 334 was used to discharge the liabilities of another
year of account without security and as such the Association considered the trustees were in breach of their duties. The trustees borrowed
from solvent Names in order to pay the liabilities of insolvent Names.
Clive asked for assurance demonstrating that there was requisite information and segregation of individual Names' accounts. Lloyd's bylaws
may give encouragement to the practice of inter-year and inter-syndicate lending, but it could not diminish the liability under the Trustee
Acts – maybe Lloyd's Central Fund had acted as guarantor of last resort.
The last published report showed that Lloyd's Central Fund had some

£600 million in cash with earmarkings of £1.2 billion ascribed to Names who could not or would not pay. This suggested that the Central Fund was insolvent and as security, it must be deemed doubtful or worse.

On 21 April, Alasdair Ferguson analysed the last three years' losses of the Merrett Group totalling £6.7 million, summarised in two tables as follows.

Merrett Group PLC Losses by Year

Year (Ending 30/9)	Losses (£'000)
1991/92	649
1992/93	3,507
1993/94	2,558
Total	**6,714**

Merrett Group PLC Balance Sheet Items for 1993 and 1994

Account Name	1993	1994
Fixed assets	2,793	4,680
Liabilities	(1,927)	(3,323)
Net assets (£'000)	**866**	**1,357**

The audit report was qualified regarding 'uncertainty as a going concern' and listed ten active legal actions against the Group, including that of Syndicate 334. It mentioned the claim against Pulbrook Underwriting Management that was held to be negligent by the court. An appeal was being considered. Names on Syndicate 418 who participated in the 1985 year were alleging breaches of duty and misrepresentation in relation to the management of the syndicate. Alasdair concluded that the Merrett Group was bust.

Newsletter, April 1995

The April newsletter reported that Pulbrook Underwriting Management had asked if the Association would like to settle. After waiting five years, this ploy seemed eminently resistible. The Association had asked for full disclosure of E&O policies. In March Mr Justice Phillips gave his ruling on 'first past the post' and licensed the Gooda Walker Action Group to scoop the pool. This judgement was immediately placed in limbo by the appeal against it from Janson Green and other long-tail Action Groups. The outcome of the appeal could have some bearing on the Association's ability to achieve restitution. The Association was unaware of any other Action Group suing on the 1985 account. Phillips showed his disapproval of his earlier ruling and limited Gooda Walker damages to claims paid away. This was relevant for the Association as the greater part of the 'long-tail losses' had gone into creating reserves for future claims.

Clive gave his new 'Hardship' address in Queen's Road, Exeter, calling the property 'Hardship House'. Poor Clive; this was a great climb-down from a beautiful house in Notting Hill, via digs and eventually ending up in the sticks in Exeter, with little income. How are the mighty fallen! Communications were disrupted as a result of a delay by BT in providing facilities.

Reporting on the Super Group meeting of 27 April, Clive said there had been an explosion of interest in Lloyd's by broadsheets and tabloids, although there was nothing new revealed. The last published value of the Central Fund was £800 million with earmarking of £1.3 billion. Consequently, Managing Agents had been forced and encouraged to mingle funds, borrowing from those in surplus and giving to those in deficit. Peter Middleton said, 'If we say we're solvent and the DTI agrees, then we ARE solvent.' In other words, Lloyd's was solvent because Lloyd's said so.

David Rowland had again been summoned before the Treasury Select Committee. Brian Sedgemore MP and Diane Abbott MP walked out, objecting to the meeting being held in secret. It was held in secret because the Committee was alarmed at the Lloyd's solvency position and wished to dig deeper. Another reason was that authentic but anonymous sources said that the Select Committee had received some minutes of board meetings of Stewart Smith, Stewart Wrightson and Matthews Wrightson at which Rowland had been Chairman. These minutes revealed beyond any doubt the Chairman knew in 1981 and 1982 of the impending disaster. They included explicit reports from a Mr Tyler who was a founding Member of the Lloyd's AWP.

During last week Lloyd's had instructed thirty-nine surviving Members' Agents and some ninety-nine Managing Agents to issue writs and sue nonpaying Names. By Thursday morning, of the four Agents contacted by the Super Group, two were 'sucking their teeth' and two had decided 'over my dead body'. If it wasn't so serious, the situation would be hilarious.

The 'rottweiling' aggressive, ruthless efforts of Philip Holden of the Financial Recovery Department (FRD) in collecting debts from Names had only brought in a derisory £43 million. As a rottweiler, he was openly called toothless and therefore had been racking his brains on how best to proceed. The Agents were aghast at the thought they had to sue their Principals, for this would raise all sorts of adverse situations – those Principals were the ones who constituted their very bread and butter. Not only that, but it was arguable that if an Agent sued his Principal, the formal Agency relationship could be held in question. Moreover, Agents were well aware of the virtual impossibility of obtaining an Order 14 judgement (an application by a plaintiff for a summary judgement) against any of their Names. They would be quite unable to cope with the plethora and complexity of legal defence and counter-claims from their Names.

True to fashion, Lloyd's loaded a huge gun and pointed it directly downwards. It issued a set of parameters outlining the type of Name who should be pursued. They defined the very types the Agents were most loath to pursue. The ideal targets were to be the nonpaying wealthy, those trading on, those who were not Members of Action Groups and those who had made no claims against their Agents, etc. One of the more interesting of the parameters was that the targets should be confined to UK Names. By Friday morning the answer was clear, for the Agents to a person rose to the Twelfth Floor, nominally the executive suite of the Lloyd's iconic building, and maintained they could find no suitable candidates to sue.

Even though it was such a serious matter, Clive found it very amusing to discover a 'rottweiler dog' in sheep's clothes!

The Litigating Names Committee had issued a writ seeking a ruling on the legality of alterations to the PTD. For expediency, they limited the summons to the single issue of litigation recoveries. The Super Group felt this was a severe mistake for many other proposed alterations carried dangers for Names. However, the executives on the Twelfth Floor were much less sanguine about winning the legal battle over the PTD alterations. Members of the Super Group heard that the Canadians had lost their case against banks over payments under letters of credit to Lloyd's. The judgement was held by all to be not only bizarre but patently wrong as it flew in the face of all previous judgements. The Canadian Names were confident of winning their appeal. A seven-hour Super Group strategy meeting with lawyers and accountants Robson Rhodes concluded that the interests of Names were best protected if Lloyd's went into a solvent run-off.

Clive declared it was sad to learn that several of the big Action Groups committed to fund the Super Group secretariat had reneged on their promises. The Super Group was an excellent clearing house for information, still strongly supported by smaller Action Groups. The Twelfth Floor had eventually acknowledged that without a cap and finality there could be no deal. Individual bills for the protection of Equitas would not be known until September, so it was clearly impractical to provide a settlement offer in May. The press had not been short on speculation and gave the impression that the Twelfth Floor was in disarray. The doomsters were forecasting the need for a levy for the Central Fund if Lloyd's wished to trade on for another year. The solvency problem depended on who was speaking. It was now a political football being booted by the two main political parties, neither of which wished to be the party in power when Lloyd's went down. Several leading Managing Agents already had limited-liability insurance companies ready to go into action. Clive concluded this lengthy report with his observation that 'sitting in Hardship House in Exeter has its attractions'.

Three directors of Lloyd's Agency were being prosecuted by the DTI for breaches of Section 151 of the 1986 Companies Act, which states,

'It is not lawful for the company or any of its subsidiaries to give financial assistance directly or indirectly for the purpose of that acquisition before or at the same time as the acquisition takes place.' Writing to Peter Middleton, the trio said it was regrettable that Lloyd's had to look to the DTI to produce satisfactory regulation at Lloyd's. They expressed concern about Agents distancing their assets and preferential stop-loss schemes for working Names, and were extremely concerned about Managing Agents intermingling funds. They said Middleton was on notice that any continuation of intermingling practices would constitute a breach of Trust Law. He would be open to action by solvent Names wishing to prevent further damage to their position by Agents lending to insolvent Names. A letter sent to Agents showed discrimination, by not treating Names equally and an attempt to use Names' money (Lloyd's funds) to fund Agents to take action against their Principals. This was seeking to force Agents in breach of privacy and privilege to obtain by extra-judicial means what was barred from being obtained judicially.

Twenty-Sixth Steering Committee Meeting, 2 May 1995

Six Committee Members were informed that some £5,000 VAT refund had been received and over £1 million was on deposit. Likely Association liabilities may amount to £300,000 should the appeal be lost. The Association had more money than it needed. Clive would be paid the second *ex-gratia* instalment of £20,000.

Mr Strauss was preparing a second Opinion, but it appeared that the legal position was not favourable and unlikely to be resolved before the end of 1995. Pulbrook Underwriting Management had offered further negotiations and Alasdair had set out matters to be considered as follows:

1. E&O policies to be seen and deductibles identified
2. expenses to be quantified
3. consider a discount for early payment
4. the payment date
5. conditions required to cancel the appeal

6. put Matthews Wrightson Pulbrook Ltd into liquidation
7. seek information from Charles Sturge of Chatset as to the poten-
    tial losses

The process of appeal had been instigated against the Members' Agent subject to an absence of a negative comment from Mr Strauss.

Committee Members were suspicious that Whittington Syndicate Management may not be giving proper value and wondering what could be being plundered. Charles Baron was asked to seek a breakdown of run-off syndicate reserves by cash, reinsurance time and distance policies etc., and a breakdown of assets between different years. He also needed the latest losses to date and estimates of IBNR, a profit and loss account, a clear statement of job specifications and performance standards. The Committee discussed whether the Association should be involved in the run-off. Matters considered included continuing with Whittington Syndicate Management, or whether the Association formed a separate company to handle the run-off of Syndicate 334, or a company to handle the management and assessment of claims. To set up a run-off company, £250,000 capital would be required to obtain a licence, possibly raised from 1,000 Members at £250 each. A credible board would be needed and a business plan. The objects of the business would be to reduce the liabilities of the syndicate and it might or might not make a profit. The Association was considered too small to start its own run-off and the Chairman agreed to invite Whittington Syndicate Management to give a presentation to the next meeting.

At the recent AGM it had been agreed to pool the winnings in respect of the court action. The intention was to preclude any discussion about who had won and how the funds were to be divided and to give a fair distribution to all Association Members. Funds received in respect of the eleven Members who had signed under seal should also be aggregated with any other winnings.

Apart from the Chairman other Committee Members who had provided services outside the confines of the Committee were Alasdair

Ferguson, Charles Baron, Jasper Salisbury-Jones and the Treasurer. The Treasurer expressed the view, 'I have always been concerned that the Committee should not whittle away sums provided by Members for legal action by paying Committee Members for work which had been taken on voluntarily. When monies are distributed, that will be the time to acknowledge work done by Committee Members.' The Chairman pointed out that the Association had been running for much longer than originally envisaged and was actively pursuing cash won from the court case. Alasdair said he did not wish to take any fees. The Committee agreed that Charles, Jasper and Keith receive £5,000 each for the 1995 financial year payable on 1 July.

Christopher Stockwell's letter of 5 May said that Lloyd's had requested information about Membership of the Action Groups in connection with a proposed offer being called 'Reconstruction and Renewal'. Concern was expressed that Lloyd's had told Agents that they would use their central database to coordinate writs against Names. He suggested that Action Groups that had not submitted details so far should say they were not willing to do so until necessary assurances were received in writing, that the information would not be used to issue writs.

Clare Sambrook in *Business News* on 15 May stated that auditors and brokers would be asked to contribute £2 billion towards the settlement to be discussed on 16 May, at a marathon Lloyd's Council meeting. William Gleeson reported that 'Lloyd's Feared US Crunch'. He said that Lloyd's solvency was causing a problem in the US and unless more money was forthcoming Lloyd's may face restrictions. A *Reactions* item headed 'Lloyd's Names Continue to Win in the Courtroom' said that rulings for Pulbrook and Feltrim litigation spelled out guidelines that should have been followed by underwriters to protect Names. Clive Boxer in *Corporate Cover* said some Names may have run out of time to bring claims against their Members' Agents. The article explained the Association's case and result.

On 16 May, Clive wrote to the Committee to say the Super Group subscription was due. As it was a valuable forum for the exchange of views and a prime source of all the latest developments in the Names' struggle, he recommended payment of £1,860. Although the Association had won its case much that affected the Association was still developing. The Super Group maintained a research caucus and the organisation was a force which the executives on the Twelfth Floor had to consider when formulating proposals.

Charles Baron reported on 16 May that John Winter was managing Syndicates 334 and 418 run-offs. Charles had worked through a typical claim and concluded that the individuals concerned appeared quite competent, but he would need to probe more deeply. Claims were handled in concert with the Special Claims Unit. He enclosed a copy of the syndicate expenses for the run-off 1985 year to 31 December 1994, amounting to over £4 million.

Charles produced a schedule of the syndicate's 1985 reserves as at 31 December 1994 amounting to £41 million.

The Whittington Syndicate Management Company Run-Off Details

	£m
Outstanding claims	34
IBNR	23
TOTAL	**57**
Less	
Time and distance policies	-16
Total liabilities	**41**
Represented by:	
Investments	35
Reinsurance recoveries due	1
Total	36
Uncalled and unpaid losses	7
Total	43
Rounding	-2
Total assets	**41**

Uncalled losses were the total of the deferred loss plus unpaid calls plus the loss called as at 31 December 1994. Unfortunately, Chatset put the IBNR at a much higher figure than Whittington Syndicate Management Company which was at the lower end of a range.

The Association of Non-North American Names said preventing deposit drawdowns was one of the most important aspects of their activity. It was necessary to prove the fraud case to be able to press claims against banks which had drawn-down deposits. It was essential to build pressure on guarantors of Lloyd's deposits to prevent compulsory drawdown. The figures for Lloyd's general solvency position did not add up and the Association of Non-North American Names had not been able to obtain answers to questions on solvency from either the DTI or Lloyd's.

Michael Deeny indicated that the Super Group was gearing up for litigation on the PTD and secured the services of Sidney Kentridge QC who agreed to appear in court with Nicholas Warren QC. He was an extremely able Chancery silk and an expert on trusts. Kentridge was a heavyweight advocate selected as number one in a top-ten list of barristers in a recent *Legal Business* survey of the legal profession.

The Names Defence Association produced a paper on 25 May titled 'Lloyd's of London: The Case Against the DTI'. This related to the DTI's regulatory failure, as it treated Lloyd's as if it was a single entity where trading losses must, if necessary, be mutualised across all traders. However, Lloyd's was a marketplace with 400 separate insurance underwriting businesses. It appeared that the DTI had assessed the solvency on a false presumption.

There were press reports that additional security from Lloyd's was being demanded by the Commissioner of Insurance for New York State and reflected how worried the US Authorities were. The report stated that several eminent Lloyd's managing underwriters knew in the mid-1970s that Lloyd's faced a long-term avalanche of product liability and pollution clean-up claims from the USA. These claims were monitored through official Lloyd's working parties. In early 1982 Lloyd's officials were informed by its panel of approved syndicate auditors that the liabilities facing

Lloyd's were massive and unquantifiable. External and most Working Names were never informed.

The DTI was aware of the problems and a two-part solution was proposed and agreed by them and Lloyd's. The first was to gradually increase reserves over the coming years. The procedure of gradually increasing minimum percentage reserves was called 'stair stepping'. Stair stepping increased the reserves to the disadvantage of certain Names on syndicates, for instance, those joining or leaving or changing their underwriting capacity. The report suggested the reserves had been fraudulently increased and used as the basis for setting RITC premiums as an essential element in the annual assessment of Lloyd's solvency by the DTI. Stair stepping was implemented throughout the 1980s and into the 1990s. The term first came to light in 1994. The procedure was totally inappropriate for Lloyd's syndicates which were annual business ventures where membership varied from year to year. New Names were neither told of the potential liabilities they were assuming nor received proper financial consideration for taking on those risks, risks believed so large as to be unquantifiable. It was a criminal act to trade when insolvent. Fundamental insolvency occurs when a trader knows he will be unable to pay in full all known creditors as the debts eventually fall due.

The second part of the solution agreed by the DTI and Lloyd's officials was to encourage the recruitment of ever-increasing numbers of new Names at Lloyd's and by this and other methods to increase the total capital available to finance trading and to pay forthcoming US policyholders' long-term claims. As a result of the substantial increase in capital funds and guarantees deposited at Lloyd's by Names, gross underwriting capacity increased from £3.2 billion in 1980 to £11.02 billion in 1988.

The actions of Lloyd's and DTI officials might be likened to those directors and auditors of a company who ignore its long-term debt when considering its financial strength and ability to continue trading. Lloyd's insiders had material information for many years which clearly indicated that many syndicates were in the bankruptcy category.

Since the late 1970s many long-tail syndicates did trade and close out their accounts. However, they were only able to do so because they in turn managed to pay out improper and fraudulently low RITC to their successors. The Names Defence Association report stated that some Names considered that the DTI and Lloyd's officials might have been criminally guilty of allowing many syndicates to trade when they were fundamentally insolvent and bankrupt.

Charles Baron saw Equitas as a dustbin and wondered whether it was 'safe'. He saw discounted liabilities at £15.2 billion and wanted to know the undiscounted value. If Equitas went broke, Names would not be able to litigate. He wondered whether Names' liabilities became joint and several. In his view Equitas should be controlled by Names and information was required about the directors and employees.

On 29 Mr T. N. Nelson of Argyll expressed his lack of confidence in Equitas and argued the Reconstruction and Renewal did not offer finality. He thought £200 million from the Agents was an unacceptably small contribution from a community that had extracted £10 billion from the Market in commissions and expenses over the past ten years. Clive responded on 6 June and commented that he was bemused by the concept of qualified finality proposed in the reconstruction plan. An executor would be unable to close an Estate on the questionable finality of Equitas. Clive replied in similar vein to William Letten of Grimsby, as the document suggested there would be considerable debt credits for syndicates in a similar situation to Syndicate 334. The court's award would not bring finality which was of paramount importance. Flexibility and compromise would be the best negotiating stance.

A Mr Shreeves, on 1 June, believed a properly structured enquiry focused on the issues of complacency and concealment would be welcomed by those seeking the truth. Mr Shreeves shared with his MP, Mr Lilley, a quotation after Rudyard Kipling, where he thought of replacing the word 'Name' for 'Saxon' and 'Lloyd's Council Members' for 'Normans'. It then read as follows:

The Name is not like us Lloyd's Council Members. His manners are not so polite.

But he never means anything serious till he talks about justice and right.
When he stands like an ox in the furrow with his sullen set eyes on
    your own
And grumbles 'This isn't fair dealing' my son leave the Name alone.

Shreeves suggested the above could become the Names' clarion call. Clive responded that the political will to keep Lloyd's alive was very strong indeed. Frankfurt and Paris were snapping at London's heels for Europe's financial leadership. Lloyd's employed directly or indirectly some 60,000 people. By comparison the plight of some 15,000 burnt Names, however cogent their grievances, seemed in political terms fairly insignificant. During the 1980s the Treasury and Civil Service Select Committee had recommended that there should be an enquiry into Lloyd's conduct. While Clive would support an enquiry, however damming, it could not provide recompense for those who had suffered and some form of restitution should come from the future trading of Lloyd's.

On 7 June Clive commented on the reconstruction plan, billed as a £2.8 billion offer to Names. Actual cash amounted to £800 million. Closer inspection revealed £1.5 billion came from Names' own funds at Lloyd's. However, success in litigating left the Association in a strong bargaining position. The nub of the plan revolved around finality. If finality was absolute Names could rush to the exit and executors would be able to get on with their work, giving the plan a strong chance of success. Nothing in the offer relieved Names of their fundamental obligation to pay up on their unpaid calls. All that was happening was the redistribution of Names' reserves amounting to mutualisation. This was entirely contrary to the concept that the Name was a sole trader underwriting on his own account. Legal ownership was the important issue and Lord Wrenbury provided an example. He said that if a person owed a debt of £590 and means were found of reducing this to £390 one did not expect the person who had the good idea of how to affect the reduction to scoff the difference of £200. This was precisely the way the settlement offer was structured. Lloyd's would take the £200 and distribute it to those pre-1993 Names with whom it wished to curry favour. He viewed the proposal as an exact replica of the story in the Holy Bible of the 'Unjust Steward' (Luke 16:1–12).

The Devonshire Action Group received an Opinion from Michael Tennet QC on 10 June, regarding inter-Name and inter-year lending at Lloyd's with liabilities to policyholders being settled out of intermingled PTF assets belonging to different Names. The 'won't pay' defaulting Names were unlikely to volunteer to repay other Names whose funds had been used to settle the defaulters' liabilities without their consent. As for 'can't pay' Names, the figures given by David Rowland raised doubts as to the sufficiency of their Lloyd's deposits and the Central Fund to cover their existing liabilities. It was by no means clear that what the PTD trustees had been doing in practice could properly be characterised as making loans. It is one thing for the trustees formally to grant a loan, it is another for the trustees simply to settle syndicate liabilities from intermingled funds. The trustees may have had no intention of making a loan but used the funds without considering whether the beneficial owners of the funds used were the same as the persons liable to pay the claims. It was not easy to see why they should be treated as having made a loan to meet defaulting Names' liabilities. He concluded that it was unlikely 'inter-Name lending' would continue for much longer.

David Tiplady replied by return to Clive's concerns about lack of progress for obtaining an interim payment. Stephen Merrett's affidavit put forward an argument that the Association would only be able to recover £821,958. This was believed to be a specious argument and it needed studying with counsel and US experts. David had a very able assistant, Mark Everiss, working exclusively on the task.

On 10 June, Harry Purchase circulated a fax following his conversation with a Lloyd's elder statesman who was of highest integrity – a rarity, he observed! The statesman had analysed the Equitas formula and estimated the company would last no longer than four years. Then outstanding liabilities would revert to the Names, who would have already paid twice, once for the losses and once for the Equitas premium to buy an illusory cap. Harry was adamant that the Association must insist on an absolute cap.

Twenty-Seventh Steering Committee Meeting, 12 June 1995

Matters discussed at the June Steering Committee meeting were as set out in the June newsletter below. In addition, David confirmed that a reinsurance policy with Equitas could be relied upon by executors so that deceased Names' Estates could be wound up. It was agreed that the Chairman receive £20,000 per year for 1991 and 1992 and £10,000 for 1995. A further £5,000 each was to be paid for the 1995 calendar year to the Treasurer, Charles Baron and Jasper Salisbury-Jones upon presentation of an invoice.

Newsletter, June 1995

In the Chairman's June newsletter Clive reported slow progress since receiving judgement in pursuing a hearing for an interim payment. The defendants had produced detailed evidence to show that any interim payment award should limited to the miniscule sum of £800,000. David Tiplady was working to produce evidence that an interim payment of some £12 million was required together with a date for the hearing.

Commenting on the Lloyd's plan for Reconstruction and Renewal, Clive confessed he was quite mystified by the concept of qualified finality. Should Equitas fail no Name would achieve finality. He thought the Lloyd's plan was spoilt by delicate euphemisms and omissions. What had been billed and hailed by the press as a £2.8 billion Lloyd's offer to Names was planned to be funded almost in total by the Names' own money. There was a charming euphemism that stated there was a slight mismatch between assets and liabilities in the USA. The latest estimate of this mismatch was $7 billion. There was no explanation of where this sum may come from. Those consigned to Equitas would have years of worry wondering whether the hulk would go down. Nevertheless, the Committee gave the plan a cautious welcome. However, the chances of an insured being able to recover from Names should Lloyd's fail was slim indeed.

The addendum to the Chairman's newsletter stated that the date for the hearing of the interim payment award had been set for 3 July at the Royal Courts of Justice. Clive invited Association Members to attend. He added that any money awarded would be held in escrow until the case of the alteration of the PTD had been heard.

Clive asked the run-off managers, Whittington Syndicate Management, about the 'loan' of £4 million from Syndicate 334, 1985 year to Syndicate 334, 1990 year. He had received assurances that the money would be repaid as soon as certain reinsurances had been credited. Managers had received a legal Opinion that Whittington Syndicate Management was in breach of trust regulations and trustees may become personally liable for unpaid amounts. Furthermore, managers had no powers to make loans. There was little doubt there was a severe cash crisis at Lloyd's. Those Names contemplating making payments in the near future might well reflect that it might be wiser to wait and see how things would develop. In conclusion Clive speculated that it might be two years before any Association Member saw a cheque for recoveries. Without cast-iron finality, the plan was unlikely to succeed.

The Names Defence Association provided a detailed analysis and explanation of the Lloyd's Reconstruction and Renewal offer by Lord Wrenbury. A review of records with Citibank and Lloyd's indicated that there was not any record of individual Names' total assets in the Lloyd's American Premium Trust Fund accounts (LAPTF). It was noted that Lloyd's instructed Citibank to draw down on a pool of funds held in certain other group accounts regardless of whether or not the group accounts were under the control of the same Managing Agent. To ensure the claim was settled a Name's funds that were drawn down may have no liability for the claim. It was one thing to negotiate a premium that appeared to be sufficient to cater for future deterioration and quite another to fix reserves at a level which did not require topping up in the future.

Clive received a letter from Adam Raphael on 17 June resigning from the Committee explaining that it was from pressure of work. Clive replied thanking him for his wise counsel and the kind, courteous and valuable contributions to the Committee's debates.

On 25 June Keith Lester's father died. It was a terribly sad day adding more difficulties, issues and complexities at a time of severe financial and business pressures.

A memorandum was circulated titled, 'Additional Material about Lloyd's Suppression of Malpractice by Lloyd's Deputy Chairman, Dick Hazell' (see also 14 November 1995). The scandal revolved round the 'garaging' of $22 million premium received from US companies for a ten-year liability risk for $490 million and the misappropriation of $12 million interest on the total from the syndicates that underwrote the risk. In 1982 Pan Am, the airline, and other US companies were advised by Tom Gallagher of a way to sell their huge tax losses to other profitable companies by way of leasing an asset for tax purposes only. The companies wanted financial guarantees against the possibility of the US Inland Revenue declaring tax benefit transfers as tax evasion any time within the succeeding ten years. Lloyd's brokers Blackwall Green quoted premiums for tax benefit transfers guarantees for a 'tax lease' on ten airliners. The lease was signed on 27 August 1982. Dick Hazell, the underwriter on Syndicate 190, was approached by the brokers to be the lead underwriter of this new package. He asked Blackwall Green to 'garage or park' the full ten-year premiums and only pay into his syndicate annually one tenth of the premiums due. Other syndicates with lines on the slip were also paid one tenth of the total premium into their syndicates' accounts each year. The slip was the document prepared by a broker describing the risks to be covered and presented to a syndicate underwriter to initial the percentage of risk the syndicate was prepared to accept. They did not know that the full ten-year premiums were being held in a specially set-up Jersey Trust and a Morgan Grenfell (Jersey) bank account. The Green family drained out the interest into Smith Bromfield Ltd, a Jersey company set up in the maiden names of the wives of two Blackwall Green directors.

There were forty-seven separate tax benefit transfer policies. News of the interest retention was given to certain Lloyd's Committee Members including David Coleridge, a Director of the Sturge Underwriting Agency, whose underwriter was Ralph Rokeby-Johnson. He was the second insurer on the slip. An enquiry was demanded into the retention of $12 million by the Green family. The enquiry started in 1990 and terminated in 1991 without disclosure or conclusion.

Dick Hazell resigned as underwriter of Syndicate 190 in 1991 and found a new job as Chairman of the UK subsidiary of Liberty Mutual, an American reinsurance company. It was very important to realise that this reinsurance company was both a policyholder and one of Syndicate 190's largest reinsurers.

Syndicate 190 was managed by Cater Allen Bank and they wanted to be rid of its Lloyd's syndicate management arm. Hazell bid to take over the management of his old syndicate under the hat of Liberty Mutual. If Hazell was made Manager of Syndicate 190 while Chairman of Liberty Mutual and controlling Syndicate 190's run-off years, he would be able to call in the houses of 6,000 Names on the 1989 and 1990 years of Syndicate 190 to offset losses.

Hazell, as Chairman of Liberty Mutual, would be able to deny liability to pay the reinsurance claims for which Syndicate 190 had paid premiums to the company. Furthermore, using the Syndicate 190 cheque book, he would be able to pay out money to Liberty Mutual for any claims that he cared to dream up as policyholder.

Hazell underwrote three layers of E&O insurance at Syndicate 190 in 1989 and 1990 above the policyholders' excess of £2 million. He took 7% of £3 million excess of £2 million (total cover £5 million) and 7% of £7 million excess of £3 million (total cover £10 million) and 7% of £10 million excess of £10 million (total cover £20 million). He made his Names liable for 7% of all claims against 400 Agents brought by litigating Names from £2 million to £20 million.

It was an insightful thought that Dick Hazell would be put by Lloyd's Council and the regulator of Lloyd's into the same advantageous position as a previous Deputy Chairman Stephen Merrett. Merrett was able to deny liability for a reinsurance contract issued by his own Syndicate 418 to Pulbrook 334 by buying the Pulbrook Agency. He arranged an arbitration which Syndicate 418 won and the reinsurance contract was voided.

Syndicate 190 was forecast to be one of the worst syndicates in Lloyd's. Hazell arranged little or no reinsurance for asbestosis. It was not known whether Syndicate 190 insured the E&O for the Syndicate 334 Managing and Members' Agents for the 1985 year but the above-illustrated practices were common in the Market at the time.

Clive wrote to David Tiplady on 3 July about the preliminary hearing which had just been sealed. The Association had thirty-five days to lodge an appeal. David indicated that the Association would oppose the Pulbrook Underwriting Management appeal relating to those Names on the syndicate in the 1979 year of account.

Tom Benyon's article in *The Times* of 4 July gave reasons why brokers must help towards Names' £2.8 billion compensation. Since 1982 there had been a practice of 'adding to premium'. Tom explained that quotations were obtained from a broker who gave a premium based on what he thought the client would accept. Sometimes the mark-up added was as much as 180%. Then the broker pretended it was the best quotation around, thereby overcharging the client. The Market invented fancy names for the ploy such as 'grossing up'. The inaccurate telexes used to convey information to potential policyholders were known as 'gimmicky' telexes. It was known that letters concerning the practice had been circulating between Lloyd's Chairmen and brokers since 23 April 1974. Brokers should make a substantial 'without prejudice' contribution to the £2.8 billion settlement, as Names would have already paid the premium without knowing it.

Alan Porter FCA IPFA, Chairman of Devonshire Names Association and a leader of two groups, one long-tail and the other an LMX spiral, welcomed the Reconstruction and Renewal initiative. He said that he considered the E&O cover to be much greater than promulgated and it would not be exhausted. He also mentioned the so-called 'double count' including secondary E&O, personal stop-loss and Estate protection plans. However, it was not only about money that litigation was important. He required a bank of favourable judgements as potential protection in case of Lloyd's meltdown and to achieve justice rather than revenge. Porter concluded that there were two parts to the settlement: part one, the litigation settlement pot, and part two, the debt forgiveness pot. Lloyd's expected the litigation pot to be at least £800 million, however, Porter thought it should be increased to £1.5 billion. He also said that Lloyd's panel auditors had been feeble to the point of negligence and this may be a perceptive insight utilising his professional experience as a Chartered Accountant. The fat cats of the Market were the brokers and over five years had made as much money as the Names had lost. Much of the loss related to churning within the Market represented by LMX spiral business. Brokers also had a reputation of hanging on to cash, which, in an efficient system, would be held by syndicates. In a well-regulated Market, Names should have the expectation that even-handed compensation should be available to all. The debt credits were currently rated at £2 billion and Names were expected to pay £2.1 billion by way of drawdowns or voluntary payment of losses. There was a groundswell of opinion that the terms envisaged for the ongoing Market were much too soft in relation to the benefits received and profits earned.

Lastly, if the pot fell a little short, Porter hoped the Bank of England would be prepared to persuade clearing banks, building societies, insurance companies and those who had dealt in Lloyd's guarantees to put together a modest lifeboat in the form of a grant or soft loan. There must be an opportunity for negotiation and Lloyd's must avoid the arrogance and haste that characterised the first failed initiative. Clive thought this article to be as objective and comprehensive a survey as he had seen.

Lloyd's List on 6 July said the courts had been much exercised by Action Groups and case law was developing rapidly. It also reported on 12 July that the plaintiff was a representative Lloyd's underwriter whose syndicate reinsured the Sturge Syndicate against such losses as US liability business. A more detailed account was given in the September issue of *D J Freeman Insurance Review* saying a novel point of general significance concerned the effect of tax on the assessment of pre-judgement interest. Interest was a significant component of any commercial claim but could not be treated as a precise science. The rate, amount and period were matters solely at the court's discretion. To allow interest on all the damages would be a windfall at the expense of the defendants. This point was very relevant for the Association as interest had yet to be decided by a court.

Lloyd's List also reported potential documentary problems in a case regarding brokers' cover notes issued in 1956. Three layers of excess of loss reinsurance (or rather retrocession, a policy in which a reinsurer lays off part or all of a risk with another reinsurer) were placed by the brokers at that time. The cover notes did not specify the names of the retrocessionaires (underwriters) with whom the brokers had placed the business. There was no other record of the identities of the retrocessionaires. The brokers argued that the syndicate's claims were time-barred from the time the documents were lost probably occurring in the 1970s and also that the syndicate had been contributorily negligent because it failed to keep any records of the retrocessionaires' names itself. In the context of the practice of the 1950s, it was not unreasonable for the syndicate to rely on the brokers to keep the relevant records. Therefore, the syndicate sued the brokers for the lost retrocession recoveries. It was reported that Mr Justice Clarke held that information must be retained for such period within which a reasonable broker would regard a claim as possible.

John Winter said some Names and Members' Agents had contacted him regarding the intermingling of funds. Terry Roydon expressed extreme concern that funds paid by Names to Syndicate 334 (1985) year to cover future losses had been lent unsecured to another year of account. Winter clarified that there were no inter-syndicate loans but there were inter-year borrowings and £4 million was outstanding from the 1990 year which should be cleared by early 1997. A commercial interest rate was charged on the loan. Outstanding cash calls from Names on Syndicate 334 (1985) year amounted to: 1989, 0.3%; 1990, 1.75%; 1991, 2.85%; 1992, 9%; and 1993, 35%. In other words, 0.03% of the cash calls for the open year 1985 in 1989 was still unpaid but of the open-year calls in 1993, 35% was still unpaid. The reason for the outstanding balances was likely to be relating to 'can't pay who have run out of cash, or won't pay' Names. Whittington was making vigorous efforts to collect these balances. Winter stated that IBNR might be five or six times more than forecast. This did not fill Clive with confidence and he realised how bad things could become.

On 13 July, David enclosed a copy of Michael Crane QC's Opinion about an appeal, which was not particularly optimistic; his views echoed those of Nicholas Strauss. However, David thought the Association should enter a Notice of Appeal. The defendants had done so. The case would not be heard until early in summer 1996. The outcome of the application for an interim payment was still awaited.

Christopher Stockwell distributed a circular on 21 July stating that apparently 370 boxes of documents were in the Adam Room at Lloyd's, containing 28,000 copies of the new secretly amended Lloyd's American Premiums Trust Deeds. He thought this was a breach of trust. The new deed sought to give Citibank the sole trusteeship, and immunity from suit for the breaches of trust. Names' rights to seek compensation for loss may be harmed by these changes. Stockwell said Names should immediately object to this action.

Non-newsletter, July 1995

The Chairman's non-newsletter of 22 July informed Members that there was no news about the result of the interim payment hearing in front of Mr Justice Potter. The one-day hearing had been postponed to 6 July and lasted nearly two days. The Association was once again in the hands of the same judge. Clive was profoundly disappointed to have to counsel patience when he grew most impatient himself, having been waiting five years for this announcement.

The Halifax Building Society sent an anniversary certificate on 29 July showing the Association's balance of £889,028.97 with gross interest of £50,099.83 at an interest rate of 6.85%. Halifax was converting to a bank, and provided the Association retained the relevant balance it would receive a significant windfall relating to the equity balance accruing to its Members.

On 31 July Mr Justice Potter awarded the Association £14 million. The Association was claiming £80 million including IBNR – so the amount awarded was considerably lower than the amount claimed. However, the amount claimed was subject to a discount relating to the time value of money. The estimated net present value might result in a monetary claim of £25 million, still £11 million short.

On 1 August 1995 Keith Lester entered into a Hardship Agreement. Keith was allowed to retain an interest in his house and to receive a modest income from his business. Any surplus was to be paid to Lloyd's to set off, in his opinion, the unjust debt calculated by Lloyd's that was covered by the Central Fund.

Twenty-Eighth Steering Committee Meeting, 2 August 1995

David Tiplady informed the eight Committee Members at D J Freeman's offices:

> I have launched an appeal regarding the £14 million awarded by Mr Justice Potter. I hoped there might be additional funds available but this may be unlikely. I have a list of Estate protection plan and stop-loss underwriters who will be exercising their liens on Names who have made claims against such policies. It is possible to have the Association's costs taxed. Usually this is a very lengthy and expensive process and I am reluctant to embark on this task. Taxation is the legal term used to describe the assessment of a solicitor's costs by a Taxing Master who is an official of the court. The Taxing Master determines whether the costs are fair and reasonable and if they are not, what costs should be paid. An application must be made within three months of the award.

Jasper Salisbury-Jones suggested that the Association put forward a reasonable figure for the defendants' costs and get it agreed without being taxed. The amount paid towards the Association's costs would not be subject to the proposed amendments to the PTD. The Treasurer confirmed that total costs to date were some £850,000. David thought the Association should expect to receive approximately two-thirds of the total, about £500,000, if taxed by a Taxing Master.

Funds from the award would be held in a solicitors' interest-bearing escrow account in the names of D J Freeman and Cameron

Markby Hewitt, the plaintiffs' solicitors. The Treasurer raised the question of the investment policy. Keith Lester and Guy Wilson were partners in Langmead Charlesworth & Co, a firm registered to conduct investment business. It was agreed the partners should contact the D J Freeman finance director who normally made investment decisions. Guy stated that he used to manage $2 billion for Gulf Oil and Chevron Corporation in fixed-income securities. He had extremely strict exposure guidelines limiting the amount placed with any one banking or financial institution. It was agreed to adopt a strict exposure policy for the Association's award.

The Treasurer observed that D J Freeman was acting on behalf of Lloyd's, such as providing Hardship documentation or acting for other Action Groups. He wondered if there was any conflict of interest. David said the funds were held in a clients' account and not controlled by the D J Freeman partners. They did not charge for handling the clients' account. The Committee agreed to seek some signatory control over the funds held in D J Freeman clients' account. The Treasurer was to enquire if D J Freeman charged for investment decisions and to discuss setting up appropriate safeguards for managing the funds.

The Association had substantial funds with the Halifax Building Society. If the funds remained long enough for the building society to become a bank there might be a £50,000 windfall. The Association's cash balance was £994,000, less some outstanding cheques.

It was accepted that the case for 1979 joiners had been won as it was not going to be appealed by the defendants. The Committee agreed that any recoveries on behalf of 1979 joiners could be used to top up the Association's funds.

Charles Baron expressed some concern about the mutualisation aspect as defined in the Association's Rules.

Nicholas Strauss had sent his Opinion on the aspect of 'duty of care in tort'. The Committee unanimously agreed to lodge an appeal against the nondelegable duty of care in tort which might cost £200,000. David said there were now five appeals on substantive issues, two by the Association and three by the defendants. If all the appeals were lost by the Association the cost would be about £1 million.

Newsletter, August 1995: A Rare but Important Victory in Court

The Association had won a clear victory in court. Money in the Premiums Trust Fund account technically belonged to the Names until it was paid to settle claims. Pulbrook Underwriting Management admitted liability for all Names on the 1979 syndicate but they were appealing against part of Mr Justice Potter's judgement, which favoured those Names who joined the syndicate between 1980 and 1985. The basis of Pulbrook Underwriting Management 's appeal was considered to be weak.

Lloyd's proposed to vary the PTD so litigation recoveries would be paid into the PTF. The Association and the Litigating Names Committee were opposing the retrospective changes to the PTD. The case was to be heard in October 1995. Stop-loss insurers were putting a lien on any litigation recoveries for those Names who had received stop-loss payments for the years concerned. Members' Agents held liable under the judgement were unable to invoke the time-bar as eleven Names had signed their agreements under seal. Names in Hardship would have to pay litigation recoveries to Lloyd's in terms of their Hardship Agreement.

A second, more favourable Opinion had been received on the prospects of success against the time-bar for those agreements not under seal. A notice of an appeal had been entered to protect the Association's position.

The Parliamentary Treasury Select Committee Report on Lloyd's had been sent to the DTI some six weeks previously. The DTI carefully launched its response on the day the Commons rose for summer vacation. In the face of all the evidence the Treasury Select Committee said nothing much had gone wrong at Lloyd's. Clive observed, 'Anything Lloyd's said was correct and to be applauded whilst those wretched things called "Names" could just jolly well keep quiet and stop being a nuisance.' The DTI saw no point in setting up an enquiry. Despite the frustrating news, Clive said the Committee was still heartily resolved to fight to obtain the recompense due to each and every Member of the Association. On the bright side as the calculations for the settlement proposals got under way, the Association had established a strong bargaining position.

The US Securities Exchange Commission had instructed Lloyd's to cease recruiting Names in the USA. The inference was that the Securities Exchange Commission no longer had any faith in the power of the City of London to regulate itself.

Clive circulated several papers on 11 August, including an extract of the Matthews Wrightson Pulbrook Board minutes of 11 September 1981 when David Rowland was its Chairman. It could be construed that Rowland was aware in 1981 of limitless asbestos, pollution and health hazard claims in the future. Asbestosis claims were accelerating. Ron Verrall, the underwriter of Syndicate 334, placed reinsurance with Merrett Syndicate 418 on 28 January 1982 to cover the early years (the slip shows 30 September 1981 at the policy signing office. There is some uncertainty over dates especially as David Carrington had informed Names that a policy had been placed in July 1981). Nevertheless, Rowland could see the impending damage if brokers were found guilty of material nondisclosure. The brokers would become liable to pay the claims.

Briefly in outline, policies were written with an excess of $200,000 in the expectation that no claim was likely to exceed $200,000 as claimants were usually individuals. However, an aggregate extension clause was included as a 'sleep easy' in 1981 and considered to be a low-risk blanket cover. The aggregate extension clause seemed not to be fully understood by the brokers as it substantially changed the risk profile. Instead of an excess of $200,000 applying to each and every claim, it only applied to the first claim. Subsequent claims would total more than $200,000 resulting in a valid payable claim against the insurer.

Newsletter No. 2, August 1995

Clive updated Names on the current situation regarding appeals. It was in the Members' Agents' E&O cover that the Association's major prize lay.

1. Pulbrook Underwriting Management were appealing Mr Justice
    Potter's earlier judgement in finding for the Names who joined the
    syndicate for the first time for the account years 1980 to 1985.

2. Members' Agents were appealing against eleven Names who signed
    their contracts under seal.

3. The Association had decided to appeal the original judgement in the
    matter of Members' Agents nondelegable duty of care, seeking redress
    from the E&O cover.

4. There was a further appeal to be launched by the Association arguing
    that the size of the interim payment was insufficient to meet the cash
    calls and claims in the pipeline.

5. The Association's fund had enough to fight the appeals and provide
    for the worst case of losing all the actions and having to pay all the
    costs. Appeals were likely to be heard in April 1996.

However, the recovery of costs may have to go through the expensive and
lengthy process of taxation.

Amended Rules of the Association were issued following the Special
Resolutions passed at the SGM (see Appendix 5).

Correspondence from David Tiplady on 4 September advised that
some £7 million cash was due before the next Committee meeting on
21 September.

The Association had raised £1.8 million, spent £0.8 million and
retained £1 million. Potentially there was the £100,000 cost of the
Members' Agents nondelegable duty of care appeal. If the defendants'
main appeal succeeded the cost may be £1 million and David Tiplady
concluded that the Association was not fully funded for the worst possible case. It would be prudent to anticipate the worst possible outcome,
thus it was not appropriate to make a payment to Association Members
at this stage.

Linden Ife wrote on behalf of her father Mr H. J. Ife, who had been
an underwriter for Syndicate 90, regarding the change of the Association's
Rules at the AGM. Rule 9 affected those Names whose contracts were

written under seal. The Rule required the distribution of awards for damages to be divided in proportion according to line. She wanted to know if proper notice was given in respect of the intended Rule change. Clive responded on 11 September, informing Ife that the notice of the Rule alterations was sent out in July 1993, providing more than the required notice period.

Anna Young copied to Clive her letter to Sir Adam Ridley, Chairman of the Names Committee. He was charged with suggesting to the Council of Lloyd's how best to allocate the Council's proposed offer. She said she started from a low base eventually underwriting with a premium limit of £500,000 and had been loss-making every year since joining in 1978. In 1991 she was obliged to stop underwriting and applied to the Hardship Committee. During the period she had four Members' Agents. The last was an involuntary transfer to Lloyd's Members' Agency Services. Losses claimed by Lloyd's amounted to £600,000. Young was involved in seven Action Groups, had twenty-four open years and was receiving legal aid. Her husband worked for the Medical Research Council examining the effect of long-term pollution on humans. She understood the harm done by exposure to asbestos and had been repeatedly assured that she was not involved in potential exposure to asbestos claims. Lloyd's had been very aware of the asbestosis problems since 1982 but kept the information from Names. Now she was deeply in debt with no prospects of an income to cover losses. Over half her losses, she considered, were due to negligence, misrepresentation, failure of regulation and possibly fraud. She would prefer to avoid lengthy litigation but sought his advice on how Names in her position would be treated in the allocation of the settlement offer. Like Bridget Milling-Smith and Clive Francis earlier, this was another very distressing example of a Name in serious difficulty.

Peter Plaskitt of Bellevue Hill, NSW, Australia, said he had read the transcript of the AGM about the 'vote' regarding compensation for officers of the Association. He found no record of the result of the vote in the transcript by way of show of hands or by proxy. He also questioned the necessity of sending unsolicited items to Members which seemed more like a vendetta against Lloyd's. He urged Clive to seek the views of the Association's Names in a convenient and disciplined way by sending out a simple questionnaire and enclosed an example of a questionnaire.

The Super Group reported on 13 September that Peter Middleton had agreed to an independent financial firm to advise Names on the settlement and the Equitas project. The Equitas board, shareholding and personnel had still not been defined. Some ongoing Names may be forced out of the Market by taxation on money they might not receive. The Super Group also produced a thoughtful and serious September 1995 newsletter dealing with the future of Lloyd's either as Reconstruction and Renewal or run-off. Lloyd's historic legacy of paying all valid claims was a marvellous marketing plus but also an enormous financial burden. The willingness of American courts to cooperate with American lawyers in extending policy cover and creating the claims nightmare that Lloyd's faced was unforeseeable before the last war.

On 21 September Charles Baron attended the Syndicate 334 and 90 Monitoring Committee meeting at Whittington Syndicate Management Company and provided a trial balance at 30 June 1995 for Syndicate 334 run-off.

The summarised information was:

Assets	£	£
Debtors		19,009,938
Including:		
Uncalled losses	6,019,544	
Outstanding losses	5,605,955	
Total	**11,625,499**	
Investments		29,762,263
Less creditors		-658,030
Net assets		**48,114,171**

Claims		
Gross		52,808,000
Less time and distance policy		-16,101,000
Outstanding claims		**36,707,000**

Net assets of £48 million and liabilities for claims at £37 million indicated a surplus of assets over claims of £11 million. Uncertainties arose regarding the values of uncalled losses, and outstanding losses to be received, and whether the gross claims figures were realistic. Subject to these considerable uncertainties the accounting statement showed adequate funds to pay expected claims. Charles expressed concern about the high level of management expenses for the six months, totalling £539,000. Computer leasing costs were particularly extortionate at £59,000 for six months. Intermingling of funds between years had reduced substantially.

The fundamental question that Names must ask themselves was, 'Was it better to preserve Lloyd's because that was better than the alternative, whatever that may be?' Litigating Names close to a judgement had the perceived advantage of receiving payment for claims. The prospect of the whole Society moving into run-off and therefore delaying compensation was not an exciting one. The supposed advantage of the Hardship Scheme was illusory. Deals were no more generous than would be forced by a receiver or administrator. Keeping the Society trading had the advantage of closing the open years and giving finality to Names.

How 'final' was 'finality'? It was envisaged that Equitas would force all syndicates to effect RITC on all 1992 and prior liabilities into a new corporate vehicle. There would be a massive aggregation of reserves. Claims would still be paid in full. Lawyers would not relish the alternative of having to pursue thousands of individual Names. Would Equitas as the sole underwriter be able to apply more pressure to commute claims? Could Equitas survive ten years? How should premiums be assessed on huge long-term liabilities that auditors had previously declared unquantifiable?

If Lloyd's went into run-off, then future liabilities would fall on Names over a twenty-year period. Crystallisation of losses at this time would create a huge tax loss exceeding the ability of Names to recover from other income. Many Names would not be able to continue underwriting, nor would they be able to recover tax on losses against future income.

If the Society made a major reconstruction, then the US standard accounting regulations would require holders of policies written many years ago to be reserved in full, creating immense pressure on Lloyd's solvency. While Lloyd's traded, assets must exceed the liabilities of the whole membership and be subject to solvency tests. Once Lloyd's ceased to trade forward, the DTI would no longer be interested in solvency. It was the fear of the unknown that was driving Names towards Reconstruction and Renewal. Some stop-loss underwriters had refused to pay out on losses and some became insolvent. Intermingling of funds continued between solvent and insolvent Names. It was thought the scale of intermingling was greater than the value of the Central Fund. Names should make it clear they would not make any payments other than to settle their own liabilities.

Bureaucrats had written the Reconstruction and Renewal document which was entirely focused on keeping the institution alive that provided their livelihood. If the business was to go forward there should be a different regulatory framework and a change to the marketing structure away from reliance on brokers and discounts. It was estimated that there would be a reduction in capacity of 15% in the next year further exacerbated as operating changes are required by the American Stock Exchange Commission.

Twenty-Ninth Steering Committee Meeting, 21 September 1995: Cash Received but Not by the Association. Held in Escrow

David Tiplady said damages of approximately £15 million should be paid to the Association and held on its behalf by D J Freeman and Cameron Markby Hewitt pending appeal results. The interim payment appeal would be heard in January 1996 and substantive issues in April 1996.

The funds were subject to third-party interests. The order of priority was stop-loss and Estate protection plan underwriters who had paid out on behalf of Names, the Names PTF and valid assignees prior to the date of the proposed PTD amendments.

The Association's litigation funds amounted to almost £1 million. The Treasurer said that funds would run out if the Association lost its appeals. However, David reported that £7 million was awarded by the court which would remain if all appeals were lost. The money was held in escrow by the Royal Bank of Scotland. He explained that the costs incurred by Action Groups were immune from the effects of the PTD amendments. D J Freeman clients' account was retaining £15,500 subscriptions that should be paid to the Association.

Mutualisation of awards and the Association's Rule 9 change raised by Linden Ife on behalf of her father were discussed. David thought her views were valid as her contract was under seal and she was entitled to the agreed recovery entitlement and not part of a mutualised distribution. Clive should write to her suggesting she defer her arguments until the results of the appeals were known. Other recovered costs should be mutualised.

Peter Middleton was in favour of the concept that litigation recoveries on behalf of Names in Hardship should be invested in a Hardship Trust Fund. Interest should be paid to Names while they were in Hardship. He had also admitted that Equitas would probably not last long. David thought that the Association should not support the Super Group initiative to fund an independent investigation reviewing the settlement offer, as it might be *ultra vires* the Association's Rules. The Chairman took the opposite view and regarded an independent review essential to safeguard Names' interests.

Clive had warmed to the idea of being elected to Lloyd's Council and realised the value of being able to represent the really damaged Names. He was not chosen in the Super Group ballot and confessed to feeling a little sore at the political traffic involved.

The *Daily Telegraph* headline of 16 October was 'Will Rowland Rat on Writ?', and reported that David Rowland was served with a summons while attending an ALM Conference in Chicago on Friday, 13 October. Maybe the Editor of the newspaper had in mind *the* Roland Rat who ran a chat show set in his sewer home, now converted into a high-tech media centre called the Ratcave. The keynote speech in Chicago attempted to persuade Names to stay in Lloyd's.

A summons prepared by the West family's attorneys on behalf of family members who were Names included documents such as the minutes of Matthews Wrightson Pulbrook meetings of 1981. Matthews Wrightson Pulbrook had been subsequently bought by the Merrett Group. The minutes showed that Matthews Wrightson Pulbrook Chairman Rowland and his board concealed huge asbestos claims to obtain a lower-cost reinsurance from Merrett Syndicate 418. This enabled Syndicate 418 to refuse to pay reinsurance claims exceeding £30 million. Similarly, the minutes also showed that directors decided to conceal asbestos claims made against (the stablemate) Syndicate 90 and pass the liability for these undisclosed claims by reinsurance on to Outhwaite Syndicate 317. The West family was told that any suit against Lloyd's had to be brought in England because of the wording of their contracts.

However, the West family decided to sue LeBoeuf, Lamb, Greene & MacRae, Lloyd's heavyweight attorneys in the US, who advised them on Lloyd's membership. Their argument was that LeBoeuf et al. were corresponding with Lloyd's throughout the 1980s about asbestos claims. They concealed from the West family their liability for undisclosed asbestosis claims on syndicates on which Lloyd's Agents placed him and his daughters. The West case was proceeding in California. The family successfully petitioned the Chicago court under US comity law to issue an immediate subpoena on Rowland to appear in Cook County Court on Tuesday, 17 October at 9 am. He was to be asked questions on his knowledge of concealed asbestos claims and what he knew of LeBoeuf's involvement in keeping the knowledge of the claims and liabilities from potential US investors (Names). They would also want to know if he could explain the damaging correspondence between several firms of US attorneys with the AWP that was chaired by a fellow Matthews Wrightson Pulbrook Director.

At the end of the keynote speech in Chicago to a large number of North American Names attending the ALM Conference, Rowland received polite applause. Thinking he had done well, he was approached by a stunning-looking girl.

The dialogue was as follows:

'Are you Mr David Rowland?'

'Yes, my dear.'

'This is a subpoena to appear in court to answer questions.'

'That is an event I will not be attending.'

'Well, that is between you and the court.'

'What day is it?'

Misunderstanding his question, she replied, 'It's Friday, the 13th. I guess it's your unlucky day.' Rowland went beet-red.

Caught by an opportunist solicitor attending the conference, Rowland was very surprised. The answers to questions to be asked in court about concealment of information were germane and material to the substantial ancient US asbestosis and pollution claims that were troubling the London market. The result of the subpoena is not known but documents supporting conspiracy to conceal existed.

Following the order of Mr Justice Potter on 31 July, David Tiplady informed Clive that all matters relating to the quantum of interest had been agreed. There was a side-letter releasing the defendants from liability on payment of the agreed figures. Two matters remained outstanding, the apportionment between the Members' Agents and the Managing Agents and the precise terms of the escrow account. Monies were expected shortly. Nevertheless, David was taking the precaution of restoring the summons for an interim payment before Potter.

The amendments to PTD affected all Names who were Names for 1987 and subsequent years. Compensation received for underwriting losses at Lloyd's should be used to settle their obligations regarding outstanding cash calls and Central Fund drawdowns. David Tiplady said he appreciated the strong reservations by the Association regarding the amendments. However, it was important to assist Lloyd's, otherwise there

may be difficulty in obtaining damages. The PTD undertaking to Lloyd's
was addressed to D J Freeman and the Association. It undertook to the
Society of Lloyd's and Simmons & Simmons, solicitors, that all amounts
received in respect of the main Action and all interest earned on any
such amounts to give ten days' prior notice in writing to Lloyd's. *For the
avoidance of doubt the undertaking shall only apply to those amounts received
absolutely by D J Freeman and shall not apply to monies held in escrow,
distribution of which is subject to leave of the court, unless and until such
amounts are received absolutely.'* Dr Tiplady clarified his advice regarding
distribution on 19 October and said he was satisfied that Lloyd's would
not attempt to exercise a prior claim over litigation costs and would allow
them to be repaid to successful litigants. He was concerned because the
Association was still involved in litigation which may require all the litigation funds. The last thing he would wish to happen was that Members of
the Committee would attract a personal liability for litigation costs in the
event there was a shortfall in funds.

Charles Baron believed he had obtained immunity from the proposals
to amend the PTD. Immunity meant that receipts from the legal action
could be paid to Association Members. David believed this to be a grey
area and it may need to be tested in court. Written dispensations given
by Lloyd's Members' Agency Services Ltd could convince a judge that
immunity had been given. However, it might be argued that other Agents
giving similar advice could well be sued. This situation only added to the
complexity of the Committee's task in arriving at a scheme of distribution.

On 30 October Keith Lester's mother died and he suddenly became an
orphan. This very sad tragedy following the recent passing of his father added
more complexity and anxiety to an already exceptionally stressful situation.

Cameron Markby Hewitt confirmed to D J Freeman on 31
October that a tranche of monies due to clients on the 1979 year
would be paid around 10 November. Various calculations arrived at a
sum of £9,668,200.29. This included interest at 8% from 1 August of
£209,389.56. It was like getting blood out of a stone and the immediate
comment was 'hooray'!

Thirtieth Steering Committee Meeting, 2 November 1995

Six Committee Members attended the meeting plus Mark Everiss in place of David Tiplady. The Treasurer reported that Mr Lakelore's name was on the writ, but he was not a Member of the Association. D J Freeman had held his subscriptions for some years amounting to £4,400. There were also other monies received by D J Freeman for Names on the writ which had not been received by the Treasurer. The Association's fund amounted to £900,000 after settling fees from D J Freeman of £101,000, whose fees were running at about £13,000 per month.

It was estimated that £9 million was due to the Association from the legal action plus interest at £1,726 per day. This interest was reducing the size of the finite pot available for damages. The Committee found this extremely disconcerting. Ray Cook pointed out that the longer negotiations went on, the more was paid in legal fees and the less the Association was recovering. Money controlled by the Association could be placed on deposit and earn interest without depleting the pot available for damages. It was resolved to exert considerable pressure on D J Freeman to ensure a substantial payment was made by the defendants in the very near future.

Mark Everiss explained:

The 1979 Names' Interim Payment of £10,003,215 will be paid on or around 10 November. A further amount of £553,546 was due in respect of Members' Agents. The award against the Managing Agents was 100% but the award against Members' Agents was limited. If the Pulbrook Underwriting Management funds were exhausted, the Members' Agencies' Indemnity would become worthless. I have lodged an appeal about the total £10.5 million interim payment. Funds received will not be available for immediate distribution but held in escrow until the outcome of the PTD amendment hearing.

The Committee instructed D J Freeman to give notice to Cameron Markby Hewitt that if funds were not paid by 10 November the matter would be referred to the court without any further communication. Clive expressed his alarm, 'I am utterly dismayed and exasperated that interest accruing simply diminishes the E&O pot and there is no disadvantage to the E&O insurers by delaying payment for as long as they possibly could.'

A distribution subcommittee was formed to review the apportionment of funds, scrutinising amounts and discrepancies in the figures produced by Cameron Markby Hewitt. Once funds had been received, the Association would give ten days' notice that reasonable litigation costs would be paid to litigating Members as a return of their contributions.

LSS had been reconciling subscriptions and Names' lines on the syndicate. It revealed that four Names had overpaid and thirteen had underpaid. It was agreed to repay overpayments and write to those who had underpaid.

At the Whittington Syndicate Management Ltd Monitoring Committee meeting on 9 November, John Winter said he expected to receive syndicate-level quotation indications on 15 November from Equitas. Non-asbestos pollution and health claims for Syndicate 334 amounted to about 20% of future claims.

Some 750 syndicates were organised by Equitas. Forty staff had been recruited in syndicate focus teams. There had been an increase in the claims filed in the USA. Some large claims had been settled and other large pre-1985 policies repurchased at heavy discounts. These changes would not affect quotations. The cost of a pollution clean-up estimated in 1989, previously featuring 'doomsday figures', were not nearly as bad as had been thought. Regarding unpaid cash calls, the amount of 'set-aside' of the Central Fund for all Whittington Syndicate Management Ltd syndicates was £10 million but a comparatively small sum for Syndicate 334 at £6,000.

Clive was concerned about the judicial declaration to legalise the alterations to the PTD and wrote to David Tiplady for advice on 13 November. The Litigating Names Steering Committee believed it could drive a harder bargain with Lloyd's over settlement details by wielding the threat of such a hearing. The Committee justified this stance by maintaining that a cocked pistol was more valuable at this juncture than a discharged pistol missing its target. The Association's Committee may be asked to endorse a resolution to challenge the legality of the PTD proposals. There was a general apprehension that the litigation recoveries won by the Association would be quietly shovelled up into the big settlement bag. Clive asked David for detailed advice on whether the circumstances and conditions under which the Secretary of State signed the relevant instrument had been properly fulfilled and still obtained. The Committee may decide to challenge PTD validity and as D J Freeman acted for Lloyd's and the Association, could a serious conflict of interest arise? Clive was informed that the hearing testing the legality of the PTD amendments had been postponed until April 1996.

On 14 November the Association received a circular from Epstein Grower & Michael Freeman. They recommended that this be forwarded to banks and insurance companies. The circular said Mr Justice Cresswell found that the Merrett syndicates had acted negligently in taking on certain run-off contracts and were guilty of deliberately concealing from Names the true nature of these contracts. In addition, he found that the Merrett Syndicate (Merretts) was negligent in closing certain years of account for Syndicates 418 and 417 and deliberately concealed from Names potentially huge liabilities which were not capable of reasonable quantification. The judge said Stephen Merrett himself was in breach of his duty of care in closing certain years of account and he personally had deliberately concealed from Names potentially huge unquantifiable losses.

In the past Lloyd's Audit Committee kept the procedures of Lloyd's panel auditors under review and issued annual instructions as to the conduct of their audit of Lloyd's syndicates. It was for this reason that on 24 February 1982 audit firm Neville Russell wrote to the Manager of the Audit Department of Lloyd's on behalf of themselves and major firms of Lloyd's panel auditors. The minutes of the Audit Committee of 2 March 1982, attended by Merrett, recorded the reinsurance of underwriters' asbestos liability, effectively reinsuring the 'asbestos tail'. Concern was expressed that such liabilities could fall on comparatively few syndicates. Merrett considered that it would be inappropriate for such reinsurances to go unnoted and unreserved by panel auditors, and improper for a syndicate taking such reinsurances not to tell its own Names. The judge said that the point of concern was that '*such liabilities could fall on comparatively few syndicates*'. Merretts did not inform their auditors Ernst & Whinney about writing the run-off contracts until year three. The judge said he had not heard from John Emney, the deputy underwriter, and concluded that concealment by him was deliberate. He was also extremely troubled because Stephen Merrett was the active underwriter of Syndicates 418 and 417. The RITC was the most important function Merrett should have performed. Merrett knew about the run-off contracts and the developing problem with asbestos-related claims. Reports in year-four accounts contained a mixture of truth, half-truth and falsehood. Merretts knew the underwriters' report in the accounts was deliberately written to conceal the true facts and deliberately aimed at keeping Names in the dark. The judge referred to accounts, stating 'a series of conservative assumptions had been used to calculate what was believed to be a conservative premium … for the "run-off" book, as well as the balance of the old years' exposures'. The detailed knowledge within the Lloyd's Market of the potential scale of asbestos risks and that of Lloyd's and Stephen Merrett in particular could be traced to 1980 when Lloyd's set up the AWP.

The AWP assumed responsibility for handling asbestos claims on behalf of the Market. By 1980 certain major defendants had been identified and underwriters exposed to claims had been notified of their participation. Lloyd's set up the AWP to monitor the asbestos problem and inform the Market. Letters and reports were sent directly to underwriters involved. An example was quoted from a letter of 10 February 1981 which stated that, 'During the past year the number of cases in suit had increased from some 5,500 to over 8,000. It is not possible to project how many more claims would be filed.' Lloyd's had thus far claimed that it did not have knowledge of the extent of the asbestosis problems during the period of the early 1980s. It was now impossible for Lloyd's to continue maintaining the position. The Market regulator was responsible for initially setting up the AWP and market-wide distribution of AWP material could not have gone unnoticed. There were responses to the Neville Russell letter of February 1982. Murray Lawrence, Deputy Chairman of Lloyd's, wrote to inform all underwriting Agents and active underwriters as well as Neville Russell. David Rowland admitted at the 1995 AGM that the letter was not sent to Members' Agents. Lloyd's had always maintained that the conduit for all information from Lloyd's to Names was via the Member's Agent. Whilst Lloyd's recognised the magnitude of the problem it ignored its own procedures. Throughout the 1980s Lloyd's misrepresented the true state of affairs as it continuously published material as to the nature, role and function of Lloyd's, declaring:

1. Lloyd's conducted itself with utmost good faith.
2. the ownership, control and activities of underwriting Agents operating in the Lloyd's Market were strictly regulated by Lloyd's.
3. Lloyd's required syndicates' annual reports and accounts to show a true and fair view of the profit or loss of syndicates for closed years of account.
4. Lloyd's Insurance Market was properly regulated by Lloyd's.

The Epstein Grower & Michael Freeman circular summarised key information and evidential material to show that Names had not been informed or kept informed of the full scale of the catastrophe as it unfolded. Lest Lloyd's took the impossible stance that it was unaware of the events leading up to 1982, it listed some of the senior personnel in 1982:

1. Peter Green, Chairman of Lloyd's, Chairman of Janson Green Syndicates, which were heavily involved in writing asbestos-related risks and a Director of Blackwell Green, whose Managing Director was his brother
2. Murray Lawrence, Deputy Chairman of Lloyd's
3. Stephen Merrett, Council Member and Member of the Audit Committee
4. Robert Kiln, Council Member to 1981 and Chairman of the Audit Committee

5.   Ted Nelson, Council Member and Chairman of the AWP
6.   Henry Chester, Council Member and Member of the Audit Committee (deceased)
7.   Charles Gilmour, Council Member and Member of the Audit Committee

On the *assumption* that the External Members of Council were as much in the dark as non-Working Names, seven out of sixteen Members of Council were inextricably linked. They had the same knowledge as Stephen Merrett. The introduction to the Lloyd's Act of 1871 set out the objects of the Society, including 'the advancement and protection of the interests of Members of the Society … collection, publication and diffusion of intelligence and information'. Members were entitled to rely on the continued representation of the statutory protection. Throughout the 1980s Lloyd's misrepresented the true state of affairs when it continuously published material as to the nature, role and function of Lloyd's. The solicitor's circular maintained that no sane Name having been made aware of the potential liabilities associated with asbestos would have commenced, or increased, underwriting at Lloyd's. The commercial interests of Lloyd's insiders caused them to abrogate their regulatory responsibilities, so as to nullify the very objects of the Society.

On 20 November the Names' Committee Interim Report by Sir Adam Ridley was circulated. (Extracts from Sir Adam Ridley's letter and the Names' Committee Interim Report are shown as Appendix 4.)

David Rowland's covering letter expressed surprise at the sudden resignation of Peter Middleton. Council had unanimously approved the appointment of Ron Sandler, who had been one of the architects of the reconstruction plan. As CEO, Sandler would be working with Action Groups and Names' Committees to formulate a settlement offer that was fair and acceptable to Names. Rowland said it was unsurprising that Names' Committees would like to see a larger settlement to fund its preliminary proposals. Council was continuing strenuous efforts to maximise the settlement. However, there was no assurance that the offer would exceed

£2.8 billion. Council continued to see the plan as the best prospect of an affordable solution to past liabilities and its final decision would be reflected in finality statements to be sent to Names in May 1996.

In order to mutualise the Market under the Reconstruction and Renewal scheme Sir Adam Ridley's Interim Report estimated the losses to finality for the purpose of calculating the amounts due from Names as the cost of the finality bill from Equitas. Computer modelling indicated that further funds should be made available if the plan was to succeed. Indicative figures below taken from the report were not final.

	£(billion)	£(billion)
Amounts owed by Names called		
Receivables to finality		5.9
Less		
Settlement fund for debt credits and litigation	-2.8	
Triple profit release	-0.8	-3.6
Add: Payments to Names in surplus		0.2
Finality bill		**2.5**
Funded by		
Drawdowns of Names' funds at Lloyd's	1.5	
Payments from Names in deficit being new money	0.6	2.1
Names residual receivables – unlikely to be received		0.4
		2.5

The division of the funds was not done equally but weighted as described later. The basic amount allocated to each Name was known as a debt credit. Only Names who had been litigating participated in a separate Litigation Settlement Fund.

The task of the Names' Committee was to advise the Council on the allocation of the settlement offer proposed in Lloyd's Reconstruction and Renewal comprising an estimated £2 billion of debt credits and

£800 million Litigation Settlement Fund (total £2.8 billion). The Committee was given three objectives: to assist Names in achieving finality, to help the hardest-hit Names, and to settle litigation.

The Committee proposed that debt credits should be allocated in three tranches.

- **Tranche 1:** Allocated debt credits as far as possible pro rata to a Name's cumulative net loss as a % of their premium income limit over a standard threshold measured as a % of each Name's own average premium income limit.
- **Tranche 2:** Allocated debt credits to those who, after they have used some or all of their funds at Lloyd's, were still likely to have difficulty in meeting their finality bills because of the scale of their Equitas bills, uncalled losses and unpaid calls.
- **Tranche 3:** Could provide a reserve to assist the hardest-hit Names who demonstrated inability to pay even after the first and second allocations.

There was no mention in Sir Adam's report of a **Tranche 4**, which appeared at the time of voting for Reconstruction and Renewal. Names awaiting Tranche 4 credits were subsequently very disappointed and information regarding this became an important topic subsequently.

Some 40% of Names were active litigants, numbering 13,600 among the 34,100 Names. A table was produced analysing the breakdown across bands of loss showing the numbers of litigating and non-litigating Names. The average expected loss for a litigating Name was £480,000 but only £190,000 for non-litigants.

A vital criterion for any enterprise was to receive payment for goods or services. The Association had won its case in court but where were the assets to settle the financial award and how to obtain access to them? Surprisingly, this was far more difficult than it appeared in theory.

Summary of Key Issues

1. Issues included Lloyd's solvency questions and comments plus protection of Names' interest.

2. The Association's SGM approved Committee remuneration.

3. Clive Francis, Jasper Salisbury-Jones, Charles Baron and Keith Lester went into Hardship.

4. Premiums Trust Deeds were altered.

5. Management of Syndicate 334 run-off issues were moved to Whittington.

6. Inter-year borrowing and intermingling of funds continued.

7. Examples were provided of sharp practice, fraud and concealment.

8. Ongoing worries were expressed about the Association having adequate funding.

9. Pooling arrangements, distribution of winnings and treatment of contracts under seal were discussed.

10. Sir Adam Ridley reported about Reconstruction and Renewal, including Mutualisation proposals.

CHAPTER 8

Access to Assets by Liquidating Pulbrook Underwriting Management Ltd

The Emperor's coming in behalf of France,
To order peace between them.

Henry V, Act 5 Prologue

On 20 November 1995 David faxed that he would be taking steps to put Pulbrook Underwriting Management into liquidation. He said this was a highly sensitive and labour-intensive process. He asked Clive to advise Committee Members not to contact his staff or himself as it would be more cost-effective if Clive could handle any queries. Clive spoke to David Tiplady about the E&O underwriters:

> I'm outraged and truly appalled at the behaviour of the E&O insurers. Even during the protracted negotiations between your office and Cameron Markby Hewitt over the precise size and allocation of tranches and interest due, it was confidently expected by both sides that the money would be handed over on 10 November. Interest is running at £1,700 per day out of a finite pot. There is absolutely no incentive for the E&O insurers to pay up. While our money remains in the E&O coffers it continues to earn money for them. David, we need you *urgently* to arrange the earliest possible date to petition the winding up of Pulbrook Underwriting Management.

David insisted, 'The earliest possible date *is* 16 January 1996' – a two-month wait.

In the Syndicate 90 hearing on 24 November, Jeremy Cook QC told the judge that there was a problem with the E&O payment for Syndicate 334 because of fraud. The Merrett Syndicate 418 was the lead E&O for the Pulbrook Underwriting Management cover. The question had to be asked, how could Merrett seek to avoid payment claiming concealment and deceit when he was the one to conceal? Was he claiming that he did not pass on to himself that which he already knew? If it wasn't so serious for the Association one could raise an incredulous laugh at these gyrations.

Clive called John Winter to discuss the safeguarding of the Pulbrook Underwriting Management papers until the receiver took control. David said the insolvency arm of D J Freeman was dealing with the plans for receivership. Clive wondered how this might be handled as he was concerned about the shrinking litigation fund. Clive's letter to Ron Sandler, Lloyd's CEO, explained that the Association won an award of damages against Pulbrook Underwriting Management for £14 million but no payment had been made and the reasons for such avoidance had not been made public. Clive recalled Ian Hay Davison's pungent aphorism, 'I found the whole barrel to be tainted.' The facts led Clive to believe that anyone who joined Lloyd's since 1981 or increased their line had been wilfully defrauded as concealment and deception were endemic. The only honest man in the inner circles of Lloyd's in 1981 was Peter Cameron-Webb, who from his membership of the AWP realised the game was up, grabbed the money and ran. If the Lloyd's Market hoped to march away into a carefree future leaving 20,000 Names to the dubious embrace of Equitas, then it had better find some money from the trading position. Clive lodged a formal complaint on behalf of the Association.

Clive accepted an invitation to meet Sandler to discuss the issues on 23 January 1996. Charles Baron circulated information for Clive to discuss at the proposed meeting. Eleven suicides were directly attributable to Lloyd's problems and Sandler must realise the anger and contempt many people felt for Lloyd's. Financial information included estimated Equitas release calculations and estimated Equitas Premium, in a range.

Syndicate 334

Total line	£17,725,000
Litigating line to total line	*£11,790,000
Percentage litigants	66.51

Range	Minimum	Maximum
Whittington uncalled loss	£6,019,544	£6,019,544
Less: Equitas release calculation	£3,913,000	£910,000
Based on settlement figures		
Estimated Equitas premium	**£2,106,544**	**£5,109,544**
66.51% premium due by Association*	£1,401,624	£3,398,358
Per £10,000 line premium divided by litigating line	*1,401,624/1179	*3,398,358/1179
A) Result	£1,188	£2882
Court judgement	*£21,000,000	*£21,000,000
B) Per 10,000 line *21,000,000/11,790	£17,800	£17,800
Members' shortfall A–B payable to Members	£16,612	£14,918

* Key numbers in the calculation shown

It can be seen that the higher the Equitas release figure, the lower the premium due by the Association Members to Equitas and this increased the amount due from the court award.

The amount due to the Association's Names per £10,000 line was somewhere between £16,612 and £14,918 assuming the estimates were agreed and subject to the PTD litigation and stop-loss/Estate protection plan allocations.

Clyde & Co, solicitors, acted for the E&O underwriters of the Merrett Group companies which were insured under a group policy. This had included Pulbrook Underwriting Management since the take-over. Under the group policy all insurance covers stood or fell together. On 5 December 1995, Clyde & Co had given Pulbrook Underwriting Management fourteen days' notice, which was about to expire, to provide reasons why the group cover should not be repudiated by underwriters on the grounds of fraud alleged against Stephen Merrett. The alleged fraud related to Merrett deliberately withholding information from his own Names regarding the writing of eleven run-off policies, including that written for Syndicate 334. It was unlikely that Pulbrook Underwriting Management would be able to come up with any reasons to convince E&O underwriters to avoid the cover.

David Tiplady indicated the three options that were open to the Association, firstly, taking no further action and effectively throwing the Association at the mercy of Lloyd's; secondly, attempting to negotiate with the E&O underwriters through Pulbrook Underwriting Management; thirdly, putting Pulbrook Underwriting Management into liquidation when the Association would acquire statutory rights to sue the E&O underwriters. It was confirmed that the E&O cover was £20 million with one reinstatement and only Syndicates 90 and 334 had claims in the 1989 policy year. Underwriter John Emney had been sacked by then. Was it believable that canny underwriters did not know of Merrett's problems? What were the E&O underwriters claiming that Emney concealed in placing the policy? Clive and David concluded that it was a 'try on' and decided to call their bluff. It could be a case of the E&O 'kicking a man when he was down'.

On 6 December Clive's fax said that David Rowland was making strenuous efforts to appear squeaky-clean in the matter of Stewart Wrightson Pulbrook. In a phone call Clive commented to David Tiplady:

> Rumour has it that Merrett was going to be thrown to the wolves in
> order to preserve the skins of the rest. You know, it might be possible

to play on this and enlist David Rowland's help in bringing pressure to bear on the E&O underwriters. Mind you, there could be a political counter-move to present Merrett as the victim. If we could play on this as well and involve Merrett on the Association's side it might be possible to confound the E&O underwriters. I agree with your view that we should put Pulbrook Underwriting Management into liquidation and acquire statutory rights to sue the E&O underwriters. I also think there would be no harm in exploring an option to negotiate with them. What do you think, David?

'I think you will carry the Committee on this.' David declared.

The Super Group said that Lloyd's Council had passed the enabling bylaw for Equitas on 6 December. As part of this process Lloyd's was instructing all Managing Agents to sign an agreement with Equitas before the end of the year. The interests of the individual were to yield to the perception by Equitas of what was in the interests of Lloyd's as a whole. Equitas could act without reference to a Name or Agent even where the interests of Equitas conflicted with those of the Name.

Equitas had not yet been approved by the DTI for trading. The Super Group was not satisfied with the proposals put forward by Lloyd's for the governance of Equitas. The Super Group's solicitors thought it would be a breach of contract to sign these agreements. The matter was in dispute. The Super Group urged Names to write to their Managing and Members' Agents to protect their interests and provided a draft letter for them to use.

On 7 December Clive circulated his thoughts on influencing the settlement decision. He suspected the real decision-makers would be individuals who would look at the bottom line of the Equitas bill and decide to accept or reject it. However, the Association's power was in negotiation with Sandler, who would be anxious to determine the willingness or otherwise of litigants to cease litigation. With the circular was a memorandum from the Donner Names Association. John Donner said that the Equitas proposal had the appearance of being a further fraud, specifically designed to mislead Names. The Reconstruction and Renewal settlement offer must include a clause which provided Names with a measure of protection from the situation when Equitas ran out of money. Otherwise at this point, all further claims would fall upon Names or their Estates. Under present proposals the Names would then be time-barred from proceeding against those responsible. The E&O insurers' liabilities were being commuted so that they were not settling the expected losses in full. Donner queried the adequacy of the £2.8 billion proposed settlement and said without amendment he would not be able to accept the proposal.

The Super Group sent an invoice for £9,200 for urgent settlement in respect of the 'Special Fund for Validation of the Lloyd's settlement offer'. This was to cover costs not paid by Lloyd's. The list of specific expenditure given totalled £125,000. All the listed expenses were considered to be a legitimate charge to an Action Group's litigation fund. Costs, for example, included solicitors' and counsel's fees for researching a discussion paper for £60,000 and other legal advice such as on the Equitas-enabling bylaw, £35,000. The expenditure was considered necessary to facilitate a full and proper appraisal of a settlement offer and the preservation of the Group's negotiating strength.

The *Evening Standard* of 12 December report headlined, 'Insurers Refuse to Pay £14m Names' Cash'. The £14 million had been awarded by the High Court. A photograph of Clive was subtitled 'Citing Fraud'. The insurers cited a recent judgement against Lloyd's former Deputy Chairman, Stephen Merrett, as the reason not to deliver £14 million. Clive, as Chairman of Syndicate 334 (1985) Names Association, had started liquidation proceedings against Pulbrook Underwriting Management Ltd. This was the prelude to launching a legal suit against the E&O insurers who were refusing to pay. Syndicate 334 and Pulbrook Underwriting Management were coinsured with Merrett under the E&O policy. The refusal to pay was a sign that the attitude of E&O underwriters was hardening. They were being asked to make a significant contribution to the overall Reconstruction and Renewal.

On 13 December, David rang Clive with the good news that £586,000 had been paid into the D J Freeman client account representing the damages against Members' Agents for those Names whose contracts were under seal.

On 13 December, the Super Group wrote to Rowland to advise him that they were appointing professional advisers of standing to provide Names' Associations and Action Group Committees with independent advice, on the acceptability of the forthcoming settlement offer. The Super Group was not satisfied with the interim arrangements for Equitas. The Chairmen of each of the twenty-seven Super Group Members signed the letter and enclosed a copy of the terms of reference for Action Group Chairmen and copied the Reconstruction and Renewal bylaw dated 6 December with a draft copy of the Supervisory Management Agreement for Equitas Reinsurance Ltd. Christopher Stockwell believed that significant progress could be achieved without recourse to legal action.

Clive approved the Super Group's letter to Rowland. Expressing his disappointment in the lack of progress, Clive phoned David:

> Everyone was disappointed that the efforts of some five and a half years had not yet resulted in cash being transferred into the coffers of the Association. In some conversations with Members the disappointment was also tinged with demoralisation. I would hasten to reassure anybody that this particular Chairman is more *incensed* than demoralised. I helped Terry McAllister to compile his *Evening Standard* article of 12th, banging the 'fraud' drum as loudly as he could. I think David Rowland is particularly sensitive to fraud and perceives a certain aspect of Morton's Fork. Either the E&O pay up or they confirm that fraud was rife at the relevant time; and the claims of those Names wishing to void their agreements with Lloyd's would be greatly advanced. In fact, the whole Reconstruction and Renewal plan could become quite unstitched if the E&O underwriters continue with their refusal to pay up on the grounds of fraudulent concealment.

He replaced the telephone handpiece and pondered as to what more he could do to extract the cash that rightfully belonged to Members of the Association.

The sterling efforts made by the Super Group organisation were reflected in the substantial income and expenditure for the year ended 30 September 1995, with the previous year figures in parentheses. The financial statements showed an income of £207,946 (£254,124) and expenses of £201,594 (£238,535). Net assets were £20,815 (£14,463).

Writing to David on 19 December Clive declared that it was not known whether there was a reinstatement on the E&O policy for Syndicate 334, nor was it known whether the E&O policy for the relevant year was provided by Merrett as lead underwriter or whether it was insured under the Merrett Group policy. This would be revealed once Pulbrook Underwriting Management had been liquidated. Should there be a valid reinstatement, then the Syndicate 90 Names Action Group might possibly have an interest giving rise to a conflict of interest. Consequently, Clive wished to know the legal position of those Association Committee Members who were Committee Members or Members of Syndicate 90 Action Group. David's reply, on 21 December, confirmed that if a conflict arose the Committee Members with an interest in Syndicate 90 should withdraw from any discussion and not vote.

John Winter complained to Ron Sandler on 21 December about the Supervisory Management Agreement as he had not received a copy. He said the Agency would enter into the Agreement solely in compliance with the direction made by Council regarding Reconstruction and Renewal. He had not enough time to form an independent view. The Agency had received numerous letters from Names instructing the Agency not to enter the supervisory agreements as drafted. Repeated concerns had been expressed about claims management 'protecting' the interests of the ongoing Market. The Litigating Names Committee believed these proposals were not in the best interests of Names. Additional concerns related to a large number of syndicates being reinsured into Lloyd's that would have their run-off managed by Managing Agencies who also managed continuing syndicates. The present proposal was for 191 of 400 syndicates in this situation reducing to 100 by the end of 1998. This created a position where the ongoing Market would have a significant element of influence over the management of Equitas claims.

Newsletter, December 1995: Delays and Prevarication

The Chairman said November 10 had been agreed as the date to transfer £14 million into the D J Freeman clients' account. Delays occurred because of shifting delivery dates and amending consultations between the defendants' and the Association's solicitors which involved a series of precise calculations and adjustments. News broke that the E&O insurers were refusing to pay up and reserving their rights to avoid the policy. The Association's immediate concern was to protect its position by putting Pulbrook Underwriting Management into liquidation and appointing a receiver. The earliest court date was 16 January. Stephen Merrett as underwriter of Syndicate 418 was the lead underwriter for the E&O insurers. Thus, Merrett was both the insurer and the insured, being Chairman of Pulbrook Underwriting Management at the time. In addition, it was profoundly disturbing to deduce from various utterances and hints from defendants that the E&O cover may be insufficient, and consequently the Association's Members may not receive the full award.

Lloyd's response to catastrophic losses incurred from Hurricane Betsy in 1965 was to commission a secret internal inquiry in 1968, headed by Lord Cromer, a former Governor of the Bank of England. The wide-ranging scope of the report advocated the widening of Membership to non-Market participants, including non-British subjects and women, and a reduction of onerous capitalisation requirements. Lord Cromer rendered his report on the future of Lloyd's but it was kept under wraps for nineteen years as Lloyd's did not publish it. One of the report's most penetrating and critical observations related to E&O insurance. It was regarded as quite monstrous that the providers of capital, the Names, contracted for unlimited liability, whereas those who purported to be Agents of Names hid behind the protection of limited liability. Lord

Cromer said it was imperative under these circumstances that Names should be protected by adequate E&O insurance. The bylaw was ineffective in that it did not prescribe the amount of cover required. In 1990 the Council repealed the bylaw without prior warning. This iniquitous act left Names wholly unprotected with disastrous consequences. One must never forget that these Members of Council were largely those who made their money entirely out of the capital of those they purported to act for as Agents. Whilst Lloyd's had lost £8.5 billion in the last five years their faithful Agents had paid themselves no less than £6 billion in fees, commissions and salaries. This was in addition to arranging multimillion-pound personal stop-loss policies to protect themselves on preferential and advantageous terms. Once again this highlighted the utter idiocy not only of putting rabbits in charge of the lettuce patch but also, at the same time, issuing them with bulletproof coats.

Sir Adam Ridley's Names' Committee Interim Report of November 1995 was a formulation of advice and was not a Lloyd's document. However, Clive found it a profoundly humane and sensible document. One had to be careful lest the glow from this document served to obscure the drawbacks of Reconstruction and Renewal. It had one fundamental omission. It failed to observe one of the objects of Reconstruction and Renewal that was to allow an unfettered Lloyd's Market to trade happily into the future, free from any encumbrance of the past and any form of restitution. If the Reconstruction and Renewal plan was to have any chance of success, restitution from future trading must be an integral part of the solution. Lloyd's had agreed to fund an independent assessment of Equitas and settlement plans, calling it rather ominously 'The Validation Enquiry'. The Super Group had also commissioned a separate enquiry into the viability of any alternative solutions. One of the alternatives would be an orderly run-off of the entire Lloyd's Market. Not the least would be the tax treatment of losses, unlike the crystallisation in one year of a huge loss under the Equitas scheme. David confirmed subsequently that as far as Syndicate 334's claim was concerned, there was £20 million cover with one reinstatement suggesting that Syndicate 90's claims had been notified to a different year of account. Clive asked for this confirmation several times but continued to be sceptical that the figures were truly firm.

Feeling somewhat demob-happy, Clive circulated copies of documents to the Committee as the last batch of happy reading for Christmas and wished all a 'Happy Christmas'. The Committee could then formulate views and provide advice to the Association immediately after the festive season. A letter from David Newbigging of the Litigating Names Committee concerned the governance of Equitas. As an insurance company the DTI had the right to approve the Directors. Given this powerful safeguard, it seemed to Litigating Names Committee that all the trustees should be elected by the Names who in turn appointed Equitas Directors. Newbigging had previously enunciated the principle that the ongoing Market must not control Equitas. The concept of Lloyd's appointing either trustees or Directors was clearly in conflict with this and would not be acceptable to Names represented by the Litigating Names Committee. To get Equitas up and running, Executive Directors needed to be at work already. However, the Names had not been consulted on any of the appointments giving rise to profound concerns, since Names were expected to provide the great bulk of Equitas assets.

Also enclosed was a memorandum from Fred Price suggesting that the tables were turned on the E&O insurers by all post-1979 Syndicate 334 Names. These Names should void their liability on the opening RITC at 1 January 1980 on the grounds of fraudulent concealment. Success in reopening the 1980 RITC would stop any further payment being made by the voiding Names and crystallise the whole asbestos problem for post-1979 Names.

The *Guardian*'s report on 29 December, by Pauline Springett, informed readers that Lloyd's had once again defied all normal laws of business, despite notching up £11 billion of losses. One serious flaw remaining was the self-regulation system that was condemned as hopelessly inadequate by a cross-party Commons Select Committee. The 9,000-strong ALM was worried that there was too much capacity which would force down premiums and squeeze profits. Lloyd's had brought many of its Names to the brink of financial ruin and was about to limp into another year with £9.58 billion of underwriting capacity. The depleted number of Names was 12,811, dropping from over 30,000 a few years earlier. Huge delays occurred to the Equitas project and liabilities were calculated on the assumption that the US was about to pass favourable tax laws. Providing the laws passed, tax allowances would help pay the multibillion-dollar pollution clean-up, otherwise Equitas may have underestimated liabilities. Lloyd's corporate capital entered 1994 providing one third of the capital base. This would dominate in the future. Eventually Lloyd's would operate as a collection of quasi-insurance companies with a potential increase in professionalism and reduced running costs.

On 4 January 1996, *Insurance Day* published a 'Viewpoint' on the Equitas move towards finality. The more alarmist considered that the vessel being created was inherently unstable but did not point out that the whole of the world's insurance market was navigating similar unchartered waters. It estimated Equitas would take over the liabilities of some 745 open years of account by July 1996. The question concerning each Name would be whether Equitas would provide them with finality and an end to cash calls. The Names were unlikely to learn how much they would be expected to contribute until after March. Proponents of Equitas declared that it would be fully reserved when it started operations following massive, detailed analysis of open-year exposures. Judicial use of discounting, better returns on funds by investing in longer-term high-yielding securities and cost savings were designed to enable Equitas to weather any storms it may encounter. However, detractors asserted that the growth in claims from asbestos, pollution and health hazards was such as to make the accurate prediction of the ultimate loss extremely difficult. Equitas was probably better informed than any other insurer on liabilities and future growth patterns.

The article also discussed the possible failure of Equitas, collapse of the Lloyd's Market, the possibility that Names rejected Reconstruction and Renewal and the implications of business transfers authorisations being subject to the Insurance Companies Act 1982. A query was posed, would the descendants of Edward Lloyd, in whose coffee shop in 1688 business took place, want to pay a premium to Equitas?

On 4 January, Linden Ife questioned the validity of the change in the Association's Rules at the 1993 AGM regarding equalisation of awards from litigation. Her contract was under seal and therefore won against both the Managing and Member's Agent. She suggested to Jasper Salisbury-Jones that specialist counsel should be consulted regarding the validity of the Rule change. She asked to receive the money awarded to her father. Clive responded on 17 January saying her letter would be put before the Committee meeting next week. It was unlikely that any distribution would be made until the liabilities of the Association were fully determined.

A complaint had been lodged that Stockwell, who was bankrupt in 1991, was not a fit and proper person to be Chairman of the Devonshire Names Action Group. Alan Porter said he believed there was a strong likelihood that the *Mail on Sunday* attack on Stockwell had been encouraged or instigated by the Lloyd's Public Relations Department. This was part of a 'dirty tricks' campaign designed to discredit anyone who questioned the settlement process and posed a serious threat to it. It was clearly much easier to attack Stockwell than to debate the argument. Porter said he intended to throw all his personal energy into defending and supporting Stockwell and encouraged all Super Group Chairmen to do the same.

David Tiplady confirmed that he had made an application to the Secretary of State for an immediate appointment of a liquidator for Pulbrook Underwriting Management instead of the Official Receiver. The hearing to wind up Pulbrook Underwriting Management had been set for 17 January. Immediately following liquidation, he said he would demand from Pulbrook Underwriting Management's E&O insurers, through their solicitors, all the documentation pertaining to the cover and its alleged repudiation. The Association had no rights to other documentation. However, the liquidator would have access to papers such as Board minutes. An expert, Vivian Tyrell, would be the D J Freeman Partner to take the necessary steps to place Pulbrook Underwriting Management into liquidation.

Ian Chalk, Chairman of the Rose Thompson Young Action Group, faxed Clive to inform him that a Deputy Chairman of Lloyd's, John Stace, was unwise enough to confide in him saying he did not expect Equitas to last more than a few years. Could it be that the long-suffering Names were about to be conned again? Chalk also said Equitas was already formed and was in operation. Names would be reinsured into Equitas whether they liked it or not. Equitas would then pursue outstanding debts. The only vote on Reconstruction and Renewal would be one taken by all Names to accept or otherwise the individual offers of financial terms made to Names. The following day, Clive faxed the information to the Committee saying that it startled and alarmed him such that it was difficult not to regard the 'Sandler Process of Consultation' with complete cynicism. It appeared that Equitas would come into force regardless of the views of Names and safeguarding the financial future of those Names. The situation of some 30,000 Names was estimated. There were 12,000 Names eager to support Equitas who would be continuing to underwrite. Another 10,000 Names could cope with their Lloyd's losses out of income and tax recoveries and would probably vote for Equitas. Roughly 2,000 Names were in Hardship and Clive suspected another 6,000 Names would find it difficult or impossible to cope with their Equitas bill.

Lloyd's had written to D J Freeman requesting details of their clients who had issued writs prior to 31 May 1995. The information was required to ensure it was considered under the proposed Reconstruction and Renewal settlement offer. Lloyd's also wanted a copy of the writ following their request on 7 September 1995. Clive was of the opinion on 16 January that there may be disadvantages in preserving the Committee's decision to supply no information to Lloyd's.

On 18 January a copy of the *NewsScan* by SoN published the problems of the Association, reporting Clive's rather bitter comments that E&O insurers appeared to be quoting fraud as a reason not to pay. *NewsScan* said that Equitas permissions to trade were to be agreed by the DTI by the end of 1995. It transpired that any permissions granted were so full of qualifications as to be useless and bad public relations. It also reported details of Equitas Board Membership.

Clive distributed three important documents on 19 January 1996. Firstly, a thoughtful study by Stockwell dealing with the distribution of debt credits between different groups of Names; secondly, a letter from Clyde & Co solicitors, stating the case for avoiding payment under the E&O policy; and, thirdly, a letter from Barclays Bank.

In the first paper Christopher Stockwell considered Names such as those who had stop-loss and those who did not. He suggested stop-loss premiums should be repaid to Names to ensure fairness.

Several syndicates had uncovered fraud incidents and were not pursuing them in negligence actions. However, leading counsel was giving these fraud actions a good prospect of success. It was impossible to evaluate the financial implications for different groups of Names continuing to underwrite. A factor that would impact on some Names would be choosing to join defence groups rather than Reconstruction and Renewal, resulting in guarantees being drawn down, many secured on people's homes. Some 80% to 90% of the 'losses' that were the cause of nightmares was for fattening reserves, and a further 10% for paying incompetent Agents and brokers. Many would feel that such a 'settlement' was only an exchange of one creditor for another, the second being harder to fight since liability would have been accepted and crystallised.

Many Names were induced to pay losses in earlier years by borrowing from their banks or financial institutions, leaving their deposits untouched so that they could 'trade through'. A significant number of Names were concerned about how they would meet such liabilities outside Lloyd's if they had to accept a Hardship deal or a Reconstruction and Renewal offer, and they were left with substantial external indebtedness and no income to service it.

In the second paper, the Underwriters' Steering Group had written to Pulbrook Underwriting Management advising that it anticipated the avoidance of group cover. Underwriters would not indemnify Pulbrook Underwriting Management in respect of the interim payment offer which had been made in the Association's litigation. Clive thought that E&O insurers of Pulbrook Underwriting Management may be able to void the policy.

The third paper comprised a copy of a letter from Barclays Bank dated 8 January quoting a guarantee and debenture from Pulbrook Underwriting Management dated 19 December 1994. The letter mentioned all rights and claims relating to any policies of insurance in which the company may have an interest. It said the proceeds of such claims and rights should be paid to a notified bank account at Barclays. Clive suggested overall that Pulbrook Underwriting Management may be heavily indebted to it.

Thirty-First Steering Committee Meeting, 23 January 1996: The Committee to Meet CEO Ron Sandler!

Eight Committee Members attended the meeting, plus Mark Everiss.

The Treasurer reported that £586,000 was in D J Freeman's clients' account at 5.125% per annum interest. This was subject to undertakings given by David Tiplady and liens from the Estate protection plan for £45,212.97, personal stop-loss underwriters, Lloyd's and Linden Ife on behalf of her father. The funds were nominally in the name of the Association. Nevertheless, the Committee did not have the power to spend these funds even though 'winnings' were first to be applied to payment of expenses. The Treasurer had met a Mr Floyd, an insolvency practitioner, who quoted £10,000 to wind up Pulbrook Underwriting Management. David said the Association might need to wind up the whole Merrett Group and may need a more heavyweight liquidator. Clive raised the issue of the letter from Barclays Bank, suggesting it was nothing less than fraudulent preference. An assignment had been made after the hearing but before the judgement had been given.

David mentioned that Clifford Chance was attempting to restore the credibility of Stephen Merrett by means of arbitration. If this occurred, then payment by the E&O insurers was almost certain, as they would have no reason to withhold payment. The Committee agreed to proceed against the E&O insurers although costs could be in six figures involving a counsel's Opinion.

When arranging the date to meet Sandler, Clive informed the Committee:

> Ron Sandler told me that he had allowed an hour for the meeting. I decided it must be a negotiating meeting and wanted the whole Committee to be present. 'Oh no, you can't do that!' was the horrified response. Nevertheless, I arranged the meeting for today after the Steering Committee meeting.

The appointment with CEO Ron Sandler at 5 pm on the Twelfth Floor at Lloyd's was attended by six Committee Members and two solicitors from Freshfields, Lloyd's solicitors. Sandler confirmed that Equitas was not yet trading and was awaiting authorisation from the DTI. The RITC would be conditional on acceptance by Names. The Council of Lloyd's would declare Reconstruction and Renewal unconditional if the bulk of litigation was brought to an end and sufficient funds were available resulting from Names paying into Equitas. A judgement had to be exercised by Council based on the profile of Reconstruction and Renewal acceptances. Sandler said that 'finality' statements would be issued but nobody could be absolutely certain whether Equitas might fail. He seemed confident that Equitas would succeed and last for fifteen or twenty years rather than five to ten being the Market view mentioned by Harry and supported by Chatset. Sandler confirmed that Lloyd's should not have any influence over Equitas. Trustees would own the shares and the Directors would be elected by Names plus some nominations by the Bank of England.

Sandler said he was doing his best to raise more money for the settlement offer by talking to brokers, auditors and future Market traders. He was contemplating a tax on the future trading of Lloyd's. He thought the Association had not got much to show for its litigation except a judgement and suggested the Association might find that 'the cupboard was bare'. Furthermore, there was an extremely remote possibility that the liabilities would come back to haunt Names should Equitas fail. Harry Purchase told Sandler that he owed Lloyd's nothing and that he had been duped.

Sandler outlined various details of Reconstruction and Renewal. He said a ballpark figure of 30% of total losses to date as well as uncalled losses to infinity may be expected in the Reconstruction and Renewal package, and there would be no retribution. Clive told Sandler:

> You can forget retribution and Member restitution. Thousands of Names had been defrauded and hoodwinked by Agents who did not know their business. My definition of 'restitution' is paying cash to 'burnt Names' so that they could have lifestyles that were not 'breadline'. Furthermore, writing off debts does not constitute restitution.

Sandler explained that there would be a differentiation between litigating and non-litigating Names and that £800 million would go to litigants. He also thought a high proportion of the £2.8 billion would go to litigants. The Syndicate 334 Names Association, having received a judgement in court, would sit alongside Gooda Walker and other Associations that had won their court battles but he confirmed that Syndicate 90 would not receive an uplift. He agreed that litigation subscriptions paid by Names would be paid out in cash to their Associations for distribution, or directly to Names.

Alasdair Ferguson asked if he could keep litigating if he refused the Reconstruction and Renewal offer. Sandler said he could. However, he would not receive any debt credits and would get billed by Equitas. Equitas would reinsure all Names only if the settlement offer succeeded. Harry Purchase again told Ron Sandler that he had nothing and did not owe any money.

A Freshfields solicitor present dissertated on fraud and gross incompetence. He explained the difficulty for Names attempting to avoid contracts with Lloyd's as it was necessary to prove fraud. The standard relating to fraud was now spelt out in the 1996 trial of Kevin Maxwell, Robert Maxwell's youngest son. After his father's death and the collapse of the Mirror Group media empire with debts of some £460 million, Kevin

Maxwell was tried on fraud charges arising from his role in his father's companies. The charges were not proven and he was acquitted.

Newsletter, January 1996: Winding-Up Petition Granted

The Association's petition to wind up Pulbrook Underwriting Management was granted unopposed on 17 January 1996. The Association would be able to pursue the Pulbrook Underwriting Management's E&O policy under the Third Parties (Rights Against Insurers) Act 1930. Pulbrook Underwriting Management was co-assured under the Merrett Group E&O policy on which the E&O insurers had given notice of avoidance on the grounds of fraudulent concealment. There was disbelief at this prospect in view of the conspiracy and concealment that reportedly had been rife amongst Lloyd's underwriters. However, there were many precedents whereby co-assureds had escaped avoidance in similar situations. Pulbrook Underwriting Management had virtually no assets except for the E&O policy with which to satisfy any judgement against it. Barclays Bank had written to say that proceeds of any call on the E&O policy were hocked to the bank. A valid claim would be necessary for money to be released.

Sandler was an efficient technician managing the single job of launching Equitas. Clive said the stark meaning of Reconstruction and Renewal was that some £1.5 billion would be lifted off the 'haves' and given to the 'have nots'. The benefits to the Market of the Equitas project seemed markedly greater than those accruing to the Names. There were now Actions in some thirty-nine US States. The basis of the Actions was a report by the Parliamentary Treasury Select Committee on which the UK Government refused to act. Some 10% of Lloyd's losses emanated from the US and if successful they would be an additional burden on Names. The publicity was having a markedly adverse effect on Lloyd's business. The sad paradox of the situation was the line taken by David Rowland in the relentless pursuit of Names. This was regardless of the wholly immoral creation of those losses and was resulting in the disappearance of the very Market which Rowland hoped to preserve. These were terrible tactics and a suicidal strategy.

The newsletter noted an *Independent on Sunday* report about INTAC, the consortium of all the large continental reinsurers who reinsured a very substantial amount of Lloyd's business. As a result of the fraud exposed in the Merrett trial, these reinsurers, such as Munich Re, Cologne Re and Zurich Re, were reconsidering their relationship with Lloyd's, with a view to voiding not only Merrett but a number of other Lloyd's syndicate reinsurances with them. If this report was true the consequences for Lloyd's Names were not pretty to contemplate.

There were a number of reports of increasingly harsh Hardship deals. Names who had won in Action Groups and whose money was frozen by the Premiums Trust Deeds argument were being pursued for debts irrespective of any set-off claimed.

On Thursday, 1 February 1996 the Chairman and Treasurer went to see the Official Receiver, a Mr Pett, regarding the liquidation of Pulbrook Underwriting Management. Pett outlined the situation, saying:

Speed is of the essence where fraud is concerned. The Official Receiver's representative will recover all the books and records next Monday. A sworn statement of affairs will be required within twenty-one days, a creditors' meeting arranged and a liquidator appointed. Under the Insolvency Act 1986 all actions are stayed except by leave of the court. Pulbrook Underwriting Management may be contractually obliged to defend an appeal, as puppets of the E&O insurers. Rule 4.182 of the Insolvency Act 1986 permits the Official Receiver's costs to be transferred to the liquidator and settled by the first assets to be realised. The Barclays Bank fixed and floating charge guarantee debenture on property and assets was filed on 6 August 1993. A further charge was filed on 20 December 1994, on the E&O policy which also specified leasehold property. Barclays is owed £1.4 million jointly and severally. Other companies in the Group are profitable and solvent. If the bank was paid off from other resources, there would be no call on the E&O policy of Pulbrook Underwriting Management. Stephen Merrett informed me that he was not aware of any assignment and understood that an undue preference was a fraudulent preference.

He continued:

> Cameron Markby Hewitt visited my offices yesterday. Stephen Merrett denied offering Barclays Bank the proceeds of Pulbrook Underwriting Management E&O insurance recoveries. Cameron Markby Hewitt said they were owed £8,000 by Pulbrook and enquired whether they were going to be retained to conduct the resistance to the Association's Interim Payment appeal. I told them it was something to be decided later. The appointment of a liquidator is urgent and I will give you a few hours for the Association to come up with a firm's name for a liquidator.

As Mr Floyd was not in a suitably sized firm, a Partner of Pridie Brewster, a medium-sized City firm, was interviewed. Details of the proposed appointment were faxed to the Official Receiver before the deadline. The Chairman subsequently explained to the Committee that he and the Association's Treasurer had to take swift action without the opportunity to consult the rest of the Committee and hoped it would receive approval.

One of the E&O underwriters had written to Clive saying Barclays Bank was going flat-out to claim the E&O proceeds. Apparently, the insurers intended to pay the money into court for the court to decide between Barclays and the Association. The Official Receiver had opined that the assignment to Barclays had the appearance of unlawful preference.

Cameron Markby Hewitt had written on 5 February to interested parties that the Official Receiver had to consider the position and take independent advice. They had also written to the Court of Appeal stating they could not file Pulbrook Underwriting Management information by the deadline because of changed circumstances. A later submission was allowed. On 9 February, David wrote to say the Official Receiver as the liquidator of Pulbrook Underwriting Management thought it was unnecessary to appoint another liquidator. He disagreed and said there were distinct advantages in appointing another liquidator. It was open to the Names on the petition resulting in the winding-up order to request the Official Receiver convene a creditors' meeting to appoint a liquidator. He was obliged to call such a meeting, if at least one quarter in value of Pulbrook Underwriting Management's creditors made such a request. Thus, David's letter to the Official Receiver of 15 January requested the Secretary of State to appoint a liquidator of the petitioners' choice. He cited the complex affairs of Pulbrook Underwriting Management and the purported withdrawal of the E&O insurers' cover and assignment of the proceeds of such E&O cover to Barclays Bank, on which only a liquidator could take action. Requisitioning the creditors' meeting and compliance with statutory time limits would take some time. Once the Official Receiver had received a request, a meeting must be summoned within thirty-five days and give creditors twenty-one days' notice of the meeting and its venue.

The Super Group distributed a lengthy February newsletter. It was critical of Reconstruction and Renewal as there was negligible reconstruction envisaged and doubtful renewal. Lloyd's suggested that Reconstruction and Renewal could be completed if 50% of Names accepted. New York insurance commissioners thought that Equitas could not give finality and concern was expressed about solvency and the length of time Equitas cash would last. Many of the 'won't pays' had suffered disproportionate losses and were worthy of special treatment.

A Litigating Names Committee report made it clear how unequally the losses had been divided. Lloyd's FRD and Agents insisted Names should 'pay now and sue later'. The Super Group queried who should they sue. Lloyd's had denied responsibility and the only hope was to withhold payment and await a settlement or some form of compensation. If Names paid the cash calls, they would certainly never see any money back.

The complexities of the winding-up of Pulbrook Underwriting Management were illustrated by a letter from David to Clive on 13 February. The text of the letter, slightly modified, was as follows:

Yesterday, I received a phone call from Michael Pugh of the Official Receiver's Office inviting me to a meeting with himself and Michael Steiner of Messrs Denton Hall, solicitors. Mr Pugh informed me that Clyde & Co, solicitors, on behalf of the E&O underwriters, had agreed to pay his expenses in investigating Pulbrook Underwriting Management's standing in the various legal actions against it or on its behalf. Mr Pugh told me that he had instructed Messrs Denton Hall to provide him with objective legal advice.

Mark Everiss and I attended a meeting with Michael Steiner and Michael Pugh yesterday afternoon. Mr Pugh then told us that Clyde & Co had threatened that the E&O cover would be vitiated, assuming it was not already vitiated from Stephen Merrett's various defalcations, were the Official Receiver to refuse to allow the E&O underwriters to continue the defence of the Syndicate 334 and 90 actions.

Mr Pugh said he was now minded, contrary to earlier indications given both to me, my colleagues and I believe to Clive and Keith, to make a Secretary of State appointment. However, he would only do so if he was satisfied as to the standing of the liquidator we chose. He made it quite clear that he was not satisfied with either of the Treasurer's choices to date but would accept Paul Evans of Price Waterhouse. He clearly believed that a liquidation of this complexity and probable notoriety required the skills of a very-high-class technician indeed. As you know I tend to be of the same opinion myself. In view of Mr Pugh's comments, I have taken the liberty of inviting Paul Evans to address the Steering Committee at its meeting next Friday. I trust this meets with your approval but if not, I can easily cancel the appointment.

Clive phoned an officer of the Official Receiver's Office and asked if someone could address the Committee meeting the following week. Michael Pugh volunteered to attend the meeting himself. Clive explained to the Committee that the situation was approaching Gilbertian levels when he remarked to the Official Receiver that the Committee was undecided whether to sue him if he defended the Association's interim award appeal or sue him if he did not. He did not demur when Clive suggested that the Barclays Bank situation was one of fraudulent preference. However, there seemed little point in the appeal on quantum and scoring an academic victory only to discover there was nothing in the pot. Jasper Salisbury-Jones alerted Clive to danger in the current arbitration, should Merrett compromise on a low-figure settlement. He said it was important not to get caught up in an arbitration.

The net assets of Pulbrook Underwriting Management comprised mainly office furniture and equipment and it was doubtful whether they could be sold for the value indicated. A note in the auditors' report stated that there were cross-guarantees relating to an overdraft facility. The directors believed that the support of the group's bankers would continue beyond the expiry of the current overdraft facility.

Following a telephone discussion, the Treasurer wrote to David on 14 February about the £9,603 cost to date of winding up Pulbrook Underwriting Management as there appeared to be some excessive charges. He also queried the comment that if funds were in D J Freeman's clients' account the first call upon the money was to pay the Association's expenses. This did not appear to be the case and thus one concluded that the Association had not received any funds following the award from legal action. Lastly, the Treasurer complained that fees were reasonably estimated up to the judgement, but subsequently there had been no estimate of likely costs for subsequent phases.

Thirty-Second Steering Committee Meeting, 16 February 1996

A meeting at D J Freeman's offices was attended by eight Members of the Committee as well as Mark Everiss from D J Freeman, Paul Evans, a Price Waterhouse Partner, and Michael Pugh, the Official Receiver. The Official Receiver confirmed that Pulbrook Underwriting Management was in liquidation. It was noted that Members' Agents were also a creditor of Pulbrook Underwriting Management. David said that the E&O policy could only be voided on the grounds of fraud. The Association's claim fell into the 1989 year. He also confirmed that the Barclays Bank 1994 Assignment may be valid, but it could probably be set aside; and that the debt due to Barclays was in the region of £1.4 million. Regarding avoidance of E&O cover, arbitration proceedings had been instituted by Clifford Chance, solicitors, acting for the Merrett Group. The Association would be bound by the arbitration decision. It was essential the Association attempted to sever all relationships with the other parties involved and take the matter to court under the Third Parties (Rights Against Insurers) Act 1930 on a technical point of law.

David thought the Association could go for a summary judgement Section 24(2) of the Arbitration Act 1950 which gave the High Court the power to transfer the arbitration to itself where an issue of fraud was raised. Counsel's Opinion would be sought to determine whether such a transfer was the best tactic, whether to seek arbitration independently, or to agree the steps taken by Clifford Chance which involved the consolidation of arbitrations on behalf of all the Merrett Group Companies. David's instinctive preference was to litigate the issue in the High Court.

The Official Receiver confirmed that no reliable declaration had been made by Merrett concerning the Barclays Bank liability. The E&O underwriters were probably creditors of Pulbrook Underwriting Management for the deductible under the E&O policies. The Official Receiver said he had a duty to investigate the affairs of Pulbrook Underwriting Management regardless of who was appointed liquidator. He said there were no assets to warrant calling a creditors' meeting. He also thought it improper to pursue the appeal which could use funds in the Pulbrook Underwriting Management pot and this would not be in the Association's best interests. It might result in another reason for the Pulbrook Underwriting Management underwriters to repudiate the contract.

The Official Receiver said he needed to be satisfied that the nominated liquidator should be sufficiently experienced and clearly understood possible conflicts of interest. If he could liaise with someone of sufficient standing, he could arrange a Secretary of State appointment for an hour, within twenty-four hours. This would avoid the need to call a creditors' meeting. The Official Receiver confirmed that he would continue his investigations relating to fraud, impropriety and unfit conduct. These investigations would be funded by the taxpayer. It would take six to eight months to report. The Chairman asked, if there were no real assets, why appoint a liquidator, and the reply was the potential recovery of £1.4 million that might otherwise go to Barclays Bank.

Paul Evans of Price Waterhouse was invited to outline what he would do if he were appointed liquidator. He said there were four commercial issues to be faced.

Firstly, other creditors such as non-litigating Names. Secondly, Barclays Bank's contingent claim as a secured creditor by virtue of this assignment. It would be a prudent move to have this assignment set aside by the court in the immediate future. Thirdly, the debt due from Merrett Holdings PLC amounting to approximately £150,000. Fourthly, the difficulty of concluding the liquidation of a Lloyd's Agency Company particularly if Reconstruction and Renewal was accepted.

Evans thought he might look at such matters as wrongful trading, unlawful transactions and transfers of assets elsewhere in the Group. The protection of the E&O policy would be the top priority. He mentioned that he had five years' experience in the insolvency of insurance companies and Lloyd's Agencies. His view was that E&O underwriters would have to pay Barclays Bank all the funds under assignment before paying the liquidator and the balance to the Association. He said that security for his costs would be required in the event that no funds were forthcoming from the liquidation. The Chairman said there would need to be a regime of cost control and a ceiling.

The Official Receiver confirmed that he had no problem with the appointment of Evans as liquidator should the Committee decide to appoint him.

In the absence of the Treasurer, Guy Wilson raised a query on his behalf that the Association should not proceed with the appeals as the costs were becoming out of hand, and he was concerned about their recoverability. David observed that if Reconstruction and Renewal was accepted later in the year all litigation subscriptions would be paid to Names in cash. Thus, litigation should proceed with haste, particularly on the Barclays Bank issue.

The Official Receiver and Paul Evans left the meeting which then discussed the appeals. Two main appeals were discussed with the substantive issues appeal in the matter of Members' Agents' nondelegable duties being the more important than the quantum appeal. It was agreed unanimously to go ahead with the substantive issues appeal of nondelegable duties. Counsel's costs would be in the region of £5,000. If the appeal was lost the maximum cost would be £40,000.

It was resolved to appoint Evans, and Guy was asked to contact him to define the work to be done and the costs of the liquidation. Harry Purchase wondered if it was possible to obtain the minute books of Pulbrook Underwriting Management, as he was convinced there would be evidence helpful to the investigations.

Guy Wilson wrote to Evans on 20 February confirming his appointment as liquidator for Pulbrook Underwriting Management and wished to know specific charge-out rates. The Committee had agreed to guarantee a fee of £25,000. Guy said that the Committee had earlier agreed a fee of £10,000 with another prospective liquidator. In view of Evans' past experience there should be no learning curve, which should help to keep the costs down. At the meeting on Friday, Evans had mentioned there were some severe problems to overcome. Guy acknowledged that while the Association was likely to be the largest creditor there may be others, such as Names who had not taken legal action. Advice may be needed as these creditors might be time-barred. Guy suggested that he and the Treasurer met Evans to discuss proposed strategies.

A Mr North of Bampton said that litigation settlements had been totally removed from any benefit attributed to the Names. This Reconstruction and Renewal proposal was not fair. He was incensed that the objective of Tranche 2 was to reduce the cost of finality without disadvantaging those who had paid their debts in full. However, Tranche 3 produced a cap of £100,000 to all Names, however little they may have subscribed towards their losses. In his case he had wasted £880,000 trying to pay losses.

David wrote on 21 February saying that the Pulbrook Underwriting Management liquidation itself was reasonably straightforward and inexpensive. The Association wished to control the liquidation and determine whether any assets had been improperly removed and challenge competing claims for remaining assets. He wished to challenge a Barclays Bank claim with a priority interest in the whole E&O policy. Most importantly of all was the need to reinstate the E&O cover, as such a reinstatement would increase the potential amount of funds. Reinstatement required refuting the grounds for repudiating the cover. This was based on Merrett's allegedly fraudulent behaviour towards his Syndicate 418 Names. All this had involved a considerable amount of work including a consultation with counsel resulting in revising amendments to the petition.

David also commented on the lack of a budget since the conclusion of the trial as subsequent events were beyond D J Freeman's control. The E&O repudiation and Barclays Bank assignment had exposed far higher costs than usually anticipated. As a result of the queries he reduced an invoice and Clive was delighted to see that his fees were under constant scrutiny.

On 21 February Clive wrote to the Chairman of Barclays Bank explaining that the Association had recently won a negligence case and an interim payment from Pulbrook Underwriting Management. The only asset of the company was an E&O policy. According to Mr Justice Cresswell in the High Court, Merrett had deceived his Names through a mixture of truths, half-truths and falsehoods. As a result, the E&O insurers of Merrett Group intended to void the Merrett Group policy on the grounds of fraud. The Association had received documents purporting to show that Barclays Bank should benefit from the proceeds of any claim under Pulbrook Underwriting Management's E&O policy. This arrangement was made in between the Association's hearing and the delivery of the judgement. Legal advice to the Association stated this to be unlawful preference and that it could easily be overturned. Clive expressed moral repugnance at the behaviour and intentions of both parties to the arrangement. He contacted the Chairman of Barclays, saying:

> You may like to reflect on the opprobrium your bank might attract should it be publicly perceived to have entered an apparent conspiracy, with an adjudged fraudster, to attempt to filch from the Members of this Association the proceeds of five and a half years litigation. I ask you, politely, to renounce promptly any claim to monies due to Members of this Association.

Subsequently, on 4 March, Andrew Buxton, Chairman of Barclays Bank, wrote to Clive stating that the bank's solicitors were satisfied that the security held by the bank for a loan to Pulbrook Underwriting Management was valid. He was not prepared to renounce any claim against the E&O policy.

The editorial of the February issue of Chatset League Tables did not approve of the Equitas premiums sent out the previous November. The indicative premiums were incomplete and inconsistent. It said Lloyd's must be fair and even-handed with Names. The *Independent* of 22 February reported that Chatset demanded an extra £1 billion for Equitas. Seemingly, Lloyd's ploy was not to involve Names in the consultative process. It slated Lloyd's for sham 'consultations' with Names and for missing deadlines, indicating that brokers should cough up another £300 million, Managing Agents £350 million and E&O underwriters £300 million. Fat salaries paid to Equitas staff could also be cut to reduce costs. John Rew of Chatset said insiders were not yet frightened enough to stump up. Loss-making Names were celebrating the first step in their fight for damages. The High Court ordered that Stephen Merrett and the Merrett Managing Agents should pay 80% of the damages awarded to Names and that Merrett personally should pay £500,000 within six weeks. The other 20% was payable by Ernst & Young the auditors.

On 27 February the Super Group wrote to the Chairmen of the Action Groups about the difficult decisions facing Council the next day regarding Reconstruction and Renewal. There was a widespread desire for a settlement of litigation but not at any price and disgust at the way the Hardship Scheme guidelines and undertaking had been abandoned to be replaced by an indiscriminate and uncaring 'cash grab'. There was a very deep resentment at the idea of means testing which was held to be insulting. Many did not accept they had any moral responsibility for losses as they believed they were the victims of regulatory failure, negligence and fraud. Finality must be meaningful and Names should have control of Equitas. The Litigation Settlement Fund was too small to achieve a settlement. The debt credit package was inadequate for its supposed objectives and stretching it with means testing was unacceptable.

The Reconstruction and Renewal package was seen as a fudge, allowing Market insiders to distance themselves from historic problems left with Names. A substantial body of litigants did not believe the package was in their best interests. A significant number of solvent Names were unwilling to mutualise their reserves. Whatever package was finally proposed it had to be agreed by the majority Names and even then, some Names would not consider it to be fair. However, all would be pleased that the current unsatisfactory situation would be resolved.

The Times of 28 February was optimistic that a conclusion to Lloyd's problems was expected as soon as Reconstruction and Renewal progressed. Nevertheless, it was critical of the Society, stating:

> Lloyd's resembles a nest of competing vipers, some of which were stubborn, some deluded, and others unable to distinguish reality from imagination. The symptoms were evident in all the constituent parts of Lloyd's, the Agents, the Council, ongoing Names, burnt Names, E&O underwriters, personal stop-loss underwriters, the brokers and the syndicates' auditors.

On 29 February, Ian Young of KPMG Cork office wrote about the key deficiencies of the Reconstruction and Renewal proposal. Comments included the following.

1. The consequences of the proposed settlement were not set out. If there was an indemnity offered to Names how secure would it be?

2. £2 billion debt credits seem to be mere book entries. Debt credits were nebulous and remained carefully undefined. What legal and financial reality lay behind the phrase?

3. Despite the efforts to portray it otherwise the 'Litigation Settlement Fund' would not be focused solely on the litigants.

4. In a number of places the document suggested that failure of Reconstruction and Renewal would be catastrophic, though there was no evidence to support such assertions.

5. What assistance did Hardship or FRD ever provide in the past?

6. Why would a change of a department name make an iota of difference? Re-spraying the department would not alter anything or improve the Names' financial position.

7. There was little in the document that was attractive to litigants who were effectively being asked to bear the financial burden compared with those Names who had done nothing to protect themselves and were exposed to a much heavier burden than those who were culpable.

8. The proposals did not seem to recognise the serious implications of the numerous US and Canadian legal actions.

Overall, these detailed observations showed it was difficult to be optimistic about the outcome of the Reconstruction and Renewal initiative in its present form. Too little was offered to litigants, too little financial redress, too little was made clear and too much was obscure.

Mr S. A. D. Maybury of Petersfield provided an extremely negative view of Equitas, illuminating the extensive ramifications of failure. He commented on 29 February that if Names consider the probability of Equitas' failure to be remote his analysis would not disturb them too much. Lloyd's had proved disastrously unreliable at assessing liabilities in the past. If Lloyd's could obtain reinsurance of the tail for Equitas at an affordable price, from reputable insurers outside the Lloyd's Market, Names would have some grounds for believing in the sustainability of Equitas.

On 1 March 1996 Clive faxed the Committee with the very sad news that Committee Member Jasper Salisbury-Jones had passed away on Thursday, 29 February. He had gone into hospital the previous afternoon with a stomach complaint requiring an operation. It was discovered that he had been suffering from a massive cancer for which nothing could be done. He did not regain consciousness. His knowledgeable, astute questioning and fervent involvement would be sorely missed by his friends on the Committee, his family and more widely.

The same day the Super Group provided up-to-date information about US cease and desist orders which were to prevent furtherance of the 'fraudulent or illegal offer'. State Security Commissioners had received substantial evidence to two basic effects, firstly, that being a Name at Lloyd's was a security for the purposes of state security laws and that Lloyd's had sold this security without receiving state approval first, and secondly, the sale of the security was obtained through misrepresentation and that this representation was fraudulent. Cease and desist orders had been issued in six states and shortly four other states would declare. Some 1,392 Names would have received orders by the end of the month, nearly half the US Names. If the order was upheld in court, it would freeze Lloyd's operations and cause Lloyd's to cease trading immediately.

Tim Freeborn wrote in *City & Finance*, 'Lloyd's Big Guns Facing the Mother of All Writs'. He reported that the retired underwriter John Donner alleged bad faith, which meant fraud, by nine of Lloyd's leading lights. US claims for asbestosis moved from a trickle to a flood in the 1980s. The writ was signed off by leading Queen's Counsel Michael Gadd, a fraud specialist. The list of defendants included former Chairmen of Lloyd's Sir Peter Green plus Sir Peter Miller and Murray Lawrence. The last was cast in a central role, as on 1 March 1982 he placed all the asbestosis risk of his Syndicate 362 with Syndicate 317 which was run by Richard Outhwaite. Less than three weeks later as Deputy Chairman of Lloyd's, Murray Lawrence wrote a letter which he said was sent to all active underwriters and the auditors. The letter warned of potential claims arising in connection with asbestosis and represented a major problem for insurers and reinsurers. Managing and Members' Agents were strongly advised to inform their Names. Subsequently forty Agents wrote to say they had not seen the letter. However, there was a letter in circulation from Cameron Markby Hewitt, solicitors, instructing Agents not to reply to enquiries. This effectively acted as a gagging order and left Lloyd's accused of concealment.

A previous report for Lloyd's, produced in November 1981, warned that between 8 and 11 million workers had been exposed to asbestos, four months before Lloyd's said it had alerted the Market. The same month Lawrence attended a meeting of panel auditors and said that if syndicates had reinsurance the scale of losses may be sufficient to bankrupt reinsurers. Events were moving quickly in the litigation-happy United States. In state after state the authorities had granted orders stopping Lloyd's from drawing down funds held by Agents. Lloyd's risked losing access to $2 billion. This could blow a hole in the plan to dump old Lloyd's claims into Equitas. John Donner expected outside reinsurers who took on risk from Lloyd's to rally behind the case. In its defence Lloyd's pointed out that it had made two investigations into the charge of concealment, one by Sir David Walker, former Chairman of the Securities and Investments Board, and the second by Freshfields, Lloyd's solicitors. Neither found there was a case to answer. Donner reckoned his team had amassed compelling new evidence. He said that in reality Lloyd's may have been insolvent in 1980 and he would like the DTI to answer why it allowed Lloyd's to continue to trade and recruit an extra 25,000 Names to share the burden. In 1980, information in the market was imperfect, and potential asbestosis claims were unknown, and unquantified. Underwriters would have taken a view based on the information of which they were aware and created appropriate reserves as they thought fit. With hindsight, speculatively some of these may have been fudged in the hope that the situation might not be as bad as rumoured. A fudged solvency statement by Lloyd's may not have been spotted by the DTI.

Clive circulated the notice by the Secretary of State of the appointment of Price Waterhouse as liquidator of Pulbrook Underwriting Management Limited on 7 March, together with a notice of a creditors' meeting on 21 March. He wanted to be assured that the statement of claim and proof of debt was submitted correctly. Clive requested as many Committee Members as possible to attend, in order to pack the meeting and to vote, thus determining the composition of the subsequent Creditors' Committee.

The same day John Flynn, Chairman of the Portfolio Selection Action Group based at Chantilly, Rathmichael, Dublin, wrote to Sandler saying Names were not being properly recompensed by the forward Market for the value of the Lloyd's name and ongoing business net of past liabilities. He quoted Peter Middleton who thought the Society's future was best secured as a public limited company (PLC). According to Lloyd's the business had produced a profit of approximately £1 billion for the past three years. If this entity was floated on the stock market as a PLC without its past liabilities and as an ongoing concern it would be capitalised at a multiple of ten or twelve times' earnings, i.e., some £10 to £12 billion. In equity and law, Lloyd's name and ongoing business was rightly an asset of the Names. The greed and deception which were factors in bringing Lloyd's to its knees continued to be demonstrated by those who controlled the destiny of the Society.

The *Financial Mail* reported that more than 32,000 Names had been told they may have to contribute to a £5.9 billion plan to rescue the ailing Market and Lloyd's had asked building societies to set aside traditional lending criteria. The average age of Names was fifty-eight and many were considered unsuitable as they did not meet current lending criteria. Names had so far reclaimed £3 billion from the Inland Revenue. The Inland Revenue was extremely slow, sometimes taking years to pay tax refunds based on losses. The only way for some Names to survive financially was to borrow on the value of losses agreed by Lloyd's but not necessarily agreed and paid by the Inland Revenue.

Newsletter, March 1996: What Is 'Finality'

Clive stated in the newsletter that Equitas, like most novel ideas, had its proponents and opponents. In some areas the battle between the two sides had become vituperative and unpleasant in the extreme. This resulted in truth and objective judgement to become utterly clouded and he questioned precisely what in Reconstruction and Renewal was being Reconstructed and Renewed? Riddance of the Ravaged would have been just as appropriate. Were practical expressions of Remorse and Restitution to be on offer then one could react more charitably. The meaning of the word 'finality' had been corrupted to disguise the situation which should be described as 'you are now entering an area of definite risk'. Finality meant the premium to be paid in cash to reinsure all past and future Lloyd's liabilities into an insurance company, the liabilities of which were not fully and accurately established. The insurance company, Equitas, needed to pass an annual solvency test. It could become insolvent at any time that its liabilities exceeded its assets. Clive speculated that if Equitas became insolvent a liquidator would be appointed and it would take years to sort out the muddle. Meanwhile the Names' money would be locked up. The track record of insurance companies in liquidation did not fill one with confidence. The conundrum was, if Equitas was going to succeed, why was it needed? Lloyd's could have coped with the existing mechanism and funds available to it.

Clive thought that one had to admire the spin doctoring which had induced the national press to repeat constantly the entirely fallacious message of 'Lloyd's £2.8 Billion Offer to Names'. The reality was that funds and levies totalling over £2 billion would be extracted from those Names who still had money to be turned into debt credits for those who could not pay their liabilities. The actual sum on offer from Lloyd's was £100 million, less than the last offer, but dressed up with Names' own money to look like something far more benevolent. In the original plan the money was coming from '£1.5 billion from funds at Lloyd's'. What the drafters cunningly left out was the word 'Names'. Those funds at Lloyd's really should have been billed as 'Names' Funds at Lloyd's', i.e., 'all their deposits and reserves'. Clive's observations precisely expressed the state of play which was not favouring External Names, especially the burnt ones.

Clive commented on alternatives to Equitas and the fear that the DTI would take over and pursue Names if Equitas did not succeed. He pointed out another danger, taxation, when deposits were turned into cash by the sale of securities and consequently resulted in an unwelcome capital gains tax. Debt credits would be deemed by the Inland Revenue as income and result in a large income tax bill. Lloyd's would leave the Inland Revenue to finish off the job they started, that is, the ruination of the Names. Many Names had pledged their houses as security in order to pay losses. The Names would find the guarantee would be encashed and ultimately their houses would be sold.

On the strength of the present proposals, one could liken Lloyd's to a snake shedding its skin, gliding away to a golden future, leaving the sad, sorry and discarded epidermis to be digested by a swarm of scavenging accountants, lawyers, bank managers and the Inspector of Taxes. The question must be asked, 'Why is it so vital to crystallise all the losses of Lloyd's into one tax year?' The advantages seem to be excessively one-sided. Clive's view was that unless the Lloyd's Market actually guaranteed finality and provided restitution, the Reconstruction and Renewal proposals would not succeed. It could be that current American litigation may decide the issue. He suggested Association Members wrote to their MP.

The Association formed a subcommittee to handle the affairs relating to the liquidation, which comprised Clive Francis, Chairman, Keith Lester, Treasurer, and Charles Baron, Committee Member. These, together with Harry Purchase, Committee Member, and Guy Wilson, Secretary, were willing to be appointed as Members of a Liquidation Committee to represent the creditors. On 12 March Daniel Schwarzmann forwarded a form to Treasurer Keith Lester, for him to consent to act as a Member of the Pulbrook Underwriting Management Liquidation Committee, together with a copy of the Insolvency Act 1986. The proof of debt form was completed and returned.

Jasper Salisbury-Jones had passed away on 29 February and for a few moments Clive wondered about his own mortality. He started voicing his views to no one in particular, 'Oh dear! How should I present this sad news to our Members? I could write a letter to them all or just put it in a newsletter but it is probably best in a personal letter even though it will cost a bit.' Clive stopped and referred to the Committee minutes and continued his conversation:

> Jasper came to the Committee meeting on 16 February and gave his usual penetrating contribution but gave no inkling of anything being amiss. His legal training as a barrister and acute mind were of the greatest help to me in guiding the fortunes of the Association. His Opinions were always delivered with pragmatism and unfailing good humour. His contribution to the work of the Association's Committee had been incalculable and his wise counsel will be sadly missed. Committee Members have lost a wise colleague and a great friend. Not only was he one of our Committee Members but also a tireless Member of Syndicate 418 Committee, the Syndicate 90 main Committee and was Chairman of the Syndicate 90 (No 2) Committee.

Pausing to think about his lifestyle, he noted:

> Jasper's constant travelling to and from his home on the Isle of Man on work for these Committees, as well as visits to Australia and the USA to meet Names, could not have been conducive to his health and well-being. He was indeed a doughty fighter in the cause of seeking justice and redress for those who believed that they had been wronged by their Agents and by Lloyd's. I will ask Celia to let me know the arrangements for the funeral.

Clive subsequently travelled to the funeral on the Isle of Man and received a most appreciative letter from Jasper's widow, Celia.

The *Evening Standard* reported that Barclays Bank was laying claim to money from an E&O policy on the basis of a secured loan to Stephen Merrett's failed Pulbrook Underwriting Management business. It mentioned that the money was also claimed by Syndicate 334 (1985) Names Association awarded after a five-year battle with Pulbrook Underwriting Management. Clive Francis, Chairman of the Association, had contacted Andrew Buxton, the Chairman of Barclays Bank, saying that legal action could be avoided if it dropped its claim. The bank rejected the argument and refused to say how much money it wanted.

Thirty-Third Steering Committee Meeting, 20 March 1996

David Tiplady informed the six Committee Members at the meeting held in his offices that the solicitors were awaiting a date for the appeal on the quantum issue which was likely to be in June. It was thought there were seven policy years which had been repudiated. Writs had been served on all the E&O underwriters who had avoided cover. David confirmed that he expected to be in court to have the avoidance overturned under the Third Parties (Rights Against Insurers) Act 1930. The Merrett Group had started arbitration proceedings. A claim from a £50 million fund had been made under a Lloyd's bylaw 15/89, and it appeared that Syndicate 387 had also made a claim.

On 12 March, Syndicate 418 Action Group had forwarded a copy of a legal Opinion about the responsibilities of the Committee regarding cessation of litigation. This Opinion needed careful study by all Committee Members. Compliance may be vital to avoid Lloyd's finding an excuse not to make approved payments.

The Equitas indicative statements had been distributed. At a recent ALM meeting, Sir David Berriman posed the question, 'If more funds are available under Reconstruction and Renewal, please indicate whether you would be likely to accept the indicative statements?' A straw poll was held and 248 were in favour of acceptance and 2 against. The Chairman was requested to write to Ron Sandler to request that more funds should be contributed by the Market. David said that if Action Groups wanted to act against the auditors they must go against the Agents. This raised the question of foregoing litigation rights on acceptance of the Reconstruction and Renewal proposals. It was clear that Names wanted a settlement but not on the Reconstruction and Renewal terms currently offered.

As part of the settlement, Clive had received an offer of £2,172,000. However, he made the point that many Names would be made bankrupt by the Inland Revenue if assessed to large amounts of debt credits with insufficient losses being carried forward to offset them. This was a potentially serious side-effect of the proposals as presently envisaged.

Lloyd's had requested authenticated information about Membership of the Association. Failure to produce the data would result in none of the Association's Members receiving debt credits. The Committee agreed to provide the information but the Chairman refused to release a copy of the Rules of the Association.

A creditors' meeting to wind up Pulbrook Underwriting Management was held on 21 March when it was approved that the company be liquidated.

A Special Report by *Reactions* in April on the London company market said too many companies entering run-off were doomed to insolvency. It listed six insurance companies declared insolvent between 1992 and 1994. It was postulated that Lloyd's appeared to be on a knife edge between solvency and insolvency.

The Lloyd's Settlement Validation Steering Group circulated their conclusions on 2 April and recommendations included:

1. an increase in the £2.8 billion may be required to achieve acceptance of Reconstruction and Renewal
2. a contract reinsuring Names' 1992 and prior business into Equitas must provide 'proportionate cover'. This meant having enough assets to meet 80% of forecast claims
3. names should be able to derive a level of comfort about Equitas comparable to what would be available to members of the public being invited to subscribe for shares

4. procedures needed to be in place to elect directors who would not be influenced by the ongoing Market

5. as part of the funding of Reconstruction and Renewal Names underwriting on 1993, 1994 and 1995 years of account would be asked to contribute 1.5% of their allocated premium limits in each of those years. Those Names ceasing after the end of 1995 should have their special contributions repaid

Charles provided an estimated calculation comparing 'Finality' from Equitas with rejection of the settlement. The cumulated loss for all litigating Members was 263% of line, of which cash had been called of 229%. He showed that those Association Members accepting Reconstruction and Renewal resulted in an overall recovery of 119% compared to 127% of line for those rejecting the settlement offer. There seemed little to choose between acceptance and rejection although there might be significant taxation implications where taxation rebates were due from Inland Revenue.

The Super Group's latest circular suggested that Lloyd's problems lay in the USA and that had probably been underestimated by them. With acceptance of Reconstruction and Renewal, the ongoing Market would be one of the few Markets or insurance companies in the world that no longer had to make provisions for historic liabilities. Equitas was not about creating finality for Names but creating finality from historic liabilities for the ongoing Lloyd's Market. The Super Group proposed a 2% levy on the ongoing Market for fifteen years.

The Super Group complained to David Rowland on 11 April about the debt collection from Names which caused undue hardship. Previous undertakings allowed Names in Hardship to continue to live in their houses on which Lloyd's had a charge, and now such arrangements were being cancelled. This policy escalated uncertainties and stress for Names in Hardship. They wondered if they would have sufficient money to live on and ever get free of Lloyd's in their lifetime. For them, this was a profoundly depressing thought.

The next day Clive reported to Members that indicative statements were in the process of being amended with the result distributed towards the end of May. He asked for guidance from Members and supplied a questionnaire considering the pros and cons of supporting the majority and minority to Members of the Association. Lloyd's had allocated the Association £16 million of litigation credits plus the return of litigation costs in cash. The best that could be achieved by further litigation was approximately £19 million. There was the moral question whereby the Market was insisting on extracting £2 billion from the 'haves' to settle the debts of the 'have nots'. The City was poised to pour in huge amounts of capital once the battered and bewildered Names had given in. Clive's missive contemplated upon the report that George Soros was investing considerable funds in the Lloyd's corporate vehicles which had increased 20% in share value in the past ten days. The Market was sensing the capitulation of Names. In an Equitas survey by Willis Faber & Dumas (Agencies), James Sinclair had written that there was no future for individual Names at Lloyd's. Should the Equitas scheme pass then Lloyd's Market would have lost its backers £14 billion over the last six years. With an eager source of alternative capital Lloyd's was consigning those original backers to oblivion practically without a cost to itself and openly exulting in the manoeuvre. That Names should have fallen for Equitas astonished Clive, although he could sympathise with the general war-weariness under the splendid pressure of the Lloyd's Public Relations Department. Michael Deeny and apparently several Action Group Chairmen had ceased pursuit of the PTD litigation. Clive said his phone had been going all day with those expressing anger and incredulity. Some 12,000 Names were still hoping to continue underwriting and supporting Reconstruction and Renewal. About 14,000 Names appeared able to live with Equitas bills, leaving some 6,000 of the financially weakest at the bottom of the pile facing ruin or having been ruined. Some people would have to raise mortgages or even sell their house to satisfy their Equitas bill. In the meantime, the Market hopped happily and unscathed into a patently rewarding future. To Clive's mind this was obscene and morally indefensible.

Clive's conclusion was that Deeny and his tribe had surrendered the last and most powerful negotiating position of the weakest, almost without a shot and certainly without any careful thought. The last chance of the hardest-hit to obtain some form of recompense from future trading of the Market had been sabotaged. Clive had heard the Twelfth Floor were ecstatic. From the American faxes coming through they could not believe the supinity of the Brits. Clive regarded the situation as a game of poker against a set of extremely ruthless and greedy men. These were attempting to lift large sums of money off a group of relatively defenceless people in pursuit of their own selfish betterment. He had no romantic illusions about Lloyd's as a British institution, nor was he trying to rectify a 'cads and bounders' situation. The bottom line was money. The Association had to demonstrate to Market practitioners that if they wished to continue, they would have to provide some form of restitution. The response of the corporate vehicle shares demonstrated vividly enough the future expectations of Lloyd's and the City. He believed injured Names should share in the fulfilment of those expectations.

On 19 April, Henry Young of Kildare suggested that once Equitas functioned it would be three times better reserved than any other UK trading insurance company. Consequently, he proposed that Equitas should trade. From a solvency point of view, it would unravel the conflicts between trading and non-trading Names. Reserves which would otherwise be static could be used to attract new business. The advantages of Equitas trading included unravelling double counting, maximising investment income, centralising control, and reinsurance recoveries could be performed more efficiently. However, Young listed a number of potential benefits for a captive reinsurance business that were not available to Lloyd's. These included the use of offshore jurisdictions with lower tax levels, reinsuring its own risks to other commercial insurers, sustaining a less severe solvency margin and floating on a stock market to generate more capital. In conclusion the author regretted the probable passing of the club that was the Society of Lloyd's with individual underwriters and syndicates blazing a trail across the insurance world. Finally, he emphasised that the trading of Equitas would enable the mini-economy that surrounded Lloyd's to flower instead of withering.

Thirty-Fourth Steering Committee Meeting, 24 April 1996

The meeting of eight Committee Members in D J Freeman's Fetter Lane offices agreed to send £2,500 to Mrs Jasper Salisbury-Jones and mentioned that a further sum would be considered in due course.

The Treasurer expressed astonishment at the size of D J Freeman's £219,370 outstanding fees and commented that he had written to David Tiplady about the lack of a budget in February. David said some of the fees were outstanding since last July and some related to counsel's disbursements. D J Freeman's firm was concerned that they were working without being paid. Harry Purchase proposed that the Treasurer and Mark Everiss should jointly audit the invoices. It was agreed to pay £184,000 in the next few days. Keith Lester explained:

> The Treasurer's task is to ensure good husbandry of the income and expenditure and the security of the Association's assets. Throughout the history of the Association the focus was on collecting what was due and questioning what was spent. Without that careful attention to financial management there may have been no Association that won its legal case in court. The money would have dribbled away in solicitors, other fees and payments to volunteers. The Treasurer had to be a bit dramatic at times while keeping an eye on the downside risk.

David mentioned that letters had been received from Members of the Association and other parties and Mark Everiss was receiving letters from insurance companies, Estate protection plans and stop-loss underwriters requiring a reply. Guy Wilson suggested the response should be a standard letter saying that the correspondence had been passed to the Association. He added that he would reply with a view to cutting legal costs and leaving the solicitors to deal with the appeals. David said he found it distasteful that D J Freeman invoices were not paid as they had not been challenged. The Treasurer said that D J Freeman costs of the Pulbrook Underwriting Management liquidation so far was £27,000, and would probably be over £50,000, if Price Waterhouse fees were added. The Official Receiver had said there should be a report on the winding-up of Pulbrook Underwriting Management within six months. This should stop the drain on cash. The Treasurer expressed concern that expenses were dipping into the 6% tranche of £650,000 which was reserved for the defendants' costs should the Association's action fail.

In the ongoing uncertain situation, the Committee never knew if there was enough cash to pay all potential liabilities. The Committee retained a highly competent specialist solicitor from a very reputable firm and had to be prepared to pay the exceedingly high fees that were demanded. It was important to keep costs to a minimum, and that unjustified or unnecessary costs be rejected.

David reported that the quantum appeal would be heard before 31 July and the four other appeals should be listed by the court by 14 May. David considered that Lloyd's had been in a state of chaos – and there was no change in this situation! He was resisting the underwriters' solicitors Clyde & Co's attempts to force the Association into arbitration regarding the E&O policy. Furthermore, an application by the Association for compensation, under Lloyd's bylaw 15/89, had been submitted six weeks ago.

Alasdair Ferguson suggested all legal action should cease on the basis Reconstruction and Renewal would be successful. David said the Association should keep the defence, otherwise the appeals would be lost by default. The full legal protection for Members required maintenance of the Association's legal presence, with a minimum of cost.

Charles Baron was not present at the meeting, so David Tiplady read out a copy of his letter to Ron Sandler complaining about the reduction in settlement terms for Syndicates 334 and 90 from those he had been given some weeks ago. Charles said that based on the earlier figures he had recommended the Reconstruction and Renewal settlement to three

Associations. He commented that the proudly vaunted new methodology was already in doubt. The views of those who had always held Equitas to be less of a marvel of modern technology than a noisome dustbin would gain ground once the tremendous fluctuations, which were not limited to the above-mentioned syndicates, were more widely known.

There were 202 responses to the Association's recent questionnaire; 172 were likely to accept Reconstruction and Renewal.

Henry Young's paper of 19 April was discussed and there were general expressions of support and endorsement of the paper's constructive proposals. The Committee refused a request to spend £20,000 on promoting the paper as the expenditure was not covered by the Association's objectives.

It appeared that Lloyd's intended to force all Names into Equitas whether they liked it or not. The Super Group circulated a note on 25 April of Lloyd's proposals for the establishment of a Global Substitute Agency and to remove Names' rights to decide on the Reconstruction and Renewal settlement package. The Super Group had received legal advice that Lloyd's proposals to implement the Global Substitute Agency was an abuse of the Council's powers and should be subject to a judicial review. The Super Group intended to obtain legal advice immediately on seeking an injunction, should it be necessary to prevent the implementation of the Global Substitute Agency. A subscription of £100 was requested as Action Groups did not raise funds for judicially reviewing Lloyd's.

The Treasurer wrote to Paul Evans on 29 April as the prime objective of the compulsory liquidation of Pulbrook Underwriting Management had been achieved. The Association had information relating to the E&O policy. He wondered if it was necessary to continue with the liquidation and asked if there was anything further that could be achieved.

Clare Sambrook in the *Daily Telegraph* of 30 April said that the DTI was set to move on Names' debts and classify Names' outstanding insurance liabilities as statutory debts. This would sweep aside defences and allow debt collectors to seize assets. The DTI declined to confirm or deny such draft legislation existed. This may have been a circulating Market rumour picked up by the journalist. Was this a fact or just another confusing rumour?

The Association was slow to start and set up, similarly there were unexpected facets to issues that created delays to the approaching end game.

Summary of Key Issues

1. A petition was made to wind up Pulbrook Underwriting Management Ltd.
2. Pulbrook Underwriting Management Ltd appointments were made and issues discussed.
3. Lloyd's Council approved Equitas and Equitas premium estimates.
4. £586,000 winnings were banked in escrow.
5. Barclays Bank claimed some of the E&O pot.
6. Falling capacity and Names at Lloyd's occurred while losses were increasing.
7. The need for more money in the proposed Settlement was emphasised at a meeting with Ron Sandler.
8. Mr Justice Cresswell made a statement on evidence of concealment and fraud.
9. The Reconstruction and Renewal proposal had deficiencies.
10. Tributes were paid to the Committee's barrister Member, Jasper Salisbury-Jones, who died.

CHAPTER 9

Solution: Reconstruction and Renewal Plan to Mutualise the Market

Princes Katharine: Is it possible dat I should love de enemy of France?

King Henry: for I love France so well that I will not part with a village of it; I will have it all mine; and, Kate, when France is mine and I am yours, then France is yours and you are mine.

Henry V, Act 5 Scene 2

Clive was quite unhappy about Clare Sambrook's article of 30 April 1996 and decided to get hold of Mr Neill Collins, the City Editor of the *Daily Telegraph*, stating:

> I am Chairman of a Lloyd's syndicate action group and very worried about the potential damage from last Tuesday's article by Clare Sambrook. Threats to reclassify Names' debts may leave them without assets, especially accommodation. The situation is much more complex than that set out in the article which was misleading to the point of causing wholly unnecessary alarm and distress.

Clive continued his explanation:

In the event of Lloyd's collapsing and a policyholder wanting to make a claim on a particular policy, in the first instance he would have to pursue Names on that policy whether it was written for example in 1980 or 1950. Only Names on the actual policy were entitled to be pursued. Mr Hobbs of the Department of Trade and Industry had maintained that Lloyd's had been a mutual affair since 1972, although Names were induced to join subsequently under other beliefs. The net effect therefore of any claimant on a valid policy would be to pursue the Names on that policy most likely to respond. Such Names might include very wealthy individuals such as former Chairmen of Lloyd's like Messrs Green, Miller, Murray-Lawrence and Rowland rather than the long-suffering Name in the street of today. Roger Henderson QC argued forcefully that a direct claim cannot follow through the Reinsurance To Close chain which would obtain were Lloyd's still extant. Thus, apart from hitting one or two well-heeled Market practitioners any claimant would find it unprofitable to pursue the claim. The Department of Trade and Industry's powers to pursue Names were far weaker than those Lloyd's possessed and whatever the Department of Trade and Industry may be considering to enact, it could not be retrospective. Moreover, before any claimant could turn to the Department of Trade and Industry it must be shown that the policy had failed to respond. Mr Henderson was absolutely clear that any present-day Name would have an almost impenetrable defence against such a claim from the past. I ask you to update your readers with my comments.

It was not evident that the *Daily Telegraph* reported Clive's worries and concerns. However, the proposed policy was not implemented by the DTI.

Following Henry Young's paper of 19 April, Clive spoke to thirteen chairmen of Action Groups as to whether Equitas should trade. Young's paper received enthusiastic support. Ron Sandler was most complimentary about the constructive tone of the paper, which had gone to the DTI for their consideration. Clive had also discussed trading by Equitas with James Sinclair of Willis Faber & Dumas (Agencies), who was in favour of the scheme provided the assertion as to reserves was correct.

Dick Rosenblatt of the American Names Association said that Tennessee had ignored the moratorium and come out with a full-blown, immediately effective, injunction against Lloyd's. However, the biggest story was that on Monday, 6 May the US Stock Exchange Commission would enter lists effectively allowing any American to sue Lloyd's in the US. The Americans were out for blood and Reconstruction and Renewal meant Rescission and Restitution to them.

On 3 May, David Rowland was advised that the Committee had expressed abhorrence at the obvious attempt to circumvent the undertaking given to the Secretary of State the previous July to have the legality of the PTD alterations tested in court without delay. The Committee had received with some distaste various reports that Sandler had attempted to ensure the PTD case was adjourned to the point where it would never be heard. The Committee had also expressed repugnance that Deeny had apparently been induced to betray a trust. One incensed Member rang Clive to complain about Rowland's posturings on television the previous Sunday where integrity and transparency sat ill with the devious and shady deal ascribed to him. The same old fudges were still appearing. For an increasing number of Names, Reconstruction and Renewal was coming to mean Recidivism and Reoffence. It came as no surprise to those who had been ravaged by Lloyd's to learn that 'Fiddlentia' endured.

On 3 May Clive emailed the Committee that at 5.30 pm the previous day, all Managing Agents were informed of another emergency meeting to be addressed by Rowland at 9.30 am the following morning. Relations between Managing Agents and Equitas staff were finding new depths. Instead of serious and researched calculations for each Managing Agency there were guesstimates, plain fudges and naked horse trading. Equitas staff was under severe pressure to meet time scales which they were not only failing to meet but they were failing to arrive at any accurate results. Previously David Tiplady had told the Committee that the

Twelfth Floor was in disarray. This was becoming increasingly apparent as Rowland was seizing all the levers and pulling them by himself to a pattern which nobody could follow. In addition, the American scene was getting grimmer by the day. Young's paper supporting the idea that Equitas should trade was endorsed by Joe McBrien, who was Chairman of Syndicate 126 North America and of Managing Agency ASM. In addition, there was endorsement by thirteen Action Group Chairmen in a fax of 1 May. Sandler had sent the paper to Freshfields for comment. A month earlier, the paper would not have stood a chance, so sure was the Twelfth Floor that the Equitas battle had been won. Twelfth Floor morale was very low. Whether or not the concept of trading Equitas reached fruition, the scene was highly political.

Clive wrote to say dear old Major M. Edwards MC of New Zealand, the octogenarian with one arm, was visiting England. He had called in for a chat and produced a copy of the Syndicate 90 newsletter and a related Equitas analysis sheet. Clive was aware that Equitas figures were bouncing up and down. He asked Charles to prepare a similar factsheet for the Association.

On 10 May Clive discussed in a memorandum the possibility of a 'success bounty'. Potential recoveries were now in view, either through debt credits from Reconstruction and Renewal or compensation direct from Lloyd's, because of fraud or if the E&O underwriters were forced to pay the Association's claim. Clive had been discussing the subject with other Action Group Chairmen and agreed a basis of some form of reward. Resolutions would be put to a General Meeting of the Association's Members and would include a postal vote. Many Members had expressed deep gratitude to the Committee for their tireless involvement over many years with a ratio of 6:1 in favour. Payments must be discretionary and based on a formula to be decided by an independent body as it would be improper for Committee Members to be in control of such a distribution. No contractual arrangements existed between the Committee Members and the Association. The concept of such a bounty would be payable to those who had borne the brunt of responsibility relating to the litigation process over several years.

It was reported that Deeny had been paid a 'success fee' and remained on a substantial salary. Action Groups were arranging their awards on the basis of what they had achieved either through as-yet-incomplete litigation or enhanced debt credits, because of winning in court or being just about to go to court. The Reconstruction and Renewal indicative statements were heavily weighted in favour of those who had won or were about to have their cases heard this year. The Association fell into the category of having won its case but was having difficulty collecting. Under Reconstruction and Renewal, the Association had achieved a cash/debt credit settlement of approximately £16 million and had played a major role in extracting an offer from Lloyd's which many Names might find acceptable. In addition, Lloyd's had agreed to repay litigation costs to the Association if Reconstruction and Renewal was accepted. Acceptance looked likely with an extra £1 billion being placed on the table, according to a *Times* report of 10 May.

Clive pondered upon taxable aspects of the bounty payment and whether for those in Hardship, monies could be put in trust with a 'Remuneration Subcommittee' to advise trustees. He was keen to avoid another Lloyd's trap.

On the same day Lloyd's issued a circular giving a substantial improvement to the settlement offer. It increased the offer from £2.8 billion to £3.1 billion and reduced the Equitas premiums by £900 million to approximately £1 billion. The total increase to cover the 1992 and prior liabilities was likely to be about £1.2 billion. Rowland said that Reconstruction and Renewal was the only practical route forward. The largest change in the Equitas reserving figures derived from a thorough analysis of liabilities. More than half of the total 1992 and prior liabilities related to Lloyd's main businesses such as marine, aviation and transport, but excluded long-tail risks like pollution and asbestos and a number of catastrophe risks. Lloyd's analysis of these risks revealed a significantly more robust reserving position than previously envisaged. Lloyd's would enhance offers to give more assistance to those Names who had paid all their obligations, and extra assistance for those with extreme losses, thus improving prospects of settling litigation with Agents and auditors. Brokers were close to agreeing a fund of £100 million. Lloyd's would sell and lease back some assets such as the Lloyd's building, and others like the Lloyd's of London Press, its own in-house printing company, would be mortgaged, totalling around £270 million. Some £200 million would be paid by Agents. Leading auditing firms had offered collectively £100 million. E&O underwriters had agreed to make a contribution of £800 million.

Names underwriting in 1993, 1994 and 1995 years would be asked to approve a contribution of the equivalent of 1.5% of their overall premium limit each year. A further indicative statement would be issued by mid-June. Clive's covering letter was sceptical about the assistance for 'those at the bottom of the pile'.

On 15 May, Ron Sandler replied to a letter from the Names Defence Association saying that the reinsurance of Names 1992 and earlier liabilities would be mandatory, subject to the settlement offer becoming unconditional. The Council of Lloyd's and the DTI had agreed that Equitas was a suitable and appropriate vehicle to provide reinsurance. Names would be provided with information to enable them to have a proper basis for deciding whether or not to accept the settlement offer. Brokers had not been and would not be involved in the Equitas scheme. For reasons of professional privilege, he could not provide a copy of the advice showing the strongest possible legal Opinion that the Equitas scheme did not infringe the Lloyd's Act. Clive observed that the letter employed breath-takingly draconian and sweeping powers to force Names into Equitas whether they liked it or not.

Guy Wilson entered correspondence about bounty payments with some Members on 17 May. He pointed out that a discretionary trust might be open to attack in that litigation subscriptions had been given tax relief as an expense of underwriting. He was not convinced that income tax on bounty payments could be avoided. Making a 'gift' to the Chairman was unlikely to be approved by Association Members. In his letter to Alan Porter of Cuthbert Heath Names Association, a cost of £750 per Name was mentioned. An alternative was to use a percentage basis. In terms of a discretionary trust, it would not be appropriate to disclose payments and if it was offshore, it would not fall within the scope of VAT as Committee Members would not receive invoices. However, Guy was circumspect since the payments would not escape the attention of the media or the Inspector of Taxes, so he thought that avoiding income tax should not be a top priority. He preferred VAT to be avoided. Guy posited that Reconstruction and Renewal would be successful and supposed that Lloyd's was so anxious to settle the litigation that it was prepared to pay litigation expenses in cash. It was only as a result of litigation that Lloyd's was prepared to grant such large debt credits to Syndicate 334 litigating Names.

Guy's fax of 24 May outlined a brief history of the Committee since 1990 and its achievements, suggesting something similar should be included in a newsletter to Members. This would be the opportunity to give some consideration to the bounty proposal discussed in Clive's recent memorandum.

An official letter from Sarah Wilton at Lloyd's dated 21 May mentioned that should the entire Membership of the Action Group agree to settle its litigation, reimbursement of expenses would cover the winding-up. The letter provided a basis for the calculation of the Association's expenses and a form was included for completion by 9 June. Expenses had to be analysed in total between incurred and expected. Another section required receipts from defendants, held by D J Freeman, amounts received by the Association and anticipated receipts. An estimate had to be made of the costs of winding up the Association. The form had to be signed by an independent accountant, the auditors in the Association's case. On 30 May, Clive followed up a telephone conversation stating firmly that the Rules of the Association did not compel Members to either accept or reject the Reconstruction and Renewal. He said it would be wrong to deny winding-up expenses to an Action Group which ceased litigation if 2% dissented from the 98% majority.

Newsletter, May 1996

In the May 1996 Chairman's newsletter Clive reported on the 202 responses to the questionnaire from Members showing that a majority of 127 were likely to accept the offer. An interesting analysis showed the extent of Association Members who were, or were likely to be, in financial difficulty. Some not in difficulties might have had big losses elsewhere and decided it would be beneficial to join the Association.

A high proportion of those who did not join the Association could possibly have had profits or minimal losses covered by stop-loss insurance, resigned and ceased underwriting, or had died and the trustees of their Estates decided not to engage in litigation.

He gave a breakdown of the Association's Membership for Syndicate 334.

Members still underwriting with no losses	25
Members still underwriting with losses but no unpaid calls	71
Members ceased underwriting but with no unpaid calls	66
Members ceased underwriting with unpaid calls	108
Members ceased underwriting with debts to the Central Fund	70
Members refused by the Hardship Scheme	14
Members accepted by the Hardship Scheme	18

Association Membership total*	**372**
Names not Members of the Association	190

Syndicate 334 total Names in 1985	562
	-----

* A total number of Association Members reconciled to Members on the writ. This had been increasing over the months with new Members joining. For instance, the total number on 19 July 1991 was 264, on 25 October 1993 was 366 and was currently 372.

At the outset David Tiplady had said he would be disappointed if fewer than 300 joined the Association. At the time it seemed a high target which would be helpful, if met, in generating the essential finance to achieve the Association's objective.

Ninety-six Association Members would continue underwriting while 276 had ceased, of whom 32 were effectively ruined. Lloyd's was due to issue a second finality statement in mid-June and the Lloyd's AGM was scheduled for 15 July. The Committee was planning to hold the Association's AGM in September.

The Association had a valid claim against Lloyd's Central Fund for £13 million through the Members' Compensation Scheme under bylaw 15/89. However, as soon as the Association entered its claim the Council of Lloyd's revoked bylaw 15/89 without prior warning and cancelled the scheme. Lloyd's said subsequently that the only Names who could continue their claim for compensation under the Members' Compensation Scheme would be those refusing the settlement offer.

As noted, under the Lloyd's business plan in late 1993, two panels were set up in an attempt to obviate or settle the threatened avalanche of litigation. A legal one was headed by Sir Michael Kerr and a financial one under Sir Jeremy Morse. The Kerr Panel was to assess the relative strengths of each Action Group's case. The Morse Panel was to assess what monies were available for settlement. The claims had to be quantified as to what had been paid, outstanding calls and estimated future amounts. Clive recalled that the panels rated the chances of the Association's success at 2%. In the event the Association had achieved 100% success. The Association's final percentage award under Tranche 1 of the Settlement Fund had increased from 32% to 38%. In addition, Lloyd's would pay in cash the litigation expenses. Thus, the benefits would have been obtained at little cost to each Association Member.

On 24 May, Guy Wilson offered some tax considerations regarding payments to Committee Members who were office-holders. The Rules of the Association referred to 'remuneration' and 'ex-gratia' payments and they appeared to be taxable as earned income but outside the scope of the employment rules. Some Committee Members had been paid fees gross, either to the individual or to family companies which were not VAT-registered. No Committee Member had submitted invoices including VAT. Income derived from the Association was classified as 'earned income' and as such was 'pensionable'. Paying into a pension plan could be a tax-efficient way to shelter some income from income tax.

Thirty-Fifth Steering Committee Meeting, 28 May 1996
In D J Freeman's offices, the Treasurer reported that Price Waterhouse had been sending fee notes for settlement under their interpretation of the Association's 'guarantee', irrespective of recoveries. The first Barclays' charge appeared to be valid. The second charge may be one of fraudulent preference but there was little point in establishing this if it would not be called upon. As there were no more financial benefits, no further costs would be incurred.

Lloyd's Legal Services Department clarified the Members' Compensation scheme on 29 May. It appeared that if Names accepted Reconstruction and Renewal to eliminate any possibility of a double recovery, compensation from the Compensation Scheme would not be available. Clive lobbied Ron Sandler to query the Lloyd's Legal Services Department's edict. He said Lloyd's had no power to make such an administrative edict. By way of a suggestion Clive thought the Association should receive similar treatment as other Action Groups with money in escrow. But for fraud allegations by Pulbrook Underwriting Management the Association would have had £15 million in escrow. To deny this could give rise to the charge that here was Lloyd's once again attempting to escape the consequences of fraud. As Sir Richard Scott QC put it, 'One of Lloyd's short-cuts'. Sandler replied on 27 June saying that there were insufficient grounds for the compromise suggested. There were other Action Groups that had not received payment from the Members' Compensation Scheme for one reason or another and he was not convinced the Association should be treated differently from them.

On 31 May Clive sent a letter to Association Members requiring urgent attention. He explained that the Super Group, the ALM and most

Chairmen of Action Groups remained dissatisfied with the inadequate financial contribution to Reconstruction and Renewal by Market entities. This related to Managing Agents and the ongoing Market, post-Reconstruction and Renewal. It was proposed to apply pressure on Lloyd's by convening an SGM on 9 July. The SGM was not intended to damage or obstruct the Reconstruction and Renewal process. Some 1,500 signatures were required by 4 June.

Harry Purchase sent his fee note for £1,000 on 4 June indicating there was more work to be done. Clive's defensive financial hackles were raised in his response to Harry. He reminded him that the Treasurer properly insisted upon supporting vouchers for expenses, and acknowledged an unfortunate remark made jokingly by Jasper Salisbury-Jones regarding the lack of rigour in the Treasurer's examination of expenses claims submitted by Committee Members. He thanked Harry for past press cuttings and market intelligence helping him to function so effectively as Chairman. The Treasurer wrote to Harry that the Rules of the Association said vouchers should be attached to the expense claim. In the absence of vouchers, he asked if it was possible to provide a detailed breakdown of how he arrived at the overall fee.

Mark Everiss said the appeal on the interim payment award was to be heard on 11 to 12 July with Nicholas Strauss QC appearing for the Association as plaintiffs. There were five appeals, including:

1. two regarding an interim payment following Judge Potter's interlocutory judgement
2. liability of Members' Agents in tort as well as contract
3. limitation in respect of contracts under seal
4. liability to 1980–1985 Names, where the Names were disputing that the Members' Agents duty owed only to 1979 Names

On 24 April, Clyde & Co, acting for the E&O underwriters had issued a summons seeking a stay of the plaintiffs' High Court action that was listed for 14 June 1996. Mr Strauss QC and Adam Fenton's advice on

28 May was that the stay was mandatory under the Arbitration Act of 1950 as there were foreign Names amongst the defendants and plaintiffs. David Tiplady and Mark Everiss believed that the court had the power to retain the matter within its jurisdiction on the grounds there was an allegation of fraud despite the mandatory stay provision. To avoid unnecessary cost, it was advised that the Association should consent to the defendant E&O insurers' application to proceed with the arbitration.

David's letter on 6 June to the Legal Services Department set out the reason why the Association's claim for compensation from the Central Fund was valid, since it was presented before the withdrawal of the scheme by Lloyd's Council. Clive expressed concern that the claim would not be accepted. He refused to accept that Lloyd's had the power to make such administrative arrangement curtailing the rights of redress of defrauded Names.

Harry wrote to Adam Raphael as Chairman of the Syndicate 90 (1982) Names Association on 10 June and counselled that the Association should not take a decision to discontinue litigation. He said there was no substitute for attack. The damaging result of the Committee behaving like gentlemen was clearly apparent, having lost out by appeasement, and the Association might have had a judgement by now. Instead of a litigation credit of 32% it would have been in Tranch 1 with 38%. The Council of Lloyd's had already reneged, changed the rules, backdated amendments and was now in complete disarray. Harry explained to Clive the reasons for the letter:

> Rowland is said to be in a state of absolute panic. Those of us who work with him know how dangerous he can be. He is now making offers without consultation and then counter-offers. It is a very muddy situation indeed, with no certainty that Equitas will become a reality. The Syndicate 90 Committee could not accept the settlement offer. Each individual Name will make the decision. I cannot believe that Adam or the Committee would recommend acceptance when there is still more cash to be found. You may recall that Peter Middleton gave

Equitas five to seven years' survival and then the Name or his Estate
would become insurer of last resort. Any hint of appeasement now
would let Members down badly.

In a handwritten appended note to a copy of his completed letter, he
hoped Keith Lester and Guy Wilson would express similar views.

On the same day Clive wrote to the Association's Members about an
early AGM following the improved offer from Lloyd's and the Association's
survey suggesting that a majority of Members would accept the settlement
offer. Nevertheless, the Association was conducting five separate appeals
and must devise plans for minimising expenditure whilst maintaining
various legal positions pending the outcome of the settlement offer.
Lloyd's had indicated it would refund Action Groups' expenses and properly voted success rewards for Committee Members. The Committee had
decided to harmonise the rewards as recommended by the Super Group.
Consequently, an SGM would be called and voting allowed by proxy.

Clive received letters approving payments to Committee Members
for their service; among them were Alistair Strathnaver (Lord Strathnaver,
of Golspie), who said he would be very pleased to reward the Committee,
as did Fernley Allen of Sunningdale; Peter McGovern of Mosman, New
South Wales; Ralph Clark of Street; Lawrence Jones of Sudbury; John
Holder of Ellesmere; Geoffrey North of Bampton; and Hazel Levine-
Freeman of Herts. One arrived from James Leitch, who said Clive had
been an inspiration in the dark days and no doubt the hierarchy at Lloyd's
would be glad to have him off their backs. Leitch said he had joined in
1971. He was placed on Syndicates 334 and 90 and was sorry that so
many of the perpetrators were apparently coming out of it scot-free. Clive
replied on 18 June expressing grateful thanks for James Leitch's comments
but pointed out that without the support of a singly united hard-working
Committee the achievements might have been much less.

Following his letter of 4 June, Mark Everiss confirmed that the
hearing of the interim award was removed from the list and was proceeding towards arbitration. Mark had spoken to Clifford Chance, solicitors,

and there was general desire to avoid incurring costs, and, pending the Lloyd's settlement, he believed Clyde & Co on behalf of E&O underwriters would apply to stay the arbitration. However, points of claim should be served within twenty-eight days.

Daniel Schwarzmann of Price Waterhouse confirmed on 20 June that there was an intercompany debt due to Pulbrook Underwriting Management that might be recoverable of £115,727. He also thought it may not be beneficial to continue with the liquidation. Price Waterhouse required a signature from each Member of the Liquidation Committee that they did not wish to proceed with the liquidation.

Thirty-Sixth Steering Committee Meeting, 9 July 1996: SGM Overwhelming Support

At 11 am in D J Freeman's offices, the Chairman reported that by 2 July, 160 proxies for the SGM had been received with an overwhelming vote in favour of the resolutions. Guy Wilson circulated a form to Committee Members asking each one to complete and return confidentially a form for allocating percentages of a sum to be distributed to Members as 'ex-gratia' or 'remuneration' for services. The projected expenses including 5% of £16 million bounty of £800,000 amounted to £1,056,758. Clive considered abandoning the Members' Compensation Scheme claim and asking the liquidators to recover the original E&O premium. If the Members' Compensation Scheme was going to be pursued, he wondered if the Association should engage a professional public relations consultant to hammer the fraud theme.

Keith referred to an inaugural ALM's lunch at which Robert Hiscox was speaking, observing, 'At the lunch I met Clive and persuaded him to come to the initial Syndicate 334 legal action meeting. Subsequently he agreed to become Chairman and he has been a truly excellent Chairman.'

Clive commented on LSS:

I find it difficult to muster sufficient words of praise for Louth Secretarial Services run by Julia Barkworth for the support they have given me as Chairman and the Association as a whole. They played such a supportive role I could not have done my job without them. They have provided information at the drop of a hat on every conceivable Membership topic. They had rushed out newsletters and various circulations with astonishing promptness, most efficiently, and helped me devise various campaigns. Julia's pragmatic solutions and suggestions have played a very significant part in the operation of the Association. I understand, Charles, you and Julia are to be married soon. I am quite sure we all wish you both a very happy and contented marriage.

Sandler was admitting in public that the American actions could derail Reconstruction and Renewal. There was undeniable anxiety on the Twelfth Floor. The Association's claim for compensation was but a pinprick by comparison. It may be that the Association's nuisance value was greater now than after Reconstruction and Renewal had succeeded. Charles told Clive that Rowland and Sandler were both upset by the representations of the Association.

SGM, 9 July 1996
Following the Steering Committee Meeting the SGM was held at 2 pm. Resolutions were put to the meeting as follows.

Resolution 1
Once Lloyd's settlement offer is declared unconditional the Association should cease all litigation. In favour 207, Against 0, Abstentions 4.

Resolution 2
Association Members may have a valid claim for compensation which lies outside the settlement offer and instructs the Committee to pursue the claim. In favour 179, Against 30, Abstentions 3.

Resolution 3

Members of the Association's Committee shall be rewarded according to the Super Group proposed scale. For each year of service, the Chairman should receive £30,000, Officers £15,000 and other Committee Members £7,500.

There was an extended discussion about fees as some Members were unhappy at the level and their distribution. Daniel Salbstein said that he would have been happier if the amount was decided by, for example, the ALM, the Names Distribution Committee, the Super Group or Lloyd's. Guy said that Lloyd's did not wish to get involved in this matter. Ray Cook said he would object to the ALM being involved. Alasdair Ferguson uncharacteristically had remained silent but now said:

> I have never been happy about these success fees at all ab initio – from the beginning. I feel it easier for me as a Member of the Committee to vote against than it is for other people who have been hit much harder. We have all played our role. It was extremely difficult to say how much one had contributed over another. I had mentioned that a formula was more acceptable rather than trying to have any discrimination between Committee Members. If there was another formula, I would welcome that. I would hate the possibility of Members thinking they had been ripped off, because that was not the motivation.

The Treasurer commented, 'Alasdair has never drawn any expenses from the Association. To be clear, for everyone present the statement that Alasdair just made carries very great weight.'

Alasdair had made an invaluable contribution to the Association's Committee. This was not surprising considering aspects of his earlier life. On 19 August 1942, as Lieutenant Alasdair Forbes Ferguson (decorated subsequently MBE. DSC and Bar, RNVR), he commanded one of the landing crafts which carried Canadian soldiers into a hail of fire at Puits during the Dieppe raid. As second-in-command of the 10th Landing Craft Assault Flotilla, he had the task of landing on Blue Beach. Dawn was breaking, and the element of surprise had been lost. The Allies learned valuable lessons from the raid, but the Canadians suffered appalling casualties: on Blue Beach alone, 485 out of 545 Canadians were killed, wounded or missing. For the rest of his life the lieutenant measured everything by Dieppe, saying that nothing else could possibly worry him. He was educated at Loretto, where he was head boy and captain of athletics, swimming, rugby and boxing. His engineering studies at Clare College, Cambridge were interrupted by the war. After the war he began business with engineering companies at Poole. His yacht, *Swan of Arden*, was as well-known on the French coast as in the Western Isles and he had helped found the Poole Maritime Trust. In the Association's meetings and communications, he always exhibited his perceptive moral compass suggesting and encouraging the right thing to do in the circumstances. The *Daily Telegraph* announced his passing on 21 February 2005.

Charles Baron felt he had to further clarify the situation, explaining:

> If no action had been taken six years ago, there would have been no Equitas and no Equitas release. With no action, Names would have paid out another 500% of line according to Chatset. Instead, the Association won a case in the High Court, received the maximum from the Litigation Settlement Fund which was 38% of loss over 82% of line. Each of us had debt credits. None of that would have happened without the litigation. I have also been a Member of the Syndicate 90 Action Group Committee since its inception, over six years ago. Our Committee had achieved more for this Association than any one of us, including Mr Salbstein, would have believed possible a year ago.

The Chairman asked the Secretary to read out the result of the vote on Resolution 3, 'In favour 177, Against 27 and Abstentions 8; all the resolutions are passed.'

The appeal for an increased interim payment was lost. Although the judges applauded Mr Strauss's arguments, they refused to deviate from a principle established previously.

A paper on 10 July from the Super Group drew attention to the lack of audited accounts in respect of 1992 in the syndicate reports and accounts being distributed for the year ending 1995. Some lawyers were taking the view that lack of audit certificates breached the Lloyd's bylaws. Consequently, Names who refused the settlement offer would not be able to prove Names' indebtedness if they brought writs subsequently.

Christopher Stockwell wrote to Sandler on 11 July that the 'finality' statements issued to Names may be misleading. Firstly, there was no warning in the Reconstruction and Renewal documentation that tax would be withheld from the 1993 profits which would reduce the available profit figures and their cash distribution by the tax due. Secondly, there was no mention of winding-up fees when Names resigned their Membership. Confirmation was needed that no winding-up fees would be charged under Reconstruction and Renewal.

The offer required Anna Young of Edinburgh to pay £170,000 which was £50,000 more than she had. She wrote to Philip Holden of Lloyd's Financial Recovery Department that she would like to continue litigation as it appeared to be the only route to protect her interests. Holden said it was not possible to process her application before the end of August, the closing date for acceptance of the settlement offer. Clive explained that until Tranche 4 credits were known it would be impossible to accept the Reconstruction and Renewal offer. The offer she had received would lead to insolvency, and any future offer may not improve the financial position. Reconstruction and Renewal acceptance would remove all rights to further litigation. Her suggestion was to form a residual Action Group consisting of those Association Members who wished to continue litigation. Clive received no information about the eventual outcome.

There was a letter in *The Times* on 18 July in support of remuneration for Action Group Committee Members. The Action Groups pushed the settlement offer from £900 million to £3.1 billion. The Association had got its case into court and won full liability, obtained Tier 1 debt credits with a chance of further benefits from the Members' Compensation Scheme. Clive thought that in terms of cost-benefit, the Committee did not feel there was anything about which they could be reproached.

On 23 July Clive wrote to thank Committee Members for their support during the SGM and he had noticed that all Committee Members addressed the meeting. It was clear from the assembly that the main point of objection was the remuneration resolution. Daniel Felbstein had objected to the method by which it was achieved. It seemed to Clive that motivation sprang from Felbstein's personal dislike of Stockwell and the Super Group. Clive had also received a long letter from Peter Levy, firstly, objecting to any form of remuneration and, secondly, that any remuneration should be assessed by an unrelated remuneration committee. The Super Group had revised their recommendation which was now the independent remuneration committee approach. This followed Sir David Berriman's proposal whereby all professionally qualified Members of the Committee ought to have charged professional fees from the inception of the Action Group. This revised basis caught the Committee a little flat-footed through its desire to be in the forefront of things administratively. By virtue of the twenty-one-day notice period for the SGM it was only possible to promulgate the fixed scale proposed by the Super Group. If the Berriman formula had been adopted, the Committee would have been dunning the Association's Members for a great deal more than the fixed-fee calculation now firmly adopted by resolution.

Charles had sent Clive on 24 July a bald statement of his expenses. Clive explained that he was most appreciative of the help he had received from him. He fully supported the expenses route for the proper recognition of Charles' endeavours. However, he now needed help to get the transaction through. If Clive sent the statement to the Treasurer, he would refuse it straight out of hand. Clive discussed the matter with Guy, Keith Lester's business partner, who was also entirely sympathetic with the payment of just rewards. Guy suggested a detailed annual account for each year of service by job description and hourly professional charges.

The greater the detail that Charles could summon, drum up or plain invent, the better. Moreover, this approach not only allowed the Treasurer to convince himself that proper scrutiny had been exercised but would enable him to claim under the heading of 'proper expenses expended annually' and stand a greater chance of being able to reclaim the whole from Lloyd's. Only a certain proportion of expenses was likely to be refunded by Lloyd's. Therefore, the greater amount of bona fide expenses the Association submitted, the less would be the burden on the shoulders of Members, a burden which he knew Charles would wish to diminish. In summing up, Clive asked Charles to help him by submitting an impressive wedge of any guff but the thicker, the better, to ease the Treasurer's susceptibilities. He hated to be bureaucratic but, in this instance, a suitable weight of paper was the key to success. He realised it was nothing but a chore and a pain in the ass but he fell back on quoting the old motto 'per ardua ad ackers'. For the uninitiated Clive's bastardised Latin phrase meant 'through work add benefits' and its use might reflect his senior age and education.

The headline on 2 August in the *Independent* was 'Double Trouble Is Brewing at Lloyd's Rescue Plan'. David Rowland had admitted in the past that the rescue plan included some rough justice. The plan had to be approved before the DTI solvency test at the end of the month. The Paying Names Action Group was seeking to apply to a judge for permission to seek a judicial review of the settlement offer. Rowland had been forced into compromise and arm-twisting, at every turn, by the reality of life in the Market. There had been unfairness on both sides of the balance sheet, among those finding the money for the rescue as well as those receiving it. Agents, auditors and brokers had escaped lightly. The financial reconstruction was a masterpiece of ingenuity. Rowland and colleagues were making ends meet with resources that were less than they seemed and they had done it with brilliant ingenuity. On 7 August the Paying Names Action Group was granted permission to apply for a judicial review.

Christopher Fildes in the *Daily Telegraph* said he would stay away from Lloyd's as it was past the point where he would be ready to take it on trust. Its Names had to make a poker players' choice: whether to continue with Lloyd's with potentially increased losses, or to leave and cut losses. Leaving at this point was not simple as legal action and associated funding was required.

On 1 August 1996 David forwarded a draft Action Group Settlement Agreement and Clive called an unscheduled Committee meeting. Three days later Freshfields delivered the Action Group Settlement Agreement package to Clive at Exeter, and after discussion with David Tiplady he hoped to be able to obviate a tedious journey to London on Tuesday to attend the Committee meeting. He faxed a draft of minutes for the meeting together with a resignation document for use by those persons not wishing to participate in the Action Group Settlement Agreement.

Thirty-Seventh Steering Committee Meeting, 6 August 1996: Action Group Settlement Agreement

The Meeting was held by proxy in D J Freeman's offices and convened solely to consider the Association's response to the Action Group Settlement Agreement. Under the Rules of the Association the Committee was authorised to conclude any form of settlement on its behalf. The agreement was signed by the Treasurer in Clive's absence and by David Tiplady, and then despatched to Lloyd's.

This was an important decisive step in drawing to a close the efforts of six years to obtain justice on behalf of those Names who had joined the Association to take legal action.

Charles Baron supplied an amplification of his invoice on 7 August for services to the Association at £15,000. He said he was a retired Chartered Management Accountant and his professional experience had been used extensively throughout the Association's existence by the Chairman. In the first two years he set up and supervised the accounting systems at LSS. He resolved inevitable errors in the initial stages. He set up a database for over 300 Members which had run smoothly. He was instrumental in appointing and dealing with the auditors with whom he had been in contact throughout from time to time. In the past two and a half years he had been the Association's representative on the Wellington Monitoring Committee and the work was largely of a financial nature. At the Chairman's request he had attended various meetings including the Litigating Names Committee and provided reports. He had charged travelling expenses from Louth at £100 per visit which was woefully inadequate. His invoice was certainly good value for money.

Settlement offers to those in Hardship were automatically accepted. Keith Lester's finality statement showed losses of £293,448 but these were reduced by debt litigation and stop-loss credits to an amount due of £93,692. This offer was a great improvement on potential losses estimated at one point in the past of £800,000 which had created the need to apply for Hardship. It seemed possible that Keith may eventually be able to settle the Lloyd's account which was a phenomenal relief. Nevertheless, the stresses of recent years were still the cause of difficulties. There were tens of thousands of pounds in tax refunds due. They were extremely slow to be repaid although the remuneration voted and paid by the Association was very helpful. A cash-positive situation appeared to be on the far-distant horizon, but at least now there might be an horizon.

A circular from Lloyd's acknowledged receipt of the Expenses Certification Form and set out a timetable for signing the Action Group Settlement Agreement and subsequent steps, together with factors determining the amount of the refund.

Newsletter, August 1996: The Acceptable Offer

Clive explained in the August newsletter that the Committee voted unanimously to enter the Action Group Settlement Agreement which provided for the return of Association's expenses for pro-rata distribution in cash, entirely at Lloyd's discretion. Members would have already received the 'finality' statement. The advantage of the offer promised peace for a time and a period during which those Names who had any Estate left could legally make such dispositions without fear of subsequent challenge. Nevertheless, the offer figures had not been audited or received the discipline required of a prospectus. They were not open to challenge once the offer had gone unconditional. A number of mistakes had been reported and Association Members were advised to check their statements carefully. If errors were discovered, it was vital to pursue Lloyd's or the relevant Agent for satisfaction prior to signing. There were 12,000 Names stuck on orphan syndicates, where there was no successor syndicate, for whom 'finality' was not achieved in 1993.

Many Names who applied for Tranche 4 credits had not received a response and should not sign the settlement document. The 'hardest-hit' at the bottom of the pile had received no more than vague assurances that 'something will be done'.

Enclosed with the newsletter were some press comments and not all were favourable. The offer conferred on Lloyd's a complete exculpation for all the misdeeds of fraud and deceit in return for peace in our time. 'Haven't we heard that before?' asked Clive. Circulated with the newsletter was a notice of vital importance to those Members of the Association who decided as individuals to refuse both the Lloyd's settlement offer and Action Group Settlement Agreement. The Committee had received legal advice that it was in the Association's best interest to agree to the Action Group Settlement Agreement as it would simplify recovery and distribution of refunded litigation expenses. It had been resolved at the SGM to cease litigation. Under the Association's Rules the Committee resolved to execute the Action Group Settlement Agreement. Those persons rejecting the settlement offer and wishing to continue litigating should immediately resign from the Association and inform D J Freeman if they wished to continue litigating.

Fernley Allen wrote on 21 August to Clive expressing his gratitude to him and the Committee for all the time and effort devoted to the protection and pursuit of Members' interests during the past six years. The successful litigation as reflected in the terms of the final settlement offer was a great tribute to the team. It was a happy release for many Names from years of financial anxiety.

Mark Everiss's letter to Clive on 21 August raised several issues to do with the Action Group Settlement Agreement. A Mr Knipp had ignored all correspondence and without his permission his name could not be included on the Action Group Settlement Agreement. Mr Laidlaw had belatedly decided to join the Association which would require financial adjustments for subscriptions and payment to the Association of fees received by D J Freeman. Letters were to be sent to five Members. A Mr Turner was no longer a litigating Member of the Association and four others had resigned. Mark was awaiting advice from Lloyd's regarding Mr Pulbrook's position.

Guy Wilson received a taxation memorandum from the Super Group on 21 August containing several misleading and incorrect statements which would have been corrected by a professional accountant. The payment of fees to Committee Members was a result of litigation success and there was no reason for delay in payment. Other matters included the following.

1. Guy met a counsel and was told 'one-off' awards were not subject to VAT and there was no reason for invoices to be raised by Committee Members or their companies. However, there were differing views about the taxation of fees.

2. Consequently, indemnities should be obtained from those to whom fees were paid just in case there was a problem. Individuals were subject to income tax and companies to corporation tax. The indemnity should hold the Committee Member responsible for the taxation of his fee. A precedent had already been set by making payments to service companies.

3. Guy said that the Association should set aside 10.2% of the fees paid to other Committee Members for Employers' National Insurance just in case the Inland Revenue determined that the Committee Members were employees. In his view it was the responsibility of the Association as a purported employer to reserve the appropriate amount. As there was a ceiling on Employers' National Insurance, he estimated the potential cost to the Association to be in the region of £60,000. Employees' Class 1 National Insurance cost to each Committee Member would probably not exceed £2,300.

On 7 September the Treasurer informed the Committee that the Halifax Building Society was to become a bank. Consequently, building society members would receive a significant pay-out. During the qualifying period the Association had substantial funds on deposit. The Treasurer asked Committee Members not to draw down their full entitlement so that the building society could retain a minimum deposit balance of £50,000, enabling the Association to receive the maximum benefit when it changed to a bank.

On 11 September it was learned that the Inspector of Taxes had heard that some Action Groups were making payments to Committee Members and to others for services. The letter said such payments were taxable under PAYE and subject to National Insurance regulations. A form was enclosed which was to be sent to the relevant tax office. As this was the Revenue's opening position no action should be taken until the Super Group had consulted tax counsel and met the Inland Revenue. This was a trap and the Inland Revenue form should not be used. The Super Group categorically stated that on no account should Committee Members names be given with allocations of income to Lloyd's. However, there was probably no harm in showing what had been paid as professional costs.

The eighteen pages of certified expenses were submitted to Lloyd's by the due date of 18 September totalling £2,198,563 including winding-up costs. The Association was required to be wound up by 31 July 1997.

Newsletter, September 1996: Lloyd's Settlement Offer Unconditional
The settlement offer was unconditional and, to the relief of many the shouting was now over. According to the figures supplied by Lloyd's, some 355 Members of this Association had accepted the settlement offer whilst a further 21 had refused it. David Rowland acknowledged, 'some "rough justice" was involved', and our gallant Trade Minister, Anthony Nelson, in ringing the Lutine Bell so joyously, opined that 'some degree of financial hardship had occurred'.

Clive was exasperated and commented critically to a Committee Member:

What has been so astonishing had been the strength of the political will on both sides of the Atlantic to keep Lloyd's afloat. Some £14 billion had been lifted out of middle England in one of the most disgraceful episodes in British commercial history. Yet the politicians, in the face of all the documented evidence of fraud, failure to regulate, the misleading of Parliament and pervasive crookedness had refused to act, other than to blandly condone.

He went on:

Even more astonishing was that the Names' representatives sent to the Council were unable to extract a better deal given the political climate and one had to ask why? Especially as two leading Lloyd's Agents in that morning's papers were openly trumpeting just how marvellously well they had done out of the settlement. Underwriters Ockham pre-tax profits went from £2.9 million to £10.9 million having paid a paltry amount into Reconstruction and Renewal, whilst Archer maintained that it had made £7.8 million out of Reconstruction and Renewal. Meanwhile, whilst Lloyd's had persuaded some 12,000 Names to part with enough money to induce another 12,000 Names to cave in, some 6,000 Names were left at the bottom of the pile in virtual ruin with tax bills to follow. At the same time the Market men brayed to the world just how well they had done out of the settlement.

With a grim-looking countenance, he paused for a moment:

But is the shouting *really* over? Some 12,000 Lloyd's Names were on orphan syndicates and left open on the 1993 and subsequent years of account. Moreover, 4,000 applicants for Tranche 4, for instance, had still not received any offer. The information relayed from the Super Group was that whilst Lloyd's were claiming 94% of all Names had accepted the settlement offer, some 4,000 of those acceptances were conditional upon Tranche 4 offers being made. This was a perfectly understandable position as it would be a very foolhardy man who would sign away all his rights only to find himself unable to pay the final bill.

Shaking his head, reflecting his incredulity, Clive added:

All those who refused the settlement offer have now received a threatening letter from Philip Holden of Lloyd's FRD. In the end, I suspect, many of the refuseniks (Names refusing the settlement offer) would be able to close a deal on much more favourable terms than the settlement offer. Thus, for 12,000 Names on orphan syndicates, the 4,000 conditional acceptors and the 1,200 offer refuseniks, the trouble at Lloyd's still goes on and on. This has led to the setting-up of the United Names Organisation. The inaugural meeting of this Organisation will be held on 26 September. Moreover, for the twenty-one Members of the Syndicate 334 Association who refused the settlement offer or who resigned earlier, a new association is being formed called the 334 Syndicate (1985) Association for the Compensation of Fraud. The new Association will be pursuing the claims already lodged under Lloyd's Bylaw 15/89 (Members' Compensation Scheme). These claims arose from voiding Syndicate 334 E&O policies by the underwriters claiming fraudulent misrepresentation by Stephen Merrett. Details of the Association are being sent to all those eligible to join which precludes those who had signed the settlement offer.

Clive gave further information regarding the Association:

You may be interested to know that eighteen pages of returns demanded by Lloyd's to support the Association's claims for the return of litigation expenses were lodged with Lloyd's on time, namely 18 September. The Committee knew just how important this return of cash is to Members for it is the only cash return being made by Lloyd's. However, I strongly urge some words of caution. Firstly, you will recall the offer from Lloyd's to refund litigation expenses would be 'at Lloyd's sole discretion'. There are already ominous sounds at Lloyd's that there is insufficient money to meet the claims of the various Action Groups. Some disallowances may well be made and following that, scaling-down of the final figures is almost inevitable. The refund of cash would be paid within fifty-six days of the offer being declared unconditional.

The Committee was now faced with terminating five appeals. The costs of doing this and winding up the Association had been included in the expenses claims. The Association would receive and distribute the refunds. In preparation for the return of litigation expenses the Committee was seeking confirmation from each Member of the Association that their record of litigation subscription amounts tallied exactly with the records kept by the Association's secretariat. A form for completion was enclosed with the newsletter.

Clive continued to receive letters of grateful thanks. Michael Jump, a tax barrister who had initially indicated he would join the Committee, had retired to Malta and wished to add his name to those who had expressed appreciation for the work of the Committee. John Chappell, an actuary of South Yarra, Victoria, said it had been very lonely and at times a frightening experience over the last six years being so far away from the Lloyd's debacle. He said he felt somewhat hopeless and wondered whether he was the only Name with such a level of loss and had been more stupid than all the others. He enthusiastically supported the motions to recompense the Committee. The peace of mind that had been afforded to Members was priceless.

Payment of the Association's winding-up costs depended on producing a list of 100% acceptances. Clive wrote to Mark Everiss on 24 September asking him to reconcile the lists of Members to achieve 100% acceptance and exclude those who had not accepted the offer and had resigned. Once agreed he would like Mark to write to Lloyd's accordingly.

Finality bill payment forms had to be submitted. The revised settlement offer to Keith Lester was an amount from him of £107,862.

Tom Boyce of Shipton-under-Wychwood complained about the
SGM resolution to remunerate the Association's officers and possible
scaling-down of recoveries. He said that it was an unfortunate decision
to disregard so arrogantly the request for a remuneration committee. He
would be very unhappy if the recoveries due to Names were reduced as a
result the Committee slavishly following a scale of 'rewards' set by such
a discredited body as the Super Group. Ten days later Clive discussed
with Committee Members suggesting his reply, stating:

> I thank you for your letter but from your tone I am inclined to
> doubt whether any productive dialogue could ensue. At the SGM
> I mentioned that scaling-down of returns were at 'Lloyd's sole
> discretion' and until the end result was known I am not sure how
> valid recriminations could be offered. Although constrained by
> notice periods the Association had acted quickly to convene the
> SGM to pass requisite resolutions. Let me tell you, some Action
> Groups appointed remuneration committees causing delay and
> missed the deadline. Some of the Action Groups were much larger
> than the Association with offices and salaried staff. I see you have
> accepted the settlement offer and presume it was to your benefit.
> I am a Member of the Super Group which had forced Lloyd's to
> increase its offer from £900 million to £3.1 billion, a substantial
> increase that benefitted Association Members. I suggest that if
> I and the Association are so discredited by taking such a robust
> part in ensuring the best possible deal out of Lloyd's, then you
> may care to return the litigation credits and your subscriptions
> will be refunded. The resulting cash would be welcomed by
> those needier than you. Furthermore, Tom, I may have observed
> that there were those in life who accept benefits and carp only
> when the hat was being passed around. You might not wish to be
> counted amongst those!

Clive continued: Mr Justice Cresswell had delivered his judgement earlier in the year and said of a former Deputy Chairman of Lloyd's, 'He has deceived his Names through a mixture of truths, half-truths and false-hoods.' Judging by Lloyd's frantic efforts to exculpate all who might be guilty, by insisting that Names renounce in the Action Group Settlement Agreement any redress for fraud, recklessness, dishonesty and misappropriation, there was a great deal to hide. Of the past Chairmen of Lloyd's Chairman Green was ejected for stealing from his Names, Chairman Miller misled Parliament and Chairman Coleridge was shown to millions on live TV as a liar over his Membership of a baby syndicate. If Chairman Miller had kept his promise to Parliament to ensure all Agents carried sufficient E&O insurance to protect their Names, little of the ensuing disaster would have occurred. Very quickly the rising price for such cover would have revealed the fatuous and crooked behaviour of many Agents. When the price did rise the Agents protected themselves at the expense of their Names by failing to take out the requisite cover, abetted by the Council of Lloyd's and in a number of cases, proceeded to take out large concealed stop-loss policies with each other. In discrediting the Super Group for publicising these little peccadilloes I think you, Mr Boyce, have acquired some very strange values. Those who had not been badly damaged at Lloyd's appeared to be content to overlook the astonishing transgressions of Market men whereas those who have been badly damaged or ruined, do not have the same forbearance.

The Committee gave their whole-hearted support to Clive's robust, precise and to-the-point response to Boyce. Accordingly, Clive despatched his cogent reply.

Mark Everiss sent a complete list of Association Members accepting the Action Group Settlement Agreement on 18 October. Some 95% of Members accepted numbering 358 of a total of 377. He also confirmed that damages held on behalf of those Names who accepted the settlement offer had been transferred to Lloyd's. The total number of Association Members had increased from 372 in the May newsletter.

Thirty-Eighth Steering Committee Meeting, 22 October 1996

Adoption of the minutes of 6 August was deferred so that a precise extract could be incorporated regarding the Action Group Settlement Agreement.

The Treasurer reported that the Halifax Building Society account had not yet been closed. He was waiting for the society to become a bank and the proposed windfall relating to the Association's deposit on the relevant dates.

The Chairman read a letter dated 17 October from the Super Group concerning the costs being levied on non-accepting Reconstruction and Renewal Names. E&O underwriters were seeking to make the twenty-one non-accepting Names responsible for all the E&O underwriters' costs. David totally disagreed with the letter, saying it would be an abuse of the court.

Clive suggested a waiver indemnity from Association Members was required prior to refunding litigation subscriptions to them. Interest received on the Association's funds had been charged to corporation tax and there was no need for Members to include such an amount in their income tax returns. David thought that future claims made by Members against the Committee were very limited.

It was agreed that a balance of £10,000 should be retained for some years and the Association put on a care and maintenance basis.

Specific information was requested by Lloyd's about remuneration. It was thought that if Action Groups refused then Lloyd's would not pay Committee remuneration voted after 26 May, the date on which it said Lloyd's would reimburse litigation expenses. Guy said there were three Lloyd's project officers investigating different aspects of submitted claims.

David Tiplady presented the legal report and said that the Association had decided to cease all litigation although there were some appeals outstanding and five Names were continuing to litigate. All resigners were removed from the Action Group Settlement Agreement so that the list represented 100% acceptors and thus qualified for reimbursement of expenses. It was agreed to pay a proportion of the litigation expenses to Members as soon after reimbursement as possible.

David Tiplady reported that he had been in contact with Paul Evans of Price Waterhouse who confirmed that no legal rights regarding Pulbrook Underwriting Management had been surrendered by him as liquidator. Pulbrook Underwriting Management was being kept alive and not struck off the Register at Companies House.

A resolution was passed for the Association to pursue claims on behalf of twenty-one Members under the Members' Compensation bylaw. The estimated cost was £2,000. The maximum claim per Member was £50,000.

Fourth AGM of the Syndicate 334 (1985) Names Association, 22 October 1996

The AGM was held on 22 October by proxy in D J Freeman's offices when the resolutions to adopt the report and accounts for the year to January 1996 and the appointment of auditors Forrester Boyd were approved. The Committee Members were re-elected, being Clive Francis, Keith Lester, Guy Wilson, Charles Baron, Ray Cook, Alasdair Ferguson and Harry Purchase.

A letter from Darrell Ling's department at Lloyd's arrived on 31 October asking for confirmation of the accuracy of expenses and that remuneration had been approved by resolution at a meeting of Members prior to 21 May 1996. A copy of the resolution was requested as certified by the Action Group's solicitor. Information was required by the next day. Clive responded to Ling and confirmed the subscriptions to third-party organisations were in accordance with the schedule provided. He understood it was Lloyd's intention to wriggle out of its commitment to refund all proper litigation and settlement expenses such as the Super Group subscription. Clive said as the Association's Chairman he was a Member of the Super Group. It was accepted by this Association that the Super Group was the main instrument in forcing Lloyd's to up its previous final offer. In every way this was a proper expenditure complying with the objectives of the Association. It was conceivable that unless these proper expenses were allowed the Association Members would no longer feel bound by the Action Group Settlement Agreement or the settlement offer. Clive enclosed a copy of the SGM resolutions passed on 9 July 1996, and did not understand the significance of 21 May 1996 mentioned in Ling's letter. He pointed out that the cut-off date of 21 May 1996 appeared in a settlement offer date document about three weeks after the SGM, which was held on 9 July 1996. If there was any diminution of the return of expenses by reference to his newly stipulated date, resulting in a reduction in the expected payment of expenses, the Association would have to consider whether or not Lloyd's had broken the terms of its settlement offer promises. Clive followed this up with a fax on the same day saying that the change to the rules which allowed Committee remuneration was held at an SGM on 15 March 1995. This was well before 21 May 1996. Lloyd's was trying to wriggle out of its promises.

Clive replied to David Tiplady's letter of 30 October regarding future strategy. The overriding factor in the tactics was the full and timely reimbursement of the Association's litigation expenses. Although Association Members were established creditors of Pulbrook Underwriting Management, they could not pursue their E&O claim through a liquidator as the Action Group Settlement Agreement had been signed. The Pulbrook Creditors' Group was defunct.

There were some twenty refuseniks and once the expenses refunds were safely banked Clive would launch a publicised reiteration of the Members' Compensation Scheme. Almost coincidently with that could a claim be made by the liquidator for the return of the Syndicate 334 portion of the E&O premium amounting to some £530,000, for each of the years the E&O insurers purported to avoid. At that stage Clive imagined the E&O underwriters changing their minds and the policy was not to be voided.

It might be that a new Action Group would have to be formed to obviate any possible compromise of the Association's reimbursements. All Members of the 'old' Association who were forced to resign over the Action Group Settlement Agreement were registered creditors of Pulbrook Underwriting Management and did not have to conduct any litigation to establish this status. David thought that all 'old' Association Members could join the new Action Group. It was noted that the Barclays Bank claim was in the background and the E&O insurers may think twice before they unvoided the policy. Clive speculated that an even bigger prize to be wrested from the Merrett Group E&O insurers would be £18 million in cash, less the Barclays claim, which he understood to be £1.5 million.

Clive's suspicions increased about Lloyd's intentions on 5 November. A very unsatisfactory picture was developing over the allocation of Tranche 4 credits which were so far below expectations as some Names were unable to meet their finality bills. This was an indication that Lloyd's was running short of money and seeking to pare down where possible. He expressed that view in his correspondence with Lloyd's adopting his usual soft, delicate and diplomatic approach. Several Action Group Chairmen had asked the Association to join in an approach to counsel with a view to obtaining an injunction against Lloyd's behaving in the fashion now anticipated. Clive had assented as expenditure was expected to be very modest. He hoped that the Committee would concur with the expenditure together with his employment of stridency as being the proper weapon for the moment.

A disturbing fax from Christopher Stockwell on 7 November said a total of £67 million expenses would be reimbursed to Action Groups while total claims amounted to £102 million. Christopher wanted to know the total claim made by Action Groups. Clive immediately wrote to David about the disquieting rumour and quoted terms included in the settlement offer such as 'incurred and committed after 26 May 1996', 'other expenditure' and 'contingent remuneration'. He also mentioned the rumour that Lloyd's was about to rush out cheques, excluding any remuneration voted after 26 May. He believed this treatment of expenses was contrary to the spirit of the settlement and in breach of the Action Group Settlement Agreement. Clive had been counting the days since the settlement offer date declared that expenses refunds would be paid in cash within fifty-six days. Now it was 12 November and the fifty-six days had passed and he wanted to be sure of his calculations before charging Rowland with being out of time.

The *Sunday Telegraph* of 17 November stated that as many as 100 of 130 blacklisted Names had won an unexpected reprieve from unlimited losses as a result of a Lloyd's internal bungle. The blacklist was drawn up to reassure Names and public opinion that Lloyd's would not use the settlement to reward the wrong people. Blacklisted Names such as Stephen Merrett, Anthony Gooda, Derek Walker and Richard Outhwaite had been excluded from the settlement. They were thought to have brought Lloyd's into disrepute as their activities caused hundreds of millions of pounds in losses. However, the committee compiling the blacklist did not liaise with another committee which worked out the final exit package. The 100 would now be paid enough to clear their personal debts to syndicates. This could mean relief to insiders blamed for causing many of the Market's recent problems.

Mrs E. A. Stephenson of Ramsey accused Rowland of moving the goalposts. Some £40 million had been conjured up to buy off American Names. Insiders had paid themselves bonuses and found £20 million to pay Freshfields, Lloyd's solicitors, to keep the business from foundering with livelihoods in the Market at stake. To crown it all she was paying the losses of 'fraudsters' who had been at the very centre of the whole disastrous business. All this money was pulled from Names, like her, fooled by false prospectuses and a conspiracy of silence in the 1980s. She was still waiting for Tranche 4 promises to be fulfilled. Another letter to Rowland mentioned the article in the *Sunday Telegraph* of 17 November regarding 130 Names, including some of the major villains, who were to have their debts met. After all the sacrifices that had been made could he imagine how incensed Names were?

The Super Group said Lloyd's was refunding up to 50% of some Action Group legal expenses but for others the percentage of total costs was derisible. Sources were saying that Lloyd's was delaying its trade bills several weeks, paying late and in part rather than in full. Lloyd's was in danger of breaching its £300 million overdraft ceiling and was having difficulty collecting dues from Names and Agents. It was thought that the bad debt element was between £500 million and £1 billion. The Super Group also observed that brokers had agreed extended terms for money to be paid under Reconstruction and Renewal. The £100 million payable was being delayed and interest earned on the sum was being treated as brokers' income rather than that of Names. It was a pity that future Lloyd's had done a deal with brokers surrendering Names' claims to this income. Stockwell said it was the basis of Warren Buffet's fortune through Berkshire Hathaway. Buffet had started a business in insurance. The theory was that the business collects cash for premiums and invests them to earn interest. Claims have to be paid from realisation of the investments. The key is having more assets than claims to produce a profit.

On 22 November Lloyd's sent a cheque for £565,691 as an interim refund of 49% of legal expenses promising more by 31 January 1997. The total claimed by the Association was £2,198,563, including Committee Members' remuneration.

The Inland Revenue at Salford on 26 November informed the Association that payments to Committee Members were taxable under Schedule E, in 1996–97 fiscal year. Tax should be accounted for by the payer. It said the Inland Revenue administration would be operated as Lloyd's Names' Associations' Central Accounting Scheme. Tax and National Insurance should be deducted in accordance with PAYE regulations. A copy of a letter was supplied which payees might find convenient when completing their tax returns. Clive 'blew his top' and could hardly contain himself, expressing total disgust at the demand, liberally punctuated with fruity phrases, as the Association had no employees and no PAYE scheme. The Treasurer only wanted to record printable comments from Clive.

On 1 December Stockwell circulated a memorandum saying Lloyd's was going to issue a fourth 'finality' statement. This was because the pound sterling had weakened against the US dollar and increased the cost of Reconstruction and Renewal. It was estimated there would be a 5% charge. He also said there were some problems with stop-loss underwriters and Agents did not understand the very unclear explanations. When finality results were issued Christopher wondered who checked the numbers and if the calculations could be trusted.

Sarah Wilton's letter of 18 November informed Clive she wished to disallow claims after 21 May 1996. Clive replied that a formal offer was made without qualification in the settlement offer document which was accepted by the Association. Lloyd's was in breach of the terms of the offer as it did not have discretionary powers and was likely to be subject to legal challenge. A further breach occurred by failure to apply Lloyd's own criteria that may have invalidated the Action Group Settlement Agreement. Clive requested an explanation as to why 21 May had been selected as the cut-off date. Only two syndicates had complied and they were chaired by Members of Lloyd's Council. He wondered why it was not considered to be a straightforward case of insider dealing. Lastly, he queried the acceptance percentage for calculating the refund which was underpaid and asked for an extra £3,000.

Thirty-Ninth Steering Committee Meeting, 11 December 1996: Extracting Cash from Lloyd's

Mark Everiss and all Committee Members attended D J Freeman's offices.

The Treasurer reported that D J Freeman's costs since 4 September amounted to £104,000 compared to an estimate of £20,000 for winding up, the amount claimed from Lloyd's. Winding-up costs had to be certified by the auditor. Committee remuneration from July to December would be included in the winding-up costs. Calculations were based on a formula per litigating Name. The Association was in Tranche 1 and the amount would be £375 per litigant. It was unlikely that Lloyd's would reimburse the remuneration. Solicitors' fees always seemed to be substantially more than budget or forecast and without care, funds disappeared at the 'blink of an eye'!

Approximately £1.2 million should be received. Lloyd's had not accepted conditional acceptors. Conditional acceptances under Reconstruction and Renewal had not been given Tranche 4 debt credits on the grounds there was no such thing in law as a conditional acceptance. This was incredibly bad news for the non-acceptors. Lloyd's was dragging out the allocation of Tranche 4 credits, causing difficulties for Names expecting to receive them.

David Tiplady confirmed that appeals would be signed off in court and legal rights would remain intact. This was important to safeguard against future uncertainties. He could think of no reason to avoid the Action Group Settlement Agreement. Matthews Wrightson Pulbrook should be wound up as there was no reason to prevent that.

Lloyd's wanted the Association to be wound up before they would pay all winding-up costs. Clive agreed that no publicity would be given to the Members' Compensation Scheme regarding fraud until all the cheques from Lloyd's had been banked. Hardship Names being assigned into Equitas may have a tax liability. Names' tax losses brought forward could be offset against the Equitas release.

A second cheque from Sarah Wilton for £597,954 was received on 19 December. It was for the balance of expenses refunded to the Association amounting to approximately 86% of eligible expenses, making a total recovery of £1,163,645. The original claim was £1,959,693 plus eligible winding-up costs estimated at £238,870 which would be received in February 1997. This was the only cash paid by Lloyd's following successful litigation by the Association. Lloyd's declined to pay remuneration expenses and trimmed all other expenses to 86% of claim. Following part repayment of expenses, Clive wrote to Wilton on 14 January complaining that there was an increased shortfall in the calculation of the refunds totalling £6,500 and referred to his letter to her of 3 December.

It was not known quite why it was always difficult to settle the exact number of Association Members, but it looked as though the final number was 375. On 4 February David confirmed to Wilton the number of the Association's Names on the Action Group Settlement Agreement and the percentage payable to the Association following Clive's earlier statement. He said the applicable percentage for 371 Members was 98.93% of 375 in total. Four Members rejected Reconstruction and Renewal.

Legal fees since the submission of the initial claim amounted to £144,225 including a provision for future costs of £10,000. It was understood that D J Freeman would have to retain documentation for fifteen years and four months to take account of claims under the Latent Damage Act 1986. The four months allowed time for a writ to be served after the expiry of fifteen years. The Association would need to consider procedures and financial arrangements regarding any enquiries after it had been wound up.

On 9 January 1997 Lloyd's issued a circular about a settlement with Merrett and the underwriting agencies. As a result, Lloyd's had decided to halt their enquiry into Merrett's business activities. It appeared that Lloyd's was mightily relieved they did not have to inquire into Merrett's suspected dubious underwriting and other practices – an inquiry for which they could have had little enthusiasm.

On 14 January Clive wrote to Sir Alan Hardcastle, Chairman of the Regulatory Board, expressing astonishment at the decision to cease the formal investigation into the transactions of his quondam former Deputy Chairman Merrett. He explained that the Association in a judgement had been awarded full liability against Pulbrook Underwriting Management. The losses were estimated at £64 million. The only satisfaction was Pulbrook Underwriting Management's E&O policy for which the cover was £20 million. Through Merrett's allegedly fraudulent misrepresentation at the inception of the E&O policy the Association lost in the Lloyd's settlement. If Merrett had been fraudulent then all Members of the Association were due for the maximum compensation under the Members' Compensation Scheme. If Merrett had not been fraudulent then all the Members of the Association would have benefitted in the settlement offer. The Association was formally notifying Hardcastle of the allegations and required him to conduct a formal investigation. The Association had sufficient grounds to repudiate its Action Groups Settlement Agreement and reserved the right to do so.

Hardcastle's response to Clive was regarded as a fudge and totally inadequate. Clive replied on 12 February that the Committee wished to thank him for the masterly way in which he had managed to avoid the issue. The argument was, if the E&O policy was repudiated on the grounds of fraud then certain Members of the Association would be able to take action under the Members' Compensation bylaw. If the E&O was voided and there was no fraud the E&O policy should be reinstated and make recompense for losses. The Committee told him, therefore, that evidence of fraud was held by the E&O insurers and requested him to investigate. Alternatives were reviewed including an approach to the insurance ombudsman or going to the DTI. Hardcastle replied on 19 February saying that in view of the Lloyd's settlement offer there would be no enquiry into the business and management of Syndicate 418. Merrett's business had suffered and he had resigned as Deputy Chairman of Lloyd's. Clive was not surprised by Hardcastle's response but it left him feeling that there was no prospect of justice.

Mr F. Daniel Bee and his wife had both conditionally accepted the settlement offer based on their Tranche 4 credits application. They had received a letter from Lloyd's intimating that the Tranche 4 credits had been refused and thought the Committee should be apprised of Lloyd's latest tactic. They had an amount owing that would be impossible to pay. Daniel said in the last five years he had participated in six Action Groups. He was financially ruined. It was his understanding that Lloyd's would not hound people to their grave and added that he was sixty-eight years old, ill and recently had surgery. Clive replied on 12 February and said that there were a number of Names who made their acceptances conditional upon receiving Tranche 4 credits. Some Names failing to receive Tranche 4 credits found themselves as non-acceptors. Clive recommended contacting Stockwell who was running the conditional acceptors' group. The matter was urgent as the defence of the conditional acceptors was approaching the court stage. The Association did not wish to be involved further in this case and the ultimate outcome was unknown. The true human cost to so many Names will never be known.

Steve Boggan's article in the *Independent* on 7 February was titled 'Names' Fury as Lloyd's Sends Further Bills'. Lloyd's had previously reserved the right to send out further bills. Securities offered against debts failed to realise the amount owed by the Name, such as changes in foreign currency exchange rates, life assurance policies and letters of credit. He reported that Stockwell said, 'We have feared a further recalculation for several weeks.' The reality was that Reconstruction and Renewal was not going according to plan. Hundreds of the hardest-hit Names had yet to see any evidence that Lloyd's would honour its pledges.

Names received a letter on 10 January 1997 that Municipal General Insurance Limited had gone into liquidation. Names with personal stop-loss policies underwritten by the company were asked to confirm the amounts outstanding. This affected some Syndicate 334 Names. Some stop-loss recoveries were delayed for many years and into the second decade of the next century.

Fortieth Steering Committee Meeting, 20 February 1997: Pound Strengthens against Dollar but Costs Increase???

Following the acceptance of Lloyd's settlement offer all legal actions by the Association had been discontinued. Although an action previously mentioned, the Members' Compensation Scheme, would be pursued separately and not under the auspices of the Association. To tie down final costs D J Freeman's fees for winding up would not exceed £10,000 under any circumstances.

Members giving a conditional acceptance was rejected by Lloyd's. The rejectees had made a counter-offer and brought a disadvantageous situation upon themselves. The legal and moral stance of the Association was considered. David pointed out that the Rules of the Association prevented it from acting on behalf of a few individuals. The rejectees were 'on their own' and no further action should be taken by the Association.

Sterling was strengthening against the US dollar. When the pound sterling was weakening against the US dollar Names faced increasing bills. Logically when the sterling strengthened against the US dollar this should reduce the US dollar costs in sterling terms. However, in the latter case, unbelievably, Lloyd's had indicated it would make an additional charge! The Chairman was asked to discuss the situation with other Action Group

Chairmen and demand an explanation from Lloyd's for increased costs associated with an appreciation of the pound against the dollar. Lloyd's idea for increasing costs was, spin a coin and falling as heads, Lloyd's wins, tails, Names lose. It was a familiar story.

Newsletter, March 1997

The March Chairman's newsletter detailed unfinished business. It was sad that those who were relying on Trache 4 assistance having given 'conditional acceptance' to the settlement were not receiving the credits. A counter-offer to the original offer had ceased to have legal substance. These rejectees were in addition to refuseniks who had refused the settlement outright. The latter were pursuing a claim under the Members' Fraud Compensation Scheme.

The rejectees who were among the financially weakest of the Association's Members were now being dunned for the full amount of their debts as though there had been no settlement offer. They were entitled to be treated as though they had not subscribed to the Action Group Settlement Agreement and to proceed against the Pulbrook Underwriting Management E&O underwriters of the E&O policy. It is not known how this was concluded.

A questionnaire had been included with the March newsletter. Two-thirds responded saying they had received a settlement cheque, none had received a further finality bill, two-thirds were not willing to help rejectees using the Association's funds and required repayment of their litigation subscriptions. About 50% were inclined to pay an increased finality bill and 50% would not. Most did not require further help or information but three did and details were forwarded to Stockwell.

David Tiplady commented on the alleged fraud by Merrett and his behaviour clearly fell within the definition of misconduct. However, 'If the Council considered that a person had carried out an act of misconduct, it may institute disciplinary proceedings against that person.' In other words, there was no obligation upon the Council to institute proceedings; so, it did nothing.

Mr G. S. was short of £70,000-worth of Royal Dutch Shell shares from his deposit on which Lloyd's was receiving dividends. He said that Lloyd's were just as much bastards as ever, perhaps even more so now they think they had gotten away with so many shady practices.

Geoffrey North, a lawyer, did not believe that Lloyd's would be induced to be honest. They had shown a remarkable ability to disregard both the law and their own bylaws. He did not believe it was the Association's task to bring them to book and Clive agreed.

Forty-First Steering Committee Meeting, 17 April 1997

Seven Committee Members attended the meeting in D J Freeman's offices. The Treasurer tabled Financial Statements to 31 January 1997.

Summary of the Audited Syndicate 334 (1985) Names Association Signed Financial Statements to 31 January 1997

	1997	1997	1996	1996
	£	£	£	£
Income	1,239,384		54,317	
Less expenditure	1,601,821		304,614	
(Loss) for year	-362,437		-250,297	
Funds available at beginning of year (1996/95)		819,474		1,069,771
Less loss for year		-362,437		-250,297
Funds available at end of year		**457,037**		**819,474**
Represented by				
Banks and building societies		511,779		943,716
Less creditors		-54,742		-124,242
Net assets at end of year		**457,037**		**819,474**

Tedious bureaucratic points followed that were discussed and determined as it was important to resolve all the issues and loose ends completely satisfactorily.

All honoraria under the SGM resolution could be shown in one financial year enabling the Committee to demonstrate a single windfall payment for the whole sum, thus clearly a one-off payment that was not repeated. Consequently, the Association was making no provision for taxation. Should the Association become liable to pay any tax indemnities had been received from all Committee Members.

The honoraria could not be paid in one instalment because of a shortage of funds received from Lloyd's. When the Halifax Building Society converted to a bank the shares arising from the Association's Halifax account were valued at about £50,000, and were sold and monies credited to the Association's bank account. Committee Members provided interest-free loans to ensure that the Association had sufficient qualifying Halifax funds available. The windfall of £50,000 set off about 2.5% of the total expenses.

Lloyd's would only pay winding-up expenses provided there was a resolution to wind up the Association by 31 July 1997. David confirmed that the Rules of the Association covered Committee Members should any legal action be contemplated against them for whatever reason. It was agreed that the purpose of the Association had been fulfilled as a settlement had been proposed.

David Tiplady mentioned that Mr Strauss's clerk requested a further £27,000 in fees for the exemplary task that Mr Strauss had performed in court acting as counsel for the Association. He had responded that the Association was not prepared to pay anything further. The Committee unanimously agreed not to use the Association's funds for action against Merrett claiming fraud. Names interested in such an action should act on their own account and fund their own legal costs.

A small trust comprising the Chairman, Treasurer and Secretary was proposed with a £10,000 fund to cater for consumables and storage for up to fifteen years and four months. The officers accepted responsibility on a minimal fee basis. The final distribution to Members was planned for 10 July and the Association wound up by 31 July.

Charles Baron suggested the Association take out an insurance policy to protect Committee Members from being sued. David wondered for what Members could be sued and observed that no individual was likely to win. He said that the Committee had acted in the best interests of the Association's Members and to the best of knowledge and belief had not been negligent in any manner.

Willis Faber & Dumas (Agencies) Limited issued their April 1997 Lloyd's Market Update. James Sinclair said that the Agency had been much quieter following the success of Reconstruction and Renewal in bringing a resolution to years of squabbling. However, the Reconstruction and Renewal exercise struggled on to completion. Lloyd's Central believed they had done a good job in the circumstances, but Names and Agents took the view it was a 'complete shambles'. He said that the reconciliation statements had been sent out with numbers so different from the second indicative statements. Only an experienced organisation such as Lloyd's could pull off a stunt where agreement was given on one set of figures, but settlement was made on a completely different, lower, set of numbers. Ironically, good underwriting results were being reported for 1993 to 1996 and coinciding with strong stock markets worldwide.

Jack Hulton of Potters Bar queried the 'delay' in sending his cheque and considered the Association to be tardy and parsimonious. He said he had received money from other litigating Action Groups the previous December, January and March. Clive informed him that Syndicate 90 did not receive Tier 1 credits in the settlement offer whilst the Association did, giving a better return under debt credits. Clive explained that following the E&O underwriters voiding the Syndicate 334 cover on the grounds of Merrett's fraud, the Association had virtually no money in escrow enabling it to bargain with Lloyd's over reimbursements. Furthermore Syndicate 418 did a special deal with Lloyd's and Merrett. This had the net effect of disadvantaging the Association, as disciplinary proceedings against Merrett were stayed and the Association was unable to conclude its fraud case. So, if Hulton had a nice lump from Syndicate 418 it was at the expense of Syndicate 334.

Clive also circulated a letter addressed to Syndicate 90 Names from Adam Raphael, the Chairman, who said it would take some time to tie up all the loose ends in winding up the Association. The Association had purchased insurance at a cost of £50,000 providing £3 million of cover for six years. This cover would give protection from claims against the Association, including the costs of defending them. There were circumstances in which each Member of the Association could be liable in respect of a claim. The insurance was for the benefit of all Members. Clive's covering letter said a couple of Committee Members had expressed misgivings about the decision for the Association not to take out insurance cover.

David Tiplady and Christopher Stockwell signed a letter with eleven other influential persons on 22 April, addressed to Ron Sandler, complaining that contrary to Lloyd's undertakings there were instances of Lloyd's failing to reply to letters or negotiate a reasonable standard of living. They felt a bitter aftertaste had developed.

Forty-Second Steering Committee Meeting, 2 June 1997

At the meeting of the Steering Committee on 2 June the Committee was of the opinion that the objects for which the Association was established had been accomplished. Therefore, in compliance with Lloyd's requirements the Association would be dissolved and the assets distributed in accordance with the Association's Rules.

Clive wrote to his Member of Parliament, Ben Bradshaw, drawing the MP's attention to the cogent findings of the last Parliamentary Treasury Select Committee on Self-Regulation in the City and particularly to the report on Lloyd's. The Select Committee's investigation was penetrating and comprehensive. It was uncompromisingly damning in recording the fraudulent nature of the conduct of Lloyd's over the past two decades. The report recommended a full-scale enquiry into Lloyd's. Lloyd's bankruptcies could have cost the Conservative Party its parliamentary majority. However, the Conservative Party resolutely ignored the findings of the Committee. Because of collusion between the then President of the Board of Trade and Lloyd's, a scheme called Equitas was concocted. The result was £11 billion abstracted from Lloyd's Names whilst those Market men of Lloyd's who had perpetrated the debacle not only went unpunished but grew measurably richer. In the period from 1987 to 1997 when External Names of Lloyd's lost £11 billion, Lloyd's brokers received £6 billion in commissions and brokerage. Clive suggested that 'the losses of Lloyd's Names during the past two decades constituted one of the greatest frauds in British commercial history' with this thesis supported by the Treasury Select Committee's report.

Newsletter, June 1997

The Chairman's June newsletter mentioned a recent valedictory article in the *Daily Telegraph* by Thomas Fellowes, the retiring Deputy Chairman of Gerrards, a City discount house. Fellowes reflected on a lifetime in the City and affection for its many institutions. He concluded, 'I will not miss Lloyd's that was dominated for much of my life by a group of insensitive and often incompetent individuals, with little sense of remorse for the pain they caused innocent and duped people.'

One life-long Tory helper put it, 'I and thousands of other relatives of Lloyd's victims up and down the country would not be running old ladies to the polls to help this lot – if they were content to ignore the scandal at Lloyd's then they were not fit to be in Government.'

Clive added that if anyone had any complaints to please let the Committee know at once. He said he chaired the Association of his old Air Force squadron and by way of thanks he was recently given a flight in the squadron's two-seater Jaguar fitted with ejector seats. An immensely competent and thorough briefing was given by one of the Stern Young Men of today. The Stern Young Man concluded with the words, 'If I say "eject" and you say "what" you'll be talking to yourself.' Clive might have added that while a serving in the RAF he had ejected over Newark, Nottinghamshire, from a Vampire jet when the elevator controls failed. He survived but subsequently always suffered from back pain.

Some 60% of the original litigation subscription was returned to Association Members and Clive had already received a complaint that the percentage compared unfavourably with percentages paid to other Action Groups. Clive explained that Lloyd's originally promised to refund only 87% of the costs incurred. This Association had expended nearly all the litigation subscriptions by winning in court and were immediately disadvantaged compared to those Associations like Syndicate 90 which did not get as far as the courtroom. The costs incurred by the latter were much lower and received a higher proportion of the original subscription. However, this Association achieved Tier 1 in the settlement offer whereas Syndicate 90 did not. Consequently, Members of this Association achieved a considerably better return from debt credits but did not do so well in cash terms.

Lloyd's promised to reimburse Associations which had passed a resolution granting honoraria to their Committee Members. Such a resolution was passed at the SGM but subsequently 'at its discretion' Lloyd's declined to honour its promise.

Clive received a letter on 16 June and a final cheque for winding-up expenses including interest amounting to £72,934 from Sarah Wilton. The letter said that by banking the cheque the Association acknowledged that Lloyd's had met its obligations.

On 24 June Tom Boyce of London thanked Clive for the newsletter. He noted that Lloyd's had declined to honour its promise to reimburse the Association for the honoraria paid to Committee Members. He wanted to know a detailed breakdown of the £675,800 shown as honoraria in the accounts and how these individual amounts were made up. He also had a discrepancy query about the figure of £65,000 for Committee expenses for 1996. Lastly, he wanted to know the percentage of Committee honoraria to total recoveries by the Association. There was no record of Clive's reply but based on a recovery of £18 million the honoraria cost approximately 4%.

Forty-Third Steering Committee Meeting, 10 July 1997

The Treasurer tabled final Financial Statements to 31 January 1997. Net assets for distribution amounted to £457,037 and a balance for reserve amounted to £10,265.

	1997 (£)
Income	195,779
Expenditure	642,551
(Loss) for period	(446,772)
Funds available 1/2/1996	457,037
Funds Available 31/7/1997	**10,265**

On 14 July, Guy Wilson and David Tiplady drafted letters for Clive to a Mr Batchelor of New South Wales, who together with a Mr Plaskitt and five others had written to Clive with a list of sixteen questions some of which had earlier been answered by the Treasurer and recorded in the June newsletter. Guy said that the Committee entered the legal fight with Lloyd's to win. The Committee had worked tirelessly for seven and a half years. The early bleak outlook was for a loss of 500% of line and Guy hoped he would share the Committee's sentiments that the fight was worthwhile. David Tiplady drafted a letter to accompany Guy's response to Batchelor, saying the questions asked were considered at great length at the Steering Committee Meeting. He concurred with Guy's reply which attempted to encapsulate the decisions of the Committee. David Tiplady was writing independently saying that at the inception of the Association it had been part of his task to ensure that decisions fell within the Association's Rules. The question of remuneration was one of extreme sensitivity. He had to be satisfied that the Committee was acting in accordance with both the letter and the spirit of the Association's Rules. The satisfaction of the Association itself was demonstrated by the overwhelming vote in support of the resolutions. The sums in issue represented in his experience an extremely modest reward for substantial achievement. He could think of no other Steering Committee which had achieved so much and had accepted so little in return.

Clive submitted his last expense claim. He said he could not have let the opportunity pass without saying a big personal thanks and for the way the Treasurer had looked after them all and dealt with the minutiae of the Association's treasury. Even more grateful he said he was for the constant support and wise advice given to him over the years. He concluded by saying it had been a real good team and he would miss it. On 30 July Clive said this was the last letter on his Syndicate 334 (1985) Names Association notepaper. After seven years of support and encouragement Clive summed it all up by saying 'Thank you.'

Newsletter, July 1997

In the Chairman's July newsletter Clive announced that in accordance with the Rules, the Association dissolved on 31 July 1997.

Commenting on Equitas, Clive pointed out four pages of qualifications to the accounts which he thought did not bode well and many Names expressed nervousness. The only prudent course was to guard against the possible failure of Equitas. It was necessary to bear in mind that the Chairman of Lloyd's had promised the Insurance Commissioners of the United States that they would always have recourse to Names should Equitas fail. The newsletter concluded that he and the Committee joined in saying farewell and thanked Members for their unfailing support.

However, all was not quite ended as Harry Purchase had asked the whole Committee and legal advisors plus one guest each to a valedictory bean feast barbeque at his Thames riverside 'palace' followed by a river trip in his launch.

Keith Lester wrote a personal note on 24 August 1997 to Clive to congratulate him on being such an able and excellent Chairman. The outcome was much better than appeared possible at times but obviously below that which it had set out to achieve. Nevertheless, it was a good effort. He also sent a personal note of thanks to Julia Barkworth and the staff at Louth Secretarial Services Ltd. He felt that they dealt with the Association's affairs and financial matters very efficiently.

A former Managing Director of an Agency resigned as a Name. He said that after twenty-five years of underwriting his overall result was zero. It was only the Action Group settlements that brought him to zero. He suggested that what wounded the Market and bankrupted many Names was Ronald Reagan putting in place the Super Fund Act which required the owner of land to clean up their patch regardless of who contaminated it. New purchasers of polluted land were liable by US law to clean it up regardless of time or cost. The owners claimed on their domestic insurance policies, some of which were reinsured with Lloyd's syndicates, costing their Names dearly. He said Lloyd's Names cleaned up the USA. Pollution and asbestos were the two big events that troubled Lloyd's.

It was a great relief that Lloyd's agreed on 9 December 1999 to terminate Keith's Hardship Agreement for £50,000. Keith's cash flow had been a serious problem and the Inland Revenue were dreadfully slow in settling many thousands of pounds in loss claims that eventually brought to him an overall breakeven position for Lloyd's activities. Keith and his wife were able to leave for a motor home holiday in Australia taking the southerly route from Perth to Brisbane.

On Keith Lester's sixtieth birthday they arrived at a sheltered campsite at aptly named Peaceful Bay, with the resounding thump of an ocean gale raging on the other side of a shelter belt of trees. It was time to celebrate the release from the Lloyd's debacle with a bottle of wine, but they had no one to celebrate with. However, two 'elderly' ladies were spotted passing by on their evening walk and they were asked if they would care for a glass of wine. 'Oh, yes!' they said. The next hour was filled with fascinating conversation. They were two nurses married to farmers who came from Denmark. As a student Keith had a holiday job farming in that country. When he suggested they were far from home, 'Not far', they said. 'Forty kilometres down the road.' The grey sky changed from daytime into dusk and the two ladies set out to finish their walk. There was an uncertain inebriated waddle as they disappeared down the trail. Truly a celebration to remember, letting go of the past and moving into a world of new horizons.

Keith's Lester's Membership of Lloyd's ceased on 17 August 2004.

Summary of Key Issues

1. Equitas, management, trading and survival matters were discussed.

2. Lloyd's negotiations were seemingly not in good faith.

3. Reconstruction and Renewal settlement offer was increased to £3.1 billion.

4. Rules regarding Action Group expenses were repaid by Lloyd's.

5. Progress was made on appeals.

6. Committee Members' remuneration was approved at SGM.

7. The Action Group Settlement Agreement was approved.

8. The taxation of Committee Members' remuneration was discussed.

9. Despite mounting evidence, Stephen Merrett escape formal censure.

10. The Halifax Bank paid a £50,000 windfall.

A Saviour? The Sage of Omaha

Our bending author hath pursued the story,
In little room confining mighty men,
Mangling by starts the full course of their glory.

Henry V, Epilogue

Although Keith had settled his debts to Lloyd's in December 1999 following Hardship, there had not been a final release by Equitas. Berkshire Hathaway Group based in Omaha, Nebraska agreed to provide the necessary security for Equitas. Letters were eventually received allowing total disengagement from anything to do with Lloyd's.

On 20 October 2006 Hugh Stevenson, Chairman of Equitas, wrote to reinsured Names that an agreement had been reached with the National Indemnity Company, a Member of the Berkshire Hathaway Group. The company would reinsure all Equitas liabilities, provide up to a further $7 billion of reinsurance cover (about £3.7 billion) and take on the staff and operations of Equitas and run-off of Equitas liabilities. Berkshire Hathaway Group expected to make a profit on the premium they received, a paltry sum compared with that group's profits or assets.

A letter informed Keith Lester on 25 June 2009 that Mr Justice Blackburne had approved a transfer of all the 1992 and prior year non-life Lloyd's liabilities of open- and closed-years Names to Equitas Insurance Limited.

The letter detailed the steps taken to complete his involvement with Lloyd's. It said the transfer took effect on the previous day and it followed that no Name had any further liability whatsoever under English law, in respect of 1992 and prior non-life Lloyd's liabilities and throughout all the jurisdictions of the European Economic Area. In the unlikely event that Equitas became insolvent no policyholder with an unsatisfied claim would be able to enforce that claim in any court of the European Economic Area to recover it from any Name. Equitas would explore how far it may be possible to seek judicial recognition of the major overseas jurisdictions, in particular the United States of America. Names were indemnified by Equitas Insurance Limited should any claims be made against them directly in a foreign jurisdiction. The Chairman believed that the likelihood of Equitas ever becoming insolvent was extremely remote. Equitas had purchased for a further premium of £40 million all the additional reinsurance cover of $1.3 billion from the National Indemnity Company under the terms of the Agreement entered into in October 2006. As a result, policyholders benefited from a total of $7 billion of reinsurance from National Indemnity Company over and above the Equitas reserves at the 31 March 2006. Equitas would be maintained on a care and maintenance basis. No more Equitas Open Meetings would be held or report and accounts distributed. Names would no longer have to keep Equitas informed of their addresses although they may wish to do so in case the company was ever in a position to pay a further return of premium, although this was something not in the foreseeable future.

After more than thirty interesting but also some very traumatic, stressful years of involvement with Lloyd's and aged nearly seventy, Keith Lester's ordeal of the Lloyd's debacle saga was finally over. It was not an experience anyone would wish upon themselves... but that's life!

E. A. K. Lester

11/10/2023

Summary of Key Issues

The end of the end... or was it?

John Neal CEO on Why Lloyd's of London 'Had to Change'

A precis of Charlie Conchie's interview in *City AM* on 25 April 2024
John Neal, Lloyd's Chief Executive Officer, explained that since his appointment in October 2018, he had been pushing through a huge modernisation effort. The Market has had to become more digital, more interactive and more professional in the way it measures, manages and resolves risk. Profits have surged to £10.7 billion from a loss of £800 million the previous year.

Since starting as a motor syndicate underwriter in 1985, Lloyd's has been his workplace – apart from seven years in Sydney as Chief of QBE Insurance. Insurance covers placed by Lloyd's have been transformed; climate change and cybersecurity risks have shot up the agenda. Much growth results from the crystallised concept of risk. Premiums rocketed following crises caused by Brexit, Covid and wars in Ukraine and Gaza.

Physical interaction face to face is important, to explain the story behind numbers on a piece of paper. Arguably, the world is considered to be much riskier than five to ten years ago. Complications arise when providing cover for fossil fuel projects and ESG risks.

Neal says one of his strengths in the 1980s was that he avoided lunchtime alcohol and would be behind his underwriting box at 2.30 pm while colleagues and others were still in the pub. The dark side of a tradition was brought blisteringly to the fore in 2019 by a Bloomberg investigation exposing the culture of hard drinking and misogyny. Neal has set about stamping out booziness and bringing in a policy to exclude those under the influence of drink and drugs.

'I have tried to create the belief that the Market wants to be inclusive and therefore the best talent will want to come and work at Lloyd's.' About 25% of women are in leadership positions and in terms of the gender balance in the workforce it is 50:50.

Finally, Neal has been zealously sounding the alarm about the Capital's lack of competitiveness. London was the gateway for America to Europe and the rest of the world. Neal says 'there is a bit to do' to ensure London remains one of the three main financial services markets in the world.

The author, Edmund Lester, found it quite astonishing to read that, after Ernest Moore's policy statement in December 1991, his message had not gone viral and alcohol-related issues still plague Lloyd's.

Ode to the Committee of the Syndicate 334 (1985) Names Association

Author's note: after reading the book, read the Ode aloud and the characters come alive!

Could this story have been Shakespearian
with losses so great they're wearyin'?
Clive pursued his clear vision
most ardently, with high precision.

Baron of Louth fixed the syst*i*ms
so sweetly ran, all the admins.
Ray inspected every penny,
and ensured there were very many.

The financials could have been much worse
Except, the Treasurer held the purse.
Harry 'per ardua' of many hours,
took time to 'add akers', in showers.

Alasdair's analysis of extensive schedules
laid bare others' wrongs, and their scruples.
Adam Raphael came and went
following his journalistic bent.

Legal skills were needed most.
Sadly, Jasper's intellect was lost.
However, David gave us good advice, you see,
a judge was convinced, by Nicholas Strauss QC.

We won our case; and David Rowland at slow pace
mutualised the marketplace.
Guy finally wrapped it up, quite true
without too much more ado.

These few lines, all but one,
were seemingly written by 'Anon'.

E. A. K. L., 11.10.2023

Timeline

Past centuries	Asbestos mining for thousands of years.
1940s & 1950s	Increasing number of claims on past policies received by Lloyd's.
1980s	Estimated value of claims incurred but not reported (IBNR) became unquantifiable.
1985	Syndicate 334 1985 year of account due to close on 31 December 1987 was left open.
1988–89	Syndicate 334 claims arising became unquantifiable.
1990	Huge cash calls demanded of Syndicate 334 Names.
6 Jun 1990	A number of Syndicate 334 Names met to challenge the validity of the cash calls.
16 Jul 1990	First Steering Committee. Meeting formed to take legal action.
16 Aug 1990	Second Steering Committee. Agreement in principle to form an Association.
26 Sep 1990	Third Steering Committee. Standing for election to Lloyd's Council.
15 Oct 1990	Newsletter. Legal strategy and communication considerations.
16 Nov 1990	Fourth Steering Committee. Inadvertent libel.
10 Dec 1990	Fifth Steering Committee. Syndicate 90 issues, elaboration of circumstances.
16 Jan 1991	Sixth Steering Committee. Inflicting commercial damage. Rules for an Association.
13 Mar 1991	Seventh Steering Committee. Dodgy secret internal reinsurance arrangements.

1 May 1991	Eighth Steering Committee. Withdrawal from Merrett Syndicates. Jonathan Gaisman QC gives his Opinion.
15 Jun 1991	Newsletter. AGM notice.
19 Jul 1991	Ninth Steering Committee. Lack of control at Lloyd's. AGM strategy.
15 Aug 1991	Newsletter. Association Membership still open for new Members.
18 Sep 1991	Tenth Steering Committee. Unfair distribution of losses. Raising Funds and dealing with distressful stories.
3 Dec 1991	Eleventh Steering Committee. Syndicate 334 losses might rise to £50 million.
15 Dec 1991	Newsletter. The Association's strong, simple case. Cox & Bell dispute.
15 Jan 1992	Newsletter. Settlement of Outhwaite and Warrilow cases stimulates hope.
25 Feb 1992	Twelfth Steering Committee. Shocking increase in losses. Discovery had to precede the request for a court hearing date.
13 Apr 1992	Thirteenth Steering Committee. Concerns about collapse of Lloyd's.
2 Jun 1992	Fourteenth Steering Committee. Standard & Poors downgrade. 10,000 insolvent Names and another 8,000 to follow.
3 Jul 1992	First Annual General Meeting. Discovery requirements and possible court dates.
22 Sep 1992	Fifteenth Steering Committee. An unacceptable offer.
2 Dec 1992	Sixteenth Steering Committee. Inklings of hope. Problems in finding a judge and a date in court.
15 Jan 1993	Newsletter. Asbestosis history and issues coming to light.
4 Mar 1993	Seventeenth Steering Committee. Fear of impending meltdown of Lloyd's.
26 May 1993	Eighteenth Steering Committee. Nineteen judges required? Mr Justice Saville informs about the shortage of judges.

15 Jul 1993	Nineteenth Steering Committee. No excuses from lawyers. Lloyd's business plan considerations.
15 Aug 1993	Newsletter. Determining trials for court.
31 Aug 1993	Newsletter No. 2. Kerr Panel issues.
9 Sep 1993	Second AGM. Stephen Merrett resignation as Deputy Chairman of Lloyd's.
17 Sep 1993	Newsletter. At Special General Meeting bylaw resolutions passed.
15 Nov 1993	Newsletter. Counsel, Nicholas Strauss QC.
15 Dec 1993	Newsletter. Rejection of the Lloyd's settlement offer.
22 Dec 1993	Twentieth Steering Committee. Mr Justice Cresswell involvement.
13 Jan 1994	Twenty-First Steering Committee. Strengthening funding. A 6% levy proposed.
15 Jan 1994	Newsletter. Ballot for 6% levy.
10 Feb 1994	Twenty-Second Steering Committee. Presentation of a strong case by Nicholas Strauss QC.
15 Feb 1994	Newsletter. Appointment at court timing.
15 Mar 1994	Newsletter. Judge retired to consider his judgement. Judgement expected in seven weeks?
15 May 1994	Newsletter. Power politics. Vicarious responsibility judgement awaited.
15 Aug 1994	Newsletter. An anxious wait for a judgement.
15 Sep 1994	Newsletter. Still waiting for judgement, still fairly imminent.
15 Oct 1994	Newsletter. Dates for submissions.
31 Oct 1994	Newsletter No. 2. Disappointment, anxiety and irritation in slippage of judgement.
15 Nov 1994	Newsletter. Mr Justice Potter will be taking over the Commercial Court.
18 Dec 1994	Newsletter. Judgement delayed due to pressure of work.
15 Jan 1995	Newsletter. Premiums Trust Deed proposals.
19 Jan 1995	Twenty-Third Steering Committee. Approach to be made to the judge.

10 Feb 1995   Newsletter. Judgement favours the brave.

24 Feb 1995   Twenty-Fourth Steering Committee. Nicholas Strauss QC retained for further legal action.

15 Mar 1995   Twenty-Fifth Steering Committee, Third AGM, SGM. Approval of Special Resolutions for Committee remuneration.

15 Apr 1995   Newsletter. Delays due to appeals.

2 May 1995   Twenty-Sixth Steering Committee. Preparing for an appeal by the Association.

12 Jun 1995   Twenty-Seventh Steering Committee. Committee remuneration considerations.

12 Jun 1995   Newsletter. Slow progress on interim payment award.

15 Jul 1995   Non-newsletter. No news about the interim payment.

2 Aug 1995   Twenty-Eighth Steering Committee. Winnings to be held in escrow.

15 Aug 1995   Newsletter No 1. Premiums Trust Deeds considerations.

30 Aug 1995   Newsletter No 2. Amended Rules of the Association.

21 Sep 1995   Twenty-Ninth Steering Committee. Revelations of concealment.

2 Nov 1995   Thirtieth Steering Committee. Dealing with actual and prospective receipts.

15 Dec 1995   Newsletter. Errors & omissions underwriters refuse to pay up.

23 Jan 1996   Thirty-first Steering Committee. Winding-up Pulbrook Underwriting Management Ltd.

30 Jan 1996   Newsletter. Winding up granted.

16 Feb 1996   Thirty-Second Steering Committee. Dealings with the Official Receiver.

15 Mar 1996   Newsletter. Funding and life expectancy of Equitas.

20 Mar 1996   Thirty-Third Steering Committee. Distribution of indicative statements.

24 Apr 1996   Thirty-Fourth Steering Committee. Financial housekeeping matters.

15 May 1996	Newsletter. Questionnaire response.
28 May 1996	Thirty-Fifth Steering Committee. Members' Compensation Scheme amended.
9 Jul 1996	Thirty-Sixth Steering Committee. Response to remunerate Committee Members.
9 Jul 1996	Special General Meeting. Resolutions on remuneration passed.
6 Aug 1996	Thirty-Seventh Steering Committee. Considering of Action Group Settlement Agreement.
15 Aug 1996	Newsletter. Approval of Action Group Settlement Agreement.
15 Sep 1996	Newsletter. Settlement Offer unconditional.
22 Oct 1996	Thirty-Eighth Steering Committee. Halifax bonus on moving to a bank.
22 Oct 1996	Fourth AGM. Housekeeping matters and appointments.
11 Dec 1996	Thirty-Ninth Steering Committee. Calculations of final costs to closing the Association.
20 Feb 1997	Fortieth Steering Committee. All legal actions discontinued.
15 Mar 1997	Newsletter. Rejectees of the settlement offer are the weakest Names.
17 Apr 1997	Forty-First Steering Committee. Financial statements and Halifax bonus.
2 Jun 1997	Forty-Second Steering Committee. Association's objects completed.
15 June 1997	Newsletter. Dissolution.
10 July 1997	Forty-Third Steering Committee. Goodbye.

Guide to Terminology

Action Group Settlement Agreement: Agreement implementing Reconstruction and Renewal proposals.

Active underwriter: A Working Name employed by a syndicate to accept or reject risks.

Agency: An intermediary acting on behalf of Names or syndicates.

APH: Asbestos, pollution and health hazard.

Arbitrators: Persons appointed by parties to resolve a dispute.

Asbestos: Comprising several minerals that may separate into long, flexible fibres. It is a magnesium silicate and the fibrous form of the mineral serpentine.

Asbestosis: Cancerous disease, also called mesothelioma, that damages human health caused by exposure to a naturally occurring fibrous silicate mineral called asbestos.

Asbestos Working Party (AWP): Committee set up to monitor asbestos claims.

Assisted Name: Name at Lloyd's allowed to underwrite, supported by a guarantee or assets of their employer.

Association: The Syndicate 334 (1985) Names Association, consisting of Syndicate 334 Names, also referred to in the text as Members, being co-plaintiffs joining together to pursue an action for compensation, and managed by a Committee.

Baby syndicate: A syndicate with a few members who were senior Names at Lloyds that underwrote highly profitable business.

Bodily injury – negligence: A form of insurance policy; asbestosis is an example of bodily injury.

Broker: The intermediary between a client and the Lloyd's Market.

Box: The underwriter's desk at Lloyd's, large enough to seat a few people.

Bylaws: Rules made by Lloyd's Council.

Capacity: Maximum value (the turnover) supported by Names that could be underwritten. Lloyd's capacity was the total of all syndicates' capacities.

Capital gain: The profit on sale of assets is called a capital gain. Usually, a capital gain was made but sometimes there was a loss: a capital loss. When there was a loss on trading (premiums less expenses) losses could be set off against other income for tax purposes.

Carry back: HM Inspector of Taxes allowed losses to be used against income in earlier years.

Cash call: At the end of a trading period the result may be a loss and the loss is due and payable to the syndicate. This is payable through the Members' Agent and is known as a cash call.

Central Fund or Central Guarantee Fund: Names paid a subscription to enable the Council to fund Names' unpaid calls.

CentreWrite: An organisation renamed Equitas, formed to provide support for mutualising exceptional losses.

CEO: Chief Executive Officer, e.g., Alan Lord, Peter Middleton, Ron Sandler and John Neal.

Chatset: Consulting firm for measuring syndicate performance run by John Rew and Charles Sturge as joint editors.

Claim: Policyholder who incurs a loss seeks recompense from the insurer.

Collateralised reinsurance: Market underwriters create a trust account for participants at inception of a contract term to take on reinsurance risks.

Council of Lloyd's: The governing body of the Society of Lloyd's.

Counsel: Barrister or other legal advisor providing a professional Opinion on a matter of law.

Cover: Arrangement subject to the terms of an insurance policy, under which a syndicate undertakes to pay to the beneficiary the admissible benefits in respect of an insured, on the happening of specified events in the policy.

Debt credit: Amount allocated to each Name following the division of assets under Reconstruction and Renewal.

Deductible: Amount of money an insured is responsible for paying towards an insured loss.

DES (diethylstilbestrol or diethylstilboestrol): Synthetic form of oestrogen prescribed to pregnant women giving rise to an increased cancer risk for their daughters and other long-term issues.

Discovery: Compulsory disclosure, by one party to an action to another, of relevant testimony or documents.

D J Freeman solicitors: Employer of Dr David Tiplady and Mark Everiss.

EGM: Extraordinary General Meeting. A meeting of members of an enterprise; not an Annual General Meeting.

Errors and omissions policy (E&O): Insurance policy covering professional liability and negligence, for example.

Escrow: Assets held by solicitors on behalf of others.

Estate protection plan (EPP): Insurance policy that covers underwriting losses incurred by a deceased.

Excess of Loss: Insurance policy which covers losses above a prescribed limit.

External Name: Underwriting member of Lloyd's providing capital for, but not employed by, a syndicate.

Fax: A copy produced by a facsimile or telefacsimile machine used for transmitting information, which came into use during the 1980s.

FCA: Fellow of the Institute of Chartered Accountants in England and Wales.

FRD: Financial Recovery Department at Lloyd's.

Garage or park: Terms for holding premiums temporarily.

Hardship: Names unable to pay their calls could apply to the Hardship Committee which agreed financial arrangements preventing bankrupt Names from becoming destitute.

HM Inspector of Taxes: The United Kingdom's Inland Revenue service.

Income limit: The total amount of premiums the Name is permitted to underwrite.

Incurred but not reported (IBNR): Estimated amount to be provided for likely claims not yet notified at the end of a financial three-year period.

Insider: A person working in the Market with privileged sensitive information not generally available to Names.

Insurance: Arrangement by a syndicate or company providing a guarantee of compensation for a specified loss in return for a premium.

Laid off, or lay off: Reducing risk by passing some or all of it to another party.

Layers: Dividing insurance cover for potential loss into bands with an agreed spread between different levels of loss. Demonstrating the development of layers: up to £1 million is paid by the client as an excess, the insured layers then step up as £1 million excess of £1 million (total cover £2 million), £3 million excess of £2 million (total cover £5 million), £5 million excess of £5 million (total cover £10 million) and the top-layer £10 million excess of £10 million (total cover now £20 million). Above £20 million the loss is uninsured and falls on the client.

Lien: Right to keep possession of property belonging to another person until a debt due from that person has been settled.

Line: The proportion of risk an underwriter agrees to insure.

Litigating Names Committee: A group of Names taking legal action.

Litigation Settlement Fund: Fund set up under Reconstruction and Renewal to settle litigation.

Lloyd's Central Services Unit (CSU), or Lloyd's Central: Comprehensive database of Market, syndicate and Names' information.

Lloyd's Defence Shield: An umbrella organisation sponsored by the Super Group.

Lloyd's Names Association Working Party (LNAWP), or Super Group: Comprised of Action Group Chairmen.

LMX, London Market Excess of Loss: Lloyd's syndicates and insurance companies providing cover for single risk accumulations and pure catastrophe covers, for example.

Lloyd's settlement offer (LSO): Unacceptable plan to resolve the legal action.

Long-tail risk: The length of time, say, in excess of three years, between a policy being written and a valid claim causing incident which may arise many years later.

MAP: Modified arbitration procedure where the parties agree to change a procedure.

Marine: Risks associated with ships and associated activities.

Market: Lloyd's syndicates collectively trading insurance business (other markets: companies authorised to conduct insurance business outside Lloyd's).

Means: An individual's assets recorded by Lloyd's to support a Name's underwriting.

Mesothelioma: Another name for asbestosis.

Member of Lloyd's: Also known as a Name at Lloyd's. (See also **Association** for Members of Syndicate 334.)

MP: Member of Parliament.

Name: Member of Lloyd's providing capital, accepting unlimited liability and authorised to conduct insurance business as a member of a Syndicate.

Neill report: 1987 report by Sir Patrick Neill QC on regulation at Lloyd's.

Names' Individual Action Group: For pooling resources to achieve massive savings in time and lawyers' fees.

Non-marine: Business other than marine underwriting, for example, non-marine business including motor, aviation and life assurance underwriting conducted at Lloyd's.

Off-balance sheet: Financial arrangements for assets and liabilities properly attributable to a syndicate not included in the syndicate's balance sheet thus changing the syndicate's risk profile.

Offshore: Business conducted and balances held outside the UK jurisdiction.

Open year: Either one of the first two years of account, or one for which the IBNR cannot be satisfactorily estimated.

Opinion: A written view on a matter of law provided by a barrister or similarly qualified professional.

Orphan syndicate: Syndicate that cannot be closed because there is no successor syndicate.

Park or garage: Terms for holding premiums temporarily.

Personal stop-loss: Stop-loss policy attributable to a Name.

Placed: When an insurance policy slip is agreed, dated and signed by underwriters.

Pleading: A written presentation by a litigant in a lawsuit setting out the facts and contentions is relied on in a claim against another party to a legal remedy or which he relies on in his or her defence to a claim against him or her by another party.

Policy: A legal contract between the insurer and policyholder that provides the rules determining the criteria for a valid claim.

Pre-emption rights: First option to buy or acquire an asset before it can be offered to any other person or entity.

Premium: Consideration paid by an insured to an insurer.

Premium limit, or premium income limit: Maximum amount of premium a Name was authorised to underwrite expressed in sterling, also called the total line. It is restricted by the value of the means a Name showed to, and is accepted by Lloyd's.

Premiums Trust Deeds (PTD): Documents containing rules for controlling the Premiums Trust Fund.

Premiums Trust Fund (PTF): Receiving premiums on behalf of Names and paying out claims and profits.

Product liability – negligence: Types of insurance policy.

Proxy: Person who is given the power to do something, such as vote, on behalf of someone else.

Quantum: How much, amount.

Queen's Counsel (QC): Barrister or solicitor advocates recognised for excellence in advocacy, leaders in their area of law, taking on complex cases requiring a high level of legal expertise. Since the 2022 accession of King Charles III, they are titled King's Counsel (KC).

Reconstruction and Renewal: The Market mutualisation plan to settle syndicate legal disputes.

Refuseniks: Names refusing the settlement offer under Reconstruction and Renewal.

Reinsurance: Laying off some of a risk to another party.

Reinsurance to close (RITC): The estimated sum to be passed to next year's syndicate and intended to have a zero effect on that syndicate's year's profitability.

Reserving: Making provisions for liabilities known or unknown.

Retrocession: A policy in which a reinsurer lays off part or all of a risk with another reinsurer.

Risk: Anything that threatens a commercial business, preventing it from achieving its financial goals.

Rollover: Reinvesting funds from a security that has reached its maturity term into a new issue of a similar security.

Run-off: Winding up a syndicate. Managing incurred or possible claims.

Short-tail risks: Insurance policies where claims arise during the period of cover or shortly after the policy has expired.

Silk: Barristers are said to have 'taken silk' or 'received silk' and become 'Silks' when their outstanding ability has been recognised by appointment as Queen's Counsel (QC) or, since the accession of King Charles III, King's Counsel (KC).

Slip: Document prepared by a broker describing the risks to be covered and presented to a Syndicate underwriter to initial the percentage of risk the syndicate is prepared to accept.

Society of Lloyd's: Comprising all those who work in or are associated with the Lloyd's Market.

Solvency: Ability of a syndicate and Lloyd's overall, to meet long-term debts and other financial obligations.

Standstill agreement: An agreement which has the effect of suspending or extending a statutory or contractual limitation period.

Statutory Statement of Business: Lloyd's Statutory Statement of Business required by the Lloyd's Act 1982.

Stop-loss: Insurance policy to reduce a loss incurred by a Name.

Successor syndicate: Each calendar year a syndicate may have different participants from the previous and the following one but the business was continuous; consequently arrangements have to be made for the syndicate in the following year to continue with the business. The subsequent syndicate was called a successor syndicate.

Super Group: Lloyd's Names Association Working Party (LNAWP) Members were Action Group Chairmen.

Suspension: Name who had not paid calls and was required to cease underwriting.

Syndicate: Association of Names trading as individuals. Collectively able to receive premiums from clients in return for providing a policy underwriting risks covering potential loss for the client and paying valid claims.

Syndicate Underwriting Management Ltd (SUM): A company formed to manage unclosed run-off syndicates.

Syndicate 90: Included Syndicate 82.

Syndicate 334: Included Syndicate 85.

Tax benefit transfer: A scheme for avoiding taxation and disallowed by HMIT.

Taxing of legal costs: Determining fair and reasonable costs of solicitor's bills by a court official called a Taxing Master.

Telex: International system of telegraphy with printed messages transmitted and received by teleprinters using the public telecommunications network.

Time and distance policy: Policy maturing at some future date and matching expected cash flow requirements for claims.

Tort: Civil wrong that causes a claimant to suffer loss or harm, resulting in legal liability for the person who commits the wrong.

Trust Fund: Assets belonging to a trust held by trustees on behalf of beneficiaries.

Twelfth Floor: The executive suite at the top of the iconic Lloyd's building.

***Uberrima fides*, utmost good faith:** Contractual legal doctrine that requires parties to act honestly, not to mislead or withhold any information that is essential to the contract, and to make a full declaration of all material facts in an insurance proposal.

Underwriter: A person, business or company that accepts an insurance risk.

Underwriting: Signing and accepting liability under an insurance policy guaranteeing compensation in case of loss or damage.

Value-added tax (VAT): Tax added to the cost of goods and services.

Vicarious liability: Liability in law for the actions of another person – for example, the liability an employer may have for the negligent act of an employee.

Willis Faber & Dumas (Agencies) Ltd (WFDA): A Names' Managing Agent.

Working Name: A Name employed in the Lloyd's Market.

Year of account: A calendar-year account of a syndicate.

Extracts from Sir Adam Ridley's 1995 Names' Committee Interim Report

Chairman Sir Adam Ridley
20 November 1995

Communication

Sir Adam said that the interim report is a work in progress as a contribution to the process of guidance and information for Names. The Committee is comprised of twelve members representing a wide range of interests and expertise.

Report Structure

The six parts to the report includes a summary and a background to the Names' Committee. The remaining sections are: meeting the cost of Equitas, allocation of debt credits, allocation of the Litigation Settlement Fund and issues in achieving an acceptable finality.

1. Summary

The task of the Names' Committee is to advise the Council on the allocation of the settlement offer proposed in Lloyd's Reconstruction and Renewal comprising an estimated £2 billion of debt credits and £800 million of the Litigation Settlement Fund. There are three objectives: to assist Names to achieve finality, help the hardest-hit Names and settle litigation.

The Committee has tested alternative allocations of the settlement funds to find the fairest distribution and the majority of Names would have sufficient funds to meet the finality bills from Equitas. However, with only £2.8 billion it is unlikely that the objectives would be achieved without additional funds.

2. Background

The Names' Committee was formed in July 1995. By the end of October, the Committee had received 250 letters, held sixteen lengthy meetings and reported four times to Council and used Lloyd's Central Services Unit (CSU) comprehensive database. The database held information about 34,000 Names and participation in syndicates over the past ten years. Details of outstanding cash calls, uncalled losses and other information needed for modelling fund allocation. There was no information about Names assets held outside Lloyd's and no comment on whether Names' could meet their finality bills.

3. Meeting the Cost of Equitas

In Reconstruction and Renewal, the outstanding cost to finality is estimated to be £5.9 billion. The funding can be expressed as a finality bill as follows.

Unit		£ billion
Receivables from Names		5.9
Settlement fund	-2.8	
Triple profit release	-0.8	-3.6
Payments to Names in surplus		0.2
Leaving: finality bill		2.5
Funded by:		
Drawdowns of Names' funds at Lloyd's	-1.5	
Payments from Names in deficit (new money)	-0.6	-2.1
Names' residual receivables*		0.4

*Residual receivables are doubtful debts unlikely to be received.

The figures remain subject to change while the cost of reinsuring 728 syndicate years into Equitas is undetermined.

4. *Allocation of Debt Credits*

The task is to assist those who have suffered disproportionally large losses and may have the greatest difficulty in meeting their 'finality bills'. Principles of fairness are considered and the definition of 'disproportionately large losses'.

All Names should be eligible for debt credits.

Debt credits should not be used to compensate for normal commercial losses.

The allocation should be defined in proportion to a Name's overall underwriting experience over a number of years.

The disproportionate loss should be defined in relation to a Name's Premium Income Limit.

For 1986 and 1987 are years in which Names generally made profits but Members' Agents failed to keep accurate records. It is estimated that a Names' overall loss amounted to 100% of the Premium Income Limit (PIL).

The gross loss will be reduced by E&O payments to Names who are litigating against Agents. There is an element of 'double count' reducing the loss to 94% of PIL. Settlement of litigation and finality requires personal stop-loss (PSL) and Estate protection plan (EPP) reserves to be considered. However, the Committee has no information about a Name's tax position and potential amount of tax relief.

Schedules of the range of profit and loss Names experience by banding have been produced, e.g., loss £0–£200,000, £200,000–£400,000, etc. These show the number of Names per band and the projection after distribution to finality as a percentage of PIL.

The main conclusion is that it would cost £2.3 billion at 80% of average Names' PIL to provide a comprehensive cap for the losses. Even so, Names would require additional help to meet their finality bills.

Alternatives have been considered and discarded. One alternative would be to pay all Names an equal amount such as £60,000. This would not help the hardest-hit Names and would leave about £2 billion of unsecured debt. Merging the £2 billion debt credit fund and the £800 million

Litigation Settlement Fund would eliminate the distinction between litigants and non-litigants. It would leave some litigants with less than they had already won in court and is unlikely to achieve the objective of settling litigation.

The proposal is to allocate debt credits in three tranches.

- <u>Tranche 1</u> allocates debt credits as far as possible pro-rata to a Name's cumulative net loss as a % of their PIL over a standard threshold measured as a % of each Name's own average PIL.
- <u>Tranche 2</u> allocates debt credits to those who, after they had used some or all of their funds at Lloyd's, are still likely to have difficulty in meeting their finality bills because of the scale of their Equitas bills, uncalled losses and unpaid calls.
- <u>Tranche 3</u> could provide a reserve to assist the hardest-hit Names who demonstrate inability to pay even after the first and second allocations.

Modelling suggested that 20% will have no finality bill. Over 50% will be able to meet their finality bills from some or all of their funds at Lloyd's. Around 30% would have a finality bill greater than their funds at Lloyd's. The Committee hopes it will be possible to cap these bills at a figure that exceeds their funds at Lloyd's by a relatively modest sum.

5. Allocation of Litigation Settlement Fund

By definition, Names with disproportionately large losses are members of one or more syndicates with disproportionately large losses and some but not all are the subject of litigation. 728 syndicate years are to be reinsured into Equitas of which 151 will have lost 100% of capacity at finality. Serious litigation was concentrated on seventy syndicate years with losses estimated at £6.6 billion. In short less than 10% of the syndicate years closing into Equitas will be responsible for 60% of the overall loss.

There are now 13,600 active litigants among the 34,100 Names being 40% of the total. A table has been produced analysing the breakdown across bands of loss showing the numbers of litigating and non-litigating Names. The average expected loss for a litigating Name is £480,000 but only £190,000 for non-litigants.

The Committee believes the litigation fund should only be allocated to litigants. The definition of 'active litigant' covered syndicates-specific action groups, their active members and the years to which their claims relate, but also to those litigating individually; and those arbitrating individually or in a group. The Committee is very concerned that the £800 million litigation fund may be insufficient to settle the growing mass of litigation threatening the Society.

6. Issues in Achieving an Acceptable Finality

All sections of the Lloyd's community are deeply involved and need to achieve consensus. There may be a contribution from the auditors otherwise there is unlikely to be assistance from outside the Society.

The consistent message from Names with which the Committee concurs is not to reward the 'won't pays'. Distinguishing 'can't pays' from 'won't pays' requires a detailed examination of individuals' circumstances about which the Committee has no information.

Important facts about unpaid calls includes £1.5 billion still outstanding and 13,500 Names with unpaid calls. 1,500 Names have accepted an offer of hardship and many more are in discussion. About half the Names with unpaid calls are litigating and have a claim to offset their losses.

About 6,000 Names will have a surplus on their finality bill after the release of profits from the 1993 account. They will receive a cash payment. The Committee proposes that litigation subscriptions will be paid in cash. Debt credits will not provide cash payments but can only be used to extinguish the finality bill debt. About 8,000 Names who are no longer underwriting and have met the finality bill can leave the Society and withdraw the balance of their funds.

There is a commentary on tax efficiency, but it shows only limited relief for those who have ceased trading.

Rules of the Syndicate 334 (1985) Names Association

Issued August 1995

Second Edition

Incorporating the amendments adopted at the General Meetings of the Association of 1993 and 1995.

Name and Address

The name of the Association is 'the Syndicate 334 1985 Names Association'.

The address of the Association shall be c/o Louth Secretarial Services, Louth, Lincolnshire

Objects and Powers

2.1 The objects of the Association are the co-ordination, financing and prosecution of claims of members of the Association for compensation for losses suffered as a result of being members of the Syndicate for the 1985 Year of Account and to make provision for the apportionment of such compensation between the members of the Association and its subsequent distribution to them.

2.2 The Association by its Committee shall have power to do anything which in the opinion of the Committee is calculated to facilitate, or is conducive or incidental to, the achievement of the objects of the Association.

Membership

3.1 Any person who is alleged to be liable as a member of the Syndicate in respect of the 1985 Year of Account (or the legal personal representatives of such a person) shall be eligible to be a member.

3.2 Subject to Rule 3.3 an eligible person who wishes to become or remain a member shall submit to the Secretary a signed application in the form set out in Schedule 2 to these Rules together with the Initial Subscription (where not already paid) and the first instalment of the Litigation Subscription.

3.3 Where an application for membership is received by the Secretary after the Minimum Participation Date the applicant shall if required by the Committee pay to the Association (in addition to any subscription payable under Rule 3.2) such additional legal costs and disbursements (if any) as the Association's Solicitors shall having notified the Committee in writing of the same require to give effect to such applicant's participation in any Authorised Proceedings including (but not limited to) the costs of amending any proceedings issued and served prior to such application or of issuing and serving further proceedings as a result of the same.

3.4 When an application for membership is received by the Secretary after the Closing Date, the Committee may at its discretion impose such additional terms and conditions as it considers necessary and such application shall only take effect subject to the same.

3.5 The Committee may refuse to admit to membership any person whose membership would in its opinion be injurious to the interests of the Association.

Basic Obligations of Membership

4.1 On and by virtue of admission to membership:

   (1) grants irrevocable authority to the Association and to the Association's Solicitors in relation to any proceedings which the Committee having obtained the advice of the Association's

Solicitors shall deem expedient for the purpose of achieving the objects of the Association.

(i) to commence such proceedings in his name (whether alone or jointly with others and whether in the United Kingdom or elsewhere);

(ii) to carry on and prosecute such proceedings to judgement and execution of judgement or (where appropriate) make application to a superior court for leave to appeal against such judgement and subject to Rule 5.2 to initiate appeal proceedings in respect thereof or to resist any appeal against such judgement;

(iii) to settle, discontinue or otherwise compromise such proceedings.

(2) grants irrevocable and exclusive authority to the Association and the Association's Solicitors to conduct on his behalf any negotiations and agree any settlement which the Committee having obtained the advice of the Association's Solicitors shall deem expedient for the purpose of achieving the objects of the Association;

(3) grants an irrevocable authority to the Association to give a good receipt in respect of any Recoveries and to apply the same in the manner provided for by these Rules;

(4) agrees with the Association to furnish the Association and the Association's Solicitors with all such cooperation and assistance as may reasonably be required in connection with the successful prosecution of any Authorised Proceedings and (without prejudice to the generality of the foregoing) shall comply at the member's own cost and expense with any request made by the Association's Solicitors to the member to produce and deliver to them documents in custody, possession or power of such member where such request is made for the purposes of complying with any obligation in relation to Discovery in or in connection with Authorised Proceedings.

(5) agrees to indemnify the Committee and each of its members for the time being in respect of all liabilities incurred by them or any of them in exercise or purported exercise of their powers under these Rules so far as such liabilities cannot be discharged out of the Association's funds;

(6) waives all rights which he may have against any member of the Committee resulting from the exercise or purported exercise by the Committee or any of its members of any of their powers under these Rules, save to the extent that such exercise or purported exercise is or subsequently proves to be unlawful; and

(7) agrees to execute such document or documents confirming all or any of the foregoing matters as the Committee may from time to time require.

4.2 If in the opinion of the Committee any member is for the time being in breach of any of the foregoing agreements the Committee may declare him to be Defaulting member.

Appeal Proceedings

5.1 If any Authorised Proceedings shall give rise to a right of appeal, or leave to appeal shall have been granted in respect of the same by a superior court or appeal proceedings have been commenced against any judgement in favour of any member of the Association, then the Committee having taken the written advice of the Association's Solicitors and Counsel on the merits of commencing appeal proceedings (or where appropriate resisting such proceedings):

(1) shall circulate such advice to all members of the Association;

(2) may at its discretion initiate (or where appropriate resist) such proceedings; and

(3) shall, in the event that it decides to initiate (or where appropriate resist) the same, convene a Special General Meeting as soon as possible thereafter to determine whether or not such appeal proceedings shall be continued (or where appropriate resisted) by the Association.

5.2 Where appeal proceedings have been initiated such proceedings may be continued (or where appropriate resisted) only if a Special General Meeting convened pursuant to that Rule shall by a simple majority of those present and voting have passed a resolution to that effect.

5.3 Where the Committee is empowered under Rule 5.2 to act in relation to appeal proceedings, any member not wishing to participate in such proceedings must give written notice to that effect to the Secretary within seven days of the meeting and may thereafter be declared a Defaulting member of the Committee.

5.4 Subject to Rule 5.2 above Rule 4.1 shall apply to any appeal proceedings.

Subscriptions and Finance

6.1 Subscriptions shall be as follows:

The Initial Subscription of each member shall be the sum of £250.00, and

(i) The Litigation Subscription shall be 10% of line written by the member on the Syndicate in the Year of Account to be paid in the following manner.

(ii) A first instalment of 1% of the said line by the minimum participation date (28.2.91).

(iii) A second instalment of 3% of the said line not later than six months after the minimum participation date.

(iv) A third instalment of the said line not later than twelve months after the minimum participation date.

(v) A fourth instalment of 2% of the said line not later than eighteen months after the minimum participation date.

(vi) A fifth instalment of 2% of the said line not later than two years after the minimum participation date.

6.2 If in the opinion of the Committee it is desirable that further sums be raised for any purposes the Committee may subject to Rule 6.3 below raise the same by levying an additional subscription or subscriptions.

6.3 Any additional subscription levied under Rule 6.2 (but not one required by Rule 8) must be supported by either:

 (1) a resolution to that effect passed by two-thirds of those present and voting at a General Meeting; or

 (2) if such a ballot is held in accordance with Rule 18, a majority of the votes cast in a Postal Ballot.

6.4 Subscriptions shall always be calculated as a percentage of line written on the Syndicate in the Year of Account.

6.5 Any additional subscription or subscriptions shall become due within thirty days of written notice thereof being given to members.

6.6 If a member fails to pay any subscription by the due date the Committee may declare him a Defaulting member.

6.7 In relation to any application for membership the Committee may at its discretion postpone or waive payment of the whole or any part of a subscription (including the initial Subscription) if following a detailed investigation of the applicant's means it is satisfied that not to do so would cause extreme financial hardship to the applicant.

7.1 The Association shall maintain an account at a bank (to be selected from time to time by the Committee) into which subscriptions and other receipts of the Association shall be paid and the signatures of any two Officers of the Association shall be sufficient for the operation of the account. Money not for the time being required for the purposes of the Association shall be placed on deposit with such financial institution which, in the judgement of the Committee, shall be of first-class security.

7.2 The Treasurer shall be responsible (under the supervision of the Committee) for the management of the finances of the Association. The Treasurer shall cause accounts to be prepared and audited in respect of each year and such accounts shall be laid before the Annual General Meeting in the following year.

7.3 The Association's auditors shall until the first Annual General Meeting be appointed by the Committee and thereafter appointed by the Association.

8   If as a result of or in connection with Authorised Proceedings any member becomes liable to pay the costs of any other party thereto the liability will be met out of the funds for the time being held by the Association. In the event of there being insufficient funds for the purpose, the Committee shall levy an additional subscription or subscriptions to meet the deficiency.

Recoveries

9   Recoveries shall be held by the Association upon trust to apply the same as follows and in the following order:

(1) in paying or providing for the payment of any outstanding liabilities, costs or expenses of the Association;

(2) in repaying to each member, the Subscription paid by such member; and

(3) subject thereto and provided that the Committee with the approval of a General Meeting shall not decide otherwise by distributing the balance to members (other than Defaulting members) in proportion to the line written by each Member on the Syndicate in the Year of Account.

Officers and Committee

10.1 The Officers of the Association shall be a Chairman, a Treasurer and a Secretary.

10.2 Until the close of the first Annual General Meeting (when they shall retire) the Committee shall consist of the persons specified in Schedule 1 together with up to two further co-opted members. Not more than two members of the Committee may be persons who are not themselves members of the Association.

10.3 The Committee shall consist of not more than ten persons (of whom not more than two may be persons not themselves members of the Association). The members of the Committee shall be elected at the Annual General Meeting and shall hold office from the close of that meeting until the close of the next Annual General Meeting. The

Officers shall be elected by the Committee at its first meeting follow-ing each Annual General Meeting. The Committee may at any time co-opt additional members, subject to the limitations aforesaid.

10.4 Nominations for election of any person as a member of the Committee may be made by the Committee or by written notice given by twelve members of the Association and signed by the candidate. Nominations other than those made by the Committee shall be delivered to the Secretary not less than seven days before the Annual General Meeting. Retiring members of the Committee shall be eligible for re-election. Nominations made by the Committee shall be dealt with in accordance with Rule 12.4.

10.5 In the event of the number of nominations for election to the Committee exceeding the number of vacancies, the Chairman shall announce this at the Annual General Meeting and (unless the Annual General Meeting shall, with the consent of all candidates, decide otherwise) the Committee shall arrange a Postal Ballot of all members to be conducted by single transferrable vote. Such election shall be completed within twenty-eight days of the Annual General Meeting in accordance with detailed rules to be decided by the Committee, who shall remain in office until completion of such election.

Committee Powers and Meetings

11.1 So far as not otherwise provided in these Rules and subject to any directions which may be given by a resolution of the Association in General Meeting the affairs of the Association shall be controlled and directed by the Committee which shall have an absolute discre-tion as to the manner of exercise of the powers vested in it on behalf of the Association provided that unless the Committee see special reason to the contrary the Committee shall not commence any Authorised Proceedings unless reasonably satisfied that the funds of the Association are sufficient to defray the costs of such proceedings and any costs in connection therewith for which any member might become liable.

11.2 The Chairman of the Association shall take the chair at any meeting of the Committee. In the absence of the Chairman the members present at the meeting shall elect a chairman. In the event that the votes of the Committee on any matter shall be tied, the Chairman shall have the casting vote.

11.3 The quorum at any meeting of the Committee shall be four.

11.4 The meetings of the Committee shall be convened at such time and place as shall be agreed by the Committee and may also be convened on the requisition of any of the officers or any two members of the Committee. The Secretary shall give to each member of the Committee not less than seven days' notice of any meeting, but the notice may be abridged in case of urgency. Accidental failure to give notice to any members in due time or at all shall not invalidate the proceedings.

11.5 The Committee may appoint and delegate its powers to sub-committees for specific purposes and may co-opt any person (whether or not members of the Association) on to such sub-committees. Where it appears that the interests of specific groups of members may be in conflict, the Committee shall refer the matters out of which the apparent conflict arises to sub-committees. The respective sub-committees shall have power to appoint their own solicitors, instruct their own experts and take all such other action as shall be deemed appropriate to the resolution of the matter in conflict.

11.6 The committee may employ and remunerate such administrative or consultative staff (whether or not such persons are members of the Association) as it may in its discretion consider are necessary for the purposes of achieving the objects of the Association.

11.7 Members of the Committee shall not be entitled to receive any remuneration for their services to the Association other than that provided below:

(1) Where Members of the Committee provide work and services to the Association outside the Committee room, they may by vote of the Committee receive for administration and or professional

services or other functions performed remuneration at a rate not exceeding that recommended from time to time by the Lloyd's Names Association Working Party. In any case the aggregate of such remuneration shall not exceed £25,000 in any one calendar year. This clause shall be capable of retrospective application as though it had been in force at a date not earlier than 1 January 1991.

(2) Should the Association receive a favourable judgement or settlement then Members of the Committee may receive such remuneration reflecting the success of their endeavours as may be voted at a General Meeting of the Association.

(3) Members of the Committee shall be entitled to claim reasonable out-of-pocket expenses upon production of receipts in respect thereof.

11.8 The Committee shall at each Annual General Meeting report to members of the Association on its conduct of the affairs of the Association.

General Meetings

12.1 The Committee shall cause the first Annual General Meeting to be held not later than 31 October 1991.

12.2 Subject to Rule 12.1 an Annual General Meeting shall be held at least once in every calendar year. It shall be held on such day and at such time as may be appointed by the Committee.

12.3 The business to be conducted at the Annual General Meeting shall be such as may be required by the Rules or directed by the Committee.

12.4 Notice convening the Annual General Meeting shall be sent to members not less than twenty-one days before the meeting and shall specify the business to be conducted and shall include all nominations made by the Committee in respect of elections thereto.

13.1 A Special General Meeting may be convened at any time by the Committee and shall be convened in accordance with Rule 13.2

within twenty-eight days of receipt by the Secretary of a requisition in writing signed by not less than fifty members of the Association specifying the object of the meeting.

13.2 Notice convening a Special General Meeting shall be sent to members not less than twenty-one days before the meeting and shall specify the business to be conducted.

14 Accidental failure to give notice of a General Meeting shall not invalidate the proceedings at the General Meeting.

15 The Chairman of the Association shall take the chair of any General Meeting. In his absence the members present at the meeting shall elect the Chairman. In the absence of the Secretary the Chairman of the meeting shall appoint some member to take the minutes of the Meeting.

16 The quorum at any General Meeting shall be twenty-five members of the Association.

17 If the business of a General Meeting is not concluded within the time available the Meeting shall be adjourned to such time and place as the Chairman of the Meeting shall direct.

Voting

18.1 Voting at any General Meeting shall subject to Rule 18.2 be by show of hands of those present and entitled to vote unless the Chairman shall be of the opinion that a Postal Ballot should be conducted, in which case he may at his discretion direct the same. Any member unable to attend a General Meeting but who wishes to be represented may appoint a proxy who shall be entitled to vote on his behalf. Written notification of such appointment identifying such proxy must be given to the Secretary not less than seven days before the meeting.

18.2 Where at any General Meeting (other than one convened pursuant to Rule 5.1) a vote is taken by a show of hands and either:

(1) the result of such vote is inconclusive, or

(2) at least one quarter of those persons present and voting require it;

The Chairman of the meeting shall order that matter be put to a Postal Ballot and the Secretary shall as soon as practicable thereafter give notice of such ballot by sending a ballot paper to each member.

18.3 Where under these Rules a Postal Ballot of the Association is conducted:

(1) each member eligible to vote may cast an indivisible block of votes computed in accordance with his line written on the syndicate in the Year of Account on the basis of one vote for each £1,000.00 of his said line.

(2) the closing date for such a ballot shall be decided by the Committee at its discretion but in any event shall not be earlier than seven days after the day on which ballot papers are despatched by the Secretary.

(3) the result of such ballot shall be notified to the members as soon as it is practicable following its closure.

(4) accidental failure to give notice of a Postal Ballot shall not cause such ballot to be invalidated.

Resignation

19.1 A member may resign from the Association upon giving seven days' notice in writing to the Secretary of the Association.

19.2 Upon resignation becoming effective, the resigning member shall cease to be liable to the Association to meet any further calls for payment. However, the resigning member shall remain liable to the Association for payment of sums outstanding at the date of resignation. If the resigning member is a party to any proceedings commenced by the Association, the resigning member shall be removed from said proceedings, but shall remain liable for his or her proportion of costs incurred in prosecuting such proceedings up to the date of resignation, including defendants' costs, where appropriate.

19.3 The resigning member shall cease to enjoy the benefits of membership of the Association as from the date of resignation. The resigning member shall continue to enjoy such benefits of membership as have accrued to or vested in that member prior to date of resignation.

Winding-Up

20.1 If either:

(1) the Committee shall be of the opinion that the objects for which the Association was established cannot be achieved and shall be authorised in that behalf by a resolution passed by not less than 75% of the members present and voting at a General Meeting of the Association convened for the purpose; or

(2) the Committee shall be of the opinion that the objects for which the Association was established have been accomplished; The Committee may resolve that the affairs of the Association be wound up or in the case where sub-Rule (1) above applies, the Committee may instead, having taken the advice of the Association's Solicitors, circulate to the members of the Association an alternative basis upon which the objects of the Association may be pursued.

20.2 On a winding-up the property of the Association shall be applied as follows:

(1) by paying or providing for the payment of all outstanding liabilities of the Association (out of income in preference to capital) and subject thereto;

(2) so far as not provided for under sub-paragraph (1) hereof by making such provision in such amount and in such manner as to the Committee shall seem reasonable in respect of any outstanding liabilities (whether actual or contingent) of any members of the Association in connection with any Authorised Proceedings then in progress and subject thereto; and

(3) by distributing the same amongst members of the Association other than Defaulting members in the proportions inter-se in which they have been liable (or would but for any waiver have been liable) to subscribe to the funds of the Association but so

that no member whose liability to subscribe has been waived shall receive any share until all other members have received sums equal to the sums subscribed by them.

20.3 On completion of winding-up the Association shall be dissolved.

Alteration of Rules

21.1 Neither this Rule nor Rule 20.2 nor any provision in these Rules providing for the proportions in which members may share in the benefit of Recoveries or other distribution of the assets of the Association shall be capable of alteration.

21.2 Except as provided in Rule 20.1 these Rules shall be capable of alteration. All such alterations must be supported by either:

(1) a resolution passed by two-thirds of those present and voting at a General Meeting: or

(2) if such a ballot is held in accordance with Rule 18, a two-thirds majority of the votes cast in a Postal Ballot.

Notice

22 Any written notice shall be deemed to be given to a member if it has been sent by post or delivered to a member's address last notified in writing by such member to the Secretary.

Definitions

23 In these rules:

"Authorised Proceedings" means any proceedings which are authorised pursuant to Rule 4.1(1) and where the context admits any appeal proceedings commenced in accordance with Rule 5.1;

"the Association's Solicitors" means D J Freeman & Co or other solicitors for the time being retained by the Committee;

"the Minimum Participation date" means 28/2/1991;

"the Closing Date" means 31/5/1991;

"Defaulting member" means a member declared to be such by the Committee pursuant to any provision of these Rules.

"the Initial Subscription" and "the Litigation Subscription" have the meanings ascribed to them in Rule 6.1;

"Postal Ballot" means a ballot conducted in accordance with Rule 18;

"Recoveries" means any sum ordered or agreed to be paid to any member by any Defendant to any Authorised Proceedings whether in respect of damages interest or costs;

"the Syndicate" means Lloyd's Syndicate 334;

"the year of Account" means the Syndicate's year of account for 1985;

"the date of resignation" means seven days from the date of despatching a letter of resignation by Recorded Delivery to the Secretary of the Association;

References to proceedings shall include references to arbitration proceedings and references to judgement shall be construed accordingly.

Members of the Committee

Clive Francis	Chairman
Keith Lester	Treasurer
Charles Baron	
Raymond Cook	
Alasdair Fergusson	
Michael Jump	
Harry Purchase	
Jasper Salisbury-Jones	

Secretary

Guy Wilson

Application Form

Full Name & Address
Line 1985

Declaration

I have read and understood the Rules of the Association and agree to be bound by their terms.

Insofar as it has not been given, I hereby give my authority for proceedings to be commenced by the Association in my name and on my behalf and I understand that such proceedings may not be commenced until I have satisfied the subscription requirements set out in the Rules of the Association.

Signed   Date

ACKNOWLEDGEMENTS

The story is a history of true events based on extant documents that were initially written up as a diary.

Keith's wife, who he first met when she was twenty years old, was so damaged by the stress caused by his membership of Lloyd's that she was totally disinterested in this script, although kept informed of its development. During the period of acute difficulty, he was never blamed for 'their' predicament. They worked as a team addressing the issues step by step, for which he was enormously grateful. His former business partner, Guy Wilson, was also immensely supportive.

In producing this book, the author would like to acknowledge and thank those who encouraged him to write the text or contributed to and/or commented on drafts including Clive's widow Claire Francis, Edmund's brother Professor Robert Lester and Nicholas Strauss KC. Others who were very encouraging or contributed included Kishorilal Shah, Rona Aldrich, Tom Chalmers and Cherry Paler.

I would like to thank most sincerely the staff at Whitefox Publishing Ltd. John Bond the CEO provided a clear, costed plan for the production of the book, Rosie Pearce the Senior Editorial Project Manager competently guided its development and Jess King advised on marketing. Thanks also to Paul Roberts for his structural report, Peter Salmon for copyediting, Dan Shutt for proofreading, Marie Lorimer for the index and Harvey Starte for legal advice.

Lastly, it was the former Committee Member Ray Cook, who reflected with emotion, 'It brought it all back to me'.

BIBLIOGRAPHY

Brodeur, P., *Outrageous Misconduct: The Asbestos Industry on Trial* (Pantheon/New York, 1985).

Cameron, A. and Farndon, R., *Scenes from Sea and City: Lloyd's List 1734–1984* (Lloyd's/London, 1974).

Cornwell, B., *Azincourt* (HarperCollins/London, 2009).

Flower, R. and Wynn Jones, M., *Lloyd's of London: An Illustrated History* (Lloyd's of London Press/London, 1981).

Lloyd's Act 1982, UK Legislation, www.legislation.gov.uk/ukla/1982/14/contents/enacted [accessed 12 April 2024].

Merrett, S., 'Lloyd's of London Insolvent Again. Government in Denial. Action Required', Open Democracy (25 May 2012), www.opendemocracy.net/en/shine-alight/lloyd-s-of-london-insolvent-again-government-in-denial-action-required/ [Accessed 12 April 2024]

Lester, K., 'Protecting the Environment: A New Managerial Responsibility' in Owen, D. (ed.), *Green Reporting: Accountancy and the Challenge of the Nineties* (Chapman & Hall, 1992), pp. 39–48.

Raphael, A., *Ultimate Risk* (Corgi/London, 1995).

Shakespeare, W., *Henry V* (Macmillan and Co Limited/London, 1924).

Sharman, S., *Sir James Martin: The Authorised Biography of the Martin-Baker Ejection Seat Pioneer* (Patrick Stephens Ltd/London, 1996).

INDEX

LIST OF ILLUSTRATIONS

p. v: Photograph of Clive Francis reproduced with kind permission of Claire Francis.

p. ix: Lutine Bell © User:Colin / Wikimedia Commons / CC BY-SA 4.0.

p. 6:   Winchester Bowring broker's slip.

p. 40:   Candidate for election to Lloyd's Council.

p. 213:   Shenton's cartoon reproduced with permission of the *Solicitors Journal*. First published in the *Solicitors Journal* in 1994.

p. 217:   Loss development chart.

www.ingramcontent.com/pod-product-compliance
Lightning Source LLC
Chambersburg PA
CBHW031505180326
41458CB00044B/6701/J